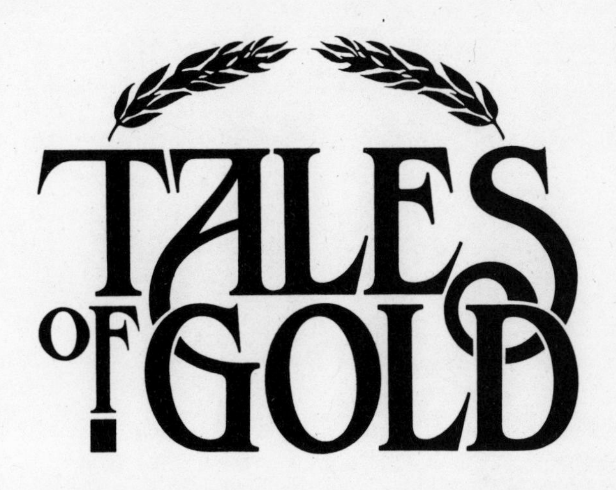
TALES
OF GOLD

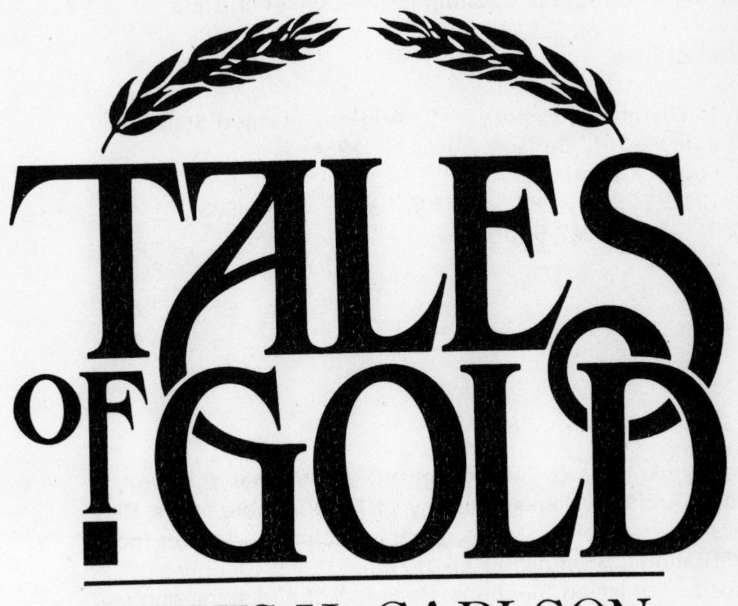

LEWIS H. CARLSON
AND JOHN J. FOGARTY

CONTEMPORARY
BOOKS, INC.
CHICAGO • NEW YORK

Library of Congress Cataloging-in-Publication Data

Tales of gold.

1. Olympics—History. 2. Athletes—United States—Interviews. I. Carlson, Lewis H., 1934– II. Fogarty, John J.
GV721.5.T35 1987 796.4'8 87-24583
ISBN 0-8092-5067-5 (pbk.)

Front jacket photos (left to right): Peter Vidmar © Dave Black; Archie Williams courtesy of *Track & Field News*; Billy Mills courtesy of Billy Mills; Eleanor Holm courtesy of the International Swimming Hall of Fame; Helen Stephens courtesy of Helen Stephens. Back jacket and spine photos (left to right): Dorothy Poynton courtesy of the International Swimming Hall of Fame; Jeff Blatnick courtesy of Jeff Blatnick; 1936 opening ceremonies courtesy of Francis Johnson; Carl Lewis © Cor Eberhard (Amsterdam, Netherlands); Wyomia Tyus courtesy of Women's Sports Foundation.

Published by Contemporary Books, Inc.
180 North Michigan Avenue, Chicago, Illinois 60601
Manufactured in the United States of America
Library of Congress Catalog Card Number: 87-24583
International Standard Book Number: 0-8092-5067-5

Published simultaneously in Canada by Beaverbooks, Ltd.
195 Allstate Parkway, Valleywood Business Park
Markham, Ontario L3R 4T8 Canada

The important thing in the Olympic Games is not to win but to take part; the important thing in life is not the triumph but the struggle.

—Pierre de Coubertin, 1896

To the world, Olympic heroes tend to stay suspended in amber at their moment of victory. There they are, flushed with youth, exalted by triumph, crystallized in time like a work of art—afloat above a crossbar. Perhaps our own intimations of death are held at bay by the image of other mortals preserved as eternally young. Perhaps that is the essence of the Olympics—a single, intense, splendidly theatrical instant of triumph shared by competitor and spectator alike. There are the medals stamped from some precious metal, hymns, and flags and transcendent applause—it is so fleeting, yet so beautiful that it can only be called perfect.

—Excerpt from *All That Glitters Is Not Gold*
by William O. Johnson, Jr.,

CONTENTS

ACKNOWLEDGMENTS

Primary gratitude is owed the Olympic champions themselves for their patience, enthusiasm, and compelling stories. Finding their addresses and establishing first contact would have been an impossible task without the generous help of Bob Paul and Rochelle Evans at the United States Olympic Committee; Bill Schroeder, Director Emeritus of the First Interstate Athletic Foundation; Buck Dawson, Director of the International Swimming Hall of Fame; and George Dales, editor of *Track & Field Quarterly Review*. Dawson and Dales also read parts of the manuscript, correcting errors and offering helpful suggestions. In addition, Dawson contributed photographs of many of the gold medalists, as did Jon Hendershott, editor of *Track and Field News*, and Mike Chapman at USA Wrestling.

Across this country many friends offered accommodations, transportation, and much needed encouragement to two road-weary travelers. Specifically, we wish to thank Phil and Remi Baker, Murray Cohen, George Colburn, Tony and Joan Haigh, Janine Johnson, David Kennard, Keith and Emily Long, Charley and Ellen Proctor, John and Constance Rieben, Pat Russell, David and Sally Schreuder, Carl and Lois Spinoso, William and Barbara Start, and A.G. and Ann Thomas.

We also thank our offspring, Ann and Linda Carlson and Julia and Patricia Fogarty, for the tape transcriptions, typing, and research they so cheerfully did as partial payment for their college educations. Also helping with the preparation of the manuscript were Paul Devlin, Don Hanzek, Gloria Hendrickson, Jack McNamara, David Rozelle, and Steve Voorhees. The title of the book was the creation of Becky Quinlan.

Lew Carlson is grateful to Western Michigan University for time made possible by a faculty research grant and a sabbatical leave.

Special thanks to Kyle Roggenbuck and Libby McGreevy, our editors at Contemporary Books, Inc., and to Jane Jordan Browne, whose preliminary work made all this possible.

Finally, we wish to thank our wives, Edna McManus Fogarty and Simone Conrad Carlson, for their enduring patience over the past five years.

PREFACE

This is oral history, history as recounted by those who actually lived it. Through the recollections of these remarkable men and women, who range in age from 24 to 95, we share the frustrations and triumphs they experienced and sometimes the tragedies they endured on their way to victory and beyond.

A few of these champions have managed to hold on to the fame that came with their Olympic triumph or have achieved distinction in other areas, but many of the older ones have been forgotten, and a few prefer it that way. Yet all of the gold medal winners had—and retain—those characteristics that we greatly admire as a nation and that we think of as defining our national character: courage, determination, self-confidence, and, above all, a fierce desire to win.

These champions also have other, less apparent, qualities. Without exception they are intelligent and articulate men and women, and each displays strong individual qualities as well. We will never forget the feisty wit and pride of Ray Barbuti, Helen Stephens, and Sammy Lee; the maverick spirit of Eleanor Holm, Mac Wilkins, and Harold and Olga Connolly; the quiet dignity and class of John Woodruff, Jean Shiley, and Harrison Dillard; the story-telling abilities of Benjamin Spock, Marshall Wayne, and

Archie Williams; the strong religious convictions of Shelby Wilson and Ben Peterson; and the scholarly detachment of Bill Bradley. Then there was Don Bragg, the pole vaulter who would be Tarzan.

But this is not merely a book about world-class athletes. Just as the popular film *Chariots of Fire* was less a success story of two British athletes in the 1924 Games than it was a tribute to the tenacity of the human will, so is this book less a collection of autobiographical sketches of individual triumphs than it is a testament to the magnificence of the human spirit.

These stories also provide a variety of perspectives on what is not right with the Olympics. Excessive nationalism, political intrigue, and controversy have long marred the Games, as have sexual and racial discrimination, biased judging, violations of amateur codes, and, more recently, boycotts, the use of performance-enhancing drugs, skyrocketing costs, and growing commercialism. We found among the older athletes a compelling innocence in their Olympic experience that one seldom finds today. They took the time to make friends and savor their surroundings. Today, the winning of medals is a much more earnest endeavor.

We expect much more from the Olympic Games than we do from the mundane or threatening reality that surrounds us—and that is as it should be. An international celebration in which the world's sons and daughters come together to perform their artistry is an ennobling experience for anyone who believes that human beings are capable of coexisting in some kind of peaceful harmony.

The stories in this book are the result of many interviews that we taped over the past several years. We originally planned to restrict ourselves to 1936 and earlier because these stories will soon be lost forever, but the need to establish historical continuity and the obviously compelling comparisons between then and now led us to seek a representative sampling of the postwar champions as well.

We have included 21 gold medalists from the pre-World War II era and 37 from after. Among the older athletes, our choices were dictated largely by availability; for the postwar era, the selection process was more difficult. Almost 700 Americans have won their Olympic titles since World War II. Track and field and swimming athletes have dominated, as they do in our book, but we also tried to find strong representative champions, regardless of event, whose words could recapture the flavor and history of each particular Olympiad.

Our interviews were conducted on backyard patios, in formal living rooms and parlors, and, most frequently, around friendly kitchen tables. We visited all kinds of homes in all types of neighborhoods, but nothing could have prepared us for the warm, generous, and gracious hospitality with which we were received everywhere.

In preparing these interviews for publication, we eliminated our questions and comments, and we sometimes rearranged the material to give a chronology or continuity to events and thoughts. Repetitious material was eliminated, as was some that was clearly irrelevant. But in the main, the editing has been minimal. This is the Olympians' story, told in their way and in their words.

1
STOCKHOLM, 1912

The modern Olympic Games were the creation of France's Baron Pierre de Coubertin, and from their beginning in 1896 the Swedes actively supported the baron's dream of using the Games to promote international cooperation and understanding through friendly athletic competition. The Swedes richly deserved the 1912 Games, and they turned out to be marvelous hosts.

Each of the four previous Games—Athens, 1896; Paris, 1900; St. Louis, 1904; and London, 1908—had been marred by such a staggering array of problems and political intrigue that some critics were surprised when the Olympic movement survived long enough for the 1912 Games to be held. That it did so was due almost entirely to the indomitable spirit and tenacity of Baron de Coubertin. But he was ably assisted by the enthusiastic, thorough, and efficient Swedes, whose Stockholm Games are still regarded as among the two or three best ever held.

The Stockholm Organizing Committee, under its president, Colonel Victor Balck, and its vice president, J. Sigfrid Edstrom, overcame many obstacles to prepare a comprehensive list of official Olympic events, oversee the construction of a swimming pool and a beautiful new stadium that seated 22,000 spectators, and provide housing for the athletes and officials from 26 countries. Among the important innovations introduced at Stockholm were electronic timing devices, a system for photographing the finish of the track events, and the thorough training of those who officiated at the various competitions.

The Games were declared open by King Gustav V on July 6, and it soon became apparent that, as had been the case in the previous four Olympiads, the track and field events would be dominated by Americans. Ralph Craig, the great University of Michigan sprinter, won both the 100- and 200-meter dashes. Thirty-six years later at the 1948 Games in London, Craig again appeared in Olympic competition aboard the Dragon class yacht, *Rhythm*, which came in 11th.

The 400 meters was the first such Olympic race to be run in lanes. The only European contender running against a field of four Americans in the 400-meter race was Hans Braun of Germany, who finished second to Charles Reidpath, a University of Syracuse football player who set an Olympic record of 48.2 seconds.

The 800 meters was one of the most exciting races in Olympic history. Among the competitors were the three medalists from the 1908 event—Mel Sheppard of the U.S., Emilio Lunghi of Italy, and Hans Braun—but at the finish it was Ted Meredith, a 19-year-old schoolboy, who led an American sweep in the then world record time of 1:51.9.

The 1,500 meters was also closely contested, although this time the favored Americans were upset by a young Oxford University student, Arnold N. S. Jackson. John Paul Jones from Cornell; Mel Sheppard, the 1908 Olympic winner; and Abel Kiviat, who had set three 1,500-meter world records in the three weeks preceding the 1912 Games, led the race until the last few meters, when Jackson swept by to nip Kiviat at the tape.

The most conspicuous American Olympic athletes between 1904 and 1920 were the so-called New York Whales, a group of huge, Irish-born New York City policemen who dominated the discus, shot, and hammer-throwing events. All were members of the New York Irish-American Club, where their beer-drinking exploits more than matched their athletic accomplishments. John J. Flanagan made his Olympic debut in 1900 when he won the 16-pound hammer throw, and he repeated his success in 1904 and 1908. Martin Sheridan won the discus in 1904 and 1908. In the 1912

Games 350-pound Pat McDonald, who for more than twenty years directed traffic at Times Square, won the shot put, best-hand event, and took a silver in the two-handed shot put. Matt McGrath won a silver in the hammer throw in 1908, and in Stockholm he won a gold, setting an Olympic record which stood until 1936. In the 1924 Paris Games, at the age of 46, McGrath won his second Olympic silver medal.

The only American to compete in the military pentathlon (now called the *modern pentathlon*) was a young lieutenant from West Point, George S. Patton. Patton had the best total score in four events, but in pistol shooting he placed 20th among 42 competitors and dropped to fifth overall. Patton was an excellent shot, but his insistence on using an army revolver rather than the standard target pistol used by the Swedes probably cost him an Olympic medal.

Then there was Jim Thorpe. The big Indian from the Carlisle Indian School was better known for his abilities on the gridiron, but in Stockholm he easily won the pentathlon and the decathlon. King Gustav V hailed him as the greatest living athlete, and in 1950 American sportswriters voted him the greatest athlete of the first half of the 20th century.

In 1913 the International Olympic Committee stripped Thorpe of his medals and removed his name from their official records when it became known that he had accepted a small sum of money for playing summer baseball.

Between 1932 and 1953, reporters and Thorpe's family periodically campaigned to have his medals returned to him. They argued that Thorpe never intended to deceive the Olympic officials, that he simply didn't know that accepting a little money to play in a non-Olympic sport made him a professional athlete, and that, in any event, he had paid for his mistake. Avery Brundage, who was President of the U.S. Olympic Committee from 1929 to 1953 and of the International Olympic Committee from 1952 to 1972, was outspoken in his opposition to restoring Thorpe's medals and reinstating his Olympic records. In one of the ironies of Olympic history, Avery Brundage was Jim Thorpe's teammate in both the pentathlon and decathlon events in 1912.

In 1973, 20 years after Thorpe's death, the U.S. Olympic Committee restored his amateur status, and 10 years later, in January of 1983, the International Olympic Committee restored his medals to his family and his name to the Olympic record book.

Photo by Fogarty and Carlson

Abel Kiviat in 1986.

ABEL RICHARD KIVIAT

Silver Medal, 1,500-Meters, 1912

Abel Kiviat was a member of the five-man team that won the 3,000-meter team race. No longer an Olympic event, it was then run as a cross-country race, and only a team's best three times were counted; Kiviat was fourth. He narrowly missed winning a gold medal in the 1,500-meter run when he was nosed out in a photo finish by England's Arnold N. S. Jackson, but as America's oldest living Olympic medalist, he belongs in this book.

Over the four years following high school, Kiviat won the national indoor AAU 600-yard championship twice and the 1,000-yard title three times. While training for the 1912 Games, Kiviat set three 1,500-meter world records in three weeks, including a 3:55.8 best in the Olympic trials at Harvard.

Until his retirement in 1971, Kiviat worked as a federal court clerk. He also served as a track official for more than six decades, including several years as chief press steward at the Penn Relays.

During the festivities surrounding the 1984 Los Angeles Games, Abel Kiviat was rediscovered. Then 92 years old, he made guest appearances on several national television programs, including "The Tonight Show." He also was chosen to be one of the Olympic torchbearers who helped carry the flame across the country to Los Angeles.

My parents were both born in South Russia. They were both employed in the clothing industry, and my father was studying to be a rabbi. One day a friend tipped off my father that the army was coming to get him, so he grabbed his wife-to-be and escaped by riding buried in the bottom of a hay wagon driven by the same friend who warned him. They went to Hamburg, Germany, and then to Liverpool, England, before coming to America. That was 1891, the year before I was born.

My father started out in New York City as a peddler—you know, with a pack wrapped up in an old, black oilcloth strapped to his back. But he didn't like peddling. So a couple of his Jewish friends from Russia said, "Why don't you try Staten Island? You'll be the first Jew down there. You could open up a general store, and you wouldn't have to go peddling." It worked out. Six of my family were born there, but I was born before they moved, on the corner of Allen and Grand streets, under the Second Avenue El.

The first town we lived in on Staten Island was Rosebank, but it was known as Little Italy because it was about 95 percent Italian. The other 5 percent were Irish, real Irish, and they ran the town. One was a policeman, one a truant officer, and two others were principal and vice principal of the school. The Italian kids I played with took me to school, and this Irish woman who was in charge of the grade school asked them, "What do you call this boy?" They said, "We call him Abe." She said, "There is no such thing as Abe. His real name from the Bible is Abel." So that's how I got to be Abel. My real Jewish name I couldn't spell or pronounce, so I never told anybody what it was. I was just Abel.

I got into running because I was into all kinds of sports, and running is the principle of most sports. I preferred baseball. You can see the results of it on my hands, the broken fingers and the sprained knuckles. In those days we didn't wear gloves. The only glove we had was a catcher's mitt, and we got that when 10 or 12 kids chipped in a cent or two each. We took turns being the catcher. We had no mask. See my nose? And our baseball in those days was called Carrs Boys' Lively. It would last two full games, and then it would start to fall apart. So we'd buy a roll of black tape and wrap that around the ball and use it for another game, but every time you caught it in your bare hand it would hurt like hell.

I played shortstop for three years at Milton High. I was so bowlegged that a sportswriter named Robert Edgren of the *New York Evening World* called me the Jewish Honus Wagner. One day I was practicing baseball, and the captain of the track team invited the ball players to come over and race. He told us he would give us a 50-yard head start for the mile, and the winner would get a bronze medal. We later found out the medal cost him $1.25. The ball players told me to go ahead because I always beat them so I ran in my baseball uniform and my spikes. I beat the track guys with the 50-yard handicap plus another 50 yards. That was the first actual race I ever ran on a track.

Then the track team captain and the baseball captain made an arrangement because several of the other baseball players were pretty fast. They would schedule matches against the same high school for the same day. We'd play baseball in the morning and run track in the afternoon, so I got to participate in two sports each day.

On the last day of school in June of 1909, I won the half-mile and the mile in the Public School Athletic League Championships. My time in the half was 2:04 something, and in the mile it was 4:40 and a fraction. One of those times was a new PSAL record. One of the officials at that meet was Lawson Robertson, who would be the Olympic coach in 1912 and in several Games after that. In 1909 he was a coach at the Irish-American Club in New York, and he asked me if I would like to join. It was kind of a poor man's club and included policemen, firemen, sanitation workers and other laborers, and school kids like myself. It was great for me because I couldn't afford to go to college. Life was tough then.

The Irish-American Club was at 60th Street between Third and Lexington avenues, right next to Bloomingdale's. Our team participated in track meets all over America—in Kansas City, St. Louis, San Francisco, Chicago, Buffalo—and it won many national championships. We didn't train that hard because Lawson Robertson had a different idea of training than do the coaches today. We did no road running, for instance. I never heard of a road runner in my time. The younger runners like myself would train only one or two days a week, and if I had to run a couple of races on the weekend, I wouldn't train all week. Robertson had the idea that, if you had ability, why the hell did you have to train so damn much? Doesn't that make sense?

The best-known members of the Irish-American Club were the so-called New York Whales. They were all Irish cops. I remember Pat McDonald. He weighed 350 pounds and won the shot put at Stockholm. For 30 years he was the traffic cop at 43rd Street and Broadway, right at Times Square. Matt McGrath was another of the Whales. He won the hammer throw in 1912 after coming in second in London in 1908. Ralph Rose was another but he was from out west someplace. He was the biggest one of them all—six feet, seven inches or so. He won the shot put in 1908 and the two-handed shot put in 1912. He was the flagbearer in 1908 who refused to dip the flag in the opening ceremony when he passed by the British king. Rose weighed 365 pounds, a pound for each day. You know, those big Irishmen protected me, the only Jew in the Irish-American Club. I remember I had a little run-in with the discus thrower, Jim Duncan, on the boat going over to Stockholm. He was a fresh mutt, about 225 pounds and ugly-looking. He started calling me names and annoying me, so Matt McGrath and Pat McDonald grabbed ahold of him and dragged him to a port-hole and threatened to push him through if he called me any more names. And then they made me track captain.

The Olympic trials of 1912 were held in Harvard Stadium, and I won the 1,500 meters, setting a world record of 3:55.4 that would last for 18 years. Something very strange happened in that race. As I crossed the finish line, several judges rushed over, yelling, "Go for the mile! Go for the mile!" I didn't know what the hell they were talking about. The mile is 120.75 yards beyond the 1,500 meters. It took me something over 20 seconds to do it, and that was terrible, but I had slowed down at the 1,500-meter finish. Still, I tied the world record for the mile of 4:15.6.

We sailed from New York on the second Saturday of June on the Red Star Lines' *Finland*, and we lived right on board ship even after we landed in Stockholm. We were anchored on the river in front of the king's castle. On the other side of us was the famous Grand Hotel—the grandest hotel I've ever been in—but we were not allowed on shore except to train.

I ran a bum race in the 1,500 meters in Stockholm, which was

Mecca cigarette card, circa 1912. Photo courtesy of Abel Kiviat

unusual. Everybody picked me to win, even the Swedish papers, because of my performance in America. Sportswriter Arthur Daley later asked me, "What the hell were you waiting for, the Toonerville Trolley?" What happened was I let England's Arnold Jackson jump me on the turn. It was an unorthodox thing for him to do. You usually don't pass someone on the turn because you have to run so much farther then. Well, Jackson shot out into the lead. I was ahead, but he caught me asleep. By the time I woke up, he had almost a 10-yard lead on me. The finish wasn't far from the turn, and I didn't have time to catch him and go ahead. It was just a stupid race on my part. I had won two trial races. A lot of the spectators thought I did catch him at the tape—that it was a dead heat. But the judges said that Jackson had won, so they gave my time as one-fifth of a second slower. Norman Tabor of Brown University came in third, a fifth of a second behind me. We argued a little about the judges' decision, but no harsh words. We were Americans on foreign soil, so we had to take their word for the finish.

I roomed with Jim Thorpe for a few days on board the ship. He was a wonderful athlete. He could do anything, but he didn't know how he did it. He would watch you do it, then he'd do it. Give him the javelin, and he'd throw it farther than the regular javelin throwers on the team.

Thorpe would eat and drink anything. He was about 5 foot, 11 inches, and, for some reason, I know he weighed 178 pounds. He had no neck and was built like a wrestler. He walked with his head sort of back of his body and always on his heels with his toes up in the air. He was a hell of a nice gentleman, but he never had a nickel. When we'd buy a beer, he couldn't. He just didn't have anything. After the Games some of us went over to France. We figured we'd get a lot of free wine and stuff. The prizes were 12 quarts of champagne for first place, 6 for second, and 3 for third. But the American officials told us no because that would make us professionals. But they did say we could help ourselves to the punch bowl after the competition, and we did.

During our three-day stay in Paris someone discovered a chandelier that must have been at least 10 feet off the floor. We all put a dollar in a pot to see if anybody could touch it. Thorpe didn't have a buck, but we gave him credit. There were about 14 of us in the room. Everybody tried it. Alma Richards of Brigham Young, who won the high jump at six feet, four inches, tried, but he couldn't. But Jim Thorpe did, and he was about four inches shorter than Richards.

Avery Brundage also competed in Stockholm. He was in the decathlon. He was a good athlete, but everybody hated him. Even when he became President of the Olympic Committee they all hated him. He wouldn't talk to anyone, and nobody talked to him. He was from Chicago. His father had a big construction business, and when he died he left Avery all that wealth. We just ignored him as much as possible. If he said good morning, you didn't have to say anything. Just bow your head and keep on moving.

I kept running after the Games and even a bit while I was a soldier during World War I. Then I quit, but I made a comeback in 1924. I went to the Olympic tryouts. I think they were in Boston. I was training for the 3,000 meters and running pretty good, but just before we had the finals, one of the Olympic coaches came over and said, "Abel, we want you to start in the steeplechase." I looked at him, but what could I do? I had never hurdled in my life and didn't know how to go over the water jump. In those days they jumped it on a diagonal. They didn't jump the entire 12-foot pit. I tried going over the corner like that, but I cracked my ankle and was laid up for eight weeks. There went my chance to be on the '24 team. I would have made the 3,000-meter team because we had no one besides Joie Ray.

I went back over to Stockholm in 1984. Bud Greenspan took me over for a documentary he was making. I remember him when he was a kid writer on the *New York Mirror*. He wanted me there to tell what I remembered about the 1912 Games. The British and Swedes also had cameramen there. Some things were still the same. The girls were still beautiful. The Olympic Stadium in Stockholm had been renovated when I saw it in 1984, but there was still something about it that hit me. There was a certain feeling.

I was kind of rediscovered on my 90th birthday in 1982. It was Stan Saplin who discovered that I was the oldest living American Olympic medalist. They gave me a wonderful dinner in New York. I think it was at the Ritz Hotel. So on my 90th birthday I became famous all over again. Of course, during the 1984 Olympics even more people took notice of me.

I was never sick a day in my life until I was 92, and I still officiate meets. I have an old saying, "You want me to go to your track meet, you got to pick me up, feed me, and take me back home." You see, I had to give up my driver's license last year when I was 92. I also used to smoke five or six cigars a day. Now I allow myself one, and sometimes I forget to smoke it.

2
ANTWERP, 1920

Olympic competition resumed in 1920, after the 1916 Games were cancelled because of the First World War. The ancient Greeks did it the other way around; they suspended wars to hold the Games.

Just 18 months after the Armistice was declared, the 1920 Games were held in a cold, wet, and dreary Belgium that had not yet recovered from the ravages of war. Nevertheless, in spite of the hasty arrangements and rather poor facilities, King Albert welcomed more than 2,600 athletes from 29 countries. Germany and Austria were not invited, and Russia could not attend because of the continuing turmoil of the revolution.

There were several innovations in these Games. The official Olympic flag, symbolizing the spirit of international cooperation, appeared for the first time. The five-colored, interlocking circles represent the five major landmasses of the world, and at least one of the colors of the Olympic circles appears in every national flag in the world. The Olympic oath was also introduced, an oath in which the contestants agree to compete in the "true spirit of sportsmanship, for the glory of sport and the honor of country."

For the first time the U.S. Army and Navy sent their own athletes, with the Navy's team traveling aboard the battleship *USS Frederick*. But the trip to Antwerp for the other 351 American athletes was something of a disaster. They sailed from Hoboken, New Jersey, on July 26, aboard the *Princess Matoika*, a military transport which quickly became known among the wags on the team as the *Princess Slowpoka*. It was slow, crowded, and dreary, and the voyage lasted almost two weeks. The men had to sleep on cots in the hold, and the dining room was so small the athletes had to eat in shifts. The generally terrible conditions prompted a near mutiny by some of the male athletes led by swimmer Norman Ross. Temporary relief was provided by another swimmer, Duke Kahanamoku, the 1912 100-meter winner, and his fellow Hawaiian swimmers, who entertained nightly by singing and playing their ukuleles.

The males athletes' foul mood did not improve much when they saw their quarters in Antwerp. They were expecting a comfortable hotel, but what they got was a barrackslike converted schoolhouse, and they again complained bitterly. The New York Whales, those more than ample weightmen from Gotham's Police Department, refused to accept straw pillows and cots whose "sides were too close to the middle," and they removed themselves to a local inn. When triple-jumper Dan Ahearn also requested permission from the U.S. Olympic Committee to move out, he was refused. He left anyway, and the next day he was thrown off the team. Two hundred of his outraged teammates signed a petition demanding that he be reinstated, and after a day of angry exchanges between the Committee and the protesting athletes, Ahearn was back on the team.

Tiny Finland produced the most spectacular athletes in the Games, led by the incomparable Paavo Nurmi, who is still generally recognized as the greatest of all distance runners. In this, his Olympic debut, he took two golds and a silver. He would go on in 1924 and 1928 to win seven more gold medals and two silvers before being declared a professional just before the opening of the 1932 Games in Los Angeles. But Nurmi was not the first of the flying Finns. In 1912 Hannes Kolehmainen became the first of only four Olympians to win both the 5,000- and 10,000-meter races. In Antwerp Kolehmainen won the marathon easily, setting an Olympic record in the process. The Finns also won the triple jump, the shot put, the pentathlon, and swept the first four places in the javelin throw. Of the 27 track and field events, Finland won 1 team and 8 individual gold medals, tying the number of golds won by the much larger American team.

Along with the ubiquitous Whales and the entertaining Hawaiians, Charley Paddock was certainly one of the more colorful American athletes. The world-record-holding Paddock was the first to be called "The World's Fastest Human." A bit of a dandy, both in his sartorial elegance and in his running style, Paddock sprinted straight up, with a high knee action, and at the finish line always leaped at the tape with arms wildly extended. He won the 100 meters but was upset by teammate Allen Woodring in the 200, a defeat Paddock blamed on too much partying the night before. Paddock at least partially redeemed himself as the lead-off runner for the world-record-breaking 4x100-meter relay team. Running the second leg on the relay team was Jackson Scholz, who was to become much better known as a very successful writer of juvenile sports fiction.

American rower John B. Kelly, a bricklayer from Philadelphia and the father of the late Princess Grace of Monaco, won the single skulls. In the 1956 Melbourne Games his son, John Kelly, Jr., won a bronze medal in the same event.

Of the 16 swimming and diving events, the Americans won 11. The men's events were dominated by swimmers Duke Kahanamoku and Norman Ross and diver Clarence "Pinky" Pinkston. Ethelda Bleibtrey won the two women's individual events and led the winning 4x100-meter relay team. The springboard diving title was won by Aileen Riggin, who at 4 feet, 7 inches and 65 pounds was the smallest Olympian at Antwerp.

AILEEN RIGGIN

Gold Medal, Springboard Diving, 1920
Silver Medal, Springboard Diving, 1924
Bronze Medal, 100-Meter Backstroke, 1924

Women's springboard diving had its Olympic premier at the Antwerp Games in 1920. At age 14, winner Aileen Riggin became the first woman to receive an Olympic gold medal in that event.

Four years later, she returned to Paris and placed second in the springboard and third in the 100-meter backstroke, the first time any athlete had won individual

Photo courtesy of Aileen Riggin

Aileen Riggin in 1986.

In the early 1920s.

medals in both swimming and diving in the same Games.

In addition to her very apparent athletic skills, the young Riggin had the keen eye of a reporter. No detail, event, or person escaped her close scrutiny. No one has created a finer, more comprehensive account of the 1920 and 1924 Games than that presented here by Miss Riggin. What emerges is a look at another era, when athletes truly were amateurs and Baron de Coubertin's Olympic ideal of international understanding and harmony through competition came close to being realized.

Sixty-six years after winning her first Olympic medal, Miss Riggin's competitive swimming career goes on. In November of 1986, at age 80, she won the 75-and-over division at the 13th Annual Castle Swim contest. This event, sponsored by the Outrigger Canoe Club in Honolulu, consists of a 1.5-mile surf course from the Royal Hawaiian Hotel to the club's facilities on Diamond Head.

I was a member of the first American women's swimming and diving team. There had been some women from northern European countries in the 1912 Games in Stockholm, but 1920 was to be the first time that American women participated in regular Olympic events. Our participation was limited in those days to swimming. Track and field events came later for women, as well as gymnastics, fencing, and various other sports that women can compete in today.

We learned that American women might participate in the Games in the spring of 1920. The American Olympic Committee and the various affiliated groups were not in favor of sending women at all. In those days women did not compete in strenuous athletics. No one swam very far. It was not considered healthy for girls to overexert themselves or to swim as far as a mile. People thought it was a great mistake, that we were ruining our health, that we would never have children, and that we would be sorry for it later on. There was a great deal of publicity against women competing in athletics at all. We had to combat this feeling at every turn. Many of the coaches on the Olympic team for men decided that they did not wish to be "hampered" by having women athletes on the team, and many of the officials felt the same way. It took a great deal of persuasion by the American women to convince them to let us participate in the Olympics at all. There were some diehards who never really got used to the idea.

In those days in New York, there was no indoor pool for women that had a 3-meter or 10-foot springboard. There was one indoor pool in New Jersey, but that meant a three-hour commute for us after school. We did practice there about once a week before the outdoor season opened. However, the water was only six feet deep under the board. This was exceedingly dangerous, and all we could think of as we dove was not about our diving and our form, but about quickly putting out our hands and cutting short our dives so we would not hit the bottom with too much force. Of course we hit bottom every dive, but the trick was to have your hands ahead and break with your elbows to protect your head. It is hard to concentrate on your diving form when all you can think of is trying to avoid getting injured or killed.

When the weather permitted, we practiced at an outdoor lagoon at Manhattan Beach on Long Island. It was about an hour's commuting time and we had to go there for diving when the tide was high, whether it was six o'clock in the morning or six o'clock at night. And the board we used was most unsatisfactory. It was just a plank and didn't give one inch when we bounced on it. The present-day boards are laminated, and you can control them by moving the fulcrum to make the board more or less resilient according to your weight, height, ability, and needs. But diving boards in the early '20s were just boards; they couldn't be adjusted.

In 1920, diving was a very new sport. There were few competitors, and the best ones for some reason seemed to be concentrated in New York, with one or two in Philadelphia. Between us we had it all to ourselves. The California girls came along about eight years later. Helen Wainwright, Helen Meany, and I were from New York, and Elizabeth Becker, who came to all of our contests, was from Philadelphia. We were all about equal, and the contests were very keen. The competition between us was so close that we never knew whether we would be first or fourth when we started out on our first dive.

Helen Wainwright and I were 14 years old. We were also very small for our age. I weighed 65 pounds and Helen about 75 pounds. Helen was dark, and I was blond, so we were foils for each other. Helen Meany was slightly older, and her specialty was platform diving. She had access to a platform near her home in Greenwich, Connecticut, and everything we learned from a low springboard she learned from a 30-foot tower. She was absolutely fearless.

We had no diving coach in those days, but we did have a remarkable swimming coach. His name was Louis de B. Handley, who is now enshrined in the Swimming Hall of Fame. He was an amateur coach, and this was a hobby with him. He developed some of the greatest swimmers of that era, swimmers such as Gertrude Ederle, Eleanor Holm, and many others. He gave us one evening a week of his time. Mr. Handley was a great inspiration to us. He was an older man who had been on the 1904 U.S. Olympic water polo team. His specialty as a coach was the crawl. In those days everybody did the Australian crawl, which is one scissors kick to three kicks on the other side. Mr. Handley improved this stroke by changing the kick. He originated the American crawl stroke, and we were the first girls to use it. It was so far superior that every time we entered the water we were breaking records. No one could understand this sudden spurt of speed and wondered how the American girls could manage to be breaking world records every time they competed. The secret was Mr. Handley's crawl stroke.

The girls from our New York team did very, very well at the trials. Helen Wainwright won the springboard, Helen Meany the platform, and I placed second and third. We were the three youngest competitors, and this seemed to cause a great commotion with the officials. They said there was absolutely no way they were going to take children to the Olympics. They had several meetings and then informed us that they would take the next-highest-rated women in our place. Our manager and several other women went to the committee and lodged a complaint. They had a bitter session, but finally we won. In the interim we had packed and unpacked our trunks several times. We were so depressed and disappointed because we felt that we had won fairly—and we had—and that we should represent our country. We also wanted that trip to Europe. Eventually it was ironed out, and we got our passports and were measured for our uniforms at Spaulding's, which donated the outfits that year.

We had navy blue suits and white flannel suits with our USA emblem on the front pocket. Helen Wainwright and I were allowed to have short skirts because we were still considered children. Helen Meany was just enough older to wear the long skirts that were the fashion in those days. We all had white shoes, and we wore ridiculous straw hats that were the same as the men's. They were the English schoolboy style that was then popular.

I think I should mention our bathing suits. In those days we wore one-piece suits for racing, with a little skirt across the front. The actual racing suit was made of silk. We usually showed ourselves only at the start. We would then take off our robes, go to the starting block, and start, because those suits were rather revealing. We did not like to expose ourselves too much. For diving we wore woolen suits. They were warmer, and we felt more comfortable in them. They also had skirts. Once in a while the skirt would fly out and spoil the line of the dive. The older girls who were in high school wore long bathing suits, also made of wool and very flattering. They gave clear, straight lines, no bulges or bumps, and they were very attractive. The girls looked something like seals when they entered the water with those pretty suits. Because we were considered children, we were allowed to wear the short suits that were something like the ones worn today.

Before the Games, we were issued new bathing suits, which caused a great deal of laughter, and we absolutely refused to wear them. They were made of cotton material that clung very much like silk when wet. These suits had legs to the knee and sleeves to the elbow. They were one piece, and they were cut out rather low in front. They were full-fashioned, and we weren't—at least Helen

Wainwright and I weren't—and we were allowed to wear our own suits because we simply couldn't fit into these. They were enormous, and we looked ridiculous in them. I don't think any of the American girls wore these suits. I saved mine for many years just as a joke to take out and look at once in a while. People couldn't believe that we had been expected to wear those things.

Our sendoff to Antwerp was from the Manhattan Opera House in New York, on 34th Street near Penn Station. We marched from there to the ferry, and then we got on the *Princess Matoika* in Hoboken, New Jersey. The *Princess Matoika* was a transport that had been in service during the war and was now carrying supplies to our forces in Europe. Our hearts sank when we saw the old tub. It was a bad wreck of a ship, but it proudly displayed "American Olympic Team" across the side in large letters but we really didn't care about how poor the ship looked because we were so excited to be going.

The morning after our departure, we went up on deck and were absolutely amazed by what we saw. The entire ship had been transformed into one large gymnasium. It was unbelievable. The decks had been covered with cork to make a track on which the athletes could run. There was a boxing ring and a fencing strip, and there was a place for calisthenics. The pistol team had their target equipment. The javelin throwers had a rope attached to their javelins and threw them out to sea. It probably didn't help them a great deal, but it kept their arms in shape. Then, when we walked off, we saw what was to be our swimming pool for 13 days. On the deck there was a framework of boards, and inside of this was a canvas tank suspended from the edges. It was filled with sea water from the Gulf Stream, so it was nice and warm, and we couldn't wait to get into it. We would swim against the clock in a stationary position with a belt around our waists.

There was a great deal to do on the ship. In the evenings before curfew we would go up on the top decks and gather around and listen to our Hawaiian team members sing and play their ukuleles and guitars. There were about 11 of them, and they were all swimmers. The most prominent was Duke Kahanamoku, who won the 100-meter freestyle in Stockholm in 1912 and was to repeat his victory in Antwerp in 1920. They were very accomplished musicians, and everyone seemed to have a beautiful, sweet voice. We were entranced listening to them and sitting under the full moon, sailing through the Gulf Stream. Even though we were supposed to be children, it was a most romantic experience.

We were all glad to arrive in Antwerp. We girls went directly to our quarters, which were in the old American Hostess House which had been used during World War I for visiting Red Cross women and any other women who had official business in Belgium. It was about a four- or five-story building, and we were on the top in a dormitory-type accommodation with about six or eight beds in each room. It was comfortable, and we didn't mind running up those flights of stairs at our age.

The men were in a schoolhouse, and they were not happy. I understand that it was very uncomfortable, and they complained bitterly about their accommodations. This was, of course, in the days before Olympic Villages.

On our second day in Antwerp an army truck came to drive us to the stadium where we were to swim. Words fail me in describing our first view of this place. I had never seen anything like it. It was just a ditch. I believe they had had rowing races there at one time. There were boardwalks around the pool—I have to call it a pool—to mark the ends. In the center were the diving board and the diving platform. On one side there was a hill, and on this were placed bleachers where some 10,000 persons could sit. This was, of course, all outdoors, and we heard later that this had been the city moat. It was a ditch that had been dug with an embankment on one side to be a protection in case of war.

The water was entirely black. It was dark, dark black. The weather was quite chilly. But we decided to quickly get into our suits and test this "pool" where we were going to practice for the next several weeks. We came running down, and the first girl who dived in let out the most dreadful shriek. The water was the coldest we had ever encountered. It was simply freezing. And the day was overcast, as most of the days were, and this seemed to make it even colder. The swimmers bravely tried to do their laps, but some of the girls were eventually carried out almost unconscious. Others were unable to climb up the stairs to get out, it was so frigid. Diving was not quite as bad, but each time we dived all we could think of was the cold water that we were going to hit. We learned to bring towels and bathrobes and woolen stockings and socks and mufflers and anything we could find to keep warm. Many of the girls helped each other by giving rubdowns between dives. We were so cold that our lips were blue and our teeth were chattering. To make things more miserable, there were no hot showers in the dressing room. It was probably even worse for the men because it is said that women can withstand cold better than men.

The water polo players had it even worse. They finally shortened the length of the water polo periods to half the usual time. They were in the water for 7½ minutes for each period, but even this was too much. Some of the men had to be rescued as they were losing consciousness from the cold.

Because the water was so cold and dark when we dived in, we would sometimes become disoriented. We didn't know which way is up. When we were going off the tower and diving as deep as possible to make a clean entry, often fifteen feet or more, it was particularly difficult to determine which way to come up. This was very frightening to me. Several times I was running out of air, and sometimes I had a feeling that I was not going to make it to the surface.

Once in a while we would have a sunny day, and then everyone would turn out from all the countries, and we would socialize and talk to various people. There was a Swedish boy who was even younger than we were. His name was Niklas Skoglund, and he was to get second place in the diving. We had lots of fun with him as we were all the same age and were doing the same sport. He spoke very good English. Later on we saw him again at the Paris Games in 1924, and by that time he spoke four or five languages. We all traded pins, which was the custom. I still have all the pins I collected at the Games.

When we were not training, we went on several trips around Antwerp in our truck, and one was to the battlefields. The mud was so deep that we could not walk, so we stopped along the line and bought some wooden shoes and learned how to walk in them. They were not too comfortable but they did protect our feet from the mud. I do not know how we happened to be allowed on the battlefields, because they had not yet been cleared. In places they were still the way they were in 1918, when the Armistice was declared. We even picked up shells and such things and brought them home as souvenirs. There were trenches and pillboxes and things like that scattered about the fields, and we looked into some of them, and they were deep in water. There were German helmets lying on the field, and we brought some home with us. I picked up a boot and dropped it very hurriedly when I saw that it still had the remains of a human foot inside. It was a weird experience, and we were glad to leave. It must have taken them another year to clear off the battlefields from the way we saw them. They were in shambles.

After about two weeks of practice, the Games officially opened. We all gathered on the opening day to march into the stadium. We wore our uniforms, of course, and as we hadn't had any practice in marching, we just walked in. But we did try to keep straight lines. We walked around the stadium, and there were the king and queen of Belgium in the royal box. We took the Olympic oath, the king welcomed us, and thousands of pigeons were let loose.

One of the first track events was the 100-meter dash, which was won by Charley Paddock, who was billed as "the world's fastest human." He was a very popular athlete. We had a cheer that went "rah, rah, rah, USA, A-M-E-R-I-C-A." And the other countries had their own cheers. The French one went "un, deux, trois; un, deux, trois; un, deux, trois, quatre, cinq," and they clapped their hands in unison.

There were only 26 participating countries in those days. There were no Russians because they were just getting over their revolution. And there were no Germans because it was right after the war. They were a defeated nation, and they would not have been very welcome in Belgium at that time. Most of the athletes came from Europe, although there were also sizable teams from Australia, South Africa, India, and Canada.

The swimming and diving events were held the second week. Our girls did very well in swimming. We got first, second, and third in the two freestyle events, and we won the relay. We had our amazing American crawl, and our girls were dominant, although the times seem slow by today's standards. In those days there were no flip turns and no starting blocks such as they use now, and the paralyzing cold water slowed everyone down. But our girls won everything and were the new champions.

In the diving competition, I was the only girl who was entered in two events. Helen Wainwright decided to concentrate on the springboard and Helen Meany on the high tower. It was a strain to do two events.

The foreign girls were very, very good at platform diving. They had a great deal of speed and force in their dives and were able to get good height from the tower and had beautiful entries. They were excellent, but at that time the contest included only swan dives. Our Helen Meany could have won so easily if they had had fancy high diving. As it was, I was the top American with a fifth-place finish. However, we did gain a great deal of experience in the high dive and did much better in 1924.

The springboard diving was held on the next-to-last day. Before the event the required two unknown dives were drawn from a hat, and we found that we were to do one forward somersault running on the layout position. This does not sound like a difficult dive, but it is if you do it slowly. It requires a lot of restraint because one is supposed to run and get height on the dive and enter the water perpendicularly. The other dive, as I remember, was some kind of gainer.

Helen Wainwright and I were fairly even until this last dive. I was fortunate that day to be diving last. This is not always considered the best position because the judges compare you with all the divers who have gone before. This time it was fortunate for me because I watched everyone else go over on this forward running layout somersault, and I made up my mind that I would not go over—that I would go almost as if I was in slow motion. It worked, and I entered the water up and down as I should—feet first.

We did not find out immediately who had won. The judging was very complicated. They did not hold up their marks right after the dive the way they do today. In 1920 each judge kept an individual score, which he turned in at the end of the contest. There was an enormous master chart that had to be filled out; it took several hours to get the results. We dressed and went back to the hostess house for lunch. When we came back they finally announced the results, and I had won. Unlike today's Olympians, the winner did not parade around and receive the medal and listen to his or her national anthem or receive any award at that time. We all received our medals and trophies on the last day of the Games.

At the closing ceremonies in the track and field stadium, we lined up alphabetically in front of the stands. The king of Belgium was on a raised platform, and he had his sons on each side of him. As the names were called, we walked up to receive our prizes, and the king awarded the first-place medal and also a statuette. The princes gave out the medals for second and third place. We spoke to the king for one minute, and he asked how old we were. We answered and said, "Thank you," and went back to our places. Then all of the athletes bid farewell and dispersed. It was very touching. We had been there so long that we had made many friends from all of the countries as well as many among our teammates.

Photo courtesy of Aileen Riggin

On the victory stand in 1920.

After the final ceremonies, the teams broke up. We American girls had been invited to Paris to give a demonstration. They had erected some kind of tower along the Seine River for us to dive from. It was on a derrick, and it was almost impossible to dive off it. Our high divers managed to climb up there and do a few tricks, but there was no place to stand for takeoff. I don't know how they ever managed to dive at all. I went off an improvised springboard. I had to do something because I was the Olympic diving champion. We also did a little water ballet, which was new then and had not been seen before.

From Paris we took the boat train to Cherbourg, where we got on another American transport. We had to wait several days in port while they were loading it, and one of the saddest sights I can remember was seeing the coffins of American servicemen being loaded into the hold. They were treated very respectfully and gently and covered with the American flag. But it was a sorrowful sight, and we felt so sad that it had happened.

After a stop in Southampton, we sailed on for home. In New York we were greeted with a great celebration. There was much excitement in the press, and there was a parade down Fifth Avenue. We started in Central Park and walked down Fifth Avenue to City Hall, which is a very long walk. When we got to City Hall, Mayor Highland gave each of us a commemorative medal from the City of New York. Later there was a banquet at the old Waldorf-Astoria Hotel at 34th Street and Fifth Avenue. The banquet hall was enormous, and it was a very elaborate dinner.

Except for some archers who gave an exhibition in 1904, we were the first American women Olympians, and there was considerable talk about whether our athletic activities would affect our health later on. Some critics thought we would develop heart trouble, and there were doubts about whether we could ever have children. There was so much discussion about the pros and cons of women in competition that my parents became alarmed and thought that I should not compete until I got older and stronger. I was still very small. So I was carted off to boarding school for a year in Greenwich, Connecticut. It was a school that did not have a swimming pool, so I didn't compete for a whole year. Of course, we know now that it was very silly to keep me away from my sports, but in those days it was the way people thought, and they had to be educated differently over the years.

When I returned to competition the following summer, I had been playing tennis and other sports, but I had not been swimming. And when I entered the national championships I took only third place. This was very hard for me to accept after having won the Olympics.

After that I kept competing until it was time for the 1924 Games, which were to be held in Paris. Of course, we all looked forward greatly to spending a summer in Paris, and we tried very hard to make the team. The tryouts were held at Briarcliff on the Hudson. I was lucky and won the springboard tryouts.

I was also competing in the backstroke. This event had not been held before. There was a girl from Chicago named Sybil Bauer who was to win the Olympics in Paris. I got second place in the tryouts, which I was very accustomed to doing behind Sybil. I did not concentrate on backstroke because I felt my best effort would be in diving, and because I was the defending champion I had something to uphold.

Things were much better on this Olympic trip. We sailed on the *America*, which was very comfortable, although we still did have the funny little pool on the deck. We had very nice uniforms. They were white flannel, and we had a navy blue suit as well for every day. We wore cloche hats and white shoes.

In Paris we were very happy in our new quarters, which were in a beautiful chateau just outside of Versailles. It was called Rocquencourt. The girls were given the gatehouse. It was all very pleasant and comfortable. The boys had quarters of their own up at the top of the hill. The grounds were beautiful, with big old trees everywhere. We had one central hall at the top of the hill where we all had our meals. We had French chefs, and the food was simple but excellent. We had no complaints.

It was about an hour's drive to our pool in Paris, and this time everything was very much better. The pool had been built for the Olympics. It was up near the Sacre Coeur somewhere, and I believe that it is still there. We had a big bus that would pick us up every morning and take us to the pool to practice. It was a 50-meter pool, and the diving board and the diving tower were in the center. This was a nuisance. We were always afraid of diving on top of somebody below, and we had to have a lookout all the time to tell us when it was safe to go. The water was much warmer than it had been in Antwerp.

I almost never had a chance to swim because I gave practically every minute I had to the diving. I would get in and swim two laps, which would cover the distance I was to race. Of course, I should have been doing a mile at least to prepare myself for the 100-meter backstroke, but I just couldn't fit it in.

In swimming we had a little more competition than in 1920, but our girls remained supreme. Perhaps the swimmer who was to become best known was Gertrude Ederle, who two years later would become the first woman to swim the English Channel.

The backstroke came in the middle of the week, and I competed and fully expected to be second because I had been second to Sybil Bauer for so long, but a little English girl got in there ahead of me, and I was third. It was too bad not to have a clean sweep for America, but I did the best I could.

We had an excellent girl diver in Carolyn Smith, who won the high diving and took it away from the Europeans for the first time. She received several standing ovations for her perfect-10 dives and was a beautiful sight to behold in the air.

The ridiculous rules that they had in 1920 for the springboard had been changed. Instead of doing 12 dives, we now did 10. There were 4 compulsory and 6 optional. However, the optional dives were chosen from any category, and this was not good because a diver could choose 6 dives from a single category. One girl actually did do 5 gainers and one other dive for her optionals. Today one has to choose from different categories, and this makes for a more rounded contest.

The competition was very, very keen in the springboard diving. When we finished, I thought I had won because people were congratulating me. I went down to dress, but when I came back up, I found that Elizabeth Becker had won and I had come in second. If I had to lose my title, I was very glad it went to such a fine person as Betty and to an American and a friend who had missed out on the 1920 Olympic team by the narrowest of margins.

By the way, the film *Chariots of Fire* was not at all the way I remembered the events in 1924. I was particularly upset about the omissions and the miscasting of the American characters. Charley Paddock was "the world's fastest human," but he was also the defending 100-meter champion. Paddock was on three Olympic teams. He was a good sport and a gentleman. He was as well educated as his British rival, Harold Abrahams. He was a writer and was on the lecture circuit. He also served as an editor of a newspaper in southern California. He was very facile with words and would not have been at a loss for words on meeting the Prince of Wales. It might have been the other way around. He also had a sprinter's build—stocky and muscular, not like the actor who portrayed him, who looked more like a miler.

Jackson Scholz was the American sprinter who placed second to Abrahams in the 100 meters, but nowhere did the film say that he had won the 200 meters, in a race in which Abrahams finished sixth. He, too, was miscast. Jack was also a well-educated man. He attended the University of Missouri and became a writer of boys' books. He was a quiet person who shunned the limelight.

This time after the Games I did not go away to boarding school or to any school. I just took a rest. I had been in training for swimming and diving for about six years, and I was getting just a little tired of it. It is a strain, and when a girl reaches 18 she thinks more of going out to parties and such things, and it is an ordeal to remain in training. However, I wanted to win the nationals and go out as a champion, which I did the following summer. I won the three-meter springboard in 1925, and then I decided to turn professional.

There were not many opportunities then. There were no college scholarships for women. There were no women coaches. There were no professional jobs. There was a stigma attached to being a professional. People were not yet ready for this. People did not think of money in those days. It was more the love of your sport. However, amateur athletics can become terribly expensive. The traveling was paid to championships and exhibitions, and we were usually entertained beautifully when we would open up a new club or hotel, but we received no salary for this.

I decided to leave the amateur ranks. I accepted a job in Florida at the Deauville Casino. At that time it was a very different setup than it is now, although it is still there. It was a club on the outside of Miami. It was a beautiful casino with dancing and all sorts of things like that. It had excellent dining and a very large pool. I was in charge of the pool. I took three girl friends with me, and we spent that first professional winter in Miami.

There was much more to follow: a world cruise, exhibitions all over Europe, although mostly in England, where I spent a year teaching and writing articles and books about swimming.

As I look back now and see how the sport has progressed, perhaps it was just as well that we did not have many photographs or moving pictures at that time because the girls who are competing now are so far superior that there is no comparison. However, we were the first ones. There was no one to copy. We had to do things on our own initiative. We invented dives as we went along. We had no coach. And because of what we went through in our first Olympiad in 1920, there have been great improvements. The water now has to be heated to a certain temperature, the diving boards have to be just so, as well as the tower. There is a separate pool for the divers so they don't collide with the swimmers. There is a little elevator to take the divers up to the 30-foot tower, which saves on climbing three flights of stairs for each dive. Now one can concentrate just on the dive and not on catching one's breath.

The bathing suits are more practical. There are new training methods. We had no such things as trampolines and harnesses to get us through the feeling of the dive the first time. The only protection we had was to put on a thick sweatshirt so when one landed flat it would somehow lessen the sting of landing in the water.

They now have jet planes to fly in, and, when the contest is over, out they fly. I think we had so much more fun in our day because we got to know each other so well. During the whole summer together we made many lifelong friends in all sports, not just swimming or diving. And we were able to see so much more of the country because we had more time.

3
PARIS, 1924

The 1900 Paris Games were so poorly run that nobody took them very seriously. A fiasco, said most critics, including Baron de Coubertin, who was embarrassed by the whole affair. The word "Olympic" was not even mentioned in the official program, and officials refused to construct a cinder running track, which meant the athletes had to run their races over the grass turf of the Racing Club de France. Twenty years later the Games were again granted to Paris, in part because de Coubertin was stepping down as president of the IOC and partly to atone for the mess in 1900.

The 1924 Games were a vast improvement. The fine track and field facilities in Colombes Stadium helped the athletes set 6 world and 15 Olympic records. A French schoolmaster helped set the tone for the new excellence when he coined the Olympic motto, *citius, altius, fortius* ("faster, higher, and stronger").

The U.S. Olympic team sailed from New York for Europe on the huge SS *America*, on June 16. Aboard were 320 athletes and officials and 250 of their wives, children, and friends. For the second time, the Navy sent its own team by battleship.

Unlike the 1920 trip, this voyage was a great success. The arrangements on board were excellent and included facilities that allowed many of the athletes to continue their training during the voyage. A 220-yard cork running track was constructed on the promenade deck, and a small canvas pool was set up in which the swimmers swam in place while suspended from a rope anchored above. For the boxers and wrestlers there were rings and mats. While it was impossible to provide facilities for all the athletes, most could at least work out, and the team arrived in France in high spirits and good physical condition.

Paavo Nurmi continued to dominate the distance events. "The Flying Finn" added four more gold medals to the two golds and a silver he had won in 1920, and he ran two of his distance races—the 1,500 and 5,000 meters—with only an hour's rest in between.

Johnny Weissmuller, who later spent 20 years in Hollywood playing Tarzan the Ape Man, dominated the swimming events. The easygoing, fun-loving Weissmuller took three gold medals, including one in the 100-meter race in which he defeated the legendary Duke Kahanamoku and his brother, Sam. When Weissmuller retired from competitive swimming in 1929, he held every freestyle record from 50 yards to one-half mile.

American women swept 3 of the 4 individual swimming races and the 4x100-meter relay. A butcher's daughter from Brooklyn named Gertrude Ederle was a member of the winning relay team, but two years later she became much better known when she became the first woman to swim the English Channel.

Head track and field coach Lawson Robertson called his American team "the greatest group of athletes ever assembled to compete in any track and field games." Among the luminaries were sprinters Jackson Scholz and Charley Paddock; hurdlers Dan Kinsey and Morgan Taylor; field men Harold Osborn, who set a high jump record that stood until 1936 and who also won the decathlon, and Bud Houser, who won the shot put and discus championships.

A Scottish clergyman named Eric Liddell, who held the Great Britain record for the 100 meters, refused to compete in his specialty because it was held on Sunday. He did set a world record, winning the 400 meters over the favorite, America's Horatio Fitch. Liddell's colleague, Harold Abrahams, also pulled an upset when he defeated the favored Paddock in the 100 meters. Both of these races were immortalized in the motion picture, *Chariots of Fire.*

The rowers were not so well known, although one of the young oarsmen on the winning Yale eight-oared team was planning to become a physician. His name was Benjamin Spock.

Photo by Fogarty and Carlson

BENJAMIN SPOCK

Gold Medal, Rowing, Eight-Oared Shell, 1924

Many Olympic champions went on to success in other careers, but none achieved the fame of Benjamin Spock, the world's baby doctor. Second only to the Bible on the best-seller list, Spock's Baby and Child Care *has sold more than 30 million copies and has been translated into 38 languages since its first printing in 1946. In recent years Spock has become one of America's best-known political activists.*

Spock attended several private schools in Massachusetts before going on to Yale, where he first took up rowing. His wiry, six-foot, four-inch frame was ideally suited to the revolutionary style of rowing that coach Ed Leader introduced at Yale and that won the Elis their gold medal at Paris in 1924.

After the Olympics Spock rowed another season for

Yale before beginning his studies in medicine, which he completed at Columbia in 1929. He practiced and taught pediatrics at several universities until he retired in 1967 from Western Reserve University. Now in his mid-eighties, Spock devotes much of his energies to the peace movement, but he also revises Baby and Child Care *and writes a monthly column for* Redbook *magazine.*

I'm considered a radical now, but I was born and grew up a Republican in a very conservative city with a conservative father who was a railroad lawyer. My father explained to me that the Republicans created all the wealth in this country, that Democrats were shiftless types who did not know how to create any wealth, but that when they saw the wealth created by the Republicans they wanted to dig out their unjustifiable share. It never occurred to me that there was any other view. My father took me to the polls in 1924 when I was just 21 years of age and a senior at Yale. As we drove to the polls on Winchester Avenue in New Haven he said, "Benny, Calvin Coolidge is the greatest president the United States has ever had." "Yes, father," I said, and voted the straight Republican ticket. I just thought he was speaking the accepted truth. It seems ludicrous now, but I had never heard any other view. I mean, all my family's friends were Republicans, and for the four years I was at Yale I never heard a political discussion of any kind. There was a total lack of interest in politics. It wasn't until I transferred to Columbia's College of Physicians and Surgeons in the middle of my medical studies that I ever spoke to a Democrat, let alone a socialist. And I was absolutely amazed to find out that college-educated people could be Democrats or socialists.

My mother was a tyrant, but she was devoted to her children. She certainly would have dashed into a burning building to rescue us. She watched us vigilantly. She wanted to be sure that our characters stayed pure. This brings up two aspects of my mother. Any of her children who were away at camp, boarding school, or college had to write two letters per week, and you couldn't get away with the kind of letters that some children wrote home. We had to explain to her what we did every morning, every afternoon, and every evening of those three or four days we were writing about. We had to tell her with whom we did it and what kind of people they were. There was always concern that we might fall in with the wrong kind of companions.

My mother also couldn't stand her children getting a compliment of any kind. She would just bat it down. If I had spent a couple of weeks with a friend, for instance, and his mother told my mother how helpful I had been, my mother would say that just proved how insincere I was because I never was helpful at home. She insisted that I was just showing off.

I alarmed my mother more than any other time by writing her about something that happened during my senior year at Andover. I was invited by about four fellow seniors to go and call on two girls who lived on the outskirts of town. I was always fascinated with girls but scared to death of them. I was terribly shy, although that's hard to believe now. We went over there, and we just sat around talking and maybe playing a phonograph. I don't remember the details. At one point one of the girls suggested I come out and help her in the pantry to get some cookies and some Coke, and there she gave me a compliment. She said that I was attractive, and this absolutely and totally startled me. I remember it as if it were yesterday. I thought, "I bet I could kiss her, I bet I could kiss her," but I had never kissed a girl. I thought, "This is the opportunity I have been waiting for all my days." Finally, the cookies and the Cokes were ready, and we brought them into the living room. The opportunity was gone, and I had never got up the courage to try to cash in on her compliment.

Anyway, I was so proud of myself for having been called attractive, and also feeling vindictive against my mother, that I wrote her and told her that a girl had said I was attractive. This alarmed her terribly, and she wrote me a letter telling me that I had lost my idealism and that, instead of living in a dormitory at Yale the next year, I would be living at home. God, what a blow. Who wants to be a towny? The whole idea of college is to be away, but my freshman year I lived at home and suffered. I was dying to be popular and a regular guy.

All through childhood I felt like a peculiar mother's boy type because she had such strict rules, entirely different from any other person's rules. We always had to wear our winter underwear at least a month longer than other kids. We weren't able to get into sneakers in the summer because my mother believed they were not good for your feet. Until the age of 12, I ate at a very short children's table. I was the oldest of six children. We sat around this table, and we had cereal and applesauce or some kind of fruit for dessert, and we had a cup of cocoa. Other kids were allowed to go out after supper, but my mother never allowed us to do so. After dinner you sat around reading or doing something else, and then you took your bath, and by quarter of seven you were in bed and you were quiet. There was no horsing around. My mother and father would then have a dignified dinner downstairs with candles on the table, served by an Irish girl. That's where cheap labor came from. The ditches were dug by Italians, and the servants were Irish in New Haven in those days.

During World War I we were supposed to conserve wool, so my mother and father cooked up the idea that I would wear one of my father's cast-off suits. It was most inappropriate for a teenager, and I was 14 or 15 at the time. Teenagers wore tight-fitting suits with four buttons on the jacket—button the top button and leave the lower three open. That was the only way to appear in public. But my father's suit was dark gray, almost black, and it was all loose and floppy, and instead of four buttons it had only two. The trousers were loose and floppy, and there were no cuffs on the bottom! I told them, "Everybody will laugh at me at school. I can't wear that." They did laugh at me, too. My mother said, "You should be ashamed of yourself—worrying about what people think of you. Don't you know it doesn't make the slightest difference what people think of you? All you have to know is that you are right." Well, of course, I didn't believe her. What my peers thought of me was of supreme importance. But after I found myself indicted for my opposition to the war in Vietnam by Lyndon Johnson's Attorney General, Ramsey Clark, and was on trial and then sentenced to two years in jail, I thought, "This is what my mother was thinking about."

I fought against my mother's moralism all through not only my teen years but my adult years as well. I wanted to be a gay dog, well dressed, sophisticated, amusing. I didn't want to be a moralist. It surprised and rather shocked me to find out that I ended up a political moralist, showing that no matter how you fight against your psychological inheritance, it captures you.

My father was a self-made man. He came from what my mother considered a rather "ordinary" family, though she thought he was the finest man in the world. My father's life was made by going to Yale. He worked his way through, and his extracurricular activity was the Glee Club. There was nothing athletic about him, and my mother had no strong feelings about athletics. It was just assumed that they were a wholesome thing to do.

Yale was where you proved yourself, and it made a lasting

impression on my father. Throughout his life he wore the Glee Club charm hanging off his gold watch chain. It was an open book of music made of gold and had blue letters. He also belonged to Delta Kappa Epsilon, which he led me to believe was Yale's finest fraternity, and he was tapped for Wolf's Head, a senior society. Wolf's Head, Scroll and Key, and Skull and Bones absolutely dominated the social and moral atmosphere at Yale. Everybody wanted to be the right kind of Yale person so that he would be tapped, thus having proven himself. It's a terrible system, but it was proof to my father that he had done well at Yale and had been accepted socially.

I tell you all this because I, too, thought I was going to Yale to prove myself, to be a competitive male at last. Up to that time, I felt very unsure of myself. I felt unpopular and unable to compete with other boys. I felt like a sissy, a mother's boy, and I was timid. I was afraid they might bully me and that I would not be able to do the things they were able to do. So at Yale I had a real ambition to try to prove that I was socially and athletically superior. As a youngster I had read those books about Dink Stover and Frank Merriwell at Yale, so I knew that it would be the proving ground.

At Andover I had gotten on the track team and won an *A* by getting half a point in the Andover-Exeter track meet. I was a very mediocre high jumper. I jumped five feet, six inches at Andover for the two years I was there and got an *A* both times. As a Yale freshman I got half of a point at the Yale-Harvard freshman track meet, and I was still jumping five feet, six inches. I never improved. I was also in a fraternity at Andover, which was a silly thing for a boarding school to have. But the combination of getting an *A* and getting into a fraternity made me feel that I was on my way to being a regular guy, if not a slightly big man on campus. I thought then, "I'll build on this when I go to Yale. I've got a start." In those days, 50, 60, 70 people went from Andover to Yale, so you went with a group, and you'd carry over your reputation. But then my mother cramped my style by saying, "Benny, you've got to live at home to regain your ideals." This was a terrible blow.

I kept going out for the high jump at Yale, although I could see that I was not making any progress. In the middle of my freshman year, I was going to the Yale gym to practice high jumping, and I passed the room where the varsity and the junior varsity rowing crews were practicing on the hydraulic machines. I stood there watching in awe because Dink Stover and Frank Merriwell had been oarsmen. The man standing next to me turned around, and I recognized him as the captain of the Yale crew. His name was Langhorn Gibson, and he came from a distinguished Virginia family. His father was Charles Dana Gibson, the artist who created the Gibson Girl. Langhorn was a very imposing, slightly arrogant person with a great big, noble head like a bust of a Roman emperor. He looked me up and down. I was skinny and chinless. He asked, "What sport do you go out for?" I said, "High jumping." And he asked, "Why don't you go out for a man's sport?"

Instead of being insulted, I was elated. The captain of the crew thought that I might be crew material! That had never occurred to me. I thought the only people who could go out for crew were those who went to Choate, Exeter, St. Paul's, and the other rowing schools. It was the middle of winter, and the crews wouldn't get out on the river for a couple of more months. It didn't matter. I rushed over to the crew offices and signed up. I got no coaching at all. I only knew whatever I had learned rowing a rowboat. I was assigned to the Freshmen M crew. There were 13 freshmen and about 6 sophomore crews, but only a couple of junior ones, because by that time people realized that they were not going to become glorious oarsmen. At that time Yale was being defeated by every other crew in the United States except Harvard, which they beat about half of the time. But it didn't matter, and crowds of freshmen went out for crew.

That freshman year, the Yale rowing committee decided it was tired of Yale being the poorest crew in the United States. Yale and most of the eastern crews were rowing an English stroke in which you took an extreme layback. You'd lie way, way back to get the length of the stroke and pull the oar up almost to your chin and shove it away. Then you'd have to pry yourself "out-of-bow." Well, the committee hired Ed Leader, who coached at Washington and who was utterly unimpressed by the English tradition of rowing. He realized that it was crazy to lie way back and then hoist yourself up this way—that you shouldn't lie back at all. But in order to compensate for the shorter stroke, the oarsmen had to be at least six feet tall. There I was, six feet, four inches tall, and I weighed 170 pounds.

You also have to realize something that is true in all athletics. It is much easier to learn an athletic skill than it is to unlearn a style that you've previously learned. What happened during my sophomore year was that some of those who had been on the varsity and junior varsity proved incapable of dropping their English stroke. So I went from Sophomore D to Sophomore C to Sophomore B to Sophomore A to the Fourth Varsity to the Third Varsity, and, eventually, at the end of my sophomore year, I got to Second Varsity.

Then we beat Harvard. "God!" I felt, "this is terrific." The Yale-Harvard boat race was just as exciting as the Yale-Harvard football game. Every yacht on the eastern seaboard came into the Thames River in New London. Anybody who knew what fun or social excitement was, was there. All the men had blue blazers or something like that. They had white flannel trousers and white buckskin shoes and colorful ties and a straw hat. All the Harvard men had their club colors on their straw hats; we had no club hat bands at Yale. It was terribly exciting. Hundreds of friends would be there. You would go up and down this railroad platform greeting your friends, and there were beautiful girls all over the place. There was a dance after the boat race at the Griswold Hotel. I was bursting with pride to have won, and I went to the Griswold and felt like a minor hero. I remember that the Harvard shirt I had won I presented to a girl whom, in my shy way, I had admired very much from a distance.

This was a real turning point in my life. In my junior year the Yale crew beat everybody in sight, and I was on the varsity. In May I was tapped for Scroll and Key, which made me a certified social success. Furthermore, I outplaced my father because Wolf's Head was definitely in third place.

Our coach, Ed Leader, had a lumpy face like an old pug, and he had piercing eyes. He was always scowling, and he talked in a harsh, intense voice. He thought of nothing but rowing and how to turn out a good crew. Actually, he was a very gentle-natured person in spite of this rough exterior. There was nothing mean about him, and he never insulted anybody. He just patiently kept harping on people's supposed rowing faults. For me, the drama of going to the Olympics was mainly watching Ed Leader. He had a hard enough time adjusting to Yale, let alone Paris. He let it be known from time to time that in the state of Washington they had hardworking young people who spent their summers in the lumber camps. Most of the people he was dealing with at Yale had gone to Groton or St. Paul's, and very few of them ever had jobs. They spent their summers in resorts. They were typical protected eastern Ivy League types. I was one of the few who had had a job in the summer.

I remember Leader would give us fight talks, and, though he meant well, we found it very hard to understand some of them. The captain in my junior year was James Stillman Rockefeller, who was a very solemn, dignified sort of person for an undergraduate. Leader would get all excited in his fight talk and would say, "A canary sings sweetest in a darkened cage, doesn't he, Rockefeller?" Rockefeller would sit there with an expression like an owl and say, "Yes, Ed."

We were asked in 1924 to try out for the Olympics. Needless to say, everybody wanted to do it. I think there were eight crews competing in the trials at Philadelphia. It was obvious that the crew to beat was the naval officers' crew. It was made up of previous Annapolis crew members who were officers in the navy and who had nothing to do but row. We won our first heat in very fast time, but the naval officers' crew won their heat in even better time. In the finals we were a quarter- to a half-length behind the navy crew all the way down the course until the last 20 strokes. But we had a sort of secret weapon that other crews didn't seem to use—a wild sprint in the last 20 strokes in which we threw all style and discretion to the winds and just rowed. You planned it for 20 strokes, and if you had to go 22 strokes, the boat practically sank because everybody was totally exhausted and the boat was wobbling all over the place. Anyway, we caught the navy officers in the last 20 strokes and passed them by something like 15 feet. Later we heard that they had complained that we had won because our lane was more advantageous than theirs. Of course, that's awfully hard to determine when you've got a curved course on a curved river. Anyway, we won.

Two weeks later we defeated Harvard in our annual 4-mile race. We hadn't practiced for 4 miles because the Olympic race was only 2,000 meters. We beat Harvard with very poor style, and that same night we went down to board the SS *Homeric*. The rest of the American athletes had gone on an earlier ship, but they left before the Harvard boat race, so we had to get to Paris on our own. The Yale Rowing Committee provided us with the coach, the managers, and the chaperon. The managers had to manage Ed Leader. They had to explain to him that on a first-class ocean liner he would have to wear a tuxedo to dinner. Ed Leader's brow beetled, and he said, "What, a goddamn waiter's suit?"

On the deck of the ship they installed rowing machines. We would practice our rowing, and that was fun because people, including beautiful, young college women, would come up to watch us row. It made you feel rather heroic to be rowing on the deck of an ocean liner with beautiful girls watching.

We were supposed to be in bed no later than 10:00 at night. Ed was always anxious about winning, but he got more and more anxious as we drew near Paris. He worried himself sick thinking we would debauch ourselves by drinking and going out with women. On board, I was too shy to make conversation with the girls, but I could dance, and at 10:00 I didn't want to say, "Excuse me, I have to go to bed." One night it was 10 minutes past 10:00, and Ed Leader came out and caught me on the dance floor. He called the whole crew out the next day to make an example of me. He announced how shockingly faithless I was. And he announced that if he caught anybody else like that, he would be sent back as soon as we landed in Paris. All my crew mates sat around looking disgusted with me, and only later in the day did I find that all of them were out past 10:00 that night. They were drinking in some other part of the ship, and there they were looking at me as if to say, "You betrayed us."

Our first morning in Paris we went to breakfast, and the first thing we got was a small orange. I sliced it, and there was nothing inside it—just seeds. I mean, there was not one drop of juice. I think the concessionnaire was cheating at the expense of the athletes. Then we got a roll and one of those curls of butter and a cup of coffee. That's it. A real American athlete's breakfast at that time consisted of two bowls of oatmeal or four shredded wheat biscuits, scrambled eggs or a couple of fried eggs, bacon, and stacks of toast and butter, all of which was washed down with beakers of milk. Well, there was none of this in Paris. We held an immediate war council right after that first breakfast, and our managers realized that you can't win a race without a decent breakfast. They moved us out into an apartment house in St. Germain-en-Laye that had several restaurants nearby. We ate in one called the François Premier. It was run by a big, beefy Frenchwoman with a black mustache. Mustaches are prized among French women and men. They are thought to be very appealing. She had one waiter. He was called Ivan, and he was a timid Russian émigré. On the Fourth of July, without consulting anybody, she put on a surprise banquet for us. She served a beautiful whole lobster to everyone. Unfortunately, to Ed Leader shellfish were potentially poisonous, and he was absolutely horrified to see this huge silver platter heaped high with lobsters. He ordered poor Ivan to take away 24 beautiful lobsters, and we ended up with cold roast beef, which was still delicious. I'm sure that Madame found something worthwhile to do with those 24 lobsters.

I'll tell you what our regular training food consisted of. The meats were steak, roast beef, roast chicken, and lamb chops. The vegetable would be peas, string beans, or spinach. At that time spinach had not yet been dethroned as the healthiest of vegetables. Later, after all those American children had eaten all that spinach, researchers found that although spinach has iron, it cannot be digested. Our potatoes could not be fried. The belief was that fried food cut your wind, so potatoes had to be mashed or baked. All this was difficult for our managers in Paris. They had to scour Paris to find shredded wheat and oatmeal, which no French person in his right mind would ever eat. That was cows' fodder. Of course, we were allowed no alcoholic beverages.

One of our managers convinced Ed Leader to let us off on a Sunday so we could see the Grand Prix, a famous horse race. As we were leaving, Ed Leader shouted at us, "Don't sit on any stone walls. You'll get piles." There were thousands of people there and all so stylishly dressed. The king of Siam and his whole entourage were there in their gleaming silk, with decorations of one kind or another and turbans. The French foreign service people were attired in admiral hats and full dress uniforms. Most of the other French wore black suits with white chalk stripes, and they all wore black homburg hats. They didn't wear them as jauntily as did the English, who would put them on at a slight angle. The French pulled them right down so their ears were slightly crushed. The real French swells were in gray cutaways with gray top hats.

We thought we were dressed in the finest eastern Ivy League undergraduate fashion. We had on white flannel trousers, white socks, white buckskin shoes, blue blazers, and straw hats. Thousands of people in the grandstand, and we were the only people dressed this way. We thought we would be cutting a dashing figure, and instead we looked like clowns.

On the day of the final race, Ed Leader embarrassed us terribly while we were launching our shell by insulting the English coxswain. They had launched their boat just before us, and they were sitting in their boat ready to shove off with their coxswain still standing on the dock when we came down carrying our shell. In the preliminaries the day before, one crew had fouled another. The coxswain had not steered correctly, and his shell had gone too close to the shell next to him. When that happens, the oars mesh, and no one on that side of either boat can row. Everybody has to stop rowing and disengage, and that is enough to cause a shell to fall too far behind. Well, the picture of us getting fouled drove Ed absolutely crazy, so he went over to this gentlemanly little English coxswain, towered over him, and shouted at the top of his lungs, "Don't you foul us, you understand?" Of course, the coxswain was not used to such crude language. We wanted to hide our heads, but there's nowhere to hide when you're launching a boat.

The race itself was an anticlimax. We won by, I think, 3½ boat lengths. You're not meant to win a race that short by as much as a boat length. We were embarrassed by the fact that our stroke, Al Lindley, who usually acted totally debonair and unconcerned about everything, apparently stayed awake all night long worrying, and as a result of this he collapsed at the end of the race. We ended up in front of a grandstand, not a huge one, but several hundred people were there, and they clapped and clapped. We were supposed to row away and relieve them of further applause. Since our stroke had collapsed, we had to stay there, and the clapping went on and on, getting thinner and thinner. This was embarrassing, as if we were gobbling up more and more applause.

That night we had a banquet at the François Premier, and the sky was the limit. The champagne flowed. Madame came waltzing out of the kitchen to start the banquet, and even though Ed Leader had been rude to her, she knew a man when she saw one. She came sailing up to him at his table, threw her arms around him, and kissed him. And Ed, never one to rise to the occasion, yelled, "She bit me!"

A majority of the members of that winning crew are still alive. The stroke, Alfred Lindley, died in a private plane accident 20 years ago. Les Miller is dead, but I don't know just when he died. Freddie Sheffield, number two, died of a coronary 15 or so years ago.

In recent years I have become very critical of the excessive competition in sports and in America as a whole society today. It may have given me confidence in my own early life, but just think

Championat du Monde Médaille d'Or

The 1924 eight-oared shell gold medalists. Spock is the seventh from the left. Photo courtesy of Charles Grimes

of all the other people who were never able to gain confidence in this manner. I find it purely accidental that I was six-foot-four and came into rowing at Yale at the same time as did Ed Leader.

But it's only been in the last couple of years that I have begun to talk seriously against excessive competition. I point my finger at the phenomenon of "super kids." Parents of young children hear that some children can be taught to read at the age of two, and they immediately become panicky, worrying if their children are going to be left behind because they're going to schools where they don't expect them to read until kindergarten. There are even nursery school people who say they won't let children do the kinds of things that I've always thought were ideal in nursery school, such as learning social skills, expressing themselves with paints, or beating drums as they march around. The parents always want them to be doing something more serious.

The problem is that everybody knows that Americans are meant to be the best in everything. I've seen the same thing in Little and Midget Leagues. Get ahead in the world, boys, get ahead now in the world of athletics, and let's not wait until high school. Let's teach them skills and perfection and how to win at an early age. I've heard of overanxious fathers landing on their sons like a ton of bricks in front of the team because the son drops the ball or makes some other blunder.

I was visiting Japan, and if any country is worse than the U.S. for competitive youngsters, it is Japan. Their educators told me that a shocking number of elementary school children commit suicide and that the number is going up every year. They commit suicide because they don't think they're getting grades high enough to satisfy their parents. What kind of a society is that in which children have to kill themselves because they can't compete?

I know that when I was practicing pediatrics in New York City I used to ask the mother and the father what their ambitions were for their boy, and I often heard the story of a father who had not been an athletic success believing that his relative lack of success in other respects of life was because he had not been athletic enough. So he says, "Goddamn it, I'm going to make my son an athlete no matter what." He takes him out to throw a ball when the kid hasn't got the coordination, and he's so strenuous about it that it spoils the youngster's taste for anything athletic. I think it's just another indication of the fact that we're unwilling to let children be children. We're trying to push them, and society is getting sicker and sicker as a result of this excessive competition.

There are studies that show that the people who are the most successful financially are very subject to ulcers. And there are other studies that show that those people who remain at the bottom of the barrel economically are not only disappointed in themselves but are depressed. They believe that they have failed America.

RUSSELL VIS

Gold Medal, Wrestling, Lightweight Freestyle, 1924

Russell Vis began his wrestling career more than 70 years ago at the age of 13 in Portland, Oregon. In 1917, he moved to Los Angeles, where he wrestled for the Los Angeles Athletic Club. He won four national AAU titles from 1921 through 1924 in the 145- and 147-pound classes and won the Olympic championship in the lightweight division.

Russell Vis, circa 1980. Photo courtesy of USA Wrestling

In 1980, Russell Vis was chosen by the Citizens Savings Athletic Foundation (formerly the Helms Foundation) as one of the Los Angeles area's greatest athletes in history, the only wrestler so honored. Vis, a member of the National Wrestling Hall of Fame in Stillwater, Oklahoma, was once referred to by Terry McCann, a 1960 Olympic wrestling champion, as "the greatest wrestling champ of the century."

Yeah, I wrestled many of the big-name professional wrestlers. I wrestled Gorgeous George a number of times. He was a nice guy, but he couldn't wrestle. He was a showman, but I liked him because he didn't pretend to be anything different. To the public he was one of the big attractions, but when he wasn't being Gorgeous George, he was just an ordinary nice guy. Up there on the mat, though, in front of the people, he was a real showman. But I wasn't. I'd get out there and make a move and get in position to where my opponent couldn't move, and then I'd have to let him go, and they'd wonder how he got out of that. It was stupid. I tried to pretend I wasn't cheating and making a show, but on the other hand I couldn't show up the promoters and the other wrestlers.

See, I'm pretty serious about wrestling—real wrestling, I mean.

The only real wrestling is amateur; the other is just show biz. In real wrestling you have to want to win, and you have to be able to win. In professional wrestling I did a lousy job because I'd get them down right away, and then I'd have to let them go. To put on a show you've got to make faces, jump up and down, pretend you're hurt, then come from underneath. I was a lousy showman, but I was a good wrestler.

I was born in Grand Rapids, Michigan, on June 22, 1900. We came out here to Los Angeles in 1902 but stayed for only a little while. We moved to Portland, Oregon, and that's where I went to high school and began to wrestle. We had this gymnasium class, and we used to do our calisthenics and run around the track and so forth. Our coach was the famous physical culturist, Leon Fabre. He had us take up wrestling. He was a fair wrestler; not too good, but fair. I was just naturally strong and fast, and you know, I beat him the first time I wrestled him. The next year, after I had a year's experience, I could beat anybody. I never lost a match. Same thing when I moved back to California.

We moved to San Francisco in 1916, and I wrestled for the San Francisco Olympic Club there. The next year we moved to Los Angeles. By then I was beginning to get a little reputation, and in 1919 they gave me a life membership in the Los Angeles Athletic Club. I wrestled in a lot of amateur matches for them, and there was never any question that I was going to win. I knew I could. I never lost a match in my weight class, and I wrestled outside my weight class and won most of those matches, too. I won the national AAU championship in 1921 in the 145-pound class, and in '22, '23, and '24 I won the national championships in the 147-pound class.

In 1924 I went to the Olympic qualifying matches out in Boston. I didn't have any trouble qualifying because I knew I could beat all of them. You see, I could always see possibilities for positions during a match, and I was able to take advantage of them quickly. Also, I had a few holds that I perfected, like the figure-four scissors, which they later banned, and the reverse face lock. Anyway, I made the Olympic team without any trouble.

We sailed for Paris on the *America.* I had never been on a big ship like that before. I remember that the food was very good, and they had facilities so you could practice on the way over. The wrestlers worked out every day. I particularly remember Bud Houser, the shot put and discus thrower. We used to sit on the deck together and talk and watch the waves go by. I can't remember the names of all the guys I wrestled there in Paris, but I do remember it was easy. I didn't have any trouble in the preliminaries or in the finals.

The reason the American wrestlers haven't done too well in Olympic wrestling is that they are trained and scored in a different way from European wrestlers. It's not that the Americans aren't good; it's just that they're different. In this country you can get points for what's called "upper time"—time you spend riding an opponent. But in Europe, if you ride a man very long, you're disqualified for loafing, so upper time doesn't mean anything.

After the Olympics, I took up professional wrestling for a while, but like I said, I wasn't really good at it, not the way they wanted it. I remember the promoter who got me started. He got rid of me the first week because every time I took anybody on I beat them in seconds, and there was no show then. So, about a year later, I agreed to put on a show for him because that's what made him some money; otherwise he didn't want me. I really couldn't stand a lot of those wrestlers. Sometimes they put on matches on the beach, and I'd wrestle two or three men at a time. Most of the time I'd take the best man first, get rid of him, and then go after the others. At other times, I'd do it just the opposite way. Most were just young kids, and they didn't know anything about wrestling and movement.

You know, I'm disappointed when I go to see amateur wrestling matches these days and see how wide open some of these wrestlers are. They try to grab each other around the body and don't know how to do it. They don't protect themselves. One arm should protect the leg and the other the head, and then you're in a position to go underneath or drop down and grip their ankle. All it takes is some intelligence and common sense.

Here I am, 83 years old. I have my four AAU gold medals and my Olympic gold medal. I'm still in good physical condition, except for a hip operation I had a while back, and that is getting better. I have my beautiful home and a '64 T-Bird that still runs like a million dollars. But you know, I'm a very lonely man. It's a nice home, but you can't get anybody to live with you that suits you exactly. They're either too dumb or too young or want to chase around and use the house for a party. Or they're too old and sedate and don't know what's going on. I would like to find somebody about 60 to stay here with me. I don't want anybody as old as I am. That's too old. And that's the problem. All my friends are dead.

Photo by Fogarty and Carlson

Bud Houser in 1983.

LEMUEL CLARENCE "BUD" HOUSER

Gold Medal, Shot Put, 1924
Gold Medal, Discus, 1924 and 1928

Bud Houser was the second and last Olympian to win the shot put and discus in the same Games. He accomplished his rare double at Paris in 1924. Four years later, while a practicing dentist, he repeated his discus victory at Amsterdam.

Houser was a high school senior in Oxnard, California, when he won his first national AAU shot put championship in 1921. He repeated his victory in the shot put while a student at the University of Southern California and added three AAU victories in the discus. He also set a discus world record of 158 feet, 1¾ inches, in 1926.

A natural athlete, Houser was considering an offer to play professional baseball in 1924 with the Chicago Cubs, but on the advice of Jim Thorpe, he tried out for the Olympic team instead.

After obtaining his DDS in 1926 from the University of Southern California, Houser began a successful 50-year dental practice in the Los Angeles area. Among his patients were many prominent athletes and Hollywood celebrities, including Johnny Weissmuller, Ward Bond, Douglas Fairbanks, Jr., and John Wayne.

I was raised in an orphanage for the first 10 or 11 years of my life, and, believe me, those years were pretty tough. I'm not looking for sympathy, but it was pretty rough going.

I was born in Missouri on September 25, 1901, and my mother died shortly after my birth. Then my father had an accident that crippled him, and he died of blood poisoning soon after. Eventually one of my sisters got settled in California, and she asked that I be sent out there so that she could raise me and get me started in school. So I went out to Oxnard and stayed with her and went to high school there.

I was one of those kids who was pretty good in just about all sports. I know that sounds like I'm bragging, and I don't mean it that way at all. It's just the truth. I'd like to say that we had good coaches, but we really didn't. Bless their hearts, they tried. Oxnard was a small school, and it couldn't afford to hire a coach that was well informed. They just did the best they could with what they had there. Our coach was the mathematics teacher. One day we watched him, from the chemistry class window, down on the field showing a kid how to pole vault. That coach was a hell of a nice guy, but that kid would never go four feet.

I was always pretty good at working with these big, clumsy-looking hands. Most everything I did with my hands seemed to work out. I had a good sense of touch and more brains in my hands than in my head, so when I graduated from Oxnard, I went down to enroll in the University of Southern California's dental college. When they saw how big I was and how big my hands were, they wanted me to play football. I told them I wanted to enroll in dental school and that I would be too busy with that to play football. They couldn't believe that anyone with hands as big as these could be a dentist, but I convinced them that I could do it. As it turned out, I guess I was right. I practiced 50 years of dentistry, and I think I helped a lot of people.

Field events like the discus and the shot put didn't require nearly as much time as football, and in 1924 I made the Olympic team. But you know, there really weren't any coaches around for field sports. Boy, we didn't know what we were doing. Honest to God, we didn't. We just had to try to work things out for ourselves.

Until the year I went over there the discus had never been thrown over 150 feet before in the Olympics. And here I was, just a kid, really, and everybody thought that Tom Lieb would win it that year. He was the old Notre Dame halfback, and we were roommates over there in Versailles where we were staying. I love old Tom. We became intimate friends, and he came to me for dental work afterward.

But Tom got in there and got frightened. He was a stronger and larger man than I was, with power galore. But somewhere along the line I had acquired some little knack with my pivot, and as I watched the others I thought to myself, I can beat these guys; I can beat every damn one of them. So I got in there, and about the second throw I threw that discus out about 151½ feet. That was a long throw in those days because we were never quite sure of our form. They improved it so much later. Nittyyma of Finland got second, and Tom got third and was heartbroken.

The same thing happened with the shot. Tiny Hartranft was from Stanford, and he and I were good friends. He was a great athlete, and we had a lot of battles in the shot put. Ralph Hills of Princeton was another antagonist. Both those guys got nervous, and I beat them both. They should have won it, but they froze up. See, I had this little God-given gift that I didn't give a hoot who I was going up against; I never got scared. I guess I didn't know any better.

After the Games were over, I came back and finished dental school and got my degree. That was in 1926. I got married in 1924, a few months after I got back. I had met Dawn on the boat going over to the Games in Paris in 1924. She was an art student going to study there. There weren't many girls on board the ship, and she caught my eye. I'm not kidding you; she was a cute girl. We got acquainted, and she came to watch me in the Olympics.

When the '28 Olympics came around I made the team again, but just in the discus. I didn't try out for the shot put. My wife traveled with me to Amsterdam and helped me a lot. We sailed from New York on the *President Roosevelt*. I was the only dentist on board. We even lived on board in Amsterdam. Several times they asked me if I'd go over to the sick bay to do some dental work, and my wife was my assistant. Usually it was just to lance a third-year molar for somebody on the team. But one time a couple of waiters got in a fight, and they called me down there about three in the morning. One guy had a couple of teeth knocked out, and the other one had some that were broken off, and I had to dig out the roots. I helped those guys out, I guess, but they probably didn't think so at the time.

I remember the day of the discus throw in 1928. One of the discus men was big, old Jim Corson, bless his big heart. He's a good friend of mine, about six feet, five inches, and weighed around 240 pounds. When they took us ashore that day and out to the stadium, Jim all of a sudden says, "Oh my God! I forgot my track suit!" I didn't know what to do. The poor guy had no shoes or anything, and it was raining like hell, which it does an awful lot in Amsterdam. Then Corson says, "I can't go out there with my street clothes on."

Well, I said to him, "OK, Jim, I'll take my sweat pants off and give you those. Will that help?"

And there was a Cornell kid on the team, and he said, "I'll tell you what. I've got a red sweater. It doesn't match the color of our uniform, but I'll give you that, Jim. And now you've got Bud's pants and my sweater."

So we went out there, and it was raining like hell, and it was awfully cold. You get a north wind blowing off Norway and Sweden down onto Amsterdam, and it's cold as the devil. Well, we went to the discus area, and I asked an official, "Can I see in what order we throw?" And he answers, "Yes."

Then he said, "You're Dr. Houser, aren't you? I recognize you from your picture."

I answered, "Yes, and I'd like to know when I throw."

"Oh, you, sir, have the honor of throwing last."

"Well, in that case," I said, "I'll go back to the stadium, and I'll wait in there. It looks to me like it'll be a couple of hours."

"Oh, no, sir," he said. "You can't go back there; no, you'll be disqualified if you do. You're on the field, and you have to stay here."

That is the God's truth. So I didn't know what to do. I walked around, and I saw Charley Paddock. He was having hard luck. He gummed up the last race that he ever ran, and he didn't make it. You know, he had gone to USC, too, but he was four years ahead of me. He won the 100 meters in 1920 and came in second in the 200 meters in 1924. He was the first sprinter to be called "the world's fastest human." He was a showman; there's no question about it. He'd wear these unusually bright suits no matter what the others were wearing. Also, he was famous for his finish. He'd always dive at the tape. Frankly, I think he'd have been better off if he had kept his feet on the ground and leaned forward. But if he thought his way was better and he was mentally set to do it that way, more power to him. But by 1928 he was well over the hill. The poor guy had been beaten in the 200-meter race, and it was raining like the devil, and he didn't feel well anyway. They must have beaten him by 60 yards, and he came to me and said, "Bud, I'm so embarrassed I can't stand it. Will you walk up to the door of the stadium with me, and I'll run into the training quarters. I don't want to talk to anybody." He was crying, and a couple of people started to come over, but I told them to let him alone because he wanted to be by himself. When we got to the door, he made a run for the training quarters, and that's the last time I ever saw Charley Paddock. Later, during the war, he was killed in an airplane crash.

While I was waiting in that cold rain, getting wetter and colder by the minute, I noticed that some of the German boys had made a tent out of some canvas and had blankets in it. Pretty soon one of the Germans who spoke some English stuck his head out and said, "Bud, why don't you come in here? We've got a blanket, and I see you don't have your sweat suit."

And I said, "Yes, there's my suit on my friend, Jim Corson, up there."

"Well," this German boy said, "you come in here with us while you wait." They were very kind and nice, and one of them said, "Everybody in Germany knows of you, and they also know that you are of German descent. Get in here in our 'bedroom.' We have a blanket on the ground, and you can get dry and warm."

I got in there, and I looked, and one of the poor guys on their team had to move out into the rain to make room. I noticed that, and I said, "Listen, I can't do that to your teammate. I'll get out and walk around and keep warm that way. I appreciate it, but it isn't fair to ask your own boy to get out there where it's raining on him." Then the boy who had moved out into the rain said, "Well, I don't think I'm going to place anyway, so you can have my place in there if you want it."

I crawled outside the tent and said, "You go right back in there; you're entitled to it. We had a little problem on our team, and we had to divide up our clothes to get that big guy over there legal. My turn is coming up soon, and I'll be fine." So that ended that.

Eventually it was my turn. These were still the preliminaries,

Bud Houser in action, 1924. Photo courtesy of Bud Houser

and each person got three throws. When Corson was up there, he broke my record on the first of his three throws, which went about 155 feet. Then some Finn also broke my record. Well, when I got to throw, I was so damn cold that my throw went about 115 feet. For the next throw I put a lot of rosin on my hand, and I got too much on, and it was raining, and that rosin was like glue. So when I tried to let go of the discus, I couldn't turn it loose. That throw went about 90 feet. I heard a bunch of duds in the grandstands telling me what I looked like. But I had one throw left. My wife was up there in the stands, and I just couldn't let her down. So I just simply stopped before I went into the circle the last time and offered a silent prayer that I could get uncorked and get one good throw, and I did. I broke the Olympic record with a throw of just over 155 feet.

When I did my last three throws in the finals, I was warmed up a little more, and all the throws were close to the same distance, but the longest was 155 feet, 3 inches, and that won it for me. Al Kivi from Finland came in second, and Jim Corson was third. I always felt that, if I had had the chance to warm up in the first place, I'd have made better scores.

I was captain of the U.S. team in Amsterdam. That came about in an unusual way. After we'd had one of our workouts on board ship, we were all sitting around shooting the bull. A navy lieutenant came down and asked, "Who's Bud Houser?" Immediately everybody said, "I didn't do it! I didn't do it! He did it!" And I said, "Yeah, can I help you, fella?" "I want you to come to the captain's quarters," he said. "General Douglas MacArthur sent me down here to ask you to come up there." I thought that there must be some mistake, that he had the wrong man, but he said, "I'll escort you right now; he's waiting for you." So all the kids got up and stood at the bottom of the stairs until I came down again. I went into the captain's quarters still thinking there was some mistake.

The first thing General MacArthur said was, "Bud, how would you like a big bowl of ice cream?" I thought, Is he talking to me? MacArthur continued, "Yes, you go ahead and have this ice cream, and I want a little discussion with you." So I sat down, and I think I spilled some of that ice cream, but soon I calmed down a bit. He was very much at ease, and that helped me an awful lot. Pretty soon I said, "Did I do something wrong, General?"

"No," he said, "I'll explain. The Olympic team does not have a captain, but you have been chosen to carry the American flag in the parade at the opening and closing ceremonies. Johnny Weissmuller will carry the sign with the name of the country on it, and I'll be walking right behind you and Johnny. That's the way it will be, and I'll keep in touch because we'll have to have a meeting at my hotel when we get ashore to work out the details."

Well, a day or so after the boat anchored at Amsterdam, Johnny Weissmuller and I went ashore to meet with General MacArthur and some other officials. The room was packed with people, and when MacArthur came in we were sort of pushed to the back of this crowd because everybody was trying to get the general's attention all at once. Johnny and I were good friends, and he said to me, "Bud, I'll tell you what: why don't we start talking loud and call each other 'general,' and maybe somebody'll notice we're here, too." So we started in. "General Johnny, how're things going with you?" "Fine, General Bud, and you're looking well."

We were yapping away like that, and General MacArthur heard us, and he turned around and said, "Listen, you generals, I'm going to take you out to dinner after this meeting. You might get back to the boat a little bit late tonight, but I think I can fix it up for you." Well, we went out with him and got to know him a little bit. You know, he could be a very nice person to be around when he wanted to be.

Speaking of carrying the flag, I guess you know about the hullabaloo we caused among some of those Europeans. Well, I was the cause of that, I guess. We were standing in line waiting to march in the opening ceremonies. Every one of the teams lined up in the parking lot for the parade into the stadium. I was watching them march in and I noticed that most all of the flagbearers, when they passed the royal box, would dip their flags. Some even dragged them to the ground. I called General MacArthur over to see that and to ask him what I should do. He answered me by asking, "Well, Bud, how does the flag look best to you?" I told him that I liked it straight up in the air, and he says, "You keep it straight up, and if you get in any trouble, I'll be right with you." So that's what I did. I marched in there, and Weissmuller was right in back of me and MacArthur right in back of him. Johnny and I turned our heads and eyes to the right when we walked by the prince, and General MacArthur turned eyes right and saluted, but we didn't dip the flag. That's not a bunch of hokum. I've got the pictures of that hanging on my wall. A lot of people over there thought we didn't have any manners, but that wasn't the point. It was just a tradition that we Americans don't dip the flag for any ruler. Well, that caused quite a flap.

Each athlete contributes a little something to his event. When I was first in the Olympics, more than 60 years ago, most of the guys didn't know how to put the shot. There I was competing against men 20, 40, 60 pounds heavier than I was. But I had worked on my technique back in high school, and I won the national AAU championship in Pasadena in 1912 before I even got out of high school. I beat big Pat McDonald. He had won the shot in Stockholm in 1912 and the 56-pound weight throw in 1920. He was one of those New York Irish policemen they used to call the New York Whales. He was one of the sweetest guys in the world. He had no hatred for me because I beat him. He came over and shook hands and said in that Irish brogue, "Well, young fella, I couldn't beat you today. You're going to be a good one." He was 43 then and past his peak.

We athletes always tried to help one another. People think when we compete against one another we're enemies, but we're not. We're friends. I remember Ken Carpenter, who won the discus in Berlin in 1936. He was a big, strong kid and also from Southern Cal. I had to tell him that the way I threw the discus was fine for me because I was just about six feet and weighed about 182 pounds. Some of the long-legged guys couldn't throw it the way I did. My God, I must have held back discus throwers 40 years! They tried to copy my form, but big kids like Carpenter—he must have been about 6-foot-6—just couldn't do it that way. But they gradually made their own changes.

I also remember Pat Ryan. He won the hammer throw in 1920. He had a hotter temper than most of the others. He was bigger too—close to seven feet—and he weighed nearly 300 pounds. He would wind up that hammer and let her go. They didn't use the form that they do today. He held the world record of 189 feet. They thought it would be impossible to beat that mark, and they didn't for more than 25 years.

Matt McGrath was another one. He won the hammer throw in 1912. And they all threw the 56-pound weight. I tried it a few times, but it damn near wrecked my vertebrae. That wasn't for me. Hell, those Irish cops always won that event.

And, of course, I knew all about Ralph Rose, who won the shot put titles and was the first to go over 50 feet, but I'll tell you who helped me the most: Jim Thorpe. I met Jim one time when I was trying to decide whether to go into baseball—I had a chance to play with the Chicago Cubs—or try out for the 1924 Olympic Games. Well, he was in town, and I asked him, and he said, "Bud, you want me to tell you the truth? If you've got a chance to go to the Olympic Games, you do it. You can always play baseball afterward, but you're going to be in your prime just once. You've got to go to the Olympics. You'll never forget it." That more or less sealed the deal for me. Thorpe was a nice guy, and he was a lot smarter than they thought he was. He was one of those fellows that had both athletic ability and brains.

Well, I'll tell you what. I have broken world records, and I have won the Olympic Games. Now what would you rather do? Any day of the week, I'd rather win the Olympic Games than break a world record. That is the biggest thrill in sports, and don't let anybody tell you any different. I've talked to a lot of my buddies from the

Games, and every one of them agrees with me that the Olympics are far better than a world record.

You know, we Olympic athletes are emotional, all of us. You just can't help it. I love sports, and I sometimes embarrass my children and my wife when the emotions get in there. I'd sock anybody in the nose that says I'm a sissy. I'm not, but it's those damn emotions. You can't help it. It took the children a while to learn that when the crucial moment of winning flashes in my head I get a little stutter. It's just one of those things. You get a flashback in your mind, and you're all alone. I've asked other Olympians, and everyone says it's true—or we wouldn't be Olympic champions. You know, it was emotion that allowed us to win in the first place. You've got to have that little something that gives you the added zip that has to be there, and that's emotion.

4 AMSTERDAM, 1928

Many Americans were disappointed after the 1924 Olympic Games in Paris because their athletes did not make their customary sweep of the track and field events. Some critics felt that the team members may not have taken the Games seriously enough and were in need of more discipline. In the hope of solving that problem, General Douglas MacArthur was selected to lead the 1928 team.

The Americans were confident as they boarded the SS *President Roosevelt.* MacArthur himself announced, "The opening of the Games finds the American team at the peak of form. We have assembled the greatest team in our history." The U.S. team, said MacArthur, was in such "superb condition for the great test [that] Americans can rest serene and assured."

Alas, it turned out not to be so. The Americans won only a single individual running race: Ray Barbuti, a husky football star from Syracuse, won the 400 meters. Perry Williams, a Canadian, took the 100- and 200-meter dashes, and the Finns continued their dominance in the longer races. The only other track events won by the U.S. were the 400- and the 1,600-meter relays, the latter anchored by Barbuti. The American track team's dismal showing lent credence to the charge that the U.S. track athletes were overcoached, overtrained, overfed, and overconfident.

The field events went somewhat better: the Americans won five out of eight gold medals. Bud Houser repeated his 1924 victory by taking a gold medal in the discus. Sabin Carr won the pole vault, Robert King the high jump, and Edward Hamm the long jump. In rowing, the University of California took the eight-oared shell event, and the amazing Paul Costello got his third consecutive Olympic gold medal in the double sculls.

These were the first Games in which women were allowed to participate in track and field competition. Reporters responded by holding an unofficial beauty contest and awarding first prize to Ethel Catherwood, Canada's winning high-jumper, but Betty Robinson, by winning the 100-meter dash, had already become the first woman in Olympic history to win a gold medal in a track and field event. An 800-meter run proved unfortunate because most women had neither trained for nor had much experience in longer races. As a result, many of the runners were overcome by fatigue and muscle cramps and collapsed on the field. This spectacle prompted Fred Steers, Chairman of the Women's Athletic Committee of the AAU to comment: "The effect and fatigue of competition does [sic] not conform to the American ideals of womanly dignity and conduct. It does not lead to the promotion of sport, but on the contrary, because of its effect on the spectators, is detrimental."

No race as long as 800 meters would be included again for women until 1960.

The American swimmers and divers dominated the swimming events in 1928. Martha Norelius won gold medals in the 400-meter freestyle and the relay; Albina Osipowich in the 100-meter freestyle and the relay; Johnny Weissmuller, the future Tarzan, in the 100-meter freestyle and the relay; George Kojac in the 100-meter backstroke and the relay; and Pete Desjardins in the springboard and platform diving competitions.

Overall, the Amsterdam Games must be considered a success. Forty-six nations entered 3,000 athletes, and huge crowds attended most events. In spite of the poor showing by America's trackmen, the United States outscored all other countries. General MacArthur was only modestly extravagant in his praise of the U.S. team when he wrote in his official report after the Games: "Nothing is more synonymous of our national success than is our national success in athletics. The team proved itself a worthy successor of its brilliant predecessors."

Photo by Fogarty and Carlson

Ray Barbuti in 1983.

RAYMOND BARBUTI

Gold Medal, 400 Meter Dash, 1928
Gold Medal, 4x400-Meter Relay, 1928

Brooklyn-born Raymond Barbuti, better known for his ability to carry the football for the Orangemen of Syracuse than for his accomplishments on the running track, was virtually unknown to track fans when the American team embarked for Amsterdam. That was soon to change when he became the only American male to win an individual running event in the 1928 Games. He also anchored the winning 4x400-meter relay team to a new world record.

Barbuti never ran competitively again, but he did become one of America's best-known football officials, working on both the collegiate and professional levels.

He also had a long career as Director of the New York State Office of Disaster Preparedness.

Barbuti, a graying, slightly bent widower, now lives in semi-retirement on a secluded lake in upstate New York. The years have not dimmed the feisty nature or quick wit and ready intelligence of Barbuti, who above all enjoys telling a good story.

I guess two things contributed to my becoming a runner. The first was when I used to come home all beat up and my father would say, "Boy, you either have to learn how to fight or how to run. It's as simple as that." So I learned to run. I thought running was the smarter thing to do.

The other thing was a fluke. I think most of them are. I had gone out for football as a freshman in high school, and the coach, Forrester Pierce, a clever man, put me in as guard on the football team. All I recall of that whole thing was that every time the opponents charged, I found myself on the seat of my pants 10 yards back of the line. I never knew what hit me. So it came spring, and RKO Keith Theaters advertised that there was going to be a modified marathon of five miles for youngsters. I went to the coach, as I thought a 14-year-old kid had to do, and said I'd like to enter. All he could visualize was me sitting on my fanny back there in the football game, not knowing what I was doing, so he discouraged me. "Go home and forget it," he said, so I watched him train other runners. He had a bicycle that he'd ride to Hook Creek, four miles and back, and his select group of runners would train by running behind his bicycle. I thought that was the only way to train, so I went home and got my neighbor, Emmett Bowker, who had a bike, and he'd ride to Hook Creek, and I'd run in back of him all alone.

I had no running equipment or anything—in those days Dad had not yet become affluent. But, as kids do when they sit around the supper table, I would brag and talk about my training. Well, the day of the race came, and I was lying in bed, and my dad said, "Come on, big shot, get up and go run your race!" I told him, "I haven't got anything to run with. I don't have any running shoes." So he said, "Call up the minister's son and borrow his sneakers."

I borrowed them, but they were three sizes too big. I had no running pants, so my dad said to my mother, "Ethel, get at the sewing machine and sew up the fly on a pair of his drawers." She did. I put the damn things on and went off to the race. There must have been a thousand kids milling around. I couldn't even find my Lawrence High School bunch. Finally I found them, and I hung back. I didn't want them to see me. I felt like *September Morn.**

I heard the coach say, "Now, remember, no one knows anything about pace here. Lie back. Lie back. And then come later." Well, only minutes later someone shot a gun, and I found myself running in this mob. I worked my way up toward the front. I was feeling comfortable and stayed in second place until maybe a half-mile from the finish, and then I let go. I was only a 14-year-old kid, and I didn't know what I was doing. I ran like hell and won by a couple of hundred yards. The first one to grab me and hug me was my high school coach. He said to me, "My boy, my boy. We did it. We did it." Hell, he never even knew I was in the race, but he was up there when they handed out the loving cup. He took credit for me for the rest of his life. That's the benefit of good coaching.

My serious track career started during my senior year in high school in 1924. I won the half-mile and the one-mile Long Island Championships. They sent me to the state meet up at Cornell, and I won the half-mile in something like a marvelous two minutes flat.

When I went to Syracuse, I wasn't much interested in running, but the track coach heard about me and put pressure on Kappa Sig Fraternity, which had pledged me, and before I knew it they had me out running. The track coach in those days was an old Irishman named Tom Keane. He had run as a professional in England, and all that man ever had in his mind when he thought of track was quarter-milers. Everybody had to be a quarter-miler. If you were a cross-country runner, he'd still have you running the quarter-mile.

About that time, Coach Keane developed a big black runner from Harlem named Cecil Cook. He was about six-foot-two, 190 pounds. He was there on scholarship, and he'd won the national quarter-mile. So my entertainment was chasing this guy. All I ever did was run behind him. He was awful good. It wasn't until my junior and his senior year that at training table one day I found myself being a little loquacious, and I said, "I'm going to take you today, Cook." Well, word got around, and on campus that day

**September Morn* is a painting of a nude bather by Paul Chabas (circa 1912).

about 3,000 people showed up, and then I was embarrassed. I thought, I got to take this guy now, but I didn't know if I could or not. Usually in the quarter you go the first 60 or 70 yards, settle down, and then come again. Well, I figured out that the coach didn't want me to beat him because it would break his heart, but I took him out, and, instead of settling down after 60 or 70 yards, I went 100 or 120 yards and got out ahead of him, and that was it. I broke his heart, and I beat him every time after that.

Then a problem developed. My football coach, Chick Meehan, took a better job at NYU, and he wanted me to transfer with him as a frosh, which you could do. I didn't want to go to college in New York, and Chick paid my father's expenses three different times to come up and convince me to come back to NYU. I said, "I'm not going to become any tramp athlete. I'm staying. I like it here." So I stayed at Syracuse. I think I would have been more prominent as a player at NYU because Chick Meehan developed some great teams there, although I wasn't too bad where I was. In fact, in 1928 I became the first football captain to graduate with my class in a long, long time.

The process of qualifying for the Olympics was a bit different in those days from what it is today. We had what they called the IC4A here in the East. Those were the meets that I used in order to qualify for the national trials. I won the 220 and the 440 my senior year in the intercollegiates up at Harvard. That qualified me for the tryouts for the 220 meters and 400 meters, but it left me in a bad position. This was in May, and the tryouts weren't until July, so the New York Athletic Club people offered me the use of their facilities because all the people at Syracuse were gone and I had a month to train before the trials. They were very hospitable people, and there were athletes there from all over the world. They said, "If you wear our emblem in the tryouts, we'll feed you down here and let you train. We have a track in our summer place on Travers Island." I said that was OK.

Well, I went up there, and I got a little disgusted because all I did at night was drink booze with the rest of the guys there. I had to tell myself, Christ, I'll never make the Olympic team if I stay here. So I called up my old coach at Syracuse. He said, "I'll get the athletic director to finance it, and I'll bring three or four of our quarter-milers back to work with you. You're going to work out twice a day."

It got so I was giving our own national champ 10 yards and some

Barbuti (far right) winning the 400-meter dash. Photo courtesy of Ray Barbuti

of the rest of them 15, and then my work every day was to go and get them. I was the only one besides the coach who thought I had a chance to make the Olympic team. And I worked and trained very hard.

The national tryouts were held in Philadelphia. They sent two events down there—the 400 meters and the decathlon. I got into the finals, and a half-tornado hit. Everyone asked them to delay the race, but they didn't. We ran into a wind that must have been 60 or 70 miles per hour. Everybody in the stands ran for cover. It rained, and the wind blew. You won't believe this, but I won the finals by 40 yards. That kind of wind didn't bother an old fullback; I used to weigh 192 pounds. I won in 53.3. Can you imagine? Why, a junior in high school could have done better, but this was because of the conditions.

I wanted to go to Harvard to try for the 200, but Lawson Robertson scared me. He was the head Olympic coach from Pennsylvania. He said, "Ray, if you go up there and pull a muscle, I'll have to leave you home." I wanted to go to Europe. I asked my father what I should do, and he told me, "Do what you think is right." So I said, "OK, I won't go to Harvard," and I didn't qualify in the 200 meters.

Our training techniques in those days were different from today's. First, you'd try to build up some endurance. A quarter-miler runs the toughest race there is. No matter how good shape you're in, during the last 40 yards the lights go on and off in your mind. They do. You see blurry things all the way. I never ran a tough quarter when that didn't happen.

There was no strength work in those days either, nothing with weights. I still don't know what the hell good it does to swing around a bunch of dumbbells. It's the legs that propel a runner; on the other hand, I don't believe an athlete can be overtrained. There wasn't a Saturday or a Sunday at Syracuse when there was no training. Even when there was three feet of snow, I got out and walked 5 to 10 miles in it. My legs never got tired in those days. I don't know what they're doing today in their training techniques. Of course, they're all worried about running time. I was a runner who ran to win. There's a hell of a lot of difference. We had a lot of guys whom we took to the Games with us, guys like Lloyd Hahn and Ray Conger, both of whom had broken world records here, but when they got over there, they got their asses beat off in their heats. They all got washed out.

Building up your ego has a lot to do with winning. The only thing that drives your legs when you're running is your mind. And your desire. Sometimes it helps to have other people help you build that. At Syracuse we had that in Tom Keane. But the greatest psychologist I ever saw in my life was our trainer, Frank Hugo, the guy who used to rub me down. He used to talk to me when he had me on the rubbing table. Sometimes he made me feel that I was invincible. You can't tell me that psych doesn't have a hell of a lot to do with the results. If a guy comes out with a desire to win, and the other guy doesn't give a damn, you know what's going to happen, everything else being equal.

For the Olympic team, they picked eight quarter-milers. The first four were to run the 400 meters, and the other four were to be on the 4x400-meter relay team. Then we met in New York City and boarded the *President Roosevelt* and went over to the Olympics.

On the boat I roomed with Jackson Scholz—you know, that sprinter from that *Chariots of Fire* film. They assigned us to a room, so I walk in, and there's this little guy with a cigar about four feet long in his mouth, just sitting there at the typewriter, writing a story for some magazine or something. He said, "Your bed is over there." I looked at him and said, "I could pick you up and throw you overboard. Don't talk to me like that." He was a very quiet, self-contained introvert, but a nice guy. I roomed with him the whole trip.

I was just a little nobody on that boat going over there. They'd heard it was a fluke that I'd won the nationals. There were a lot of name people aboard who for years had been outstanding in their events, always in the papers and whatnot. All I was at Syracuse was basically a good relay runner. Nobody ever hears of a relay runner very much, except the relay runner himself. So I wasn't prominent at all, although I was probably as good if not better all around because of football. Most of these guys just did one thing, and they didn't think I had a chance. I watched on the boat while they made a betting pool on who was going to win what. My name never came up. Nobody but my coach and I thought I would win the damn thing, so I wasn't in with Weissmuller and those people who for years had been outstanding names. Guys like him and Buster Crabbe got all the women. The rest of us didn't do much of anything. I was just a relay runner, and these guys didn't know anything about my football prowess, and they couldn't have cared less. None of them thought I had a chance. But I came back on board after it was all over, laughing like hell.

I got to know General MacArthur pretty well. He was President of the U.S. Olympic Committee and the head of the '28 team, and when we first got on board he came around and we met him in groups. The rest of the time we'd see him he'd be strolling around the deck with all those pretty little females, one or two on each arm. I never got to talk to MacArthur until after I started to compete in the Olympics. I'd won my first and second heats the first day. It got a little tougher each day, but I knew they were going to pick three or four of us for the finals, so I laid off in the semifinals, and this guy James Ball, a Canadian, went by me, but I wasn't worried about him. I let him go. You have to understand that there was only one more event after the 400 meters, and that was the marathon, and the American officials were a little concerned over what they were going to tell the American people about why this high-powered track team with all its record holders wasn't living up to expectations.

So MacArthur came into the dressing room. I'm lying there on the rubbing table, and he walks over to me. "Barbuti," he says, "you know how important it is to us to win this race?"

I told him, "General, it's more important to me than it is to anybody else. I waited a long time for this."

He said, "Well, you just got beat in the semifinals."

I said, "Don't worry about that guy. If all I got to worry about is him, I'm home. I can take him."

"I don't know," said the General. "It's very important."

We got out there at four o'clock for the finals, and they take us out pretty fast, faster than usual, and with about 100 meters to go, I'm itchy, and I open up too soon. Well, I go up about 5 yards, and during the last 100 yards there's one guy coming up. You don't have to look around. You know when there's a guy coming up. I didn't know who the hell it was, and when I got within 2 or 3 yards of the tape, I dove, and I won this thing by about 2 feet. Well, 2 feet was as good as 200 miles as far as I was concerned. I went through all the procedures of standing out there in the middle of the field, crying like a baby when they played "The Star-Spangled Banner," which, after all, hadn't been played very much during those Games. I'm a very soft-soaped guy about things like that. It's like the first time I put on my officer's uniform in World War II. I swell all up.

Everybody seemed to disappear when the race was over, and I was left to my own resources. I said, "The hell with it." I hired a cab to go back to the boat, and I told the driver to stop someplace where I could buy some gin. So I bought me a big crock of gin and a case of beer, and I sat in the cab and rode around and got back to the boat kind of late.

I was pretty well crocked. I staggered into my room, and Scholz was there. So was an army officer who notified General MacArthur that I was back on the boat. Within minutes in comes the general. He congratulated me. I thanked him. He said that the committee had just met, and they had decided that, because now I was the world champ at that distance, the next day I'd run anchor in the beginning heats of the 1,600-meter relay. I said, "Hold it, General. I'm not running anything. I don't know if I got another race in me." I'd run four tough ones.

He said, "You're going to run. That's it!"

So I told him, "Well, General, I'm not in the army."

The general stammered, and I was getting a little hot under the collar, what with some guy coming in and telling me what to do. I said, "I fulfilled my contract with the American people, with you, and with myself." And then he softened up. He was a very nice man. I admired him. And he said, "Under what conditions would you run?"

I said, "General, you realize that I was captain of track and football at Syracuse. I was a team player. The team was the important thing. Sure, here the team is the important thing too, but you picked four guys who trained all their lives to be on the Olympic relay team, and you're going to drop one because you can't run five if you're going to run me. Who you going to drop?"

He says, "Lewis."

Lewis was a black man from out in the Midwest someplace who later won the national 300 a couple of years in a row. Nice guy. I said, "If you want me to run, and I don't know if I can, the monkey's on your back. You call Lewis now in front of me, and you tell him that I don't have a goddamn thing to do with it." He told Fleming, who later became Superintendent of the Military Academy at West Point, to go and get Lewis.

Lewis was eating his dinner, but he left it and came back to my room with Fleming. The General says to him, "We have to win, and the only way we figure we can is with Barbuti at anchor, and we're dropping you." The kid started to cry, and I said to him, "Do you understand that I had nothing to do with this?" He never even answered me and walked out the door. That's how I got on the relay team.

My two Olympic gold medals are now at rest in Manley Fieldhouse at Syracuse University. I thought they belonged there. You have only one college, and they were good to me. They're still good to me. I guess I was the last Olympic winner they had.

Materialistically, my victories meant nothing to me. I think the only one to make a dollar out of the Olympics in those days was Johnny Weissmuller, who came back and became Tarzan. It never entered my head that I could do anything with it. Today these kids have contracts signed even before they go to the Olympics. But with me, it never meant that much. I said to myself, "I got to start a new quarter-mile. Where am I going to start it?"

When I came back, I started out peddling life insurance. It was tough going. It was the Depression, and you had to find yourself a job. I had graduated from college. I couldn't be a schoolboy all my life. But I couldn't make a living selling insurance. People complain today, and rightfully so, about the trouble these youngsters have finding employment. We were faced with that under worse conditions than I think there are now. We couldn't find anything to do. I had majored in business administration, and later on I became administrator of state agencies here in New York. I had budgets over $100 million. When I retired in 1972, I had 34 years in government. I was Director of the State Office of Disaster Preparedness when I retired.

I was in the Army Air Corps during the war, and one of the problems I had was that I didn't want to give exhibitions. I was officiating a football game someplace when Pearl Harbor was hit. I went down the next day and enlisted. I was 37½ years old. I felt I had to do it, that we were in a big world war, and I shouldn't wait for somebody to come and get me. They put me in OCS. I was in the class with Clark Cable, Thornton Wilder, all those guys down in Miami Beach. We were 90-day wonders. Then they put me in intelligence school. They put me in prisoner-of-war interrogation because of my Italian background. I had forgotten my Italian, but when I came out of there, I was speaking it all over again. Everything you did in that school was in Italian.

Every place I went from then on they tried to put me in a physical education outfit, but I said, "Look, I didn't get in this for that." I had to fight more with our own guys than I did the enemy. I told them, "I didn't come in the army for that. What am I going to tell my children and grandchildren, that I gave push-up training here and there?" Finally, I got a colonel who said, "I'll ship you." So he shipped me to El Alamein, in North Africa.

We got shelled every morning at 5:00 at El Alamein. You could set your watch by it. I can recall that before I joined the army I was a rough guy to get out of bed. I was lucky to get out at 9:00 or 10:00 in the morning. At El Alamein I found out that I had to get out and into my slit trench by 4:30 if I wanted to stay alive. Since then I have never been able to sleep past 5:00. It sets an alarm clock deep down inside of you, and it's hard to dispose of that alarm clock.

I thought the Olympic boycott of 1980 stunk. I thought that Carter made one hell of a mistake mixing politics with sports. I figured it would give the Russians and the rest of that bunch a chance to pull out in '84, which is exactly what they did. What this does is cheat a bunch of kids playing games. That's what the Olympics are. That's what they should be anyway. You play them hard and let them go at that. What was gained by calling it off? It didn't help Afghanistan one damn bit.

When I look back on my big race, the thing I remember most is what I felt the night before the finals. I said to myself, "I'm going to win that goddamn race, and if I don't, I'll come out in the middle of the night and put up that flag myself."

Pete Desjardins in 1983. Photo by Fogarty and Carlson

ULISE JOSEPH "PETE" DESJARDINS

Silver Medal, Springboard Diving, 1924
Gold Medal, Springboard Diving, 1928
Gold Medal, Tower Diving, 1928

When the 5-foot, 17-year-old Pete Desjardins from Miami competed in Chicago for the national indoor diving championship in 1924, the press dubbed him "The Little Bronze Statue from the Land of Real Estate, Grapefruit and Alligators." The nickname remained throughout a 25-year amateur and professional career in which Desjardins won 11 national championships in addition to his 3 Olympic medals.

In 1929, the AAU suspended Desjardins from further competition because he had allegedly taken too much expense money for a Florida exhibition. Hoping to compete in the 1932 Los Angeles Games, Desjardins fought his suspension for two years before turning professional in 1931.

During the 1930s Desjardins gave diving and swimming exhibitions around the world. Often he performed one-man shows, demonstrating his marvelous diving talent. He also toured with Johnny Weissmuller, doing "Mutt and Jeff" comedy routines.

I was 17 years old when I won my silver medal at Paris in 1924. That was a really great Olympics! I remember seeing Paavo Nurmi, Charley Paddock, Willie Ritola, and the rest of the great track athletes. I enjoyed watching the track meets, but one of the greatest races in Paris was between Johnny Weissmuller and Boy Charlton of Australia in the 400-meter swimming competition. It was very, very thrilling because they were neck and neck, turn to turn, and finally, in the last 25 meters, Johnny just burst out and won by a couple of lengths.

Later on I got to know Johnny Weissmuller very well. I stayed with him in Los Angeles for about six months in 1937. He was married to Lupe Velez at the time, and she had just left to do a musical show in New York, so he invited me to come and stay with him. He was a very likable guy. He didn't seem to have a care in the world, and he was always happy-go-lucky and never got in an argument that I can remember. When I went out with him in LA, he was too much for me; he'd be out all night. He had a little gym in his house, and he'd get up at seven in the morning and do some exercises and go out and play 27 holes of golf, and at night he wanted to go out again to a nightclub. I did that with him for about three weeks, and it nearly killed me.

If Johnny Weissmuller had trained like today's swimmers train, no one would have come close to him in a race. Today these swimmers are in the pool at six in the morning, do God knows how many laps, go to school, get out of school, and then do it all over again. But Johnny was carefree: I don't think he really trained seriously until about two weeks before a meet. He had big hands and feet and was well coordinated. He had so much natural ability that it was a pleasure to watch him swim. He was also very colorful, and by that I mean he had a lot of personality in the water.

He was also playful. He liked to get in the pool and kid around. We were a funny pair; he was about six-foot-four, a little more than a foot taller than I. We gave exhibitions together, and we used to do the comedy act that he and Stubby Kruger first did together.

I was so small that Johnny could pick me up off the board, and I didn't know if he was ever going to put me down again. But he was a lot of fun.

When Mark Spitz won his races, he had some real competitors who were pushing him, but Weissmuller won his races without too much competition. He could break any record. I remember a story going around about his coach, Bill Bachrach. When they were going around the country giving exhibitions, it seems that Bachrach didn't want Johnny to break any record by too much so that at the next pool where he gave an exhibition he would break the record again and get worldwide publicity all over again. By doing it that way he'd set a new world record just by shaving a fraction of a second off the world record that he had just set the day before. Johnny was such a fine swimmer that he was capable of doing that.

I got started in swimming and diving after I moved down here to Florida with my family. My father was a farmer up in Ontario, Canada, and after World War I he decided to move down here. We arrived on my birthday, April 12, 1917. I was 10 years old, and I remember walking from the railroad station in the middle of the night with the whole family. There was my mother and father and nine children, and we were all walking and carrying suitcases along a lonely road. We knew that Florida was filled with snakes and alligators, but luckily there was a full moon.

Some of the friends I made down here in Miami had joined the YMCA, which had just been built, and we used to swim there and fool around in the water. Also, the Royal Palm Hotel had a pool, and every Friday night they'd have a water show during the winter season. Those who took part in the show could swim free during the week. I performed in the show, along with other kids my age. The part that I took was walking a greasy pole, trying to reach a flag at the end. Being around that pool and the one at the YMCA, I got interested in diving, and one thing led to another.

In 1921, when I was 14, I saw Clarence Pinkston, who was the 1920 Olympic diving champion. He gave an exhibition here at the old Roman Pools with Norman Ross, another world champion swimmer. When I saw them, I thought, God, it must be great to do something like that! At that time I was interested in bicycle racing. Some promoters built a cycledrome down here, and I entered a lot of amateur races. In fact, we once had a bicycle race from here to Palm Beach along the old road, about 65 miles. I came in second, and it took three hours and four minutes. Another time I rode to Palm Beach and back the same day, and all I had for lunch was a bottle of olives. That just goes to show what energy young boys have.

I really got started in competitive diving when that coach at the Royal Palm Hotel pool took over the Roman Pools, which were over on the beach. There were twin pools there, and that was where the elite would go in the wintertime for swimming, and they had a little dining balcony there overlooking the two pools. They even had an orchestra playing during lunchtime. There was also a boxing ring in the back, and many of the fighters would come there to work out, including Jack Dempsey and Gene Tunney. I had a locker at the pool right next to Gene Tunney's, and I got to talk to him quite a bit. After Clarence Pinkston came there and gave that exhibition, I was so inspired that I took up diving and gave up bicycle racing. In 1922 I went to an AAU meet and won the Southeastern Championship and the Senior Diving Championship, and the next year I did the same thing.

I can remember another diver who had an influence on me. Aileen Riggin, who won the Olympics in 1920 at the age of 14, came down to Miami with the New York Women's Swimming Association, and I marveled at her diving and how graceful she was. I remember my coach asking her, "What do you think of my little Petey?" And she said, "Well, if he works hard, he might just make it." That made me more determined than ever, and I really went to work. I started diving about six hours every day.

Willis Cooling, who was my coach in 1924, took me to the National Indoor Championships in Chicago. I was scared to death because I watched those guys and they just looked terrific. I ended up taking second place to Al White, and Clarence Pinkston placed third. That meant I was on the 1924 Olympic team, and when I got to Paris I won a silver medal by coming in second to Al once more.

Aileen Riggin was also in the 1924 Olympics. She was nicknamed "the queen of the female star swimmers," and she deserved being called that. I really admired her. She was attractive and had a very beautiful smile and a terrific personality. She was just nice to be around. One dive that I was thrilled to see her do was a full twist, and she had a certain knack in the way she did that. I emulated it and developed my full twist from the way that she did hers. She also had a beautiful figure, beautiful toes, and made nice entries into the water. I can well imagine that in 1920, when she won the gold medal and was only 14, she probably entered the water like a knife.

I finally beat Al White at the National Outdoor Championships in Seattle in 1925. That was the first time they held three national championships at the same time, and I won all three. After that I won every national championship I entered through 1928. By winning the nationals I qualified for the 1928 Olympic team. You know, a kind of sad thing happened at the '28 Games. Farid Simaika was diving for Egypt. He was an Egyptian, but he was going to school and training in the United States. Farid, who was a good friend of mine, was announced as the winner of the 10-meter platform diving competition. They raised the Egyptian flag and played its anthem, but then they had to stop and pull down the flag. That caused an awful flap, and the officials had to apologize to the Egyptian government. One judge was kind of crazy, and he loved Farid Simaika so much that he had given him a high number of points but gave me just a few. Simaika won on *total* points, but you were scored on *place* points, and four judges had me in first place and Farid in second. Just that one judge had it the other way. So they had to apologize, and they declared me the winner because I had four firsts and one second.

After the '28 Olympics I returned to Stanford and majored in economics. I was all set for the banking business, but I have never had occasion to use what I learned. We were in the Depression when I graduated in 1932, and I was already a professional diver. I got into professional diving when I found out I was going to be declared ineligible by the AAU to compete in the LA Olympics in 1932. It happened this way: When I was a student at Stanford, my Miami coach asked Al White and me to come down to Miami to give exhibitions during the winter for three months. That was in 1929. Stanford runs on the quarter system, so I took a quarter off. We gave exhibitions together during the winter and had our expenses paid. The LA people tried to interpret that as showing that I was hired to go to Miami to dive, when all I ever received was expenses money. They paid my round-trip ticket and the equivalent of a daily allowance for food and hotel. I never got paid, never got any salary or anything of that kind. The secretary of the Florida AAU gave us a sanction to do those exhibitions. That secretary resigned while we were down there, and the new secretary, who didn't know anything about the background, tried to state that we didn't have a sanction. They didn't suspend Al White, but they wanted to suspend me. The political background of this was that Al was never going to compete in LA, but I was going to compete in LA when I graduated from Stanford, so the idea was to keep me out. It appeared that way from all angles because no one else was complaining except the LA people. I fought them for two years, but the AAU never did lift that sanction.

I guess I did develop some dives that no one else had ever tried before. I remember in 1925 Al White and I started working on the first back one-and-a-half layout from the 10-meter tower. The divers before were doing a tuck, and to me that was harder than doing the back one-and-a-half layout. Al thought so too, and when we got to the national championships in Seattle, all the other divers were a little envious of what we were doing. I remember that a couple of them tried that dive and fell flat on their backs. But that started the ball rolling. Al and Clarence Pinkston and I also were the first to do a one-and-a-half with a full twist, but that was not allowed in competition for a long time. I was also the first diver to do a gainer-and-a-half layout from the 10-meter tower. You see, once a dive gets started, all the divers start doing it and improving it. That's the way it works, and that's the way it should.

HELEN MEANY

Gold Medal, Springboard Diving, 1928

Helen Meany competed in each of the three Olympiads held in the 1920s. Although most of her 13 national championships were won in high diving, she won her gold medal in the springboard competition at Amsterdam in 1928.

I was just 15 years old when I was on the boat going to Antwerp for the 1920 Olympics. A lot of the people on the Olympic team complained about the food, the training facilities, and the smell. I didn't really notice a smell, but some of the others said that they could smell formaldehyde because the boat was used to carry bodies back from Europe after the war. I remember that Norman Ross, the famous swimmer, was a leader, and he insisted that we would not come home on that boat. There was almost a mutiny, and we didn't take that boat home. But being a kid, I thought everything was wonderful, just great.

Helen Meany in 1984. Photo courtesy of Helen Meany

There wasn't any Olympic Village at Antwerp. For a little while we stayed at a hotel, but then we moved to a place like the YWCA. I'm talking about the women athletes. The men stayed in a school, and I guess they weren't very happy with the accommodations. The weather there was just awful. It was cold and raining almost all the time. We swam and dove in a moat around Antwerp. Some of the women swimmers fainted when they got in that cold water, which was about 60 degrees. It was just ridiculous! The water was so cold that the American water polo team refused to compete. It was funny about the water polo team because when they wouldn't compete, some of the American swimmers—Norman Ross, Duke Kahanamoku, and others—formed a polo team and actually competed against some foreign team. They didn't really know that much about water polo and just kind of clowned their way through the game. They'd grab one of their competitors, pull him under and stand on his shoulders, and then pretend to be looking around for him. The referee, a big, fat man, was laughing so hard he nearly fell off the high chair he was sitting on.

Conditions were bad for the divers, too. Between dives it was unbearably cold. There was a nurse there who gave massages with wintergreen oil to help keep your muscles from tightening up. But for me, despite it all, it was fun. I guess that was because everything was so new and I was very excited to be on an Olympic team.

In 1924, the British and the American men were winning most of the medals in track and field, except for the long distances, and Americans were also winning the swimming and diving events. At the swimming stadium, the American flag was going up, and "The Star-Spangled Banner" was playing after practically every event. There were a lot of Frenchmen in the audience, and they all wore straw hats with colored bands on them. The Frenchmen didn't stand up and didn't take their hats off at any time. We became kind of indignant about it, so the swimmers got together, and the next day they brought some trackmen to the pool who were finished with their races. When the American anthem played and the flag went up for the first time, these men rushed the Frenchmen, grabbed all their hats, and sailed them into the pool. There were all those hats with the colored bands bobbing up and down in the water. It was beautiful! There could have been an international incident over that, and I don't know how it was avoided.

After the swimming events, some people wanted to see more high diving. No one would dive, so my coach, Charlotte "Eppie" Epstein, asked if I would do it, and I agreed. They rigged up a derrick next to the Seine, and they had to put two ladders together so that I could climb up. It was at least 40 feet high, higher than I had ever dived before. On ladders like that, I often froze, but I made it up and did three dives.

For the 1928 Olympics in Amsterdam, the Olympic team sailed on the *President Roosevelt.* We all even had to live on that boat when we got there! General MacArthur was very strict about that. He made a rule that said we all had to be in our staterooms by 8:00 P.M. The boat was anchored in the harbor, and the only way we could get to and from shore was to get a tender to take us. But, you know, when everyone finished their events, they would want to go out to dinner and celebrate a little bit. But the last tender left shore about 7:00 P.M., and if you missed it, you'd have to get one of the little kids who always hung around to take you out in a rowboat. When that happened, everyone on the ship would stand along the side and sing, "Row, row, row your boat. . . ." Of course, MacArthur was always up on the top deck, and when he heard that, he'd speak through the horn and say, "Now hear this! Have whoever came in on that rowboat report to me immediately!"

Helen Meany with Johnny Weismuller aboard ship en route to Amsterdam, 1928. Photo courtesy of Helen Meany

Some people revolted against that curfew policy. One night Betty Becker was up past 8:00 P.M. playing bridge, and someone on MacArthur's staff told her she had to get back to her stateroom. She refused, and the next day she was called in to see MacArthur. I shared a stateroom with her, and when she got back, I asked what happened. She said MacArthur patted her on the head and said, "Now you don't want to break rules, do you?" She answered, "No. But I'm going to play cards until one o'clock whenever I want." So MacArthur went along with that, gave her a little pat and off she went.

After a few days, the women divers and swimmers were able to leave that boat and stay at a hotel. Eppie, who was the backbone of the Women's Swimming Association of New York, and who always had plenty of clout, told MacArthur that the situation was ridiculous and he had to get us off that boat. On board we had to get the kitchen staff up at 5:00 A.M. so that we could have breakfast, catch the tender, then take the 40-minute drive to the swimming stadium. She told him that we were getting up too early to be in good condition for the meets. MacArthur must have listened to her; most people did.

The afternoon that I won the gold medal in Amsterdam was the longest afternoon in my life. They didn't have flights for the women divers as they did for the men, so all of us had to compete at the same time. The diving started about one o'clock and lasted until six, and you were under a strain all that time; there was no relief from the tension. I was just numb. I never watched the other divers perform. I'd just turn away, but you knew what was going on. You could hear the applause.

The divers I really worried about in Amsterdam were Georgia Coleman and Dorothy Poynton, who finished second and third behind me. In all three of my Games the competition in both women's swimming and diving was just among the Americans, so our national championships were just as tough as the Olympics.

After finally taking the gold, I was so tired that I hardly realized I had won. It was several hours before the thrill of it really sank in. Now I look back on those memorable experiences, and I feel so lucky and grateful for all that happened. I especially treasure the lifelong friendships made during those years and the wonderful people I met.

ELIZABETH "BETTY" ROBINSON

Gold Medal, 100 Meters, 1928
Silver Medal, 4x100-Meter Relay, 1928
Gold Medal, 4x100-Meter Relay, 1936

Betty Robinson became the first American woman to win a gold medal in track and field with her 1928 victory in the 100 meters. At the same Games, she also won a silver in the 400-meter relay. Her accomplishments were all the more remarkable because she was only 16 at the time, and it was only the fourth time she had ever run in a formal track meet.

One month after the Games, she set a world record of 12 seconds flat for the 100 meters. The following year she

Betty Robinson in 1983. Photo by Fogarty and Carlson

also set the world's mark for the 100-yard dash. In March 1931, she set additional world records in the 60- and 70-yard dashes. Soon after, she was so severely injured in an airplane accident that her career appeared finished. Determination and perseverance brought about a slow and painful recovery, and in 1936 she returned to the Olympic Games to win another gold medal, in the 4x100-meter relay.

I was born on August 23, 1911, in the very small town of Riverdale, Illinois. I was the youngest of three girls. I think my father was disappointed at the time that I wasn't a boy. He was always a good runner and claimed that I got my running ability from him.

As a youngster I was always very fast at the races we would have at picnics, but I never thought very much about it. I just got out and ran. I really didn't know that I was a fast runner until one day my homeroom teacher, Charles B. Price, saw me running for the train that I took home from school. He couldn't believe how fast I ran and told me that he wanted to time me for 50 yards. The next day he told me to get on my gym shoes and my bloomers, and he'd time me. I ran in the school corridor. He was very satisfied. He said it was close to record time, and he wanted me to enter a meet. It was the indoor season then, and I worked out with the men's team. There was no track for women. He entered me in an indoor track meet. I had never worn spikes before, so the day of the meet I went down a little early to a local sporting goods store and got a pair of track shoes and then went on to the meet.

I thought it was just a local meet for girls. It was March of 1928, and I was only 16. I didn't even know that women from the Illinois Athletic Club would also be competing. But I placed second to Helen Filkey. She was their outstanding runner, and after I finished so close to her, the Illinois Women's Athletic Club asked me to join them.

So I started training three days a week. I would go by train from Harvey High School 25 miles into the city to train with them.

The first meet I ran for the club outdoors was the local Olympic tryouts. I won and broke the world record. This meant that I could go to the final Olympic tryouts in Newark, New Jersey. This was the first time that women competed in Olympic track and field, so luckily I was at the right place at the right time when my teacher saw me running for the train and realized that I had some running ability. Otherwise I never would have thought about it.

In the finals I finished second in the 100 meters to Elta Cartwright, a California girl, but I made the team.

The Olympics in Amsterdam was only the fourth meet in which I had ever competed. The Canadian girls were the favorites to win. In the semifinal heat the Canadian, Fanny Rosenfeld, and I each had the same time, so in the finals we were matched against each other. I beat her—not by much, but by enough.

When I came onto the field, I discovered I had brought two left shoes. I had two pairs of shoes with me, and I had grabbed two for the left foot, so I had to run back upstairs and get a right shoe. I guess I was nervous and excited. Then there were three false starts in the finals, and two of the girls were disqualified. It was very nerve-racking, but I had the feeling that if I got Fanny on my right side so I knew where she was all the time, it would help. That's where I got her. I can remember breaking the tape, but I wasn't sure that I'd won. It was so close. But my friends who were in the stands jumped over the railing and came down and put their arms around me, and then I knew I had won. Then, when they raised the flag, I cried. Even today when I watch the Olympics and see the flag go up, I get so thrilled that I get the same duck bumps just thinking about it. It's something you never forget.

As time goes on, that victory means more and more to me—being the first woman to win a gold medal for this country in track and field.

In 1931 I was very badly injured in an airplane crash. It happened one day when it was very hot. We had finished our training, and I was wishing I could go into the pool at the club, but I couldn't because it was against our training rules. So I decided right then that I was going to ask my cousin to take me up in his plane. He said he would, and I drove out to the field with him, but I don't remember what happened from then on. I don't even remember that I took my mother and my little nephew with me out to the field. I also know that I went to a big party the night before the crash, but I have no recollection of that. The plane crashed from about 600 feet or so. They said the engine was buried in a damp field; otherwise it might have caught on fire. The man who picked me up from the accident took me to Oak Forest Hospital, which was an old people's home, because he had a friend there who was an undertaker, and he thought I was dying.

For the first 11 weeks or so I didn't even know where I was. But after that I did know that I was in the hospital. I would say hello to someone, but after they left I didn't know they'd been there. The convalescence went on for a very long time. My one leg is still shorter than the other, and my one knee is still slightly stiff because they put a silver pin through my leg, which was broken in two places. I also had a cracked hip, and one arm was smashed. But I was lucky. The doctor said that if I hadn't been in such good physical condition I wouldn't have come out of it as well as I did.

Because of the accident, I never graduated from Northwestern. I lacked only 17 hours, but I was still handicapped. I couldn't participate in practice teaching, which I had to do for my degree. So I decided to become a secretary.

After a couple of years, when I could bend my knee a little bit and walk around, I decided to try running for therapeutic reasons. Although one leg was a little shorter than the other, I could still run, especially in the relay races, where I didn't have to get down in a crouch to start.

I trained for about a year and a half and then decided to try out for the Olympic team in 1936. My starts were still not very good, but I came in fifth, and they took six girls. They put me on the

Photo courtesy of Betty Robinson

Finish of the 100-meter dash. Betty Robinson becomes the first American woman to win a gold medal in a track and field event.

The first U.S. women's Olympic track and field team—1928 (left to right): Fred Steers, coach; Olive Hayenfuss; Edna Sayer; Rema McDonald; Betty Robinson; Florence McDonald; Ann Vrana; Lillian Copeland; Dee Beckman; Mildred Wiley; Rayma Wilson. Photo courtesy of Betty Robinson relay team because I would get a flying start and I had a lot of experience passing the baton. It was thrilling to make that team, but I had worked awfully hard for the chance. In 1928 I didn't have to work—just run. Nineteen thirty-six was different.

I remember the 800-meter women's race in 1928. Dee Beckman ran in it for America, but our women were just not prepared to run that distance, so the coaches concluded that women were not physically capable of running that far. I actually said the same thing one time during an interview—that women were not built for long races. That was after I had seen the 800 in Amsterdam. I'm eating my words now, but I think what's happening today is wonderful.

The 1936 relay race was controversial. I wish the German girl had not dropped the baton, because Helen Stephens could run circles around those girls, and she ran anchor for us. The German team had run their fastest girl first. She got them a head start, but Helen would have won it for us even if the last German girl had not dropped the baton.

Stella Walsh won the 100 meters for Poland in 1932, although she was living in America at the time. I had a couple of races with her. I had defeated her in an indoor race in Cleveland. Then she beat me in a very close race in Texas. The man managing our team thought it was unfair, that the race should have been a dead heat, so he arranged a matched race between us in Chicago. This was while I was at Northwestern—just before the accident. I beat her, and I got a little track shoe with a diamond in it. When she was murdered a few years ago, the autopsy indicated that she was really part man. That was very surprising.

The two golds and the silver meant the thrill of doing something for the United States. That was the biggest thrill, to think that I got points for the United States. There was no real thought of money at that stage. I could have endorsed something after winning in 1928, but my father said, "Absolutely not, because if you do that you can't compete anymore, and you've just started." So I never did endorse any product. Nor did I take advantage of opportunities for making any money or for having a career in physical education or anything. Nothing was offered.

I thoroughly enjoyed my running. When I was training, I ran three days a week, not every day as athletes do today. I would watch my diet only two weeks before a meet. Today athletics are like a vocation, but I think it's wonderful the way athletes are allowed to endorse products now without it being held against them. Now they're given money to travel. The club used to send me, but I don't know how anybody else could have done it unless they had their own money.

It's difficult to say how Helen Stephens or I would have done against today's runners. They are only running about a second faster, and that's not very much. We didn't train as hard, and we didn't watch our diet the way they do today. Running conditions are also very different, and the tracks are faster. In fact, we didn't even have starting blocks; we had to dig a hole. In the short races today we are reaching a point where no one is going to be able to break the record. When I ran, we measured time by something like a fourth or a fifth of a second. Then it was a tenth. Today it is a thousandth of a second or less. That's all the difference there is among runners today.

5
LOS ANGELES, 1932

The Los Angeles Games surpassed all previous Olympiads in almost every way. The weather, the facilities, and the setting were magnificent, and there were record-breaking performances, crowds, and receipts. Nearly 2,000 athletes from 37 countries participated, and, in spite of the world-wide Depression, more than a million people paid a total of two million dollars to attend.

Because of the Depression and, in some places, political strife, many teams had considerable difficulty getting to Los Angeles. Brazil, for example, did not have enough money to make any contribution to its team. All it could provide was a ship full of coffee beans. The 69 Brazilian athletes had to work the ship and stop at ports along the way to sell coffee to finance their appearance at the Games. However, owing to poor sales and stiff American import laws, the Brazilians did not have the money to pay the landing tax for the entire team, and only 24 athletes came ashore. Those remaining aboard sailed the ship north along the coast in an attempt to find markets for the coffee. If the Brazilians' trip to California was sad, the Argentinians' trip back home was astonishing. The Argentine camp in the Olympic Village had been the scene of several brawls between rival political factions among the athletes. The fighting continued on board the ship returning to

Buenos Aires, and the captain was forced to confine the athletes under guard. Perhaps because he was particularly good with his fists, Santiago Lovell, the heavyweight boxing gold medalist, was escorted by the police from the ship to jail, where he spent his first night home from the Games.

Olympic records were set in 19 of the 22 men's track and field events, and world records were broken in seven contests, in large part because of the excellent facilities. The main Olympic stadium, and the site of the track and field contests, was the 105,000-seat Los Angeles Coliseum, with its track of crushed peat, which the runners said was like a springboard. Other facilities at the '32 Games included the Olympic Auditorium with seats for 10,000, the location of the boxing and wrestling events; the Swimming Stadium with a magnificent pool and seating for 12,000 spectators; and an Olympic rowing course on Alamitos Bay, where 80,000 people watched the University of California's eight-oared crew defeat the Italians in a thrilling finish.

The most innovative facility, however, was the Olympic Village. Set up on a 300-acre site in Baldwin Hills, 12 miles south of Los Angeles, the Olympic Village was a self-sufficient city containing 550 bungalows, 40 kitchens serving food to suit all national tastes, a hospital, a library, and a post office. All the male athletes lived in the Village; the female athletes stayed in a Los Angeles hotel.

Among the record-breaking performers at Los Angeles was Mildred "Babe" Didrikson, who won gold medals and set world records in the javelin and the 80-meter hurdles, and won a silver medal in the high jump. In the latter event the Babe tied Jean Shiley at 5 feet, 5¼ inches, but in a jump-off at the same height she was disqualified for "diving" over the bar and had to settle for second place. Didrikson wanted to enter several other women's track and field events, and may well have won them, but the rules at that time limited women to only three events.

A few months after the Games, Didrikson allowed her name to be used in an automobile sales promotion and as a result was banned from amateur athletics. In 1934 she became a professional golfer and so dominated the women's circuit that she won 17 consecutive tournaments in the 1940s. In 1950 the Associated Press named her the best female athlete of the first half of this century. Six years later she died of cancer at the age of 42.

The large and powerful U.S. track and field team seemed determined to make up for the mediocre performance of the 1928 team.

Of the 23 events, the Americans won 11, setting 10 Olympic and 5 world records. Eddie Tolan of the University of Michigan set a world record in the 100 meters and an Olympic record in the 200. Bill Carr of Pennsylvania squeaked out a win over Stanford's Ben Eastman in the 400-meter event. Both men broke the existing world record. Bill Carr's athletic career ended 8 months later when he had both legs broken in an automobile accident. Tragedy also struck George Saling, the 110-meter hurdles winner. Nine months after his victory, he was killed in a car accident.

The 400-meter hurdles was won by Robert Tisdall of Ireland, but the field included America's Glenn Hardin, who won in 1936; the 1924 winner, F. Morgan Taylor of the U.S.; and England's Lord David Burghley, who had won in 1928 and who was one of the most popular and respected Olympic athletes. Burghley originally decided not to participate in the opening ceremonies because of severe leg pains and because he was entered in two other events, but when he heard that his old rival, Taylor, was the U.S. flag carrier, Burghley, fine sportsman that he was, felt he had to march so as not to have an unfair rest advantage over Taylor. Hardin, Taylor, and Burghley finished in that order after Tisdall.

Led by Dallas Bixler, George Gulack, Raymond Bass, and George Roth, American gymnasts won 5 of the 10 individual events; of course, some disgruntled foreigners pointed out that tumbling, rope climbing, and Indian clubs were not regular Olympic events and had only been included as a special prerogative of the host nation. In any case, after 1932 American Olympic gymnasts would win only one additional medal until their very successful showing at the 1984 Los Angeles Games.

The U.S. men and women swept the diving medals, but the Japanese dominated the men's swimming competition with the exception of the 400-meter freestyle, which was won by Clarence "Buster" Crabbe. Crabbe made his Olympic debut in 1928, winning a bronze in the 1,500-meter freestyle and placing fourth in the 400 meters. After the 1932 Games, Paramount Pictures, looking for a suitable rival to Johnny Weissmuller's Tarzan at MGM, signed Buster Crabbe. The first of his 174 films was *King of the Jungle*, in which he played Kasta the Lion Man. Crabbe did play Tarzan in one film but was better known for his Flash Gordon and Buck Rogers roles.

The American women swimmers performed brilliantly, taking golds in every event except the 200-meter breaststroke. Helene

Madison won the 100- and 400-meter freestyle races and anchored the winning 4x100-meter relay team. Eleanor Holm, after finishing fifth as a 14-year-old in 1928, won the 100-meter backstroke, but the irrepressible Holm was destined for greater fame in 1936 when she was expelled from the team by Avery Brundage for behavior he considered unbecoming of a lady.

Eleanor Holm in 1984. Photo by Fogarty and Carlson

ELEANOR HOLM

Gold Medal, 100-Meter Backstroke, 1932

Eleanor Holm achieved greater fame in 1936, when she did not compete in the Olympics, than she did in 1932, when she won the 100-meter backstroke in Los Angeles. Holm had come out of retirement to make the '36 team and was on her way to Berlin when Avery Brundage dismissed her from the team for drinking champagne and "roistering at the bar."

Holm was only 14 when she came in fifth in the backstroke at Amsterdam in 1928. It was the last race she would lose in the backstroke, but few Americans remember her swimming skills; rather, they recall her as one of the most colorful personalities of the 1930s.

A singer in the big band era with the Arthur Jarrett Band, and married to Jarrett himself, she covered the '36 games as a correspondent for the Associated Press. Following the Berlin Games, she made $4,000 a week swimming in the Billy Rose Aquacade. Rose later became her husband, until their marriage, too, ended in a messy divorce, often called the War of the Roses in the press.

After her gold medal in 1932, Warner Brothers put her under a film contract. She starred in only one major film, playing opposite Glenn Morris, the '36 decathlon champion, in a lamentably bad Tarzan film that did poorly at the box office.

As spirited and feisty as ever, Holm is still angry over the Brundage affair, but takes out her frustrations on the tennis courts of North Miami, usually against rivals at least 20 years her junior.

I was everything that Avery Brundage hated. I had a few dollars, and athletes were supposed to be poor. I worked in nightclubs, and athletes shouldn't do that. I was married. All of this was against his whole conception of what an athlete should be. It didn't matter to him that I held the world record. That didn't mean a thing. It was just that I didn't conform to his image of an athlete. But he rained on my parade for only a very short time. He did make me famous. I would have been just another female backstroke swimmer without Brundage.

The day I got kicked off the team, I was up in first class with the newspaper guys and having a good time. People like Douglas MacArthur and Helen Hayes and others I knew were there. It was all very innocent until one of the chaperones told me I had to go to bed. I made some sort of speech—I forgot exactly what I said—but it was something like, "Look, it's my third Olympic team. I don't think you've been on any before. I know what I'm doing. And what are you doing up here? Why aren't you downstairs watching the athletes?"

I do remember very vividly that someone told me if I apologized to Brundage I would be reinstated. Of course, all the newspapermen grabbed me right away and said, "Don't you do that; whatever you do, don't do it." And I said, "Don't worry. I won't."

My husband, Arthur Jarrett, was going to sue them. That might have changed things for others later on because it was supposed to have been done by a committee, but they later all admitted they had nothing to say about it at all. When Brundage got away with kicking me off the team, he gained complete power. Later, many of the committee members said that they were sorry they didn't stand up to him because everybody, including the swimming coach, Bob Kipputh, said, "Hey, this is silly. This girl knows what she is doing."

The Germans could not understand anybody being kicked off the team for drinking wine when they had wine on their training tables. I'll never forget when Goering and Hitler said that if I had been a German athlete the punishment would have come after I had won the gold medal. I later thought, Yeah, probably Buchenwald or some other concentration camp.

Goering was fun. He really did give me a silver swastika, but it isn't silver; it's tarnishing. He took it right off his uniform. I know that some say I had it melted down into a Star of David, but that's not right. What I did do was to have this medal copied in gold—I was married to Billy Rose by this time—and had the Star of David put in it in diamonds.

A funny sidelight to Brundage kicking me off the team was that I was invited to everything in Berlin, and he would be there, too. He would be so miserable because I was at all these important functions. I would ignore him—like he wasn't even alive. I really think he hated the poor athletes. How dare I be there and take away his thunder? You see, they all wanted to talk to me.

Brundage tried to send me home, but he couldn't because the Associated Press hired me, and I had press credentials. It was Allan Gould of the AP who arranged all this. I wrote a column, and I had some mighty fine writers doing it for me—writers like Paul Gallico, Allan Gould, and Tom Walsh. I had the best time doing my column, and it went on the AP wire all over the country.

My seat in the stadium was close to Hitler's box, and sometimes I was able to get his autograph when folks would ask me to. I had met both Hitler and Goering through a reporter friend who had introduced me to Putzi Hanfstaengl, a former American who had chosen to live in Hitler's Germany. What was Hitler like? Very hard to tell, because he didn't have the sparkle that Goering did. You just knew that Goering was fun. Somebody later wrote a book about Goering that was sent to me, which I never did anything about. The author said I was supposedly at parties at Goering's place and that I gave a swimming exhibition nude, but none of that was true.

You know, Leni Riefenstahl did a whole thing on me, but it never did appear in her final documentary on the '36 Games. You see, I continued training right up until the time the backstroke went on because everyone thought that with the newspaper boys on Brundage's tail I would be reinstated. So Leni did a segment on me, but I guess it was cut out because I never got to swim, and I never got to see the film that she shot. She was a very talented woman.

Outside of the bad moments of the opening day and watching somebody else win the backstroke, it was pretty good. There were all the cables from home and one offer after another for Arthur and me to go on tour. And as the money kept getting bigger and bigger, the hurt was eased a little bit.

I was a water rat as a child. I was born on December 5, 1913, to a Swedish father and an Irish mother. My family had a cottage on Long Beach, New York, and we used to go there every summer. My mother used to tie water wings on me because I didn't know how to swim. I had no fear of the water, and I used to go way out in the ocean, and a lifeguard had to come out and keep getting me. On the way in he would bawl me out and say, "Don't do that again," but he would also teach me how to swim on the way in. An hour later he'd be out getting me again. And he'd teach me on the way in again. I was no dope. I was getting free lessons. I've never forgotten him. His name was Ralph Vail.

There was a pool in Long Beach called the Olympic Pool, and that's where I first saw all the champions. The Women's Swimming Association of New York used to come down there and have races and diving competitions. I used to sit there goggle-eyed watching them. I was so mad for Helen Meany. I was going to be a diver because of her. Then, when I saw the judges holding up their scorecards, I decided that if you touch first there's no question who's the winner.

Much to my father's objection, I joined the Women's Swimming Association of New York. I became a medley swimmer, but because there was no medley in the Olympics then, my coaches decided that I should concentrate on the backstroke.

I think I was one of the youngest girls on the 1928 team. I was not yet 15. Now these kids are what, 11, 12, 13 years old? They can do it because all they do is train. And that's why they don't last. I think I'm the only woman swimmer who has ever been on three Olympic teams. There have been divers, but no swimmers.

It seems to me that the young kids swimming today don't have any fun at all. All they do is train and train and train. I understand that they're up at six o'clock in the morning and they go and do nine zillion laps and then go to school and then come back after school and train some more. They go home and do their homework and are up at six o'clock again. That's why the girls don't last. After all, when they get to be 15, 16, 17 years old, they want to go to proms; they want to have little flirtations with boys; they want to be human.

I can't ever remember feeling any pressure. It was kind of fun. First of all, in those days I loved the water. You couldn't keep me out. I never thought of it in the beginning as being pressure. To make the '36 team—that was pressure. I was under contract to Warner Brothers, and there was my life in show biz. It was a whole different environment. And yet I was better in 1936 than I had ever been in my life. I just trained harder. I wanted to win desperately—almost more than I did in 1932. In 1928 it was all fun. It didn't mean that much to me. I don't think I had the competitive will to win in '28. I thought, This is great. This is wonderful. But when I saw that American flag go up, I got the spirit, and I said to myself, "Next time that's going to be for me."

I was Douglas MacArthur's favorite at the '28 Games. I think it was because I was one of the youngest girls on the team. I have a picture of me sitting on his lap. MacArthur thought of us all as his broads—his little children—and he thought we were all great, and he admired us and had respect for us. He was entirely different from Brundage. He had a whole different attitude. We all adored MacArthur. We didn't find him somber or anything. He loved all our silly little pranks. I bet I wouldn't have been kicked off the '36 team if he had been there.

It's a funny thing about the 1932 Games in Los Angeles, given my later reputation as a playgirl. In 1932, when nothing was going to stop me, I used to snitch on the girls if they kept me awake. I'd say to the coaches, "Did you know she was out last night? She didn't get in until 10 o'clock." Nobody believes this now. Joan

McSheehy was a fun-loving girl, and she'd sneak out every once in a while, and I'd complain that she and her friends woke me up when they came in. Nobody believes it, but it's true.

What changed me? Well, once I got hold of that gold medal, it was Katy bar the door! That's when I started to smoke. I even became a showoff with my smoking. Of course, in those days I could cut it off at any time. The moment I started training for the '36 Games I stopped. But when I was preparing for the tryouts, I would do a terrible thing. I used to walk into the locker room and light up a cigarette, and all of the girls would look at me and whisper, "How can she do that? How can she smoke?" But I was just psyching them out, that's all.

We were all fierce competitors because we couldn't have done what we did if we had not been. I still am a fierce competitor. I can't help myself. I'm still like that with my tennis. I play with girls who are so much better than I am, but I can outrun most of them because I try. Where they might give up, I won't. No matter how hard they bang the ball at me, I go for it. I just don't give up.

After the 1932 Games I signed a contract with Warner Brothers, and I married Arthur Jarrett. I sang with his band. I never had done any singing before that, but I was still on all the sports pages, so I didn't have to sing that well. I always had a throaty voice. I used to do duets with Arthur, and he would take the tough parts. And don't forget, it was his orchestra, and the arrangements were made to make me look good. I would train at two or three o'clock in the morning in the Lakeshore Pool in Chicago. We used to work the College Inn and the Blackhawk in Chicago, and then we'd go on tour. It was fun, and I loved it.

I didn't lose my amateur standing, even though I was under contract to Warner Brothers, because they were training me to be an actress. They were sending me to dramatic school. I never thought of myself as an actress. Never. And I never had the burning desire to be one. I always thought it was such a waste. The wonderful little starlets that I knew who never got a break. It seemed unfair to me that they handed everything to me on a silver platter. Those starlets used to say to me, "Gee, I wish I could swim on my back."

When it got close to the '36 Games, I settled my contract with Warner Brothers. I must say they didn't object too much. I had been in a lot of films, but only in bit parts to gain experience. They thought I was going to be a comedienne. I did keep singing, though. I trained for the '36 Games and still sang with Arthur's band.

After 1936, Arthur and I came back and played all the theaters. In 1937 we did the Cleveland Aquacade—that was the first aquacade. I was getting $4,000 a week. I think Johnny Weissmuller got $5,500 or $6,000. Some of the other swimmers got between $400 and $500 a week. But Billy Rose made a fortune on all this. That's where all of his big money came from. I think he used to clear between $40,000 and $50,000 a week. And in those days that was an awful lot of money. As a matter of fact, that's why a lot of the swimmers think of me so fondly—because they never made that kind of money in their lives. And I got news for you: they still don't.

I quit swimming after the Aquacades of 1939 and '40. In the meantime, I had made one rather bad Tarzan film with Glenn Morris, who had won the decathlon in 1936. After the grind of the Aquacades, I said that I would never go in the water again as long as I lived, that for once I was going to be dry. And I didn't go near a pool for eight or nine years. Once in a while I'll go in now if I can't get a tennis game. I'll always do something athletic, because it's just a part of me. I always feel that swimming is my ace in the hole. When the old legs won't go on the tennis court anymore, I'll go back in the water. I will say one thing: I should never have quit. I should have continued to go in at least once or twice a week, because I would probably be better-looking, better-bodied, better-muscled. You can't use those muscles all those years and then just let them go and quit. I'm just one of the lucky ones who didn't put on a lot of weight.

My mind keeps going because I have a lot of things to take care of. Financial matters. I read the *Wall Street Journal* every day—back in the thirties I wouldn't have known what it was. After I was divorced from Billy Rose I realized that I had better learn something about money, and I took all kinds of classes. And to a great extent, I'm pretty much on top of what I've got. Figures don't come easy for me—it's a chore—but I stick with it.

How does one keep her life in perspective given all the bright lights and publicity? I'll tell you. I got so used to it, it was just like an everyday event. I mean, it was just par for the course. You know, the only clippings I have are ones that my father saved when I was very young. I never saved clippings. I just thought fame was a normal everyday thing. I never had any problems adjusting because I was never really avid. Working with Arthur's band, doing theater, working in nightclubs, being in the Aquacades, and then marrying Billy Rose, I had all the glamor in the whole world, and I was right in the middle of it. I guess I had an easier time adjusting than most people. Even today I never think of the old days except to think of the laughs. I never say, "Aw, I'm getting old now, and isn't it a shame." My generation is passing on, and I'm 74, but I don't feel like it. In fact, I make cracks about playing tennis with some old broad, and then it turns out she's only 50.

Photo courtesy of George Gulack

George Gulack, circa 1980.

GEORGE J. GULACK

Gold Medal, Flying Rings (Gymnastics), 1932

Born in Riga, Latvia, in 1905, George Gulack and his family came to the United States in 1922. After winning several national gymnastic titles, he became a U.S. citizen, a member of the U.S. Olympic team, and a gold medal winner on the rings at Los Angeles in 1932.

Gulack has spent his entire life in gymnastics. After his own competitive career ended, he became a widely respected international gymnastics judge and worked several Olympic competitions after World War II. From 1934 to 1958 George Gulack was a member of the U.S. Olympic Committee, and for many of those years he was Chairman of the National AAU Gymnastics Technical Committee.

He also served as chairman of the U.S. Olympic Gymnastics Committee in the early 1960s and devoted much of his time to reforming American gymnastics so it more closely conformed to international standards.

Kaiser Wilhelm was in a way responsible for getting me into gymnastics. It was during the First World War. Kaiser Wilhelm and his forces invaded Latvia, and in September of 1917 they occupied my hometown of Riga. Within one week we had a German official who instituted German education and language in our schools. And that's where I started gymnastics.

Everybody had to take part in a gym class twice a week. These were held in the evening so we had to do our homework first. It was very cold in Riga, much colder than here in the United States. I was only 12 years old, and my mother insisted on my wearing a sweater, a shirt, and another sweater. In other words, she gave me about five or six sweaters to wear. The teacher made us run around and do calisthenics for half an hour. Then he lined us up in a single file and talked to each of us. I was the shortest one of the 80 students, and I was very shy. When he came to me, I was perspiring because I was very hot under all my clothes. He approached and said, "What are you perspiring about?"

"I'm hot," I said.

He replied, "No wonder! What are you wearing? Take off your shirt."

I took off the shirt, and he said, "What's this? Take this off." And so on. He made me actually undress. My upper body was nude.

He then asked, "How many trousers do you have?"

I told him, "Just an undergarment and my pants."

He said, "Leave them alone." Then he asked, "Why do you bundle yourself up in all these clothes?"

"Because my mother insisted."

"The next time you come to the gym, I don't want to see any of these clothes. I want you to have just one shirt and that's all."

That was on a Tuesday. Come Friday our gym teacher divided us into eight squads according to our height, with 10 of us in each squad. From the ceiling he lowered eight ropes, which we were to climb. The first 10 students approached the rope. He blew a whistle, and from a starting position they had to climb up to the rafters. He had put lampblack on the rafters, and they had to touch this. I could see that the first group was actually struggling to get a few feet off the floor. One of them finally managed to climb halfway up to the ceiling, which was about 18 to 20 feet high. When it came time for the last group, I was naturally in it because I was the shortest student in the class. When he blew the whistle, I think it took me about six to eight seconds to reach the top, and I looked down and saw that everybody else couldn't even get started. I was then 12 years old. I don't want to brag about it, but everybody applauded, and the teacher said, "Someday you, George, will be an Olympian."

Since that time I have been active in gymnastics. I later joined two gymnastics clubs in the city, and I was always the shortest and youngest member. I became the interscholastic champion and took third in the senior meet in 1922 when I was 16.

That year our family left for the United States. I was told to forget about gymnastics in the United States because they had an entirely different system for gymnastics and I wouldn't like it. And I can tell you, that was absolutely correct, but I didn't tell too many people because they would have taken exception to what I said. It was that way until 1958, when I was appointed national chairman of gymnastics in the United States.

When we arrived in New York in 1922, I looked in the telephone book for a *Turnverein,* and there was one on the corner of 85th Street and Lexington Avenue. It turned out to be one of the best gymnastics clubs in the United States. I went there, and once again, because I was short—I was only 5 feet, 4 inches—they stuck me in the last group. The class started, but my group leader soon took me to the head instructor and told him that I didn't belong in his group, so the instructor asked to see what I could do. I figured that was my chance, and I started the giant swings and changes and all that on the horizontal bar. And the leader said, "Well, you stay here in the elite group."

In the next few years I won several national championships, and I became a *Turnwart,* which is an honorary instructor in gymnastics, although I was still very young for such an honor. I also helped train the athletes who were preparing themselves for the Olympic Games in Paris in 1924 and in Amsterdam in 1928.

I met and fell in love with my future wife about this time, and all gymnastics stopped for me for a couple of years. We were married in 1930. These were bad times. It was the Depression, and we didn't have jobs. There was absolutely no use in even looking for work. However, in 1931 I was called on to judge a gymnastics meet in New York, and one of the top officials said to me, "We are training at the 23rd Street YMCA every night, and you must come. Where have you been for the past three years?" I told him that I had got married and that there were no jobs or anything. He said, "Oh, forget about jobs. You come and train." Well, with no work, most of my time after that was spent in the gym.

Just before the 1932 Olympic tryouts, which were held in July at the City College of New York, I overheard one of the coaches say about me during a training session, "He'll never make it. He better not go to the tryouts."

That discouraged me, but I thought, I'll just have to prove that he's wrong. I knew that I was just coming back and didn't yet feel the way I should, but believe it or not, at the tryouts I took second place in the rings, and that meant I was on the team.

One day while I was training in the Olympic Village, someone came over to me and introduced himself and said, "My name is Frank Merrill." I thought, Frank Merrill? Why, he's Tarzan! So I said, "Was your real name Otto Pohl?" His real name was Otto Pohl, a former gymnast from Newark, New Jersey, and I recognized him as one of the first silent-picture Tarzans. After the First World War he was in San Francisco for a national gymnastics meet, and some scouts saw him compete and picked him as Tarzan. He later perfected Tarzan's rope-swinging routine, but when I met him at the Olympic Games he was a very successful real estate agent. We got acquainted, and I let him criticize my training routines. He criticized every little detail and said, "I wouldn't talk to you if I didn't see any promise in you. Without any doubt you have it all over every other gymnast in the Olympics."

As it turned out, he was right. I was so confident that it was the easiest competition I ever went through. It was just like play, and I easily outpointed William Denton of the U.S. Naval Academy, who came in second.

Whether or not there are politics in international judging and the Olympics is an excellent question. I served as a judge in

George Gulack in uniform, 1932. Photo courtesy of George Gulack

London in 1948, in Helsinki in 1952, in Rome in 1960, in Tokyo in 1964, and in Mexico City in 1968. You will not believe me when I say that especially in the last 20 years the judging in the Olympic Games has been 95 to 98 percent absolutely correct. The reason we in the United States believe it is otherwise is that too often we try to cover the shortcomings of our gymnasts in international competition by talking about partiality and politics. We even talk about somebody else's marks—what he should have gotten. We always criticize everybody under the sun, but we don't take care of our own shortcomings. That phase of our sport is neglected.

Most of the time if you find an Olympian who participated in Olympiad after Olympiad, it denotes weakness in the sport in that particular country. He can always make the team because he has no competition. He may be a little bit better, but he doesn't measure up to international standards where the competition is greater. That was the case in gymnastics and in many other sports such as fencing, where the same athletes competed in Olympiad after Olympiad but didn't bring home the medals. But there was one exception—Al Oerter, the discus thrower from New York who won the gold in four consecutive Games—and this seldom happens in track and field because we are so outstanding in this area.

I did go to the Moscow Games in 1980. Sports are sports. I claim that sports have nothing to do with politics. You know the history of the ancient Olympic Games. They stopped wars to let young men participate in wholesome athletic endeavors. For the United States to boycott the Moscow Games and spoil the aspirations of all these young men and women who practiced for years to get there was a terrible mistake.

JEAN SHILEY

Gold Medal, High Jump, 1932

Although basketball was her favorite sport, Jean Shiley became best known for her controversial 1932 victory over Babe Didrikson in the high jump. The press made it sound like a fluke, but the two had actually tied, and Shiley, who set a new world record of 5 feet, 5¼ inches, was generally recognized as the premier women's high jumper in the world at the time.

Jean Shiley in 1984. Photo courtesy of Jean Shiley

The product of an unusual suburban Philadelphia high school that gave full and equal attention to women's sports, Shiley excelled in field hockey, swimming, and basketball, as well as in hurdling, long jumping, and high jumping. She was only 16 and had never participated in a national meet when she qualified in the high jump at the Olympic trials in 1928 and went on to finish fourth at Amsterdam.

Shiley's Olympic victory four years later in Los Angeles certainly did not bring her the fame it did Babe Didrikson. After graduating from Temple University in 1933, she was without a regular job until becoming a typing instructor with the WPA in 1935. In the meantime, she gave occasional swimming lessons and did some lifeguarding. According to Dan Ferris of the AAU, this made her a professional, and she was not allowed to try out for the 1936 team.

I was born in Harrisburg, Pennsylvania, on November 20, 1911, but I grew up in Brookline, just outside of Philadelphia. I was the only girl of four children, and I guess being from a family of boys, I just did everything that the boys did and better, which completely confounded my father, since it wasn't very ladylike for a girl to be doing those kinds of things. At that time, there were three things a woman could do—three plus another one. Either be a teacher or a nurse or a secretary. But you only really did that until you found somebody to marry and have babies with. My father believed that girls should stay home and work and bring the money home until they got married. Girls should not go to college; only the boys should. For girls, it was supposed to be a useless investment. As it turned out, I was the only one in the family who went to college. Two of my brothers didn't even finish high school. Something drove me, but I don't know what. I think about it often, and I just can't explain it. I've always just had an insatiable curiosity. I wanted to know and do everything all at once, and I really loved learning.

I went to Haverford Township High School between 1925 and 1929, and it was the most wonderful school I've ever seen. We girls had the same money, opportunities, schedule, transportation, uniforms, and support of the principal and community that the boys had. For instance, the boys had 12 football games, and we had 12 hockey games. It was really unusual, and that's why I talk about it, because I have raised three children in various eastern and western schools and I have never found anything like it. We had competition in hockey, basketball, track and field, tennis, swimming, golf, and some minor sports in which we didn't have a full schedule. We also received superb training in music, drama, debate, and other extracurricular activities. At that school everything centered on striving for excellence.

My coach was Ethel David, and she had two rules. She got our grades every Friday, and if they were not up, you didn't play the next week or until you brought them up. The second thing was she would tolerate absolutely no poor sportsmanship. Coach David is 86 now, and I still call often and talk to her.

How I got into the Olympics had to do with our excellent sports program. A female sportswriter from the *Philadelphia Inquirer* covered one of our basketball games during the 1927–28 season. Incidentally, there were three female sportswriters with bylines in Philadelphia then, and you don't see that today, either. She commented on how high I jumped in the game, and a little boy said, "Well, she jumped 4 feet, 10 inches last year." The next day a reporter called me and asked me if I'd like to try out for the Olympics. Her name was Dora Lurie, and I also still see her.

I told her that I would like to try out. Not even my coach had really thought anything about the Olympics, because she was so immersed in her high school work. Lurie got me an appointment with Lawson Robertson, the track coach at the University of Pennsylvania and an Olympic coach. She went with me. Robertson was Scottish and very brusque. He scared me to death. After I tried out, I went in to get dressed, and Lurie came flying into the room screaming, "You made it; you made it! He's going to take you for a pupil." I didn't know at that time that he didn't take just anybody, that this was a real coup of some kind. So if it hadn't been for that little boy and the reporter and Lawson Robertson, none of this could ever have happened. All of them went out of their way for me, and not one of them asked for anything. You must realize there might have been a thousand people out there who were even better than I who just didn't have the opportunity. So I just call it something like a miracle or twice blessed by God or something like that.

After the basketball season, I worked every Wednesday with Lawson Robertson. He sort of took me under his wing. He became very fond of me, so I was no longer intimidated by him, but he certainly could be frightening. I saw him dismiss people very gruffly by saying, "Go home. Your hips are too narrow. You'll never make it." But he was wonderful to me and trained me right up to the Olympic trials.

An aunt and uncle took me to the trials in Newark, New Jersey. I had to pay my own entry fee because I didn't belong to any club or school. I just represented myself. I had never been in a national meet before, and I didn't have any expectations. I just thought it would be fun to go and try out. No one knew anything about me, but I made the team, and within a week we were on our way to Amsterdam.

The trip created a great flurry in my family. My Pennsylvania Dutch father and grandmother predicted that all kinds of dire things were going to happen to me because I was only 16 and going to Europe without a chaperone. I wasn't going to be able to have children, they said. Grandmother even wanted to put a chastity belt on me, and she practically disowned my father for letting me go. Well, that was the Lutheran side of the family. Marvelous people—sturdy, good cooks, good workers, good farmers, but very grim about life. On the other hand, my mother's family were German Catholics. They were just fun-loving. They worked hard, and they played hard. My grandmother on my mother's side took me out and bought me all kinds of clothes, and my aunt and uncle on my mother's side gave me a big party as a send-off. They couldn't have been more marvelous. But my father sort of stood off to the side and observed.

He never saw me compete, but he may have taken some pride in my accomplishments. He wasn't very verbal, and he didn't say anything except when I got back. Then he said, "Don't get a swelled head." Other than that, he never mentioned it to the day he died. I think he just didn't know how to handle it. And yet he was a wonderful man and a wonderful provider.

The trip by ship was a great experience for a very young, naive girl who had never really been away from home. I can remember the first night on board we were served this meal, and I just didn't know what to do with all the silverware and everything. But it was so very, very lovely. I think there were about 360 people on board. They were all strangers, but I learned to know them very quickly. I had this great curiosity and asked about everything. In fact, the world opened up to me, and it was a marvelous experience—the people, the different cultures, the music, and the art. On ship, Jack Kelly, Grace's father, kind of looked out for me because he was also from Philadelphia. I even got to know the "black gang" down in the bottom of the ship. These were the men who kept the machinery greased and oiled. They were covered with grime, hence the name "black gang." I spent a lot of time down in the bowels of the ship with these men because I wanted to know about everything they were doing. I even asked them to sign my autograph book, but many of them couldn't write and just signed with an *X*.

In Amsterdam, we lived aboard the ship, and I dearly loved it. You didn't have to move your gear, and there was a water taxi whenever you needed it. I learned so much in a short period of time. That was another thing when I came back. My father couldn't stand me because I wanted to hear good music, I wanted to go to art museums, and I wanted to entertain guests, including people of other colors and nationalities, but all this was forbidden.

I remember an interesting experience in Amsterdam that was really very funny. There was this little boxer, he must have been a lightweight, who was very downhearted and sad because he was so homesick. I never saw anyone that homesick, so I asked him to go on into town with me. On the dock there was a little old man—he must have been 90—who put us in his carriage to drive us into town. He said he wanted to show us something. I couldn't understand all the words he was saying, but something about the museum. I didn't think this little boxer would be all that interested in a museum, but it was something to do. When we got there, the driver escorted us in and took us to this one painting. It covered a whole wall, and it was burned on one edge. Of course, it was Rembrandt's *The Night Watch.* I looked at the painting and thought, "My God! That's hanging on our living room wall!" I didn't know, and even my family didn't know, what it was. It turned out an aunt had done some traveling and brought back the print from Amsterdam sometime before I was born. So here was this same Rembrandt we had on our living room wall.

I recall very little about the competition, to tell you the truth. I remember a very lovely young woman from Canada named Ethel Catherwood who won the high jump. Later I learned that reporters had voted her the most beautiful woman of the Games. It was difficult for women athletes then. You had no idea how men looked at you as a young woman. I don't know what they thought, but whatever it was wasn't very nice. Dating became a problem for the simple reason that often a guy would date me to win a bet or something like that. For years I had this problem. In fact, I changed the spelling of my name when I moved away because I didn't want that kind of experience anymore. You just didn't know whom to trust. Fortunately, I didn't depend on dating. I had other things to do. I was very busy going to college and working.

I enrolled at Temple University in 1929. There were no scholarships for women. The Depression had started, and there was no money. I did get a scholastic scholarship, but I think it might have been tilted a little because I was an athlete. At the time I held the world record in the high jump, though not the Olympic record. I received $75 a semester, and that paid my tuition.

There were absolutely no competitive sports for women at Temple, only intramurals. Well, for someone who is a world-class athlete, that wasn't much fun. So I never competed for my university. Instead, I competed in national meets. Every time I met one of my professors, he would say, "When are you going to quit?" But I just kept doing it. As strange as it may seem, they were not adverse to calling on me to appear with all the VIPs who came on campus. They'd take pictures, even make appointments for me when I didn't know anything about it. Then they would call me and dress me down for not appearing. Often I'd be called out of class and asked to give demonstrations. I thought this was kind of hypocritical, but I wanted my education, so I didn't say anything about it until my senior year, when I finally said, "Look, I don't understand this. The policy of the Physical Education Department is to have no women's sports, and then you call on me to give a demonstration. I don't like it, and I don't think I'm going to do it." That didn't make them very happy, but that's the way it was.

At first when I competed in national meets I had to pay my way. When I came back from the Olympics in '28, I didn't belong to any club or have any place to train except the corn field across the street, and for one more year I still had my high school field. I was only a junior in high school when I went to Amsterdam. There was a men's club in Philadelphia called the Meadowbrook Club, which was operated by Wanamaker's. You've heard of the Wanamaker Mile and Track Meet. I had to go and beg them to take me. They did, but under terrible circumstances. There was no place for me to dress. I couldn't even get to the coach's room because all the men were running around undressed. I would have to stand like 50 feet away and catch one of the boys and say, "I'd like to see Lew Speeler. Would you go tell him?" It was really pretty bad. But they did pay my way to the meets. I was the only girl, so I had to travel with the New York club or some other club that had a girls' team. I would have to get on a train, go there, and then travel with them. It wasn't an ideal arrangement, but at least it helped out because I was working my way through college and there was no money for competing. Without this help I think I might have had to quit.

When I left Philadelphia in 1932 for the Olympic tryouts in Evanston, Illinois, I had $5 in my pocket. That's all I had. I had my train ticket and $2.50 a day for meal money. Once I got to Evanston, the Olympic Committee took over, and they paid for everything that you had to have. I ended up trading in my railroad ticket for a bus ticket so I could bring presents home for the family.

What I remember most about the trials is how hot it was. I think it was 105. It was so hot that some of the athletes bought a 100-pound cake of ice and sat on it. At those trials Babe Didrikson and I tied in the high jump, and then it was on to Los Angeles.

Jean Shiley in 1932. Photo courtesy of Jean Shiley

The women's track and field events ran for a week, and at the Games Babe was the Sun King. On Sunday she won the javelin. Then on Wednesday she won a controversial decision in the hurdles. By that time the crowds were all behind her. They have their heroes and heroines. And the newspapers got into it, too. The following Sunday was the high jump, and the night before all the girls were in my room telling me, "You've got to do it. You've got to do it." Oh, boy, they were really putting the pressure on me; that is, those who didn't care for her. My coach, George Freeland of the Prudential Insurance Company of New Jersey, came into the room and chased all the girls out. He told them to leave me alone.

On Sunday I won. Everyone felt, how dare I beat the heroine? It was as though I had done a dastardly thing. Reporters like Grantland Rice and Paul Gallico kept the myth going that the Babe had been cheated out of her third Olympic victory. Actually we tied, but there are no ties in the Olympics. You jump it off, although now ties are broken on the basis of fewer misses. The rules were very strict then about jumping. You had to take off with one foot and land with the other, and your shoulders could not precede your body across the bar. Babe was not jumping according to the rules. Thus, there really should have been no controversy at all. I don't know why it took the judges until our jump-off to decide that Babe was jumping illegally. I could have claimed a foul long before then. The Canadian girl, Eva Dawes, and the German girl were standing at my shoulder telling me to claim a foul. But you don't beat Babe by claiming a foul. You just don't. It would have been murder. I still have no idea why the judges finally declared that Babe was jumping illegally and put her in second place. I was ready to keep going with our jump-off, but I also felt the judges' decision was legitimate. The Babe was angry then, but she didn't really hold a grudge because she went on to greater things anyway. We saw each other lots of times afterward with no problems.

Babe Didrikson inspired either great enthusiasm or great dislike. At that time, even though they competed in sports, girls were to be young ladies, and I think a lot of girls found her behavior a little beyond how they thought a young lady should act. The Babe was very brash, and she bragged a lot, but she was also very humorous, especially when she wasn't getting all the attention. She'd pull a harmonica out of her pocket and start to play it just to get attention. And nobody did anything better than she did. I don't care if it was swallowing goldfish; she would have to swallow more fish than anybody else. It wasn't Muhammad Ali who started this "I'm number one" stuff. Babe started it. She was just so different from all the rest of the girls that it grated on their nerves. It could have been jealousy. And she wasn't necessarily a good sport, either. That's the way the Babe was, and it bothered some of the girls, but it didn't bother me. I was captain of the 1932 team, and I had to represent all of the girls. I had been on the 1928 team, and I learned that there are a lot of people in the world, and they are very different and also very interesting. So Babe didn't bother me; in fact, she and I became friends and remained so even though we're two entirely different people.

After the Los Angeles Games, I went back to Temple for my senior year. I graduated in 1933. Physical education was my major and history my minor. I had wanted to become a doctor, but I didn't have the money to get into medical school. There were no jobs for anyone in our class. Because I was an Olympic champion I was offered a job for carfare and lunch money, but you can't go to work for just that. I was out of work for a long time. Then, thank God for the WPA.

I went to the WPA looking for work. I was being interviewed when a man came into the office and said they had just lost their teacher for that night's typing class. Out of my mouth came the words, "I can teach typing." I had no control over what I said. It just came out. But once I said it, I was it. The man told me to show up at 7:00 that night, so I had to go home and find a typewriter to learn the first lesson for that night. Things were very desperate because I didn't even have enough money for clothes. People were so poor that they couldn't even go looking for a job unless it was within walking distance.

In 1936 I went to New York to see Dan Ferris of the U.S. Olympic Committee and told him I'd like to try out for the 1936 team, but he was adamant. He dismissed me just like that. I was declared a professional because after the '32 Games I had taught swimming and had done some lifeguarding to earn some money. That's how it was then. Ferris said no, and that was that. The rules were bent for other people, but not for me. It was kind of stupid because the girl who went only jumped 4 feet, 10 inches. I could have done that without any training at all.

As I look back, it was really something to win a gold medal for your country and for yourself, but I think the biggest benefit comes from the fringe things that happen: the camaraderie of the participants, your increased knowledge of the world, and your greater appreciation of the various cultures and their people. This has enriched my life above and beyond what my expectations could have been if I had not been in the Olympics. It changed my politics. It changed everything. In fact, it's like a small microcosm of the world the way it could be, but isn't.

Photo courtesy of George Roth

George Roth in Los Angeles Coliseum, 1932.

GEORGE ROTH

Gold Medal, Indian Clubs (Gymnastics), 1932

George Roth's life has many of those qualities that made the Horatio Alger books so popular earlier in the century. Roth's father died when George was nine years old, and he and his brother were raised by his young mother, until she too died, while both boys were still in high school. Roth and his wife, Bebe, married while still in high school, and the first six years of their life to-

gether, which coincided with the first years of the Great Depression, were spent in abject poverty.

In 1935, with a gold medal to his credit, Roth got a job with Shell Oil Company as a draftsman and moved to Long Beach. Roth became a very successful geologist and petroleum engineer and eventually formed his own oil prospecting company, but he has never forgotten those early years of deprivation.

When I won that Olympic gold medal in 1932, I was so poor that I didn't even have a dime for carfare to get down to the stadium to get my medal. I had to thumb a ride down there, and one of the people who picked me up and gave me a ride part of the way was Jimmy Durante. It took three rides to get there, and I was damn near late. See, they gave the medals out at the end of the games, not right after the event like they do now.

Anyway, I got there. I didn't have to change clothes because I already had my Olympic uniform on. When it came my turn, I climbed up on the platform, and they put a wreath on my head. Then they hung that medal around my neck, played "The Star-Spangled Banner," and raised the American flag. There must have been 60,000 people there yelling and cheering. It was all over in just a couple of minutes, and I buried the medal down inside my uniform and walked out to Vermont Avenue and hooked a ride back home.

My wife and I were married while we were both still in high school, but we didn't live together until after we graduated. I went to Hollywood High, and she went to L.A. High. We were married in 1929, and by the time I was in the Olympics we had a little baby girl. I remember during the competition that I stuffed one of her booties down my own shoe for good luck, and I guess it worked because I won the Indian club swinging event. You know, the marriage worked too; it's been over 50 years now. But geez, we really had an awful time in those first years.

By the time we graduated, her parents and my parents were all dead, and we finally started living together. I couldn't find a job, and then the Depression came, and most everybody was in bad shape. From 1929 to 1935 my wife and I were on county welfare. Six years! Six bloody years! Geez, that was awful. During the first of those years we were actually starving. Can you imagine? One time we went 15 days without eating. One and 2 days without food was common, and often we went from 5 to 10 days without any food, but the longest stretch was 15 days.

The athletes stayed at the Olympic Village in Los Angeles, and they ate in a dining hall, but my wife and I had our baby then, so I wanted to stay home with them. But I also wanted to eat. So all during the Olympic Games, I hooked rides back and forth to the Olympic Village and got food and brought it home. That's what kept us from starving those weeks. Boy, those were awful times, believe me.

I got interested in gymnastics kind of by accident. While I was waiting to sign up for my classes as a freshman at Hollywood High, I was fiddling around with some of the equipment there in the gym, especially the parallel bars. I had never seen them before, but the coach noticed me and asked me if I would like to sign up for gymnastics, which was held during the eighth period every day. So I signed up, and pretty soon I became a pretty good all-around gymnast and eventually captain of the team.

In gymnastics, to be an all-around gymnast you have to do everything: rings, horizontal bar, Indian clubs, parallel bars, long horse vault, and the side horse. You could specialize in one of them, but you had to do all of them. My specialty was the side horse, and I won a lot of medals in that. As a matter of fact, in 1933, the year after I won the Olympic gold medal in the Indian clubs, I won the Pacific Coast championship in the side horse.

I didn't specialize in the Indian clubs until I began training for the Olympics. It was early in 1932, and my wife, Bebe, and I were on our own and broke, and we got the chance to look after a sanitorium that was being built up in the Sierra Nevada mountains about 30 miles from Lake Tahoe. We looked after the place in exchange for rent. That was in the winter of 1931–32. For a while that was pretty good because I had a gun up there, and we could eat deer and apples, and sometimes I caught fish. But then there was a big storm that winter, and it put six feet of snow on us. Some of those days we were really starving because we could only get outdoors once in a while in that snow.

We came back down to Los Angeles early in 1932, and I started going to the gymnasium again because it was Olympics time. When I got out of high school, the Los Angeles Athletic Club gave me a free membership, and I spent a lot of time there working out on all the gymnastic routines. They were real nice to me there. When I came back down and started working out again, somebody there suggested that I concentrate on the Indian clubs, so I did. They even put up a mirror there for me so I could practice my routine.

Indian clubs look a little like bowling pins, but they are skinny and have long necks with a small, round knob at the top end. What you do is twirl them around your body—in front, in back, and on the sides—without letting them touch each other or yourself. The routines lasted for four minutes, and you couldn't stop or hesitate or repeat any pattern that you already had done.

Indian club swinging was a standard American gymnastic event until it was dropped by the AAU after the 1953 national championships. It was an Olympic event only in the two Olympics we had in this country, in 1904 and in 1932. I guess that's because the European gymnasts didn't use them as part of their routines. That was pretty much an American event, although the Mexicans and the Canadians also included it. The Mexicans were good at it. The guy who came in fourth in the '32 Olympics was a Mexican.

After the Games, times were still tough, and we were back on county welfare. We could get pick and shovel jobs, and I had lots of those, but they never lasted very long. Then after Roosevelt became president, things got a little better because they'd try to get you jobs that you were good at. I was pretty good at drafting, and I got a few jobs doing that, and then Shell hired me as a draftsman in 1935. I started in Los Angeles, but they soon transferred me to Long Beach.

I wanted to go to college, so I enrolled in geology at USC, and every night for seven years, four nights a week, I went back and forth between Long Beach and Los Angeles. Can you imagine? I finally graduated magna cum laude. I don't know how the hell I did that, going back and forth all those years. But there's my diploma on the wall. During those seven years with Shell, I got to be chief draftsman, and eventually I was made a scout. A scout is a guy who goes out and finds out what the other companies are doing. I used to go all over the valley to the various rigs, and then at night I'd drive to Los Angeles and go to school and then come home and study until two or three in the morning. There were no freeways or anything like that then. Jesus Christ, how the hell did I do that?

After I got my degree in geology, Shell gave me a job as a junior geologist, and I worked my way up to chief geologist in four years. Then I quit and went into the oil business with another man, and four years after that I went into business for myself. I've been on my own since then, until I sold out about three years ago.

Looking back, I'll tell you something. I did very well financially after I got started in the oil business, but I'll never forget those first years. I just don't know how the hell I survived.

Pete Mehringer in 1983. Photo by Fogarty and Carlson

PETER JOSEPH MEHRINGER

Gold Medal, Wrestling, Light-Heavyweight, 1932

One of 10 children of German immigrant parents, Pete Mehringer was born in the small Kansas farm town of Kinsley, where he learned his wrestling from a correspondence course. He caught on quickly enough to become not only state champion as a 10th-grader, but also the coach of the team. Later he also coached his college team while still a student.

Mehringer was equally well known in Lawrence as a University of Kansas football player who made second team All-American in 1934 before going on to a professional career with the Cardinals and the ill-fated Los Angeles Bulldogs.

He was in many motion pictures in the 1930s but was seldom recognized by his fans. His job was usually to perform some act of daring as the leading man's stunt double.

When I was in high school, one day I was looking through a magazine, and I saw this advertisement on how to learn to wrestle by correspondence. The title of it was "Wrestling and Physical Culture," by Frank Gouch and Farmer Burns. They were a couple of professional wrestlers. So my brothers and I decided to send away for it. It cost $3 or $4. I think there were 10 lessons. And that's what got me started.

We had only one coach in the entire school in Kinsley, Kansas, where I grew up, and he was busy with basketball, football, track, and so forth. Well, he was wrestling with me one night. I guess I got a little too rough with him, and I hurt his arm, and he said, "The hell with it. You take over." So I was student coach from then on until I finished high school. We went to the state tournament in 1928 in Manhattan, and I won the heavyweight championship; the other boys took a couple of seconds. The next year was the Depression, and we didn't have any money, so no one went to the finals. In 1930, the wrestling coach from Kansas State was looking for talent, so he wrote me and said if I could get to Kansas State for the state high school tournament he'd find a place for me to stay while I was there. So I hitchhiked to Manhattan and won the state again and then hitchhiked back home.

I also started playing football in high school. I'll never forget when I wanted to go out for football my freshman year. My mother didn't want me to. She was afraid I'd get hurt. But I kept insisting, so she finally told me, "Well, if you're going to go for football, I want you to be the best player on the team." And this was an inspiration to me all during high school and ever since. I figured, if I was going to be the best player on the team, why not be the best player on the field?

I didn't want to go to Kansas State because it was a land grant school. That meant compulsory military training, and I didn't like marching. I did take ROTC at the University of Kansas, but through my football and wrestling I was excused from marching and drilling.

A scholarship in those days was different. It meant they would find you a job so you could work your way through. My first two years I waited tables at the fraternity where I was staying, and in my freshman year I also picked up after the varsity in the dressing room and worked around the stadium on weekends. The last two years I worked as a janitor. Today a kid would tell you to get lost if you asked him to do all that, but I didn't mind because it enabled me to get an education, and that's why I went to school.

I started out at the University of Kansas in 1930 in premed, but with competing in two sports, they called me in one time and said, "Pete, forget it." I just didn't have the time to study. So I majored in education.

In football I made all-conference three years in a row. I also made Notre Dame's all-opponent team, and I made the *New York Sun* and *Collier's* second team All-American. I also played in the first college all-star game in 1934.

My best memory of college football was the second game we played against Notre Dame. Notre Dame had agreed to play us two games if we would hire Moon Mullins as backfield coach. This was after Rockne was killed in that airplane crash in the spring of 1932. After the first time we played them, I made their all-opponent team. That was in 1932, and I ended up with a broken nose and two black eyes. So I psyched myself up for the game in 1933, and I told myself, Well, today I'm going to get the meal, and you guys can have the lunch. I did the kicking off, and they chose to receive. I kicked off, and the ball went right into the stands. So I said to myself, Well, I'm ready. I made about two-thirds of the tackles in the game, blocked two punts, and the game ended 0 to 0. We were inside their 20-yard line five times and couldn't score. I played tackle on both offense and defense. I weighed about 214 then. During my last two years I missed only about 17 minutes of play.

Playing in that first college all-star game was really interesting. Going to Chicago was the first time since the Olympics that I had a chance to go to a large city. I played with a couple of those Notre Dame boys again, and one of them asked me, "Hey, who let you out of the cage that day?" That was also Red Grange's last game, but he didn't do much that day.

I was only a sophomore in college when I won the Olympics. My coach at the university was Dr. Leon Bauman, and he was really something. He polished up what I had already learned and taught me a lot more. He had gone to Oklahoma A & M, which is now Oklahoma State, and they had most of the good wrestlers at that time. After the Olympics, Bauman quit coaching and went to medical school, so I ended up again as the student coach.

In that sophomore year I came in second in the NCAA heavyweight division, and that qualified me to go to the Olympic trials in Columbus, Ohio. I had six matches in the trials. I started out with a fellow who weighed about 280. I beat him and won all my matches until the finals when I wrestled Jack Riley, the same fellow I had lost to in the NCAA championship. He had a bye in the semis, and I had just finished wrestling a guy who weighed 256, whom I had pinned in just over 13 minutes. I had less than an hour's rest. I lost, but I didn't think it was quite fair to have a bye that far up in the schedule. Anyway, I lost by decision.

In Los Angeles my coach asked me to go down to 191 from about 206. In practice I wrestled the winner of the 191 class, a fellow named Carter Caldwell, and I beat him in about two minutes. He weighed only about 175. Later I wrestled Riley again when neither one of us was tired, and the coach told us this was the last tryout for heavyweight. I really took him then. I beat him twice in six minutes. He was a little bit unhappy about that, and he wanted to fight, so I said, "Well, I can whip you fighting, too." The coach gave me a choice of whether I wanted to wrestle 191 or heavyweight. I asked him where I could do the team the most good, because that was most important. So he put me at 191. By the way, Riley took the silver medal in the heavyweight division. My first opponent in the Games was the defending champion, a fellow named Thure Sjostedt from Sweden. I had no trouble with him at all. I beat him in 13 minutes or something like that.

The major difference between Olympic and college wrestling at that time was in college you had to hold a pin for three seconds, but in the Olympics, if both shoulder blades hit the mat at the same time, it was all over. College matches were 10 minutes and Olympic matches 15. The first 6 minutes you each wrestled up. Then, if a fellow had an advantage, he had the choice of whether to continue standing or to go down on the mat, either on top or on the

Photo courtesy of Pete Mehringer

Pete Mehringer in 1932.

bottom, for the next 3 minutes. That was followed by another 3 minutes on the mat, and then the last 3 minutes you were both up. In my second match I wrestled a fellow named Madison from Canada. At least, I tried to wrestle him, but he wouldn't wrestle. All he did was lie on his stomach. When a fellow goes on defense like that, it's pretty hard to beat him, but I got the decision. My last match was with an Australian named Eddie Scarf. He was a butcher from outside Sydney and very strong, but again I won the decision.

Just being an ol' farm boy from Kansas, at the time I won the gold it was just another tournament. I didn't realize until a few years later just what a gold medal really meant. So I picked up my bag and went back to Lawrence to school. The people in Lawrence had a nice luncheon for the two of us who won gold medals. James Bausch had won the decathlon.

Today it means a great deal to me. It helped me when I got back to school. I know it helped me in football and wrestling. Let's face it! If you're going to wrestle an Olympic champion—or even play football against him—it makes you think twice. I remember I was wrestling a guy from Oklahoma one time, and Bauman, who was then in medical school, came up to me and suggested that I use a little psychology on him. He said that instead of my usual firm handshake I should just give him a dead fish and conjure up the dirtiest look I could think of. So I did. I pinned the guy in about five or six minutes.

I met him a few years later, and he said, "You know when you beat me that night in Lawrence?"

I said, "No, when was that?"

He said, "When you gave me that dead fish and that dirty look. It just scared the hell out of me."

I never felt that way myself. I figured, hell, the tougher they are, the better we go.

I never went to a national tournament again, not even the NCAA. Our old athletic director, Phog Allen, said we didn't have enough money to send any of us. As a matter of fact, my old wrestling coach had had to raise money from the local businessmen in Lawrence to send me to the Olympic trials. The school wouldn't send me. There was always plenty of money for basketball and track but not for wrestling.

Amateur wrestling is not as much fun today. There was more action when I wrestled. We did a lot more wrestling on the mat. For example, when we wrestled in the down position, the man on top had to have both knees outside his opponent's knees, and that made escape much easier. With one knee in between, there's not a lot you can do. Today you have mostly throws and go-behinds, and that's about it. Right now the Iron Curtain countries make the rules, and we abide by them. The hell with them. If they don't want to wrestle by our rules, let them stay home. That's the way I feel about it.

After graduation I did quite a bit of pro wrestling, but I never did think of it as a career. I didn't enjoy it. It was boring. I didn't care for the acting part of it. It was just show biz, about like it is today. In California the announcer was required to call the matches exhibitions rather than contests or bouts. I was supposed to wrestle Jim Londos once, but his handlers backed out of the match. I did wrestle Strangler Lewis, and I think I could have beaten him in a real match. Bauman once told me that at the time I could have beaten anyone in the world.

I signed with the Chicago Cardinals after college. I didn't receive any bonus, but I did have a pretty good contract. They paid me something like $125 a game, which was good for a lineman at that time. There was no no-cut clause, and they could cut you at any time. I played for three years with the Cardinals. Then I came out here to the Los Angeles Bulldogs, which was supposed to be an expansion team. The idea was that we would get the Coliseum for our games. But in those days there was quite a rift between the pros and the amateurs, so they said they didn't want any dirty pros in the Coliseum.

I played against Bronko Nagurski. He was probably even a little tougher than they say. If you caught him behind the line of scrimmage before he got up a head of steam, you were safe to tackle him. After he got past the line, he would just leave a trail of rack and ruin behind him. He was really something.

The professional game was rough then, but not like today. You didn't have these forearm slugging matches and stuff like that. We'd hit an opponent, but it would be fair and square and without intent of taking him out of the game. I see this on TV today, and I don't like it. When we were on the field, we were all business, but after the game we shook hands and all was well. I remember one party I had after a Bears-Cardinal game, and there were more Bears there than Cardinals. Who should walk in but the coach? He was a little bit unhappy about all that mixing, but this is the way it should be.

What has really changed the game is the financial aspect of it. I was talking to Merlin Olson the other day, and he said, "When you were playing, it was fun. Today it is financial." And that changes things.

I do have a Screen Actors Guild card. I got that when I was playing football out here with the Los Angeles Bulldogs. Several of the movie people used to come to the games, and I got a couple of calls to work in the movies. That was in the mid-thirties. My first movie was *The Adventures of Tarzan in Guatemala*. It was shot on location and came out in 1935. Herman Brix, who came in second in the shot put in the 1928 Games, played Tarzan, and I played his double. He later changed his name to Bruce Bennett and starred in a lot of films, including a remake of this first one called *Tarzan and the Green Goddess*. Even though Brix was an athlete, they didn't want to take any chances with him getting hurt. I was expendable. I can remember one scene when I had to jump off a wall onto the villain's shoulders, and then I had to pick him up and throw him into what was painted like a wall but was really some bales of hay. That was my day's work. I did quite a few stunts in films. It was a lot of fun.

My next film was with the Ritz Brothers. I was the double for one of them in a wrestling match. I think the name of the picture was *Straight, Place, and Show*. They were really crazy. I doubled Allan Curtis in a fight in the rain in *Four Sons* for Fox Studios. In *I Married a Nazi* I doubled a German officer. I wrestled Ward Bond for Paramount in *The Girl from Mexico* with Lupe Velez, who at one time was married to Johnny Weissmuller. I had a lot of fun with Bob Hope and Bing Crosby in *The Road to Zanzibar*. I doubled Hope in a scene where he wrestled a gorilla in a cage. But it wasn't a real gorilla. That would have required double pay. Hope just kept everybody laughing all the time. I worked in a film with Jim Thorpe called *Knute Rockne, All-American*. Ronald Reagan was in that film, too. I always called him "Ronnie, Baby."

DOROTHY POYNTON HILL

Bronze Medal, Springboard Diving, 1928
Gold Medal, Platform Diving, 1932 and 1936
Bronze Medal, Springboard Diving, 1936

Barely 13, Dorothy Poynton was the youngest American ever to win an Olympic medal when she took the bronze in springboard diving in 1928 at Amsterdam.

A child prodigy in dancing as well as in diving, the young Dorothy performed professionally on Los Angeles stages while still in elementary school. Her natural grace and rhythm coupled with a fierce competitive drive led to a string of national championships in both platform and springboard diving before she turned professional after the 1936 Games.

In later life the confident and personable woman ran one of Los Angeles and Hollywood's most successful swimming schools, where she guaranteed the famous and the not-so-famous that she could teach them to swim in 10 easy lessons.

Photo by Fogarty and Carlson

Dorothy Poynton Hill in 1983.

I started taking dancing lessons when I was a youngster in Portland, Oregon. I was more interested in dancing than diving at the time. I even had a chance to dance at the Orpheum Theater, but the Board of Education made a big stink and insisted that a child my age couldn't do this unless my mom and dad hired a tutor. So my folks picked up the whole family and moved to Los Angeles.

In Los Angeles I gave diving and dancing exhibitions for the Ambassador Hotel, which even gave my father a job as the food checker. I was about seven or eight, but I was very tiny. I'd give an exhibition of diving, and then I'd do my dance on a little stage. My coach was Roger Cornell, and we'd have all kinds of gag acts that really packed them in at the Ambassador. We had a dive called the Monte Cristo. They used to put me in this sack and drop me off the 10-foot board. Everyone was sitting there wondering how that little girl was going to get out of that big sack. They didn't know that the bag had snaps on the side. I'd just pull them open and swim out into this diving bell that had air and stay there. At that time pool water was not as clear as it is today because they didn't have all the chemicals they now do. Everyone would ask, "Where's the little girl?" Sometimes people would actually jump into the pool to save me.

About this time the Hollywood Athletic Club asked me to represent them. It was a very exclusive club on Sunset Boulevard, and Clyde Swenson was the coach. I'd go there three times a week with my dad. It didn't cost anything, and they sent me to the junior nationals in Detroit when I was 12. It was my first big meet, and I lost by one-tenth of a point to a girl named Bunny Ferguson. Ernie Brandsten, the swimming coach from Stanford and one of the Olympic coaches, told my dad that I would make the Olympic team. I didn't even know what the Olympics were. But the next year the club sent me to the Olympic trials in New York.

After I made the team, I asked the chaperone if I could go home. You see, I was there all alone, and I was still only a 12-year-old girl. I told her, "Now that I've made the team, my mom can tell the neighbors." I wanted to go home because I had never been away from home before without one of my parents. I told the chaperone that I wouldn't go to Amsterdam, but once I got on board ship I had a good time. I even had my 13th birthday on the ship. I was in three Olympics, and I'm always the one on the left in the pictures, where the shortest athlete always stands.

I won a bronze medal in the springboard in 1928, and that made me the youngest ever to win a medal. The judging then was terrible. They first announced that I was second, then third, and finally first, all of this within about one hour. But I ended up third. The *Guinness Book of Records* has stated that I won the silver medal.

I didn't do the platform in 1928. I just wasn't strong enough. But I won that event in Los Angeles in 1932. In fact, I was never defeated off the tower from the time I started until the time I turned pro, and that includes both the Olympics and the national championships.

You're never in awe of another swimmer or diver. Divers feel closer than some of the other athletes. There's some jealousy, and there are certainly rivalries because everyone wants to win so badly. That's the silly part of the whole thing. When you hear it isn't whether you win or lose but how well you play the game, you have to ask, "Then why am I working so hard to win the gold medal?"

There's no such thing as an outsider making the Olympic team. Either they're national champions, or they've been near the top for a long time. There's so much pressure just during the tryouts; you have to be well seasoned. It's not like a swimming race where it's over in a minute. There is a long wait for everyone to go through their dives. Then you have the ladder to climb. You hear so many silly stories. You'll hear a girl say, "Well, I would have made the Olympic team but I had a headache that day." Or, "I just couldn't that week. I was busy." It's always the national champions who come through.

You also have to have coordination and the right kind of family. You had to have somebody to push you. My mother used to say, "Dorothy, you can quit any time you want to." So one day I said, "Mama, I'm quitting." Papa said, "You can't quit. You're a national champion. In a couple of months you have to defend your title." Well, I stayed away three weeks. Then I said, "Mama, I'm going down to practice. I miss it." You see, it was always because of them—to be able to send home that telegram that I had won.

I didn't have any trouble in school after I won the bronze in 1928, at least not until I got to high school. One day the gym teacher said to me, "The principal wants to see you. She says you're going to have to stop having your picture in the paper. It's not helping the other girls." How did I know when my picture was going to be in the paper? After that I didn't care much for high school.

I actually had more fun in 1928 than in 1932 because I liked being on the ship. I didn't have much of a trip to make to Los Angeles. The day before my event I was asked to give an exhibition. I said I would, and something happened. I don't know just what. Just as I was entering the water, my head must have been slightly turned, and I spun down into he water, but my head was stuck. I couldn't turn my head back. It really hurt and I thought, "God, I've got to dive tomorrow." They rushed me to the emergency room, and I was in the hospital all night. The doctor told me that I couldn't dive. I told him, "I've got to dive. My mom and pop are going to be there." They didn't have the money to go to Amsterdam, so I just had to dive.

I called my dad and told him to meet me at the pool the next morning at 6:00 A.M. because I was going to try one dive off the 16-foot platform. Well, the next morning I did my one dive, and I said, "Pop, I'll be all right." I guess I had pulled a muscle, but it didn't bother me during the competition once I started to dive.

After I won, I had different offers to turn pro, but nothing very spectacular. I had some offers of endorsements and things like that, but I said, "Mom, I think I'll go on." I asked her if she thought I could win another Olympic championship, and she said, "Why not?" My brother said the same thing. In 1936 I qualified in both the springboard and the platform. I won the gold again in the platform and took a bronze in the springboard. They gave me a tree for winning in Berlin. Everyone who won received a small tree, and this professor kept writing me asking me where my tree was. That was back in 1936. How would I know where that tree is? I do know I was not going to get on that boat with a tree under my arm.

The 1936 Games were the toughest of all for me because of the pressure. I had already made a commitment to endorse Camel cigarettes, Hollywood bathing suits, and some other things, and if I had lost, all that would have been gone. So there was lots of pressure. I hadn't signed anything, but you couldn't even mention that you were thinking about it. If Brundage had even suspected, he would have kicked me off the team.

I did do the Camel ads. I was even in the funnies. The Camel ads then were made into funnies. I also did some radio advertising and I went on the road with various swimming shows.

In 1952 my husband built the Dorothy Poynton Swim Club in West Los Angeles, and I started giving lessons. I had a lot of famous stars' children. I taught Ann Sothern's daughter, Tish, and Ronald Reagan and Jane Wyman's children, Michael and Maureen. Michael was really hard to teach. He was a very frightened kid, and now I hear he's racing boats. Before we built our swim club, I used to teach him at Ann Sothern's pool. Mr. Reagan came to watch Michael swim on his 10th lesson. He had just come from the hospital where he had been treated for a broken leg, which was in a cast. The next time I saw him he was Governor of California. Several of us who were former athletes were invited to Sacramento, and I told them on the way up there that I knew Ronald Reagan and that he was a very nice person. They just looked at me, but when we went into his office to be introduced, Governor Reagan said, "Wait a minute. There's Dorothy Poynton. I have to go over and shake her hand. She taught my children to swim." I tell you, it was like the American flag going up. That was a high point in my life, with all those other athletes just looking on in disbelief.

I had my swimming club for 18 years, and I had a lot of famous folks. I taught the Bloomingdale children, and Ingrid Bergman and Robert Taylor's daughter. I used to write out a guarantee that I could teach anyone how to swim in 10 lessons. You would be water-safe, go off the board, swim the length of the pool, and even go in with your clothes on. I never had a single failure.

I can't do anything half-way, and no one will ever change me. I know you might have more fun the other way, but I can't do anything unless I do it better than anyone else. That's why I was able to win all those diving championships, and that's why I had such good success with my swimming school.

When I look back at everything that's happened to me, I think that it's kind of nice that I won medals in three Olympics and that I'm in the *Guinness Book of Records*. You know, you only take this route once. There are so many millions of people out there, so you're lucky if you make a name for yourself in anything. It's great having been the world's best in something instead of being Suzy Klutz trying to learn how to bake a cake.

6
BERLIN, 1936

More than 4,000 athletes from 49 countries gathered in Berlin on August 1, 1936, for what was to become the most widely publicized of all Olympiads. At an unprecedented cost of $30 million, these Games became a carefully and efficiently orchestrated showcase for the Nazi regime. Mussolini might have made the trains run on time, but Hitler and his officials put on an extravaganza that, even by today's standards, remains one of the best-run, most elaborate shows of them all.

These were the first Games to be broadcast, and Harold Abrahams of Great Britain did the English-language transcriptions. Abrahams was a champion in his own right, having won the 100 meters in 1924, a feat that would come to be immortalized in the 1981 film *Chariots of Fire*.

These Games also featured closed-circuit television, advanced electronic timing devices, and countless examples of advanced sports architecture; in fact, the Germans were so proud of their Olympic Village that they brought over one of the simple bungalows from the '32 Los Angeles Games and put it on display so visitors could measure the considerable German improvements. And recording it all for posterity with her incomparable camera was Leni Riefenstahl.

Opening ceremonies—Berlin, 1936. Photo courtesy of Francis Johnson

The Berlin Games were also the most controversial of Olympic Games, particularly for the Americans. Throughout the spring of 1936 serious efforts had been made in the United States and other countries to boycott the Games because Hitler had deprived Jews of their citizenship and civil rights and had barred Jewish athletes from the Olympic trials for the German team. Late in 1933, AAU delegates, meeting in the U.S., voted for a boycott, a position supported by Avery Brundage, President of the American Olympic Committee. In June 1934, the German Olympic Committee announced that 21 Jewish athletes had been nominated for the German training camps, and Brundage was sent to Germany to make an investigation. Upon his return, Brundage announced that the Germans were observing the letter and the spirit of the Olympic code and that a boycott was unwarranted. As a result, the American Olympic Committee voted to participate in the Berlin Games.

The controversy, however, raged on. On December 8, 1935, the executive committee of the AAU met in New York and defeated a proposed resolution against sending an American team to Berlin. During the next several days, Jeremiah Mahoney, the President of the AAU and a strong supporter of a boycott, resigned and was succeeded by Avery Brundage. Thus, Brundage became the chief officer of both the AAU and the American Olympic Committee, and he urged the resignation of all officers in these organizations who were "anti-Olympic."

Another controversy surrounding these Games was the question of whether Avery Brundage and the American coaches were responsible for deliberately taking out of competition two Jewish members of the American team. Sam Stoller and Marty Glickman were both scheduled to run the 4x100-meter relay, but at the last minute they were withdrawn, even though both had faster times than one of the other members of the team.

Then there was the Eleanor Holm incident. Holm had been on the team in 1928 and had won a gold medal in the backstroke in 1932. She was favored to repeat, but she never got the chance. On board ship she was discovered drinking champagne and as a result was dismissed from the team. The whole affair was unfortunate, but it is doubtful that another swimming victory would have brought her the fame her dismissal did.

But perhaps the most famous—or infamous—story to come out of the "Nazi Olympics" was Hitler's alleged refusal to shake Jesse Owens's hand after the latter's victory in the 100 meters early in the Games. Although this incident did not happen, the American press eagerly reported it as fact, particularly after Joseph Goebbels's newspaper, *Der Angriff*, referred to the black members of the team as "America's black auxiliaries" and refused to include their winning efforts in its score charts.

There is little question that these Games belonged to Jesse Owens. He won the 100 and 200 meters, the long jump and ran the first leg for the world-record-setting 4x100-meter relay team. Jesse and his nine "black auxiliaries" were truly amazing. Together they won eight golds, three silvers, and two bronzes. Their unofficial point total in track and field events exceeded that of any other nation's track and field team, including their white American teammates.

Babe Didrikson had been the star of the '32 Games in Los Angeles, but Missouri's Helen Stephens proved a fitting successor in women's track and field. She dominated her competition even more decisively than had the Babe, winning the 100-meter dash in world record time and anchoring the winning 400-meter relay team.

The U.S. Olympic team marching in the opening ceremonies.

Swimming had long been the special province of Americans, at least until 1932, when Buster Crabbe was the only American to win a men's individual event. In Berlin, Americans Adolf Kiefer and Jack Medica took the 100-meter backstroke and the 400-meter respectively, but the others did not fare so well in the face of stiff competition from the Japanese and the Dutch. Only in men's and women's diving did the Americans maintain their dominance, sweeping 10 of a possible 12 medals. The U.S. also won the first basketball championship in Olympic history, although the team had to play the finals outdoors in a sea of mud.

Although it was a splendid Olympiad for the American athletes, the Games themselves were forever marred by controversy and the overtly political propagandizing of the host nation. Even as Germany was exuding *Gemütlichkeit* on a grand scale, the ominous preparations for war were obvious as Olympic participants and spectators mixed with squads of Hitler Youth and storm troopers on the streets of Berlin. Eighteen months after the close of the Berlin Games, Germany occupied Austria and the Sudetenland, and for the second time in the modern Games—as opposed to the practice of the ancient Greeks—the Olympics were suspended for war.

Helen Stephens preparing to throw the discus at the Senior Olympics in 1984.
Photo courtesy of June Becht

HELEN STEPHENS

Gold Medal, 100 Meters, 1936
Gold Medal, 4x100-Meter Relay, 1936

Perhaps because she came earlier and certainly because she deserved them, the plaudits went to Babe Didrikson, but Helen Stephens stands equally tall in the annals of women's track and field. A Missouri farm girl, she was dubbed the "Fulton Flash" when she won the 100-meter dash and anchored the 400-meter relay at Berlin in 1936. She was also the only American athlete invited to meet Hitler personally.

Helen Stephens thrived on all kinds of competition. In a period of just two-and-a-half years of amateur competition, she never lost a scratch race while winning 14 national AAU championships in a variety of track and field events. On five occasions she raced Jesse Owens. She was unbeatable in the shot put and standing broad jump. In the 1940s, while barnstorming with a girls' basketball team, she delighted audiences during halftime by challenging anyone in the stands to come down and race her. In 1986, at the age of 68, Helen Stephens entered 12 events in the regional Senior Olympics in St. Louis and won gold medals in 8 of them.

Still physically imposing, Stephens is a born storyteller whose sharp humor and blunt manner belie a warm and sensitive nature.

I'll have to tell you a story about my meeting up with Hitler. Before I had gone over to Germany, I had read quite a bit about him. I had read *Mein Kampf*, and I figured that somehow or another I was going to meet him. I just felt it was in the cards.

After I won the 100-meter dash, a German messenger came running up and asked me to come up to Hitler's box. Der Führer wanted to meet me. My Olympic coach, Dee Beckman, was with me, and she said, "No, she can't go now. She's made an agreement to broadcast back to America. As soon as we get through, we'll be available." Well, this messenger says, "I can't go back and tell the Führer that. He'll shoot me." But Beckman told him, "Aw, he won't shoot you. It'll be all right."

He was a little undecided, but he took off. When we came out of the broadcast booth, he was there dancing up and down, ready to take me to meet Hitler. So the two of us went down, and they ushered us into a glass-enclosed room behind Hitler's box in the stadium. In a few minutes the doors opened, and about 15 black-shirted guards came in, lined up, and stood at attention. They had those big German Lugers on their belts, and they unsnapped them. Why, it looked like an assassination squad! Then Hitler came in with his interpreter. He gave me a little Nazi salute, and I thought, "I'm not going to salute you." So I extended my hand and gave him a good ol' Missouri handshake.

Well, immediately Hitler goes for the jugular vein. He gets

ahold of my fanny, and he begins to squeeze and pinch and hug me up, and he said, "You're a true Aryan type. You should be running for Germany." So after he gave me the once-over and a full massage, he asked me if I'd like to spend the weekend in Berchtesgaden. I thought that must be the name of a big track meet down there. But Dee Beckman told him that I was in training. He said he could understand that because he had to be in shape to run the country. I then asked him for his autograph. Right when he was giving me his autograph some little tiny guy slipped in there and snapped a picture. Well, that Hitler, he jumped right straight up. Dee Beckman whispered to me, "Hey, he just set a world standing high jump record." But it wasn't funny. He was spouting German, and he began to hit and kick that photographer. Then he motioned for his guards to come and get him. They shook him, and his camera fell out on the floor, and they kicked that around like a soccer ball. Then a couple of them grabbed him and gave him a one, two, three, and threw him out the door and the camera out after him. Then everything returned to normal. I had heard that Hitler could chew carpet and stuff like that. I thought, What are you going to do for an encore after this? Anyway, he wished me well. The next morning that picture was on postcards and sold at the stadium. I got six of them.

I grew up on a farm outside of Fulton, Missouri. My father's mother's name was Snow, which I think was English. The name Stephens has been claimed by the English and even by the Germans. My mother was Pennsylvania Dutch. So I'm sort of a duke's mixture, plus on my grandfather's side I have Cherokee Indian. Even as a kid I think I related to that, although I didn't know it. I only knew this maybe 10 years ago because, when they used to show me the old family album, here was this big woman sitting in a chair, and I'd say, "Well, that's an Indian." And they'd say, "No, no, no!" The family tried to conceal this. It was something they didn't talk about. But she was a full-blooded Cherokee Indian.

I didn't discover my athletic talents myself. It came about when I was 15 and a sophomore in high school. My coach, W. B. "Burt" Moore, who doubled as athletic director, track and football coach, gym teacher, and whatnot, was holding spring tryouts for a Missouri state letter. One of the requirements was to run the 50-yard dash in seven seconds. Well, we were just running on a cinder path. We knew nothing about form and ran in tennis shoes and floppy clothes and all that sort of thing. But I remember I could run! I could outrun the boys! So I took off and finished that distance, and then the coach looked at his watch and said, "I don't believe I got your time right. I think it was six something, but I think you should run it again." So I ran it again. Then he says, "That'll be all." He took off and went to the local jewelry store and had his watch checked to see if it was OK. What had happened was I ran the first race in 5.8 seconds and the second one in 5.9, both of which would have been world records. Well, my coach leaked the story to the newspapers, and it made the Associated Press and got carried around the country. That's how my speed was discovered.

I learned to put the shot on the farm. I couldn't afford $2.50 for a shot put, but my dad had broken a 16-pound anvil pounding something or other on it. So I started throwing one of the pieces. My brother and I spent a couple of years readying me for my shot put debut. He always says that he should get some credit for this because he was my retriever.

My coach gradually worked with me and taught me something about technique and so forth. Oh, he was a lovely man! Handsome man. I secretly admired him and probably was infatuated with him. Probably loved him, and he'd like me to say that, too. He's still living. He's in Ames, Iowa. We correspond all the time.

At that time our opportunities were very limited. There was no competition back in those days. There was nothing in high school, nothing in college. But in March of 1935 my coach found out that they were going to have the national AAU championship in St. Louis, so for about two or three weeks he had me running, staking starts, and tossing the shot put around. I was then 17. I also did some broad jumping because that was one of the events. So he entered me in the 50-meter dash, the standing broad jump, and the eight-pound shot put. As I recall, the superintendent of schools wasn't too keen on our going, and he told my coach for us to leave town very quietly, and he hoped that we'd come back the same way and that we'd have this foolishness out of our systems. They didn't think too much of that stuff back in those days.

Well, I had absolute confidence in myself. All I wanted was an opportunity because I knew I had the stuff. So we came down to St. Louis. The coach's wife came along, too; she was one of my greatest supporters. And Stella Walsh, the 1932 Olympic champion in the 100 meters, was there. I had had her picture on my wall for a couple of months, sticking pins in it every day; I really had her wounded. Anyway, we had this 50-meter race. We all lined up. I was nervous. I wore a little ol' blue gym suit my mother had made for me and a pair of shoes borrowed from one of the boys on the Fulton track team and a pair of ol' gray sweat pants from another boy. And, boy, I was really ready to go! When that gun went off, Helen Stephens went off. And when that tape came up, I was there with it. Stella didn't think too much of that. She didn't like it. Burned her up. She called me a "greenie from the sticks," and that really made me mad. Stella said I'd jumped the gun. And I said, "Come to Fulton, and I'll run you over plowed ground and give you an even break." Then I told the reporters that I had never even heard of her.

I never got another opportunity to run against her again until we met in Berlin. If she had been agreeable to running against me, we could have been on an awful lot of programs around the country, even after the Olympics. We'd even have been at the big men's meets. She always got a lot of money in advance before she'd run. A lot of people have told me that, but I was one of those simon-pure amateurs, you know, trying to play it all by the rulebook.

So, anyway, that was how I got started. And once I had beaten her, I made national news, and from then on they had to pay attention to me. I was then 17 and a senior in high school. That same night in the AAU meet I went on and won the standing broad jump and the shot put. So I won three national AAU titles in my first track meet. I had worked hard with that stuff, although I certainly wasn't a finished product by any means.

It was a lot of fun. I remember an ol' gal from St. Louis who was on the *Post Dispatch* there. She came down and wrote an article and did a lot of pictures. She had me dressed up in overalls and carrying a shotgun with my brother's hunting dog. The caption read, "From farm to fame in 6.6 seconds."

Two things happened before I tried out for the Olympics. Some Fulton businessmen formed the Fulton Athletic Club, which sort of defrayed my expenses and those of my coach and chaperone. Back in those days you had to have chaperones. They saw that I got to a few meets. Then the other thing was I enrolled at a local college. I had one year there before the Olympics. I trained with the boys, and I took a lot of starch out of some of them. I did a lot of long-distance running like 400 and 800 meters. It's a crying shame that they didn't have those events for girls back in those days. They didn't have them because they didn't think the women could run them. When they ran that 800-meter race in 1928, the gals fainted because they were trained to run 50 yards, and it just killed them when they ran that longer race. But I would've loved to run those longer races because, when I ran 100 meters, my coach taught me to run 120 meters. When that tape comes up, everyone stops. I always went through that bugger like it was never there. I think a lot of these runners today don't drive through the finish line. It's like they're not going to waste an extra step. I've watched a lot of top-class people, and they're always ready to collapse.

Back in those days you qualified through the AAU. It was the only thing that was going back then. I qualified in a local AAU Ozark District meet in St. Louis. I broke the world record in the qualifying, and then they found out the track was a foot short. It went on like that back in those days. They always had to have so many officials present of a certain stature and qualification and so many watches that were checked properly. And every time I'd run I'd break a record. But when I got through, somebody had always made a mistake. And they always gave an excuse: "Oh, well, you'll beat that someday."

I never lost a race from scratch in my entire amateur career of two-and-a-half years leading up to the Olympics. I think I may have lost a handicapped race somewhere along the line when they used to give these girls 15 or 20 yards on me. But I never lost a scratch race.

It also used to burn me up that in the official meets you could enter only three events because, shoot, I could have done more.

Well, when I went to any track meet I was not overly friendly with anyone. And, of course, there was my appearance and my deep voice. I was going to kill them, you know, let them know it right off the bat. Of course, later on, after you get to know people, they become your life-long friends. But my coach was partly responsible for that. He didn't want me to become friendly with anyone. Stay aloof from them, he'd say. Don't associate with them. Just go out there and run away from them. There's a little psych in all this.

Babe Didrikson was a bit like that. She could not stand another woman. I've heard many stories about her. Back when she was on the Olympic team in '32, she was a tobacco-chewing, cursing, spitting, regular ol' tomboy and hellcat who couldn't stand anyone, and nobody could stand her.

I'll tell you a little story about my first meeting with her. It was after I returned from Berlin in 1936, and I was down in Washington, D.C., to run in a track meet. Babe, of course, knew my Olympic coach, Dee Beckman, and several of the other girls. And she came over to the hotel that night to say hello to them and confided that she wanted to see me. Well, during the course of the evening, she suggested that she and I don swimming suits and take a little swim. We weren't trying to beat each other at swimming, but after we got out of the hotel pool, she suggested that we throw some of these life preservers, which were filled and rather heavy. She said, "Let's toss a few of these out on the water." I felt right away that she was testing me, but I said, "OK, lead off." We tossed a few out, and she said, "Let's go for some distance." And I said, "All right; just head right out there." Well, what happened was we threw a few, and I decided that I could probably use a spin like a discus thrower, and I wound up and threw that thing clear across the pool up against a chainlink fence. And the Babe says, "It's time to go in. I've got a golf date tomorrow, and it's getting chilly."

I played one season with the All-American Redheads, a women's basketball team, and we toured all around the country. Eventually I had a team called the Helen Stephens Olympic Co-Eds, which was similar to the Redheads. We were booked around the country. One summer I got involved in a promotion with a baseball team similar to the House of David. These were called the House of Davidites. No, I know what you're thinking—that it was some ol' gals with beards or something. I may be on tape, and I may not be, but it doesn't make any difference. I'm going to tell you this story. I think it's good. You know, Babe Didrikson toured the country with the House of David at one time. Yes, she did. Well, one time in some town or other some old haughty gal looked over her eye glasses at Babe when the Babe was throwing a few balls with these bearded guys and said, "Babe, where's *your* beard?" And the Babe looked her over and said, "I'm sitting on it, sister, just like you are."

My first boat ride was going over to the Olympics, but a funny thing happened even before we pulled out of the dock in New York. I discovered two or three boxes of literature and letters in my cabin about the Jewish people wanting us to take a stand against competing against the Germans in the Olympics. They were wanting us to stage a protest of some type. I turned this material over to my coach, and I think she turned it over to the Olympic officials. That was the first, but more came later in Berlin—letters, telegrams—where people would write and tell you to get down on your

Helen Stephens with Jesse Owens, 1936. Photo courtesy of Helen Stephens

mark and then refuse to run and say that you wanted prisoner so-and-so released from the concentration camps. I never could understand how those telegrams got through to Germany at that time. That was always amazing to me.

Well, on the boat the most famous incident was the champagne party and Eleanor Holm Jarrett. We all thought Eleanor was very outgoing—a hell of a nice girl. Actually, I didn't know too much about her. She was living a different life from mine. She was out in the world, singing in a band, traveling around, and I was fresh off the farm. She was used to drinking champagne for breakfast, and I'd never had any of that stuff. But anyway, I remember the officials talking and saying that Eleanor was acting up. They tried to warn her that she was going to get in trouble, and a few days later she evidently did.

Back in those days those Olympic officials were authority figures to all of us athletes. They expected discipline, and by and large they got it. Call it fear, intimidation, whatever. I remember the morning after this incident—and I was embarrassed to be a party to it—they paraded all the gals through Eleanor's cabin to see her. I think she had already received her admonishment. She was going to be kicked off the team. We all went down there in a group, and this kid had a hangover. We thought she was sick, and I guess she was.

I remember her when we landed in Germany. We were going to take a train, but she wasn't with us. I remember seeing her out of uniform with her suitcases off boarding another train. I thought it was sort of pathetic in a way. As she has said, Hitler told her that he would never have kicked her off the German team; first he would have let her swim, win a gold medal, and then he would have kicked her off the team.

I think she would probably have won, too. That was one of those things. It made a lot of history. I can't say whether it was wrong or right. If we have rules, you got to stick to the rules, but she was a free spirit and used to living a different lifestyle than the other athletes did. She didn't think any more about drinking champagne than anyone else would think about drinking water.

There were three heats in the 100-meter race in Berlin. I ran the first heat, I believe, in 11.4, which was a world record, but they claimed that there was a crosswind. I never heard of a crosswind ever hurting anyone. They weren't ready to accept my speed at that time.

In my semifinal heat I ran an 11.5, which was also a world record, and then in the finals I did it again to get the Olympic and world record of 11.5. But there were some people there who were timing it by hand, and they claimed that I ran that thing in anywhere from 11.1 up. Some said 11.3. There was quite a debate. My Olympic coach was there when they decided to set that record at the meeting afterward. They just didn't feel it was possible for anyone to run that fast and cut the record down that much. Stella Walsh's time had been 11.9 in 1932. My time probably should have been better than 11.5. You got to realize that I was strong! I was really strong, and I had a nine-foot stride. And I might have been even better a few years later if I had kept it up.

My coach was always working on my start. I had a slow start because I wanted to take a big stride on that first step. By taking that big first stride I was moving right away, getting into that long stride immediately. Of course, they had the idea back in those days that you had to get those little ol' choppy steps to pick that up. I think some of these athletes today get a pretty good long first stride, and then a lot of them keep their rear up pretty high. We used to be crouched down, coming out on an angle. I think they've learned a lot about technique. I was a natural runner. I could run like a deer. I had speed. I just had it.

We'll never really know what would have happened in that relay race if that German girl hadn't dropped the baton when she was about 10 yards ahead. She received it all right, but then dropped it when she exchanged it from one hand to the other. You didn't have to do that if you were running last, but she was used to running first. I saw that happening out of the corner of my eye, but I couldn't wait to appreciate it at the time. In any case, I felt that I would have made up the difference because the Germans had their slowest runner going last. I felt that I could have chewed her up. But in retrospect, as the years pass, maybe I wasn't as fast as I thought I was. At the time, however, I thought it would have been a close finish.

Our quarters over there were spartan. We had a dormitory that was a nice, new, modern building. We had a bed in there but not a real mattress. It was just a cotton- or kapok-filled thing. There was also a little stand and a light hanging from the ceiling. There was a community bath and showers. On the first floor we had a lounge that was nicely furnished to use if you had guests or if the press came. There wasn't any luxury connected with it. The dining room was nearby, and I remember they started out by feeding us green apples for breakfast and that heavy black bread that most of us had never eaten. So we raised a lot of Ned with them until we got some bacon and eggs and some American cereal in there. I think they were trying to weaken us.

Those German girls who were attached to us as English-speaking guides could speak good English, and they were telling us that the German people were going to treat us nice while we were there, but that didn't mean that they necessarily liked us. They said they were going to beat the hell out of us come the next war, and in that very stadium there were tunnels underneath for air raid shelters. We weren't used to hearing all this. And all those training fields adjacent to the stadium were filled with thousands of German schoolchildren marching around with broomsticks and swords—the Hitler Youth, the Boy Scouts.

I met Hermann Goering before I met Hitler. I think I drank my first glass of beer with him. He offered me some, and I looked at my Olympic coach, Dee Beckman, and wondered, Is this going to be all right? Should I do this or not? She gave me the motion to go ahead and drink it—you know, you're in good company or something. Of course, he was playing footsie under the table. He was an ol' rascal, I can tell you that.

I remember that after the Olympics all of the gold medalists were invited to Goebbels's estate along with the upper 400 of Berlin society and the top people of the German army, navy, and air force. They threw a big garden party there for us. They had about seven outdoor dance pavilions and bars with champagne running freely. There were soldiers all over, standing at attention. During the course of the evening, a messenger came up to me and said, "Hermann Goering wants to see you upstairs." Harriet Bland, a relay runner from St. Louis, and I said, "Hey, this'd be a fun experience to go up there. We won't tell anybody." Well, we went up, and there was a soldier in uniform standing before the door. Now this party was later written up by the press as one of those orgies, and that's what it was. We get inside the door and there's Goering sitting on a great big divan and a couple of gals sitting there in dubious attire. He had a table in front of him, and I knew things weren't according to Hoyle when one of those girls slithered up from under the table. Then I realized this black thing he had on was his kimono, and he was sitting there in his shorts. And, of course, he gives me the Heil Hitler sign and congratulations. He told me to have a drink and brought the wine over. Well, I thought, I'm not drinking anything here. So I took the wine and toasted with it and set it back, just ceremonial-like. So he says, "You and your friend make yourself comfortable and everything, and if you would like to be more comfortable, I'll have you shown into an adjacent room, and I'll be in to see you later."

I thought, Oh, my God. And Harriet, she's over there talking to somebody. Just then Goering got a phone call, and a good-looking German officer came up and said, "Would you like to come over with me and meet so-and-so?" So we did, and he says, "I don't think you young people should be here. This is not a proper place, and things will get out of hand before the evening's over. If you'll bear with me, I'll introduce you to several well-known officers who are here." And he introduced me to old World War I generals, and then he said, "I think you all will be uncomfortable here. We'll gradually work over to the door, if it's all right with you." He told us that he didn't approve of what was going to take place there. We had a hard time catching Harriet and getting her going because she couldn't get it through her head what was going on. As I got ready to go out the door ol' Hermann Goering was still on the phone, and he jumps up and says, "Auf Wiedersehen, Fraulein Stephens." And then he blew me a kiss—and that's the last I ever saw of him. I later thought, Gee, I wonder what I missed out on. I could have had even a bigger story to tell.

After the Olympics I came back and ran for my college and wore their colors. I ran in the 1937 indoor AAU meet in St. Louis and won the 50, the shot put, and the standing broad jump for the third time. The last race I ever ran as an amateur athlete was in Chicago. That was in August of 1937.

I lost my amateur standing, I guess, because I signed an agreement with a fellow to represent me. We made ourselves available for offers. I endorsed Quaker Oats and another breakfast cereal similar to Wheaties called Huskies, out of New York. Then I started touring the country with the All-American Redheads, a women's basketball team that played only men. You really didn't have to be a redhead. You could put a rinse on your hair if you wished. I did it once for kicks—thought it would put some life in it. At the half of the game I would challenge the fastest man in town to run the 20-yard dash across the floor, and then maybe I'd do a standing broad jump, and then they'd put pads down, and I'd toss the shot. There was many a man in this country who said I beat him. I run into a lot of them in this Midwest area. They come up and say, "Remember that little ol' skinny kid you ran against about 40 years ago or so? Well, that's me. Now I weigh 200 and I'm baldheaded and walk with a cane."

I even ran five races against Jesse Owens—100 yards on ball diamonds—and he gave me 8 to 10 yards, based on our fastest times. We usually wound up with practically a photo finish. I ran him in Chicago at Wrigley Field; Muskegon, Michigan; Toledo and Columbus, Ohio; and Louisville, Kentucky. I guess you never heard of anybody getting a broken finger in a foot race, but when we were running at Wrigley Field in Chicago during World War II, the race was so close that Jesse threw his arms back to his left, and he caught my right hand as it came up and broke my little finger.

I had a lot of fun with that stuff. It was like the broad jump. I won three national championships in the standing broad jump, but that was not an Olympic event. I used to jump 8 feet, 8 inches or something. Many a time I had an exhibition in gyms with my basketball team, and I used to jump 9 feet, 11 inches. Now that's a pretty fair country jump. That was from a standing position.

I got good in the shot put later on when I put on a little weight. I remember one time, in 1952 I guess it was, the Russians were doing something with the shot put in the Olympics. I think they had set a record of 50-some feet. At the time, I was giving an exhibition in a ballpark up in Rhinelander, Wisconsin, and I told them to mark out the United States record, the Olympic record, and the world record. I said, "I'm going to break the world record." I weighed 195 pounds then. I was pretty muscular, and I had worked on that shot; it was just like a baby to me. I knew just what to do, and I tossed that sucker out there close to 55 feet—54 feet, 11 inches or something. It was better than the record that had been set just a couple of days before. [Author's note: Galina Zibina of the U.S.S.R. set a world record of 50 feet, 1½ inches at the Helsinki Games in 1952.]

I once had a meeting in Chicago about going into golf. Sam Snead was there, and he was going to be my advisor. They were going to send me to Florida for two years, and I wasn't going to have to worry about expenses. They'd take care of everything. They were going to get me the finest coaches and teach me the game. I may have blown it. But in 1937 there wasn't any money in golf. They said that they felt that there was a future in that game and they would gamble if I would. Well, I'll tell you, I needed to get ahold of some money. I needed money for my folks so I could buy them a farm. I just couldn't gamble that they were going to feed me for two years. I figured I was going to eat one way or another.

You know, in recent years many girls have got into problems with this sex bit. Avery Brundage asked me what to do about it. I'd been pestered around the world on this question. So I met him in Chicago. I was then the President of the Midwest Chapter of Former Olympians.

"I'm going to tell it to you in two words," I said.

"What's that?" he said.

"Examine them."

"How are we going to do that?"

"That's for you and your crew to figure out."

And then they came up with all those chromosome and sex tests. After that on national television he gets up and says it was all my idea. I later learned that there were a lot of people who hated my guts. They just hated my guts.

They had some pretty good examples of that back in my day.

The Germans had a gal who was a high-jumper, and she was really a man. There were no ifs, ands, or buts about it. He placed about fourth or fifth, so it didn't do him any good. After the Olympics were all over, I understand that he went to Holland and fathered two children. They used to ask him, "Gee, you must have had a great time running around in those girls' dressing rooms masquerading as a woman." And he said, "Aw, it wasn't so hot."

I've stayed pretty active in sports my whole life. I bowl and play a little golf. I did pretty well in the Senior Olympics this year. Anybody can enter, from 55 on up. They have different age classes. Well, I ran the 50-, the 100-, and the 200-meter dashes, the standing broad jump, the running broad jump, threw the discus, put the shot, and threw the javelin. That's eight events, and I won every one of them. I'd never even thrown a javelin before.

When people ask me how I rate my career, I tell them a little story that Dizzy Dean used to tell. Dizzy was one of the most unforgettable characters I ever met in sports. He was one of the great, great characters and a butcher of the king's English. I always liked what he said when he was being inducted into the Baseball Hall of Fame. Some smart-assed reporter asked, "Well, Dizzy, how do you rate yourself?" And Dizzy said, "I wasn't the greatest, but I was amongst 'em."

I kind of feel the same way.

ARCHIE WILLIAMS

Gold Medal, 400 Meters, 1936

Archie Williams was a college sophomore when he won the 400-meter dash in Berlin in 1936. Earlier that year he had set a world record of 46.1 in that event, a mark that would stand until well after World War II.

Williams was one of the 10 men on the U.S. Olympic team who were referred to in the Nazi press as America's "black auxiliaries," a term reflecting the Nazi belief in Aryan supremacy and black inferiority. But much to the chagrin of the Germans, these "black auxiliaries," led by Jesse Owens, outscored every national track and field team, including their 56 Caucasian teammates.

Archie Williams holds degrees in mechanical engi-

Archie Williams in 1986. Photo courtesy of Archie Williams

neering from the University of California, Berkeley; in aeronautical engineering from the Air Force Engineering School at Wright-Patterson Field; and in meteorology from UCLA. He also holds a commercial pilot's license with an instructor's rating and a teaching certificate from the University of California, Riverside. Modest to a fault, his self-effacing remarks fail to disguise a man possessed of extraordinary curiosity, quick wit, and a penetrating intelligence.

That moment of victory was just something that proved that I could do something. Most young guys go through life not sure of what they're doing. You study, and you say, "Well, I can read, and I can write and do math and probably do this and that," but here was something that I did. And I guess that the whole world saw it. I can't say that I filled up with emotion when the flag went up and all that. I got a big thrill out of it, but it wasn't like the end of the world because I've got to think about the guy who almost won.

Maybe I just had a step on him. People say, "Well, gee, just think, you were the greatest in the world." I say, "Bullshit. I just beat everybody who showed up that day." How about some guy down in Abyssinia chasing those lions for a living or getting chased by them? He could probably come in and kick my ass without even taking a deep breath. Forget about being the greatest in the world. You just beat the ones who showed up that day.

Everybody asks me how I prepared for the Olympics. I didn't. I was preparing to get a degree in mechanical engineering because nobody in my family had ever gone to college. They weren't pushing me, but this was something I wanted to do, a goal that I had. I lived about a mile from Berkeley, so I could walk to school. In those days there weren't any scholarships. Nowadays a guy goes to Cal because they give him a better free ride; in our days we went because a Cal man with his big *C* was something. You'd say, "Boy, I wish I could be one of those kinds of guys." The kids saw it more that way then. They didn't see athletes as the guy slam-dunking or spiking the ball. They saw a guy as an athlete, pure and simple. They didn't see athletics as a way to big bucks. It was just an end in itself. To me athletics were fine so long as I got my lessons. And it was tough, man. I wasn't that smart. So I had to bust my ass. A lot of times I wouldn't even get a hot shower because I'd be in the lab until 5 P.M. and everybody else would be home. And I'd have to work out, come in, and take a cold shower. But I don't regret it. It was great.

I picked engineering because I liked aviation and I liked flying. I wanted to be a flyboy. I used to make model planes, and I finally thought, If you want to get into aviation, you got to get in on the engineering part of it, so I signed up for that. It was kind of a challenge, I guess.

When I went to Berkeley, I went to my counselor, and the guy said, "What do you want to take?"

I said, "I want to take engineering."

He said, "Are you kidding? Be serious. You ain't got a chance. Why don't you be a preacher or a real estate man or something?"

I said, "Look, man, sign me up. Let me worry about that."

Then at the end of my studies, sure enough, the big companies like General Motors or General Electric would come on campus to interview seniors, and the same counselor told me he wanted me to take interviews even though he and I knew they weren't going to hire any black engineers. Those big corporations just weren't hiring black people. They weren't, and who else would? Look, I had a job one summer making $5 a week chopping weeds for the East Bay Water Company. Later I thought about working as an engineer for them. And I talked to the guy down there, but he said, "Sorry about that."

In college they had a student branch of the American Society of Mechanical Engineers. But forget it. I couldn't even be a goddamn Boy Scout. I went to Sacramento to the state contest because I used to make these model planes with a bunch of my white friends, and I couldn't stay in the YMCA. And guess who the guy was at the desk who turned me down? A Filipino! So I had to stay in a flophouse. It really hurt the friends I was with because it never occurred to them that this was the way it was. But I'm not bitter. It's just the way it was then.

I got into sports kind of by accident. As a kid, I wasn't that good in other sports, but I could run pretty fast, so I tried track. Even in high school I wasn't that great. I don't recall winning any races.

I finished high school during the Depression, and there were no jobs, so a friend of mine said to me, "Hey, we're not doing anything. Let's go back to school." I asked him, "What do you mean?" He said, "We can go to San Mateo J.C. and at least have something to do since we can't find any jobs." So we went down there.

At San Mateo I found out I had to take trigonometry and physics so I could enroll in a regular four-year college to become a mechanical engineer. I also went out for track, just because everybody else was doing it. I started running pretty good, and the coach said, "I think you might have a good career when you go on to a four-year school." His name was Tex Bird, and he did more than talk about running; he talked about life, and he gave me some good principles to go by. And in the process my times started to come down to where he felt I could go to Berkeley and make the team. So I did.

At Berkeley I ran into a super coach, Brutus Hamilton, who himself had been an Olympian in the decathlon. In fact, he was a super athlete because he also got a baseball offer from the New York Yankees and he had been the all-service boxing champion. And besides that he was—and many people didn't know this—an English teacher and quite a philosopher. I think he had more to do with whatever success I had, not only on the track but in life, than anyone else I can think of.

I can't recall one single time when he spoke in anger to me or any of the other fellows. He was always gentle; he was always positive; he was always constructive; it was always "How can you do it better?" and not "Why did you do that?" or "What's wrong with you?" None of that kind of stuff. It was always positive. He always made you feel like you meant something to him. With that in mind, anytime you did something that wasn't good, you felt like you were letting him down. Some people said he was too soft, that he should have been a hard-nosed disciplinarian, but he got stuff out of people that other guys wouldn't have got. For instance, me. I wouldn't have done for other people what I would do for him because he never put the pressure on. He felt that any pressure was self-imposed. He said, "You can be what you want to be, and I can't make you do it. I can't run for you. So just get out there and do the best you can."

Brutus Hamilton was Glenn Cunningham's coach and Bob Kiesel's, too. Kiesel was a sprinter on the winning 1932 relay team. All of us felt the same way. It was more like he was our dad. He had coached at the University of Kansas and then came out here to Berkeley; I think it was 1931 or 1932. I've still got letters that he wrote; they're almost like poetry. He'd talk about things from life. You know, you never see grown men cry. We were over there in Berlin. He went along as a coach, and he missed his family so much that I saw him break down and cry one night. It made me cry too.

I can't remember him even talking about anything like technique. He'd just take what you had and polish it up for you and say, "Work on this." There were times when he'd come up to you and say, "Hey, you look like you're tired. Do you really feel tired or bored?" Then he'd say, "Go home. I don't want to see you for a week." And I'd say, "But coach, I need. . . ." He'd say, "Get the hell out of here. Go." He could feel what you were feeling.

He was not a religious man in any formal sense, although he could quote the Bible, but you'd have to take it from there. He wouldn't push anything like this Jerry Falwell. He was just a great man. He was an inspiration.

Actually, I was a walk-on at Berkeley. No one even knew I was there until track season. That first spring I was running only 49.7 or something like that. In fall track I got it down to about 48.5; then, the next spring, things just started happening. It seemed like every meet I'd knock a half second off. I didn't have any illusions about being that great. My real hero was a guy named

Jimmy LuValle who later got third in the Olympic 400 meters. He was from UCLA, and I saw him win the NCAA in 1935. I was way up in the bleachers, and I thought, "I'd sure like to run that good." I never dreamed that I would. Anyway, my times in the spring of 1936 started coming down. It's kind of hard to believe, but every time I'd run my time would get a little bit better. I won the PAC 8 with 46.8, which was a record for that meet at the time. Then the papers started writing me up, asking, "Can he do it?" I thought, I don't know. I can try.

Then they had the Pacific AAU at Stanford, and I got down to 46.3, which was getting close. And the next week we went to Chicago for the NCAA, and guess what? 46.1. Right out of a clear sky. I still don't believe it. And the funny part of it is you never know when it's going to happen because this was in a trial heat, no pressure. All I had to do was be in the first four. I was just floating along. I remember it was a one-turn race at the University of Chicago, and the tape was in front of a gate, and one inch past this gate was a cement sidewalk. When you were running down the home stretch, you could see that cement. They say I let up a little bit, but I don't know if I did or not. Who knows?

But, anyway, that got me in the book with a world record. You know, it's a funny thing. Have you ever heard of biorhythms? OK, students are always kidding me about my biorhythms. I always do theirs on the computer so they always were telling me to do my own. One day just for the fun of it I did, and on the day that I set that record of 46.1 everything was perfect, one of those picture-book situations. But in the Olympics it was just the opposite. Everything was for shit. You can take it anyway you want.

The final trials for the '36 team were at Randall's Island, New York. The temperature was 100 degrees. Boy, it was hot, but I won. There was so much excitement. Here's a dumb kid who'd never been out of California and in New York City with all these big athletes. I thought, What am I doing here? It was kind of like a dream. I remember Ben Eastman. I had worked out with Ben just before we went back East, and it just happened that to go to the finals we had to share a taxi, and Ben said, "Hey, I'll pay for the ride." Every time I see him now I say, "Well, Ben, I still owe you for that taxi ride." It's funny what you remember about those things.

Then we hopped on the ol' boat. In those days they didn't have any 747s. One thing I had to watch was eating. A bunch of young kids, and all of us finely tuned and well trained. Well, you get on that big ship, and the first thing they do is start feeding you. They have before-breakfast sweet rolls, and then they had breakfast off the menu. Before this we'd been eating in the Automat. And then came lunch and tea break, then supper, and at 10 o'clock at night you could come down and pig out, just to top things off. I imagine I picked up about eight or nine pounds.

I noticed that on board ship they were very careful to put all the black guys in one compartment—"Well, you guys want to be with your own kind,"—that kind of crap. My roommate was a guy I had to compete against—Jimmy LuValle. I don't think it ever occurred to them that there might be some heavy psyching involved. Of course, I was too dumb to get psyched out.

Running styles had changed by the time I was running the 400 in the Olympics. You didn't run hard, coast, and run hard again. That was like running an 800 meters. At least when I ran, if you had an outside lane, you didn't know what was going on until you got in that last straightaway, so you couldn't afford to play games. You had to kick it and get out there. You got to know your pace, that you were not burning it all up all at once, that you were still keeping up with it because when you come out of that final turn, it's really a shocker to look up and see that you're not in the lead.

I'll tell you the biggest worry I had in that damn race in Berlin was whether or not I was going to step out of my lane just before the last straightaway because all the lines are crossing there. It's confusing, and you're tired anyway, and you're trying to run. I guess I did all right because I didn't get disqualified. But I was never quite sure whether I stayed in my lane or not.

Everything is different now. We actually ran the first 220 yards faster than the second 220. I understand nowadays that someone like Lee Evans would probably run the second 220 faster. It's kind of hard to compare what we did with what they're doing now because the training is much more rigorous today. In fact, these guys train all the time. We trained four days a week, with weekends off. These guys today train every day, twice a day sometimes. They do weight training and exercises that nobody ever thought of in my time.

I picked the 440 because I didn't like long distances. I liked sprinting, but I wasn't that fast. I was pretty good. I could run 21.2 in the 220, which would get you about a third or fourth. But it was my coach who said, "I really think your race is the quarter-mile because of your temperament."

I didn't like races like the 880 where you had to jockey around for position and mess around. I liked to kick it full throttle and let it fly. That's just the way I am; whereas, some guys, like John Woodruff, liked to mess around, jockey for position, go in and out.

John Woodruff was good. You know, he was only a freshman in the Olympics. I was a sophomore. He beat everybody. Big ol' gawky kid, he ran the weirdest race. Ran the first lap in 60.5 and the second in 50.5. He won the IC4A about four times in both the 440 and the 880. He really didn't have any competition. He was in a class by himself. I was just a flash in the pan, whereas he was Mr. Consistency. He's a legend.

We had some characters in those days. Spec Towns, for instance. Well, I'm not going to tell you about him. We used to call him Li'l Abner. He'd been in the National Guard, and he'd wear these ol' GI boots. He's the only guy in the world who would take his cigar, put it down on the starting block, run a race, and then come back for it. I don't know whether he ever lit it or not. He was just a lot of fun.

We pulled a good one on Spec in a meet in Oslo after the Olympics. He had just broken the world record in the 110-meter high hurdles. He ran it in something like 13.7. That was an unheard of time then. Well, that night we got some guy to call him on the phone and say, "Mr. Towns, we're very sorry to tell you that your record will not count because there were only nine hurdles on the track." For a while he was really shook up, but the next day somebody told him the truth.

I also knew Glenn Cunningham. He was a hard worker—real dedicated. Remember that as a child he had been in a bad fire, and I think he even had some toes missing. In any case, that guy really had to warm up a lot for his races. In fact, I would warm up with him, and when we'd finish warming up I'd say, "Hell, that's my workout." God, this guy would just run laps and laps and sprints and everything. He had a nice sense of humor. A really serious guy, but he could also joke around. In fact, he discovered that my left leg was an inch longer than my right one. He was great on rubdowns because he had to do it for himself. He was giving me this rubdown, and he says, "Relax." And I said, "Goddamn it, I am relaxed." So he shook my legs and called for the coach to come and see that my left leg was about an inch longer than my right. He said, "God, you're a freak."

Another guy was Jack Torrence. There's a guy who, if they'd made the shot put ring about a foot bigger—or if they had let him have a six-pack before the meet—would have thrown that goddamn thing 100 feet. He had the record of 57 feet, which in those days was almost like 80 feet would be now. He didn't do so well in Berlin, though. I think he only finished fifth. Mack Robinson was just a junior college sprinter that nobody was watching. I think he took third in the trials, but he came through like a champ in the finals. He finished second to Jesse in the 200. You know, he's Jackie Robinson's brother. He's kind of a quiet guy. He didn't have too much to say. Just went out there and did his job.

Cornelius Johnson was another character. Ol' Corny was a great psycher. He could clear 6.6 in his sweats. In fact, he'd never take his sweats off. In those days you didn't have this flop thing. You had to muscle your way over the bar. He'd kick way over the bar and just psych everybody out. He was from Compton J.C., and he was funny. I remember one night after the Olympics we all went into Berlin, had a few drinks, and ol' Corny was doing pretty good. We jumped in this taxi, but we didn't have enough money to pay. So we passed the hat, but ol' Corny always slept through those things. Corny's gone now, and so are a lot of the guys. The whole sprint relay team is dead. Foy Draper got killed in the war, and Ralph, Jesse, and Wykoff died in the last few years.

Ralph Metcalf was the senior spokesman for us blacks. He was a little older, a lawyer, and a beautiful man. He looked out for me. He told me what to do and where to go. He was a very polished guy. He later became a congressman from Illinois. In the 1932 Games he got euchred out of the 200-meter gold. After the race it was discovered that he had run two yards farther than anyone else. He got second to Eddie Tolan. But Ralph only said, "Well, that's life." He was very studious. I think he got his PhD at USC or UCLA, and then he taught at Dillard University in New Orleans. When I was on my way to Tuskegee during the war, I went through New Orleans and stayed with him. I can remember that we went out to play golf on a little ol' dinky golf course. He was the kind of guy you wanted for a friend. You could go to him for advice.

What can I say about Jesse Owens? What can I say about God? He was just a nice guy. He kind of kept to himself a little bit. Of course, there was always someone after him for interviews or pictures. I got to know him pretty well; in fact, he still owes me $5. But I don't want it that bad. I'll wait. All I can say is he was a nice guy, a good friend. I used to train with him, and it was like running against a deer. We'd run wind sprints, which was good for me because I got the finest there was for an example. The main thing was that everything was effortless for him.

How would he do today? He'd probably jump over Carl Lewis's head, because Jesse never trained for the long jump. He'd go out and run through the pit a few times. That's why in Berlin he almost fouled out. I watched him in the NCAA in 1935. He ran the 220, ran over to the long jump pit to check if anybody had come close to his 26.1 or whatever it was, and then ran back to the start to set a world record in the low hurdles. He was running against a guy named Slats Hardin, who, next to Jesse, was probably the greatest low hurdler in the world. It kind of hurt to see a guy like Slats, who was the epitome of form, and here comes Jesse, who didn't know which foot to jump with. He'd just zoom over—shitty form, but fast. I'm glad he didn't try the 440. I was always reminding him what a tough race it was. I kept telling him, "It'll kill you."

After the Olympics I went on this tour with Jesse Owens and a group of guys to Sweden, Denmark, and Finland. We landed in Oslo, and there was this big banner saying, "Welcome Jesse Owens." But Jesse wasn't there because Eddie Cantor had gotten hold of him and told him to come back before everybody else. He promised Jesse this nightclub tour and that he'd make millions. So Jesse jumped on a boat and went home. Well, we get off this airplane in Oslo, and there's this "Welcome Jesse" banner, and everybody asks, "Where's Jesse?"

"Well, he ain't coming," says somebody.

They said, "What do you mean, 'He ain't coming'? Do you see that goddamn sign? He's gotta come."

"Sorry, he ain't coming."

This one guy goes in the plane, looking through the seats and up in the cockpit, and finally says, "I know. You're Jesse Owens."

And I said, "No I ain't. No I ain't." But he says, "Yes you are. Yes you are." So I said, "OK." And I signed Jesse's name and walked away.

I save all the articles that say why there are so many black sprinters. Actually it's not that there are so many black sprinters; it's just that the white people take it for granted, so they say, "I'm not even going to bother with it." And they don't. Let me tell you this. Jesse was such a phenomenon that after the '36 Games they decided to do a physiological profile on him. Guess what? He turned out to be a Norwegian. All these stereotypes, you know, about the heel bone, your skull being this thick, and liking to tap dance. I have a funny joke I tell about this racial thing. They had two black guys on a rerun of "That's Incredible" the other night. Did you see it? Yeah, the one guy was seven feet tall and couldn't slam-dunk, and the other one had car insurance. So much for stereotypes.

I got a big kick out of Germany. Here's a 21-year-old kid who'd never been out of California. Hell, I didn't even know where Germany was. The German people did just what you'd expect. They'd rub our skin to see if it would come off. But the people were themselves. I didn't know that much about Hitler or what he was doing. In fact, as far as I was concerned, they were just friendly, warm people who were happy to have us there.

Remember a guy named Gene Venzke from Pottstown, Pennsylvania? He used to run the mile. He was one of the guys who used to run in the Garden all the time. Well, Gene Venzke and I were both interested in planes. There was an airport right near the Olympic Village, so one day he said, "Let's go over and take a peek at those planes." We crawled under this fence, and someone yells, "Halt!" Well, it was "Hogan's Heroes" time. We got the hell out of there. Then we saw this plane go by—whoosh. I'd never seen a plane that fast before. I asked one of the Germans, "What kind of plane was that?" "Dat's a mail plane," he said. Well, shit, that was an ME-109. I never saw a plane that fast before. And they were only supposed to be flying gliders. That was the fastest glider in the world.

In the actual Games they crammed all of our heats into two days. I ran the first heat at 10 o'clock in the morning. The second was at 2:30. The next day the semis were at 3:30 and the finals at 5:00. So you didn't have much time to think about it. My coach told me, "Don't get cute out there. You don't have to win every heat, but why not do it? If you don't, you'll fool around out there and think you'll just get a cheap second or third. But that is a good way to wind up in the bleachers." So each race was a kind of final. There was no sense in saving it for something that wasn't going to happen. In every heat you were running against some guy you never saw before. And I just wanted to keep the game honest; otherwise, the first thing you know, you're saying, "Who's he? Where'd he come from?"

One thing about the whole thing was that we were having a lot of fun. We were serious, of course, but it didn't seem to me, and not to the other guys either, that it was going to be the end of the world if we didn't win. That's one thing I notice about these meets I go to nowadays. Nobody's smiling. Everybody's grim. It's like these prizefighters psyching each other out. We'd clown around—kid around—even with the guys we were racing against. We always had jokes going on. And that's what my coach, Brutus Hamilton, said: "This is nothing but a lot of fun. And if it ever gets to the point where it isn't fun, quit." That's why he used to ask us how we felt and then sent us home if we didn't feel good.

It's a funny thing. USC was always our biggest rival. Ol' Dean Cromwell was the coach there, and he always had athletes backed up. They were stacked up like cords of wood. They had a guy named Al Fitch, a sprinter from Huntington High School. Al was running 9.6 and 21.5 while still in high school. Well, Cromwell says, "You know, Al, if you come to USC, I think I can make a sprinter out of you." Shit, he could already beat anybody they had.

And once you started to win, all these guys would ask, "Hey, what do you eat?" Well, actually, I ate anything 'cause I knew my coach would run it off of me. But I'd give these guys a line of shit.

They'd ask, "Do you eat honey?"

"Yeah."

"Do you drink milk?"

"No."

They made some kind of mystique out of it.

I didn't try to psych out my competition. Oh, sometimes I'd limp a little bit. They'd ask, "How you doing?" And I'd groan a bit. Like I said, it wasn't that big a thing. I never saw a guy fall down and cry when he lost or anything. Guys now beat the ground and everything. I think that's why we got more out of it.

Another thing was that the average guy on that '36 team was a college kid. I was just a sophomore. Jesse was, I think, a senior. So was Dave Albritton. All of us were college guys. The average age was probably 21 or 22, whereas nowdays, what are they? What's Moses? Twenty-seven or 28? And the weightmen? Thirty, 35? What it amounts to today is it takes that long to be as good as these guys are. With us it was different. I didn't even dream about the Olympics in the beginning of 1936.

A guy says, "Hey, are you going to the Olympics?"

I'd say, "Hell, I don't know."

And he'd say, "Do you think you can make it?"

I'd say, "I don't know."

It wasn't something where I had to say, "Gee, I've got to make it." Way down inside, I thought, Gee, I'd sure like to do it. But I wasn't making any big plans for it. How many guys are going to go out for the Olympics? So, consequently, I wouldn't have been too disappointed if I'd tripped over my wienie and fallen on my face.

In my case, I did what I wanted. I enjoyed going to the Olympics, but then I still had to get back to school. There was no future then for a career in track. I also hurt my leg after the Olympics in a meet up in Sweden. I pulled a muscle, which never did get well. The next year I went out, and I didn't even make my letter. I tried, but I pulled the same damn thing twice, so I decided, that's it. It got to the point that I was so scared that every time I'd run I'd be thinking about it. It held up when it counted. I got my share out of it, so, I thought, why not let some other guys have it?

I graduated in 1939. That's when I got into this aviation thing. I learned how to fly. As I said before, I knew that General Motors wasn't hiring anybody. The guy who ran the flying school where I learned how to fly—a real nice guy—said, "Hey, you want a job?" I said, "Sure." He said, "I'll give you $5 a week and one hour's flying time."

I worked 12 hours a day, seven days a week, gassing airplanes and whatnot, but I got to fly. This other kid and I—his name was Andy, and he's a chief pilot for Pan Am now—were always sneaking extra hours. We'd get out there early in the morning, and we'd be warming those planes up. We'd look around, and we'd just take off and fly around the field once and come in. I built up my flying time to where I finally got my instructor's rating and my commercial license. That was early in 1941. Again, a black guy with a pilot's licence and an instructor's rating; he's . . . well, he's nothing. Even the guy I worked for couldn't hire me as a flying instructor. He'd have lost all his business.

That's when I found out about this program at Tuskegee Institute. They were starting this program down there to train blacks to fly. So I went down there for $200 a month and started teaching flying. I worked there for about a year.

Then Pearl Harbor came along, so I signed up as an aviation cadet. Because they knew about my engineering training, they sent me to UCLA for a year of meteorology school, and I graduated from that. I got my commission as a lieutenant in meteorology; then I went back to Tuskegee to be a weatherman, but they turned me back into a flying instructor, and that's what I did throughout the war. We had our own Army Air Force unit, the Spookwaffe—

at least that's what we called it. The regular Army Air Force was segregated. The rumor was "We'll get these niggers in a bunch of airplanes and let them kill themselves, and that will be that." But the funny part of it was that they skimmed the cream of the crop out of the colleges. We had guys with PhDs, doctors, All-American football players; these guys were hand-picked, so there was no way we were going to flop. One of my students was an ace. Another one became a four-star general.

I stayed in the service after the war. After Truman desegregated the service in 1948, I was sent to Wright Field to the Air Force Engineering School for two years. I got a degree in aeronautical engineering there on top of what I already had. After that I went overseas to Korea, Okinawa, and Japan for three years, flying B-29s and other odds and ends. After that I was stationed in New York, where I was staff weather officer to the 22nd Air Division. We had the defense of the whole northeast of the country. We worked out of this so-called bombproof building. Well, one day we were in there, and a goddamn foot came through the roof. The guy was up there fixing the roof on our bombproof building. I finally ended up with the Strategic Air Command in Riverside, California, where I was discharged in 1964. I was a lieutenant colonel.

When I was stationed in Riverside, I thought, Shit, I'm young; what am I going to do? So I thought, Hell, I'll go back and be a teacher. When you're an officer in the Air Force, you're teaching all the time. So I went to the University of California, Riverside. I already had my degree, so I had to take all those square fillers like ed. psych., learning processes, and how to run the overhead projector. Heavy stuff. Oh, you had to fill in the squares. Well, I got the degree, and I've been teaching high school ever since.

I passed retirement years ago. At 65 they used to kick you out, but now they can't. If they kick me out, who's going to teach this computer stuff? Hell, I'm good for another 10 years.

How do I stay looking so young? Shit, I just buy cheap clothes. No, I just take it easy. You do what you can, and you play it one day at a time. I jog to the parking lot, and my wife and I walk about 10 miles a week. That's good enough. Stay loose. I don't know about these guys that jog. It's kind of self-defeating. I know it would hurt my knees. I find if I just take it easy with everything and get a lot of rest, I'll be OK. As ol' Satchel Paige used to say, "Think clean thoughts and don't look back."

Hanging around these kids does something to you, too. You see the energy, and it kind of transfers. They want things, and I like to feel if I wasn't here things wouldn't be happening. It's a good feeling. Every day something comes up that you haven't thought of before, and the kids will ask you about it, or they'll bring in something new. It's exciting. I may be 72, but I'm not quitting for a long time. The next generation of computers is coming out, and I want to see what they're like. I just feel good about what I'm doing.

Marshall Wayne, circa 1978. Photo courtesy of Marshall Wayne

MARSHALL WAYNE

Gold Medal, Platform Diving, 1936
Silver Medal, Springboard Diving, 1936

Marshall Wayne was a brash 24-year-old when he won the platform diving title in Berlin in 1936. In the half

century since his victory, Wayne has lost little of that brashness. A colorful storyteller with a marvelous sense of the absurd, Wayne's irreverence toward society and its institutions hides a truly multitalented individual.

After his retirement from competitive diving and a brief stint in show business, he became a pilot, serving first in World War II and then, for 27 years, with Pan Am. He now lives in a small town in northern Georgia, where he has just completed his first novel, which, he insists, is only partly autobiographical.

I was born May 25, 1912, in St. Louis, Missouri, but I left there when I was about three. My parents were stage people. They were a song-and-dance team. We went around the country doing vaudeville on the old Keith Alby Circuit. They'd play these little theaters, and they'd have maybe seven or eight acts. It was the acrobats who taught me how to do somersaults and tumbling before I ever started diving.

We finally settled down in Miami about 1923 or 1924. I went to school down there—to Miami High School and the University of Miami; actually, I was enrolled, but I didn't go very often.

I suppose because there was water all over the place and that was one way of keeping cool, I sort of gravitated toward the swimming pool, and then for some reason I took to this diving thing. It came easy for me. They had this beautiful Venetian pool in Coral Gables. At least, I thought it was beautiful at the time, although the last time I saw it, it looked as though it had been abandoned. It had originally been a rock pit, and they didn't know what to do with it, so they cemented it, added caves, waterfalls, and palm trees, and made it into quite a beautiful spot.

I think they charged 15¢ to swim all day, but I never had 15¢, so I'd sneak in. Oh, I learned some tricks. I was so skinny I could go through the rails of the wrought-iron fence. They'd throw me out, and then two minutes later I'd be back in, and then the chase would be on again. They'd chase me all day long, those lifeguards. They had a couple of these Spanish-type architectural towers at the pool, and one was about 40 feet high and the other one maybe 25 feet up. The water underneath these towers was about, oh, 3 or 3½ feet deep. So I'd run up in the towers, and they'd chase me, but I'd just keep right on going and dive out into the pool. Then they'd have to run back down. They'd finally catch me and throw me out.

This went on I guess for a year or so, and finally they just gave up and told me I could come in free. That's the way I got started diving.

Nobody thought I'd make much of a diver. Everybody told me I was too tall, skinny, and awkward. But I was having a lot of fun doing it, so I just didn't pay attention.

Pete Desjardins had an influence on me. He won two gold medals in diving in the 1928 Games and was sort of a god around Miami. He had all kinds of friends there, but our first meeting was kind of funny. They had put in a new springboard in the pool where he worked out, and I was really enamored with it. I was jumping up and down on it, bouncing off that thing 40 feet in the air.

Afterward, I came home and told my dad, "Gee, Dad, Pete spoke to me."

He asked, "What did he say?"

"He said, 'Stop jumping up and down on my new springboard, you little freckled-face son of a bitch!' " So that's how I met Pete.

My progression up the diving ladder was kind of haphazard. I won a couple of meets, so I thought I was pretty good. At the University of Miami I was about the only one who won anything. I'll tell you about their athletic program at that time: I remember one year they had only 10 guys out for the football team, so they got the biggest girl in the school, and she was the best player on the team. We really didn't have much of an athletic program in those days.

In 1932 my dad gave me $40 and a bus ticket to go to the Los Angeles Olympic tryouts. I was on that bus 10 days and 10 nights, and in those days they weren't air-conditioned, and the seats didn't recline. It was really awful. I got there the day before the high diving tryouts, and my head was still buzzing from the trip; it didn't feel like it was attached. So I just stood there and watched the high diving. The springboard diving was about four or five days later. I think I placed fifth, but I learned an awful lot watching those fellows.

One of my best friends was my coach, Don Grubbs. Don helped me more than anybody else. We were neighbors, and he loved to dive. He wasn't very good at it, but he was a genius with an almost immeasurable IQ. I can remember visiting him much later—right after we had just dropped the atomic bomb on Hiroshima or Nagasaki—and I asked him how that thing worked. Well, Don tried to explain to me about nuclear fission, about the atoms and

Marshall Wayne in 1936.

the nuclei and this and that, and I said, "Don, come on, you're not telling me a thing." So he turned to his son, little Don, and he said, "Would you explain it to this dummy?" Little Don was about five years old, and, you know, he explained it pretty well.

Well, Don Senior would try to dive right along with me. I remember we'd sit around and say, "Let's try a two-and-a-half from the platform. Think we should?"

"I don't know."

Then we'd sit around, and one would say, "You go first."

"No, you go first."

And I'd say, "We'll both go together. OK?"

When we arrived for the 1936 Games, the boat docked in Hamburg. Then we took a train down to Berlin. Of course, we had been on the boat for 10 days, but they got us out the next morning at 6:00 A.M. to do this film with Leni Riefenstahl. I could hardly stand on the platform; I was still partly seasick. I did the worst diving in that film I have ever seen, and they've been running it for the last 40 years, for God's sake. Embarrasses the hell out of me. My God, my legs were like lead; all of ours were. I mean, 6:00 in the morning and we had barely gotten any sleep and were still half seasick.

A little later Dick Degener and I went out to watch the Jap

swimmers work out, and this was funny. This one little Jap really augered every dive. He wasn't flashy, wasn't great, but he wasn't missing anything; you just couldn't fault him. And we looked at each other and said, "We might as well go home."

So instead of working out, we went to see the track and field events and whatever else was going on. We stayed away from the swimming pool. The coaches couldn't find us. The weather was terrible anyway, cold and rainy, and it was an outdoor pool.

Finally one day we looked at each other and said, "We've been goofing off long enough. We ought to go to the pool and work out." So we go to the pool, and that little Jap is still working out. It's still cold and rainy, but he does a dive, and it's right on the button. We were sitting in the stands watching him, and he came up with this funny little grin. So I said, "Listen, here's what we'll do. We'll put on our bathing suits and go on out there, but don't even bring a towel—not even a towel. And don't get any goose pimples. Let's get up there and hit every goddamn dive."

By that time the little Jap had got dressed, and he was watching us. This was the first time he'd really seen us work out. Well, we came out and hit every dive and walked around whistling between them. We psyched that little guy out, we really did.

I made the finals in both springboard and platform, and so did the Jap. On his first dive in the springboard finals the Jap did a gainer and a half pike, and he landed flat on his ass, but somebody said that someone in the stands had dropped a bottle or something. So the officials asked Degener and me if we would allow him to take the dive over again because of that loud, distracting noise in the stands.

We said, "Yeah, let him do it all day and pick his best." So he did it again and landed on his ass again. That wiped him out. He was really a nice little guy. He later gave me a kimono, a little cotton kimono.

Degener won the springboard, as was right, and I came in second. Then I won the platform. But there was lots of politics in the 1936 Games. In the first place, we had to wear a certain kind of bathing suit. Why? I don't know. German morality? Those guys? Moral? But here we were in these damn bathing suits.

We lived in the Olympic Village by team. I had to room with Elbert Root. Oh, Jesus Christ, Elbert Root! He was second to me in the platform. A crazy, wild Indian. The coaches said, "Marsh, because you and Elbert are from the same hometown and you've been friends for a long time, we're going to have you room together." Well, Elbert's climbing out the window, running down to Berlin, eating all of this wurst, coming back, and throwing up all over the goddamn room, and I'm supposed to take care of Elbert. Hell, a psychiatrist couldn't take care of Elbert.

Jesse Owens was a hell of a nice guy. Greatest athlete in the world, but you'd never know it by the way he acted. I'll tell you about that broad jump. You know he was supposed to have faulted the first two times. Well, those who were sitting right there say he didn't fault at all, but the Germans saw it that way, I guess. On that third jump he took off so far behind the board there was no way they could have faulted him. It was at least a foot in back of the board, and he broke the world record. Now the popular accounts say that this German broad-jumper named Luz Long told Jesse to start farther back. Well, how dumb do you think Jesse was? It didn't take too many brains to figure out that he was going to have to start farther back if they were faulting him. But we always hear that this German had to tell Jesse to do it this way.

I had never heard of Richard Mandell's book, *The Nazi Olympics,* until one of the guys I was flying with for Pan Am received a copy from his daughter. He came into the crew lounge and asked, "You guys want to see Marshall Wayne's ass? Look at this," and he held up a picture of a guy diving into the water. I looked at it and said, "That's an Egyptian's ass. That isn't mine." I later told Mandell he had identified the wrong guy. He said he was very sorry and asked why I hadn't got in touch with him earlier. I said, "Well, for Christ's sake, I didn't get the book until about 50 years after the Games." Actually, I guess it was in 1971 or '72.

After the Games I was asked to go to Rome to do an exhibition, but I turned it down because I was supposed to get back to the States to do a film. Somebody had written me and said they had some cameramen ready to make a big movie. So I went back, but the movie never did develop; it was a big farce.

Then that winter some promoter did a traveling show. Dick Degener and I were in it. They built a tank about six feet deep, and when the girls got done splashing their water ballet stuff, about four inches of water would be gone. Well, that flopped, but they tried again. This time they got Eleanor Holm, and they lost some more money. We played Philadelphia, Pittsburgh, East Jock Strap, and God knows where. We did all of our dives, but it was a little tricky into only six feet of water.

We later swam in Billy Rose's Aquacades. Billy Rose was one of the finest guys I've ever known. Now a lot of people will argue about that, but he was a good friend of mine. I thought he was really a nice guy and smart. He was a short, funny-looking little guy with a funny little derby hat. He always had an overcoat on, and usually it was somebody else's. He paid me $250 a week just for diving. I had never made that much money in my life before.

His shows were absolutely fantastic. Of course, he hired the best people to direct and all that kind of stuff, but he was the brains behind it all.

He and Eleanor Holm were married, and Eleanor and I never really got along well. We were always fighting for some reason. I don't know why. We'd laugh and joke and go to parties, but she'd just do something, and I'd say, "Oh, you're full of crap." She couldn't take that kind of stuff, and I didn't mind dishing it out to her. But I don't want to talk about Eleanor because we were teammates and so forth. She was a damn good swimmer, a great competitor—you can't fault her.

I dived with Dick Degener in the 1937 Aquacades show and with Pete Desjardins in 1939 in the World's Fair in New York. Then in 1940 the show that was in New York moved out to San Francisco. Johnny Weissmuller was with us then, and Esther Williams replaced Eleanor Holm. Johnny had to push Williams around the pool. She couldn't swim any better than I could.

Weissmuller was a great guy—a hell of a nice guy—but he was sort of money hungry. We'd be shooting craps or something on a blanket on the floor in the dressing room, and there'd be a half-dollar out there that didn't belong to him, but Johnny with his big foot would sort of just sweep it up. We were playing poker one night, and I was kind of drunk; so was everybody else. Johnny's first kid was being born, and his wife was in the hospital, and we were having a poker party waiting for the kid. I had a nothing hand, and I was leafing through the discards, and I finally got myself a good hand and won the pot. Well, Johnny caught me doing this, and he really got pissed off. So he grabbed me in this great big left hand and held me up against the wall. He had this fist that was as big as a ham, and I knew, what the hell, I'm dead. All he had to do was hit me with that thing, and that's the end. It would have driven my head right through the wall. So I said, "Go ahead. You haven't got the guts." I figured if I'm going out, I'm going out in style. He started laughing and dropped me on the floor. And I thought, Thank God! He saved my life.

Johnny used to play water polo on a Chicago team, and they used to play the New York Athletic Club. Well, those two were the roughest gangs you ever saw. Joe Ruddy used to carry a lead pipe in his trunks, and he actually would bash these guys over the head and then stick the lead pipe back in his shorts. He'd get them under water and "pow!" Oh, they were terrible. They'd come out with no teeth, eyes gouged out, and God knows what else.

I went into the air corps in March of 1941. It was right after that show in San Francisco. I served in the European theater, flying photo reconnaissance. I started out with P-38s. Then I became a squadron commander of 12 Spitfires. In fact, I stole a Spitfire once. I stole it with a lot of fast talk and dummied up orders. I found out that there was one with a broken main spar that a guy had landed out in the woods someplace. Three RAF mechanics were out there, sleeping in a tent, trying to patch this old thing up. So I made up these orders, got all dressed up, and got a staff car, which I'd also stolen from somebody. I snowed these guys, told them I was a lieutenant colonel and all that stuff. They're standing at attention there, and I say, "Fellows, you're doing a fine job, a fine job, I must say. I'm going to be back in 10 days or two weeks. I'll be up about tea time, and I'll fly it back."

Well, they didn't know what the hell it was all about. So they fixed it all up, and I came back and flew it to my base. I put it in a hangar and got all of the RAF camouflage off the thing and put on a U.S. Air Corps star with a bar through it. I flew it for about, oh, six months before some other son-of-a-bitch wanted to fly it, too. I told him, "You want to fly a Spitfire, you go steal your own goddamn Spitfire, but you stay away from mine!"

Well, a little later I was gone for two or three days—went to London or some damn place—came back, and I wanted to go somewhere, so I asked, "Where's my Spitfire?" I noticed everybody standing around. I said, "What the hell's the matter here?"

Then I heard the story. That son-of-a-bitch took my Spitfire. Well, it's a tricky thing to fly, and he didn't know what he was doing. He started down the runway, and everything went wrong, so he pulled this goddamn handle and locked both brakes and went over on his back. He ruined my airplane.

Spec Towns, circa 1975.

FORREST "SPEC" TOWNS

Gold Medal, 110-Meter Hurdles, 1936

Tall, lean Forrest "Spec" Towns was the world's greatest high hurdler when he won his 110-meter specialty at Berlin in 1936. Amazingly enough, three years earlier he had never even seen a hurdle, much less run over one. His considerable talents came naturally rather than as the result of long and arduous training. He had played only one year of high school football and had never run track when he enrolled at the University of Georgia in the fall of 1933. But whatever he lacked in experience, he more than made up for in aggressiveness. Weems Baskin, who coached him in both football and track at Georgia, called him "the greatest competitor I have ever known in any sport."

Except for a few years when he served as an officer in World War II, Towns has never left Athens, Georgia. For 37 years he served as an assistant football coach and head track coach. Illness forced him to retire from active coaching in 1975, but he remains one of Georgia's favorite sons.

I got the name "Spec" because of all my freckles. They used to call me "Freckles," and then that got shortened to "Frec" and then to "Spec." Ralph McGill of the *Atlanta Constitution* used to spell it "Spec," and his rival at the *Atlanta Journal*, the old-timer, Edwin Camp, spelled it "Speck." But either way, that's all anybody ever called me.

I was born the fifth of six children on February 6, 1914, in a little town in south Georgia called Fitzgerald, which had the unique distinction of being settled by Yankee soldiers after the Civil War. Evidently there were a lot of them who liked the South, and a group out of Ohio and Michigan came back and established this town. It must have been a coordinated effort, though, because all the streets going north off Main Street were named after a northern general, and everything going south was named after a southern general. The east and west streets were Indian names. And the big ol' hotel that was there was called the Lee-Grant Hotel.

My daddy was a railroad man, and we lived in Fitzgerald until 1923. There had been a big strike two years earlier that they never did settle, so we moved to Augusta, where he went to work for another railroad. I lived in Augusta from when I was nine until I entered the university, and I've lived in Athens ever since.

How I got discovered was kind of strange. You read today about kids training for years just for a shot at the Olympics. Well, I never ran track in high school. I was not athletically oriented. Oh, I played some sandlot football, and I played one year of high school football. Actually, I had gone out my senior year and didn't make the team. This was at the Academy of Richmond County, which also included a junior college, and they played the high school and junior college players together. They had a hell of a football team. But that particular year they changed the rules, and you could only play high school players. So I purposefully flunked a business English course to go back in the fall of 1931 to play football. I retook the English class and passed, and I played my one year of high school football, and in January I was out of school and started working.

I had always liked to jump things. In fact, I used to visit my grandfather's farm in the summertime, and I never went through a gate in my life. I always jumped the fence. I had developed a unique way of high-jumping. I could high-jump without any problem six feet or better. Of course, I didn't know anything about technique. I had never even seen a track meet. I high-jumped because I liked to jump. In the park near where we lived they had set up a pair of high-jump standards, and I would jump there, not knowing anything about what I was doing.

It just so happened that there was a newspaperman named Tom Wall who lived next door to us. One day he saw me jumping over a homemade stand that my brother had made in the backyard. I jumped about six feet, which was as high as the stand would go. Then my father and a brother-in-law put that ol' cane pole on top of their heads. They were both taller than six feet, and I cleared that. I'd run straight at it and curl the front foot up and drag the back leg over just like a hurdler would. All I used was speed and spring. If I had known anything about technique, I might have gone seven feet. But this reporter saw me out his window, and he wrote in his paper the next day that some college was probably missing a terrific high-jumper because I was not going to attend school. There was a judge in town named Miller who sent the paper to his son, who played football at the University of Georgia and who showed the article to Weems Baskin, the track coach.

Baskin was an old hurdler himself. In 1928 he was the top hurdler in the United States, but he fell in the finals of the trials and did not make the Olympic team. He came to Augusta and talked to me about attending the University of Georgia. At the time I was driving a taxi and doing various other things that some taxi drivers did—it was during Prohibition, you know. This was in July, and he wanted me to come up in September and try out for a scholarship. I told him that I couldn't go to college because I didn't have any money. At that time the railroads were working three days every other week, and my daddy didn't have any money to send me to school. These were really hard times. So I told him that the only way I could go was if he gave me a scholarship. Come September I was there for my tryout, and Weems came into the dressing room and asked me if I wanted spikes in both the heel and toe or just in the toe. I said, "It don't make any difference; I've never seen a pair anyhow."

So he gave me a pair of track shoes and told me to go down and warm up. I really didn't know what he meant by "warming up" except to jog around and work up a little sweat, which you could do easy enough in September in Georgia. Then he put the high-jump standards out. Now, I had seen some high-jumpers do the scissors, and I thought, Well, in front of this college coach I better jump the way you are supposed to jump. So I started scissoring, and it got up to about 5 feet, 10 inches, and I thought, If it gets any higher than that, I better quit this damn fooling around. So I backed off and jumped right at it. I actually jumped 6 feet, 2 inches that afternoon. Ol' Baskin didn't say anything, and I waited around for about two or three days. I finally went to him and told him that I had a job back in Augusta and I had to get back. I told him, "You got to tell me one way or another. It doesn't make any difference, but I gotta go to work." That night he told me he would take care of my room, board, and tuition for four years. So I thought to myself, Well, this is in the middle of the Depression, and this is a way to make a living for four years. Not that I worried too much about the college education. It was just a pretty good way to make a living—to eat for four years. So I took him up on it.

A lawyer named Hirsh, who worked for a firm that represented Coca-Cola, was the sweetdaddy of the football team. A lot of the people there were Georgia grads, and they would help get up the money for scholarships. They gave most of the football scholarships. My scholarship amounted to room, board, books, tuition, laundry, and $2 per month. It wasn't bad. You could get a haircut for a quarter, and a picture show cost 15¢. And you could get $2.50 for your football ticket on a weekend when you were playing at home. I also took Advanced Military, and they paid you $25 a quarter. Georgia was a land grant college, so you had to take two years of ROTC training.

I lettered two years in football. My best work was on defense, although the most I ever weighed was 171 when I was a senior. I loved to play defense because I loved to hit folks. I lettered two years in football and made Georgia Tech's All-Opponent Team my senior year. I was red-shirted my sophomore year; therefore, I came back in the fall of 1937 after I had graduated and played my last year of football. Harry Mehre was the football coach, and he told me if I came back and played my last year of eligibility he'd put me on the coaching staff. He got fired at the end of the year, but the athletic department fulfilled their commitment to me, and I was put on the coaching staff in January of 1938. But they didn't announce it until March because I wanted to run that last indoor season.

My training for the 1936 Olympics consisted of three spring track seasons. I sure didn't know much about track that first year. I remember my freshman year spring football was going on, and some people were working out on the track. There was a boy named Smith, who had been the Georgia high school champion in the high hurdles. He was out there on the track, which was next to the football field, and I saw him running these hurdles. That was the first time I had ever seen hurdles. Baskin, who was also an assistant football coach, was walking along with me, and I jokingly said, "Hey, you want me to go over there and show that guy how to jump them things?" He said, "You'll never see the day you can whup him." So I forgot all about it. They had another boy on the team named Harmon who was a six-foot high jumper, and I was thinking more about him than I was about Smith, because the high jump was supposed to be my event. But when spring football practice was over, Baskin had me try the hurdles, too. It was a natural thing for me once I got the front leg straightened out. I had been jumping fences that high all my life. Well, the first time I raced Smith I whipped him, and by the end of his freshman year he quit track. That's the way I got started.

The only major meet I ran in that freshman year was the Southeast AAU meet in Atlanta, and I won the high hurdles in 15.1. The next year, 1935, I won two indoor meets and all of my outdoor meets including the Southeast Conference. I ran a 14.8, and that qualified me for the nationals, but in the NCAA I didn't even qualify for the semifinals.

I didn't have a good start. Indoor racing was too short for me, although I did set a world record in the 60-yard high hurdles in the Millrose Games in 1936. I continued to improve, especially after I started running the 100-yard dash. By the 1936 season I could do a 9.6 100, and the dash helped me improve my start.

Lawson Robertson wanted me to enter the 100-meter dash in 1936, but my coach wouldn't hear of it, and with Owens, Metcalf, and Wykoff, it's a good thing I didn't try to run the 100. Robertson even wanted to change my form. He told Baskin that I was doing everything wrong as far as running the hurdles was concerned. Baskin had to tell him to lay off me. Baskin told me before I got on the boat for Berlin, "You don't listen to that guy a bit about your form. You know what you're supposed to do and what we've worked on. You do your own workouts."

But I liked Robertson, and he never interfered with me. I do think he cost us the 4x400-meter relay in 1936 because he didn't run Archie Williams, who had won the 400-meter individual race. He also did not run LuValle or Smallwood, and they and Archie were the top three 400-meter people. He ran Cagle, Young, Fitch, and O'Brien. I don't know why he didn't run the three fastest guys.

There was also controversy in the 400-meter relay when Stoller and Glickman were not allowed to run. Some thought it was because they were Jewish, but they were alternates. The three fastest were Owens, Metcalf, and Wykoff. I don't know if they could have defeated Draper or not, but I'll never forget that 400-meter relay race. That was the most beautiful race I ever did see in my life.

I was kind of a loner, but my good buddy in Berlin was Slats Hardin of LSU. I had known him for some time because we had run against each other several times. If Slats had done the things in training that other people did, he would probably have set records that never would have been broken. He was that good. But he was a free-swinging, fun-loving type of guy. He enjoyed life just about as much as anybody I've ever seen. I didn't travel with him too much, because I wouldn't participate in some of the things he did, but I knew him real well.

Slats was really a character. I first met him when we were both at the Sugar Bowl Meet of January 1, 1936. I was to run against two other great hurdlers, Al Moreau, who had gone to LSU, and Johnny Morris, who had been at Southwestern Louisiana. The three of them were good friends, and they were already out of school and were pretty high livers. We were supposed to run on Sunday, and that night they were going to have a beer and spaghetti supper down at Jack's Brewery for all the track boys. Well, it rained so hard on Sunday that they put the meet off until Monday, but they didn't put off the beer and spaghetti supper at Jack's Brewery. Morris and Moreau told me this whole story later. They wanted to go out and party after the dinner because they'd had a good start on that beer, but they didn't know how good competition I was going to be, and they didn't want to take a

Spec Towns in 1936. Photo courtesy of Sports Information, the University of Georgia

chance. They figured if they were going out and have a hangover for Monday, they wanted me to have one, too. So they saw that my glass was full all the time. What they didn't know was that I never did drink beer, and I wasn't drinking that because there was a big ol' urn behind me and I was pouring everything in it. Well, about nine o'clock I got up and acted like I was stupefied and said, "I gotta go." I took off and went to bed, but they went out and partied all night, and I just whupped the tar out of them the next day.

I have a vivid picture of John Woodruff winning the 800 meters. I think he was a little afraid of Phil Edwards, the Canadian. Woodruff's coach was along in Berlin, and I think he told Woodruff that, if he let Edwards get out in front, he'd beat him because he had more speed. So he told Woodruff to get out in front and then slow the race down. In the finals the lead changed hands about four times. Woodruff would get out in front and then slow it down, and Edwards would go around him. Woodruff dropped all the way to the rear one time. But then he'd go to the outside and go to the front and slow it down again. Woodruff beat him. He probably had the longest stride of anyone I ever saw run the 800 meters.

Jesse Owens was a personal friend of mine. I got to know Jesse real well on the way over to Berlin. Jack Torrence, Slats Hardin, and I were assigned to a table on board ship, and you'd eat all your meals there. Well, Jesse came up and spoke to us and was kind of hesitant and then turned to go, and Slats, who already knew him from past meets, said to him, "Jesse, are you supposed to be at this table?" He said that he was. "Well, sit your ass down here," says Slats. So he ate at a table with three southerners all the way over there—nine days, and it didn't bother us. Not a bit in the world. Later I got to know Jesse real well. In fact, I got a picture of Jesse and me that I doubt too many people would want to see him in. We were in Hyde Park for a London Meet after the Games, and some photographer wanted to take a picture, so he got Jesse to stoop over, and I jumped him, using him for a hurdle.

Jesse Owens was the greatest runner who ever walked on a track. If he was running today, he'd still be the greatest. He was without a doubt the most relaxed runner I have ever seen. When he was at full speed and really pouring it on, he looked like he was enjoying himself and could tip his hat and say, "How do you do?" He was that great. He was a terrible hurdler, but he was the best low hurdler in the world because he had that speed. Carl Lewis is a lot like him, but he's not quite as relaxed.

To me there are tremendous differences in track coaches. Now you take ol' Dink Templeton of Stanford. He was the most foul-mouthed person I ever heard in my life. He just cussed out his runners. If he talked to me that way, I'd have whipped him sure as hell, or he'd have whipped me. Now, Brutus Hamilton at Berkeley and Dean Cromwell of Southern California were kind of similar. Cromwell would always agree with you. If you said you thought you should try it one way, he would say, "Now, I think you ought to go right ahead and try it that way." Brutus was kind of the same way, except he would finally lead you around to doing it his way.

I knew Glenn Cunningham real well, or at least I thought I did because I had run into him several times in indoor meets. I was amazed at his ability after what he had gone through. He was to me the first man ever to make a living out of track. He went to school about eight years—got a master's and a doctor's degree, all while running track.

You know, I laugh about the rules and regulations today about who gets paid for this and who gets paid for that. That kind of thing was going on back in those days, but at the time I didn't know what was going on. For instance, when I was running indoor meets when I was in college, the university handled all my transactions. They bought the tickets, paid for the hotel, and gave me eating money, but after I finished the football season in the fall of 1937 and had already graduated, I got a letter from Lawson Robertson. They were trying to revive the old Penn AC or something like that. He wired me, "We'll give you $50 and expenses to run in this meet." Well, I didn't know anything about what was going on, and I had promised to run in the Sugar Bowl Meet in New Orleans that year, after which the university was supposed to announce my appointment as assistant coach. So I wired Robertson back, "Sorry, I'm unable to compete in your meet." Well, I got a telegram right back: "$100 and expenses." So I asked Baskin, "What goes on here?" He said, "Well, you're out of school. We can do this. If you want to run in the indoor season, we'll hold off announcing that you're going to be a track coach because that makes a pro out of you. Then you can do a little dealing for yourself." Well, it ended up that I ran in six meets indoors that season. I won three and got second place three times.

I think Berlin was the first big-time Olympic Games. They really went all out. We were treated about as well as anybody could be treated. Since then I've heard a lot of things said about those Games that I didn't know were going on then. I've got a book here called *The Nazi Olympics* by Richard Mandell, and I've read it. Some of it is true, and some of it is absolutely wrong. Of course, I did not participate in the politics of it. I went there to run and do my thing, and that's what I did. I don't think any athletes got involved in the political side of things. If anybody was involved in politics, it had to be the officials of the Olympic Committee.

After the Olympic Games were over, we went up into Scandinavia to run, and in Oslo I set a new world record of 13.7 in the 110-meter hurdles. The funny part of it was that I was almost not in that race. A few days before, we were in Paris for a triangular meet with Japan and France, and I got a telegram from my football coach at Georgia, saying, "Minor sports season is over. Football practice starts September 1. Be there." I took him seriously, though he was kidding. I liked playing football. For me it was a lot more fun than running the hurdles. I loved that contact. So I went to Dan Ferris, the head of the AAU, and asked him if there was any way I could get out of going to Sweden and Norway. I told him that I had to get back for football practice. He said, "No, you've got to go up there." Well, I was kind of bullheaded, and I didn't like it when he said I had to go to those track meets. I asked him if Fritz Pollard, who had finished third behind me in the Olympics, could go in my place. Pollard had already told me he would be willing to go. Well, our Paris meet was scheduled for the next day, and Ferris says, "It depends how he does against you tomorrow." I thought, Hummm. But I didn't think that way too long because I could never have done that. I won the race in Paris. So I went to Ferris again that night. He got a little upset with me, and I got a little hot with him, and we had a few words. I told him, "The hell with you, I'm not going up there." I just walked out. But Glenn Cunningham got ahold of me and told me he didn't think I understood what those AAU rules could mean. Actually, that's what happened to Jesse Owens. He was supposed to take that same Scandinavian trip, but somebody talked him into coming back to the United States to take advantage of all those offers, and they ruled him ineligible for amateur athletics for 16 months. I didn't understand that there was an AAU rule that said if you had been entered in a meet and it was advertised that you were going to run and then you didn't, except for sickness or death in the family, you could be ruled ineligible for 16 months. Cunningham explained all this to me. And I still had another year of track eligibility. So I ate crow. I went back to Ferris, and the next day I left for Oslo.

That's when I ran that 13.7, which is the fastest time I ever ran. The track there was extremely fast. I got off to an unusually good start that day. I was even ahead over the first hurdle. When I broke the tape I turned around and looked back. The nearest guy was just then clearing the last hurdle. There was lots of talking, but I couldn't understand it; it was in Norwegian. But then one of the other hurdlers came over and banged me on the back and told me that I had run a new world record. I asked him, "What did I do—run it in 14 flat?" He said, "No, you ran 13.7." All I said was, "Aw, hell."

I had set the old record of 14.1 in the semifinals of the Olympic Games, so it broke the record by four-tenths of a second. That mark stood until 1950, and no one would beat it in Olympic competition until Lee Calhoun ran a 13.5 in the 1956 Games in Melbourne.

I used to pull the leg of a lot of people I'd race. In some of the indoor meets they'd ask me if all the smoke in the building didn't bother me. I'd say, "Hell, no. I've been smoking since I was six years old." I used to bet my uniform shirt against my opponent's sometimes. I remember I did it against a guy from Dartmouth. I wanted that dadgum shirt with the Indian on the back of it, but I never did get it.

I admit that I was a little cocky. It never entered my mind that I was ever going to get beat any time that I ever ran. I did get beat in the national AAU in 1937 in Milwaukee, and that made me mad. I had just won the NCAA in Berkeley. We had come to Rockford, Illinois, to work out, and I went up to the coach, Herman Stegeman, and told him, "I got something wrong with my back. I feel a little tight." I meant for him to grab me around the chest and shake me a bit. But he had some new way, and he bent me way down and shook me and, God Almighty, he pulled something loose in my sacroiliac that hurt me something awful. The next morning I couldn't get out of bed. Now, this was on Tuesday, and we were going to race on Friday and Saturday. My back was still bothering me on race day, and I hit the only hurdle I ever hit in my life in a race, and this boy from Wayne University in Detroit, Allan Tolmich, beat me because I hit that last hurdle. But I wasn't running very good, either.

This made me madder than hell. Well, I came back to Athens, and the trainer got my back in shape, and the next week they had a World Labor Meet in New York. Now, I've done only a couple of things in my life that I'm not exactly proud of, and this was one of them. But I was mad. We lined up for that race, and I said, "Hold it." Then I walked out in front of them and said, "Who wants to buy this watch I'm fixin' to win?" And I whupped 'em, too.

I don't think I would have done too badly against today's athletes. I notice that hurdlers today often hit two or three hurdles during a race and still win. If they had hit the hurdles I ran, they'd never even finish the race. Those old T-base hurdles came up between your legs when you hit one, and it was all over when they did. So there was more reason for technique then than there is now. We also never used starting blocks back then, and that meant that our starts were much slower.

After I ended my competitive career in 1937, I became assistant coach in both football and track. One year later I became head coach in track. My coaching career lasted thirty-four-and-a-half years. I was finally forced to quit. In 1972 I lost about thirty pounds and I didn't know why. But then I found out I was diabetic. The doctors also found a spot on my left lung. It turned out to be malignant so they took out the lung. By 1975 I couldn't coach the way I wanted to, so I retired.

John Woodruff, circa 1985. Photo courtesy of John Woodruff

JOHN WOODRUFF

Gold Medal, 800 Meters, 1936

John Woodruff had just completed his freshman year at the University of Pittsburgh when he won the 800-meter run at Berlin in 1936. There was no award for "most respected athlete" on that '36 team, but if there had been, it might well have gone to Woodruff. Tall, graceful, and intelligent, Woodruff retains the fond admiration of his teammates even after the passage of more than 50 years.

Woodruff was the first great American black middle-distance runner. He dominated the 800 meters and half-mile as no athlete has since. The times he ran in the late 1930s would be respectable today, but strangely enough, his only official world record came in an indoor half-mile race at Dartmouth in 1940.

After obtaining his master's degree in sociology from New York University, Woodruff served five years as an officer in World War II. He was called back to active duty during the Korean War, earning the rank of lieutenant colonel before his discharge in 1957. His subsequent career was in public service, with a particular interest in working with disadvantaged youth.

John Woodruff retains that quick natural grace that marks so many great athletes, whatever their age. He is now retired and spends his time officiating track meets, advising young athletes, working in his church, and traveling.

I ran my best time in the half-mile in 1937, the year after I won the 800 meters in the Olympics. It was the Texas Centennial Meet, which was run in the Cotton Bowl in Dallas. I have to tell you the story that led up to that. Earlier that year I defeated Elroy Robinson in the half-mile in the national AAU meet in Milwaukee. My next race was the World Labor Meet at Randall's Island, New York. Now, all of these track people wanted me to run the mile. They always thought that I could be a great miler, but I never cared for the mile, even though I had run it in high school. I was always more interested in the half-mile. But they talked me into running the mile against Glenn Cunningham, Archie San Romani, and Gene Venzke. They were the top milers of the day. They were all afraid of me because they knew I had this speed, and none of them would take the pace because they figured that if I followed them I had a chance of beating them. So what could you do but get up in front? However, I ran myself out because I had no pace, and I finished fifth in that race. In that meet Elroy Robinson, the man I defeated in Milwaukee, set a new world record in the half-mile of 1:49.6. The next day the papers said if Woodruff had been in that race he would probably have won it. Of course, Elroy resented this, which he should have, because he had just set a new world record. So we were to meet in this grudge match in Dallas. Here's the man who set the new world record, and here's the man who beat him in the race before, so it had to be a good race.

Just before we left for Dallas the officials told us that we black athletes couldn't eat in the dining car on the train. Well, we got together and told them that, if we couldn't eat in the dining car with the rest of the people, we were not going. Remember, several of us were already Olympic champions. So they made arrangements, but when we got to Dallas, we couldn't stay in any hotel. What they did was put us in the black YMCA down there. We had to sleep on these little army cots in the gym at the black YMCA.

Well, when the gun cracked for the half-mile race, Elroy Robinson jumped right out in front because he was a front-runner. You couldn't take the lead from him: right out in front, just like a bullet. So I fell into second place right behind him. We ran like that for 440 yards. When we started the second 440, I pulled up beside him. I had told the fellows how I was going to run this race. We battled down the backstretch, and he broke, and I went on by him and won. My time was 1:47.8. Now, remember, the week before he had run 1:49.6.

Three watches clocked me at 1:47.8, and the Dallas papers the next day said they were quite sure that the new world record would be accepted because the track had been measured by the chief engineer of Southern Methodist University within one-thousandth of an inch. You can't get any closer than that. Well, I was very happy because that was the first world record that I had ever set. I had never run with the intention of setting world records. I ran just to win.

About a week after my race it was announced in the Dallas papers that the record would not be accepted because they found the track to be six feet short. You know what went on down there. Those people got their heads together and decided they weren't going to give that black man Robinson's record. I'll never forget. I wrote Dan Ferris a letter, and I said, "Dan, this is really a shame. Here I ran the best race of my career, probably the best race I ever will run, and this is what they did to me." He never answered the letter.

I was born in the small town of Connellsville, Pennsylvania, about 50 miles south of Pittsburgh. My grandparents were slaves in the Virginia tobacco fields, but my parents moved from Virginia to Connellsville during the early part of their marriage. There were 12 of us kids, but now there's only 3 of us left. Quite a number of my brothers and sisters died in infancy because infant mortality was very high back in those days. My father was a laborer. He dug coal and worked in the steel mills and the coke ovens. He also worked in a stone quarry. He was a powerful man, my father. He wasn't as tall as I am; he was close to six feet, but he weighed almost 250 pounds. He was very strong. I heard stories about him lifting stone slabs that normally required two or three men to lift. My mother was tall and slim. She was about five feet, nine inches. I got my slimness from her.

We had some good athletes come out of Connellsville. Johnny Lujack was a Heisman trophy winner at Notre Dame and a star for the Chicago Bears. Jimmy Joe Robinson was the first black to play football for the University of Pittsburgh. There were other good athletes, but most of them just finished high school and went to work in the mines or in local factories.

That's what I was going to do, so I quit school when I was 16 and tried to get a job. I wanted to go into a factory and make some money. They wouldn't hire me. Looking back, that's the one time I'm glad I was rejected because I was black.

I actually got started running because I went out for football, and the line coach was also the track coach of my high school. His name was Joseph Larew. He used to have us running wind sprints, and the quarterback, Ralph Marilla, was the star sprinter. The coach noticed that I was able to keep up with Marilla, so he invited me out for track.

I remember we ran from the high school to the cemetery—Hill Grove Cemetery—and back. It was a mile up and back. We didn't have a regular track at our school, just a dirt path around the football field. I ran like that for two years.

I ran the mile and the half-mile, and on occasion I would run the quarter and the sprints because I could beat anybody on the team in all of those events. But I specialized in the mile. In the first mile race I ever ran for the school my time was 4:44, and I never forgot it. I ran a 4:23 my senior year, but nobody ever pushed me.

I had a lot of natural talent, a lot of God-given talent. The summer I graduated from high school I was invited to the University of Pittsburgh to run against Pitt's best miler, a fellow by the name of Harold Tost, but he refused to run against me. I guess he didn't want to take a chance on getting beat by a high-schooler. So they decided to let me run against their best half-milers, and I beat them.

I did receive a number of scholarship offers to go to college. I wanted to go to Ohio State because Jesse Owens was there. I had met him at some meets. His head coach, Larry Snyder, tried to get me to go there, but some of the people in my hometown were Pitt graduates, and they put a lot of pressure on me to go to Pitt, so I ended up there.

I'll never forget it. It was 1935 when I went to Pittsburgh. The townspeople took care of me and gave me some clothes and essentials. The sheriff of the town made arrangements for his driver to drive me to school because I had no transportation. I arrived at school with 25¢ to my name. I went to see the coach, Carl Olson, and he let me have $5 so I could feed myself the rest of the week. And I did, which tells you something about the times.

It was after my freshman year at Pitt that I qualified at the Olympic trials for the 800 meters. It was at Randall's Island in New York, and I beat Ben Eastman; "Blazing Ben" they used to call him, and he was the world record holder. Actually, he finished fourth and didn't make the team.

We sailed out of New York on the SS *Manhattan*. Mack Robinson was my roommate going over, and we lived in the same room in the Olympic Village. He finished second to Jesse in the 200 meters. Of course, no one had yet heard of his brother, Jackie. the baseball star.

Berlin was very exciting. The accommodations they had for us were absolutely superb. We stayed in the Olympic Village right outside of Berlin about 15 miles. Our chef was from the SS *Bremen,* which was an outstanding German luxury liner. The food was excellent, and everything was immaculate. The organization was superb. The old-timers who had gone to previous Olympics said the Berlin Games were the best. Hitler really put on a show. It couldn't have been run any better. A lot of people asked me how the German people treated us. They treated us royally. They rolled out the red carpet. They were very friendly, very accommodating, very gracious, very cordial. They were considerate in every respect.

We did see soldiers marching to and fro in the city of Berlin, but we didn't pay any attention to them. Of course, we had heard quite a bit about Hitler. There was a lot of talk about how he was persecuting the Jews. But, personally, I wasn't interested in politics, and I think that was the same feeling many of the athletes had. However, we did talk to a young German athlete who visited with us one day in the Olympic Village. We asked him what the Germans thought of Hitler. He spoke English very well and told us that they thought he was a great man because he had done so much for the country from an economic point of view: everyone was working and so forth. He had opened up all of those factories to make war armaments so everybody had a job. They thought that was wonderful.

As a result of the aftermath of World War I, when the Germans had to pay all of those reparations and were brought to their knees, they were looking for a savior, so to speak, and there he was. I guess they didn't anticipate what he really had in mind; they didn't know.

Incidentally, the alleged snubbing of Jesse Owens by Hitler is fiction; there was nothing to that at all, although Jesse later used it in a lot of his speeches. I don't know just how it happened, but somebody said that Hitler refused to shake Jesse's hand. I do recall seeing Jesse while still on the track, waving and exchanging salutes with Hitler in his box. And I do remember a day that Hitler invited a number of athletes up to his box, but at the time Jesse was still competing. Hitler never even got close to any of the athletes, to Jesse or to any of us, other than those who were invited to his box. There was never any other affair when the athletes might have a chance to meet Hitler personally.

Jesse Owens received a great deal of publicity after the Games, but none of us was ever envious of what he was getting. We were very happy for him because we all liked him. He didn't come back from Europe with us. He came back early and got involved in a lot of commercial ventures. He stumped for Alf Landon in 1936. I guess you heard the story that during a welcome home parade in New York City somebody threw a bag of money into the car with Jesse. The bag contained $5,000.

He was used by a lot of people. He gave exhibitions in which he'd run against a horse. Then in later years he started to get some breaks. He worked for a liquor concern in Pittsburgh as a sales representative, but he didn't really do that well until he got to Chicago, where he had a public relations firm. Then he started working a lot with kids because he was always good with them, always trying to help them. He also started making a lot of speeches. He was a good speaker. I often thought that Jesse missed his calling; he should have been a minister.

There was that incident with Marty Glickman and Sam Stoller, the two Jewish runners who were dropped from the 400-meter relay team just before the race. I don't know exactly what happened. I've heard many stories. Marty said that they gave them the business. I did hear that Jesse did not want to run because he had already won three gold medals, and he felt that those guys should have been given a chance. I also heard some story that Hitler was objecting to the Jewish boys running on the team. Now, I don't think that particular story held water at all, because Hitler had nothing to do with our team. We were over there to run, so that didn't add up. I think it was a decision that the coaches made to keep the strongest combination together to run that relay. But we still would have won it with Stoller and Glickman on the team.

I'd had only three years of track experience, two years in high school and one year in college, when I went to the Olympics. Nobody told me how to run those trial heats in Berlin, so I decided that I would jump out in front, get the lead, and keep it. That's what I did in the preliminaries and in the semifinals. I don't know why I changed tactics and decided to follow somebody in the finals. I should have taken the same strategy that I did in the heats, but I didn't. I was going to play it cagey—drop into second place and stay in second place. This was my strategy. Phil Edwards of Canada, who had attended NYU, jumped out and took the lead, and I fell in second behind him. But Phil set a very slow pace because he was trying to conserve his energy for the final drive. I fell right into a trap. Well, we ran first and second for 400 meters, but when we hit the turn going into the second 400 meters, all of the other runners bunched around me. I was boxed in, and I couldn't get out because of my long stride. I thought, I have to get out of this. But I couldn't break through because I would have fouled somebody, and I would have been disqualified. In spite of my inexperience, I was smart enough to know better than to try to do that. So the only way I figured that I could get out of that situation was to slow down to practically a stop and let the field proceed ahead of me. Then I ran out into the third lane and proceeded down the backstretch and passed Edwards. Then, before we hit the final turn coming into the homestretch, he passed me. Then I passed him again and came on in and won the race. The Italian, Mario Lanzi, who was the European favorite to win the race, came in second. Never in the history of the Olympics had a race ever been run like that. I actually started that race twice, and usually when you break your stride, you're finished. But I had a lot of speed. God had gifted me with a lot of speed and strength.

I was happy to win that race because that's what I went over to Germany to do. I've always had that feeling of winning. When I got down on the mark, the only thing that I ever had on my mind was to win the race. I never got into any race with the feeling that I wasn't going to win.

Each of us who won a gold medal in Germany received an oak

tree. I brought mine home with me, but when I got home I was notified that the tree had to be shipped to Washington, D.C., to the Agriculture Department because they had to check it for any bugs that might be on it. Then it was shipped back to me, and when I got it, it was almost dead. I turned it over to Dr. John Lewis, the botany teacher at my high school. He revived it and planted it on the lawn of the Carnegie Library there in Connellsville. Then, when the Connellsville Stadium was built, they moved the tree out to the stadium. There it stood for many years before anybody knew anything about it. Then one weekend when I was back home I went to the local paper, the *Connellsville Courier*, and told them that it would be nice if somebody would put something out there by the tree so that the young kids would know what it represented. So they raised the money for a plaque, and now everybody knows the history of that tree.

The people of Connellsville were proud of me when I came back from the Olympics. They gave me a big parade. It was really something; it was wonderful. They presented me with a watch, a Lord Elgin watch. On the back of it was inscribed "John Woodruff, Olympic Champion, 800 meters, Berlin, Germany, 1936, presented by the Connellsville Alumni Association." Unfortunately, the watch got stolen from me the following spring back at the University of Pittsburgh. It was our first track practice, and I asked the locker attendant for a locker. He said, "Well, take one of the empty ones and when you come back tomorrow I'll assign you one with a lock on it." So I took one of the empty lockers, undressed, took my watch off, and put it inside of my pants pocket. When I came back from practicing, it was gone. I spoke to the coach about it, and he said to keep it quiet and it might turn up. He didn't want me to report it or anything because it would create a lot of bad publicity. I never did get it back, but to this day the Connellsville people still think I have that watch.

After I returned to Pittsburgh I still had three years of eligibility. I ran in the Intercollegiate American Amateur Athletic Association, the National Collegiate Athletic Association, and several other major meets, and I won all of them. I won the quarter- and half-mile in the IC4A in 1937, 1938, and 1939. I won the half-mile in the NCAA for the same three years, and you can't win any more than that. In 1940 I set a new American record of 1:48.6 in the 800 meters. That year I ran a 1:47.6 in the half-mile indoors at Dartmouth. That was a new world record, and nobody was running that fast in those years. I also ran a 440 in which three watches caught me under 47 seconds, but I got credit for only a 47 flat. I was told my coach should have made an issue of this, but he didn't. Herb McKinley wouldn't run his 46 flat for another 10 years. Larry Snyder, the track coach at Ohio State, once told me, "John, you were just ahead of your time."

I graduated on schedule from Pittsburgh in 1939 with a major in sociology and a minor in history. Then I went to NYU and got my master's degree in sociology from the School of Education because I intended to teach on the college level, but I never did. I continued to run that year while getting my master's. That was the winter I set the world indoor record at Dartmouth. I was running and training hard to be ready for the 1940 Olympics, but, of course, there were no Games in 1940.

I went into the Army in 1941, and I ran a little during that time. After the war I noticed that the fellows were still running about 1:52, 1:53, and I thought, I ought to be able to come back and do that. So I started training; in fact, I trained harder than I'd ever trained before. I finally got in an indoor race over in Brooklyn. When the race started, I jumped out in front, and for a couple laps I felt good; I felt like a million dollars, felt like my old self again. But all of a sudden it seemed like something just zapped all of my strength. I don't know what it was. Just all of a sudden I had no more strength, and I finished last. I got home that night, and my legs ached like somebody had taken a club and beat on them. I got in the tub and soaked, and I said, "This is it. This is it." That was the end of my running, and that was only the second time in my career that I ever had lost a race at either 800 meters or the half-mile.

As I look back now, I know that winning that Olympic race meant a great deal to me. First of all, I was interested in getting an education. I came out of a poor family. I'm the only one in the family who went to college. In fact, if it weren't for sports and the gift that God gave me, I could never have gone to college. I'll never forget what my high school coach told me when he found out that I had good athletic potential and had the possibility of going to college. He said, "John, whatever you do, if you get an opportunity to go to college, go, even if it's only for one year, because it'll mean a great deal to you and to your race." Those were his very words, and I never forget them. When I went to school, I said, "Well, if I don't make good, I'm not going to return home. I'll just keep right on going." You see, I wanted that education, and I wanted that college degree.

Francis Johnson in 1984. Photo courtesy of Francis Johnson

FRANCIS JOHNSON

Gold Medal, Basketball, 1936

Basketball became an official Olympic event at Berlin in 1936. Led by its captain, Francis Johnson, the 14-man American team defeated Canada in the finals in a game that weather conditions reduced to low comedy. Playing outdoors on clay courts in a driving rain and with a ball that belonged on the soccer field, the squads slipped and slid through the mud in a game that looked more like water polo than basketball.

Johnson had been an all-sports star in Hartford, Kansas, before going to Wichita University where, under the coaching guidance of his brother, Gene, he became the leading scorer in the Central Conference. After graduation in 1933, Francis played AAU basketball with the Hutchinson Reno Creamery and the Wichita Gridleys before joining the Globe Refinery Team in McPherson, a corporate-sponsored amateur team made up of former university stars. It was as a member of the Globe Oilers that he was a unanimous pick for the American Olympic team in 1936.

Proudest of his defensive ability, Johnson claims the defensive techniques his brother developed have remained unsurpassed. It might also surprise some readers to discover that the dunk, the all-court press, and the hook shot were all practiced by Johnson and his teammates years before these became acceptable practices in big-time basketball.

I met Hitler and Eva Braun one evening. We were in the Olympic Village just killing time, and lo and behold, here they came through the yard. They had come out to make a tour of the Village, and it just so happened that they came through our area and stopped for about five minutes and talked with us through their interpreter. They asked us how we liked everything. Hitler looked just like you always expected him to look. He was just like you or me or anybody else standing there with his girlfriend. Eva was an attractive woman. The German women were a little different from ours, especially in dress, but she was a very attractive person and seemed very congenial. Actually, she was the only woman allowed in the Olympic Village. A couple of days before, a couple of German girls had tried to invade the compound and as a result had their heads sheared just like sheep.

Everybody in Germany evidenced the highest regard for Hitler, and anytime you'd meet anybody, instead of saying good morning, they'd greet you with "Heil Hitler" and a salute.

Whenever Hitler came to the stadium, there was tremendous secrecy. They had 10 big, black Mercedes seven-passenger touring cars, and you never knew which one he would be in. He'd be in a different one each day. They had a tunnel under the stadium, and all of these cars went into the tunnel, and from it Hitler could go right up into his box, which had a glass shield built around it. When he left the stadium, people packed both sides of the street just to watch him pass by.

One of the interesting things we found in downtown Berlin was that on every street corner there was a loudspeaker, and there was always music playing on those loudspeakers. But the German officials could cut in and broadcast throughout the whole city of

Berlin anytime they wanted. In a matter of seconds they could shut down everything in the city through this speaker system. When an American won a gold medal, our national anthem was heard over these loudspeakers; it was quite a thrill to hear that.

The other unusual thing we saw was youth in training. They said it was the same as our Boy Scouts, but they had all of these youths out training, just going out and marching and popping their heels. It was actually a young military group. All of the younger people seemed to have everything, and the older people didn't seem to have much.

I was born on August 5, 1910, in Hartford, Kansas, a small town of about 700 people. I grew up there, and I was always rather small. When I was a junior in high school I was 5 feet, 1 inch tall, and weighed 101 pounds. I played on a basketball team, but I was the runt; however, I got my share of it done. I also played football and track. By my senior year I was about 5 feet, 10½ inches. I was the most scrappy player on our team, and our coach, Stub Mayo, felt that I had more potential than anyone on the team.

In 1929 I went to college at Wichita University, which had just been taken over by the city and its name changed from Fairmount. I received an athletic scholarship from the university, which I needed desperately. My father died when I was 12 years old, and I had four brothers and sisters. For this scholarship, which paid my tuition and $20 a month, I worked from one to three every afternoon and eight hours on Saturday, sweeping out different buildings. I lettered in football, basketball, and track at Wichita. We had an outstanding basketball team that played in the Central Conference.

When I got out of college in 1933, I wanted to become a coach. I had majored in physical education and manual training and shop work. But I never did coach. That was the height of the Depression, and the jobs I interviewed for paid $50 or $60 a month, and they wanted you to be married, have a family, and have experience. I didn't have any of the three. So I started playing AAU ball and ended up with the McPherson Globe Oilers. We would actually work for the company in the off-season, but our only real job then was to play basketball.

For the Olympic trials the officials picked the national AAU champions, the runner-up, the national YMCA champion, and the five NCAA regional champions. Thus there were eight teams in the playoff. The McPherson Globe Oilers were the national AAU champions.

In the playoff at Madison Square Garden our first game was against Temple University. After nine minutes we were ahead 26–9, and I had nine field goals. I'll never forget that after I made my ninth shot, which was a left-handed hook shot, the guy guarding me yelled, "Jesus Christ, don't you even look where you throw it?" The New York papers called it the greatest exhibition of circus shots they had ever seen.

My brother, Gene, coached the McPherson Globe Oiler team and later was an assistant coach for the Olympic team. We were among the first to use fast-break basketball, the zone press, and a man-for-man pickup all over the court from our combination zone defense. We had a defense that's never been used since. I've talked to a number of coaches about it, but they all seem to be opinionated, so they don't want to listen. We could pick up man for man all over the floor and then drop into a zone. We knew exactly where the man with the ball would have to go before the man with the ball even knew, because we forced him to always go to a certain place. It went like this: when they were standing still, we were guarding them, and when they were running, we were standing still.

We also showed those Madison Square Garden folks what you now call the dunk. We could start a team that averaged 6 feet, 6½ inches, and we had five or six fellows who could dunk. The New York papers said, "Instead of jumping up and laying it in, they jumped up and pushed it down from the top." They didn't know what a dunk was at that time. But we never did it in a game—just in warm-ups to show how tall we were and how high we could jump.

I was known as a ball hawk. I excelled at stealing the ball. I also learned to shoot with either hand as well as with both as was common then. You have to be able to shoot from all over the court, and I tried never to shoot the same shot twice. I also shot hook shots with either hand from the post. But I practiced all those shots because I was barely six feet, and that meant I had to practice harder. I used to spend hours in the gym learning to run forward and backward. I could run backward almost as fast as I could forward.

Fourteen of us were chosen for the Olympic team, but I was the only unanimous choice of the sportswriters, according to the New York newspapers.

In Berlin there were four outdoor basketball courts. They were all constructed of clay, and they could hold four games at a time.

Teammates (left to right) Francis Johnson, Carl Shy, Sam Balter, and Donald Piper in Berlin. Photo courtesy of Francis Johnson

That's where the preliminary eliminations were held. The balls were made of untanned leather. They were supposed to have used U.S. balls, but when we got there and pumped up the American balls they were a sixteenth of an inch undersize, so we had to use German balls. They weren't balanced properly, so if you threw them through the air they would just wobble. They were also too light, and when you would go to shoot outdoors, the wind would catch them and move them over three feet or so. This made accuracy rather difficult.

The night before the finals it rained about four inches. We tried to get them to move the game inside. They had a beautiful gymnasium, though they didn't have goals, yet they could have set some up. However, the officials decided that since it was scheduled to be played outdoors that's where it would be played. The sunken stadium where we were supposed to play had about six inches of water standing in it, so we had to use one of the fields that had been set up for the preliminary eliminations.

These fields didn't have regular seats for the crowds. They just terraced the levels around the field, and the people would stand shoulder to shoulder to watch. It was jammed full in spite of the rain. It was like a football game in the rain with people wrapped up in parkas and others with umbrellas, all outside watching a basketball game in the rain.

The 1936 U.S. Olympic basketball team aboard the S.S. *Manhattan*. Francis Johnson is wearing uniform number 11. Photo courtesy of Francis Johnson

Every time the ball would hit the ground, it would take up water just like a sponge. And being a clay court, when you went to stop you couldn't; you'd just slip and slide along. Our uniforms got discolored pretty good from these slides through the mud.

We couldn't play like we normally would have, and the score was very low. We got out in front easily and held it that way against the Canadians. I think the final score was about 19–8. They made two field goals the first half, and we made five, plus some free throws.

When we returned from the Olympics in Berlin, I went to play with the Antlers Hotel in Colorado Springs. In 1938 I was a member of the Kansas City Healeys, which won the national championship. After that win I decided to retire from basketball, and I went to work for the John Deere Plow Company. I started out as a territory salesman and ended up owning my own John Deere dealership. In 1941, shortly after Pearl Harbor, I volunteered for the United States Navy. I received my training at Annapolis, was commissioned a lieutenant junior grade and sent to Pensacola, Florida. While there I coached the Naval Air basketball team, besides being an athletic officer. Later I was stationed on an aircraft carrier in the South Pacific, and at the end of the war I retired as a lieutenant commander.

I now live in St. Louis, and one of the first things I noticed after we moved to St. Louis was a newspaper account about the Senior

Olympics. This has no connection with the regular Olympics. It is a program for retired persons 55 and over. It's divided into several different age categories all the way up to 75 and above. They have all different types of events. I thought it would be interesting to try the free throw event, though I really hadn't touched a basketball in about 20 years. I went down there and won the 70–75 age group in free throws. I shot underhanded, and because I hadn't shot in quite a spell, I made only 5 of my first 10 shots. I had a little trouble because the guy I was shooting against was standing right under the basket to throw the ball back to me. I think this distracted me a bit, so I asked him to stand on the side, and I made my next 14 of 15 to beat him by one.

Rick Barry was the last of the great underhand free-throwers, and I don't think there's any question that underhand is a much better, more accurate, and easier way to shoot free throws. In tough games when it's tight and the muscles tighten up, the underhand free-thrower has a big advantage over the fellow who shoots with one hand because when he gets tight or he gets knocked down and bangs up his arm a little bit, his muscles tighten up. That's why when they get into the final minutes of the game you see them shoot short or push it long or shove it off to one side or the other. If you shoot underhanded with your arms extended, it is just a matter of how far to throw it. I think I could still make three out of five even with my eyes shut.

I want to be remembered for always having played hard. I was one of the original ball hawks and used to steal the ball a lot and force them to throw it away. And when I got fouled, I made my free throws. I figured if they knocked you down and you missed your free throws, they'd knock you down again.

7
LONDON, 1948

The Olympic Games resumed in London in 1948 after the XIIth and XIIIth Olympiads had to be canceled because of World War II. For the second time in the first half of the century, war intervened. World War I had forced the cancellation of the VIIth Olympiad, scheduled for 1916.

As the President of the British Olympic Association, Lord David Burghley, the 400-meter gold medalist in 1928, was chairman of the committee responsible for organizing and staging the London Games. This was no easy job considering that England still bore the scars of war and much of London had been destroyed in the Blitz, resulting in a desperate housing shortage. In addition, transportation and food were strictly rationed, building materials were unavailable or in short supply, and money was scarce, as a severe postwar austerity program had been imposed upon the nation.

Yet in the face of all this, the British, as they so often do, persevered. The London Organizing Committee "made do" with existing facilities. Most of the events were held in Wembley Stadium, which had been remodeled for the occasion. For the male athletes the Olympic Village was a military base in the suburb of Uxbridge; for the women it was the dormitories at Southlands College.

A few political problems had to be resolved before the opening of the Games, but compared to the disputes that would plague future Olympiads, these were almost trivial. As aggressors in the war, Germany and Japan were not permitted to send teams, and the new country of Israel was banned because it was not yet a member of the International Olympic Committee. The Soviet Union was also not a member and would have to wait until Helsinki in 1952 to send its formidable athletes to the Games. The potentially thorny issue of Sunday competitions, which had caused considerable consternation in previous Games, never arose in London because the Organizing Committee decided no events would be scheduled on Sundays.

The Games were declared open on July 29 by King George VI, and the pomp and pageantry of the opening ceremonies were witnessed by more than 80,000 people who sat sweltering in the stadium in humid, 93-degree weather, and by an estimated 500,000 who watched at home on Britain's 80,000 television sets.

The competitions began the next day with the 10,000-meter race. Viljo Heino, the Finnish world record holder, was the overwhelming favorite. Yet in one of the major upsets in the Games, a Czech army lieutenant, Emil Zatopek, came from far behind to win and set a new Olympic record. Later he placed second in the 5,000-meter race. Zatopek's graceless, jerky running style and pained facial contortions prompted one observer to comment, "He runs like a man who's just been stabbed in the heart."

Equally unforgettable was the performance of Hungary's Karoly Takacs in the rapid-fire pistol shooting competition. Takacs had long been one of the world's outstanding marksmen, but in 1938 he lost his shooting hand in a hand-grenade accident. The determined Takacs learned to shoot left-handed and did so well that he took the gold medal in London and repeated his performance four years later in Helsinki.

For the American athletes there were also some surprises. Harrison "Bones" Dillard, the greatest high-hurdler in the world, stumbled after hitting a hurdle during the Olympic trials and never finished the race. However, he had already qualified in the 100-meter dash, well behind Mel Patton and Barney Ewell. Patton, the world record holder, Ewell, and Lloyd La Beach, a Panamanian, were the favorites. Patton suffered a poor start and was never a threat, and Dillard, the hurdler, squeaked past Ewell at the tape to take the gold.

The 800-meter race, which was run in the rain on a field covered with water, was won by Mal Whitfield, an Army Air Force sergeant who had attended Ohio State University, in the new Olympic time of 1:49.2. (Four years later in Helsinki, the consistent Whitfield repeated his 800-meter victory in the indentical time.) In the women's diving competitions Victoria Draves took both the platform and springboard titles. Bruce Harlan became the sixth consecutive American to win the springboard diving competition, and a 28-year-old physician named Sammy Lee took the platform.

Olympic Games often are dominated by the performances of a single individual, such as Jim Thorpe in 1912 and Jesse Owens in 1936. In London two people emerged as stars. One was a 30-year-old Dutch housewife and mother of two children, Fanny Blankers-Koen. In 1936 Blankers-Koen tied for sixth place in the women's high jump event, but 12 years later she compiled the best record of any woman in Olympic history. She won gold medals in the 100- and 200-meter dashes, the 80-meter hurdles, and the 4x100-meter relay. She was limited by the rules at the time to three individual events and therefore could not compete in two events in which she held the women's world records, the broad jump and the high jump.

The other remarkable individual at the London Games was the 17-year-old decathlon winner from California, Bob Mathias. The grueling ten-event decathlon is held over a two-day period, and Mathias had to compete in horrible weather. He finished the last event, the 1,500-meter run, on the second day at 11:00 P.M. on a muddy track after some 12 hours of competition. Mathias was the youngest decathlon winner in history. Four years later at Helsinki he won it again, setting two records in the process, for the highest total points and the widest margin of victory.

HARRISON DILLARD

Gold Medal, 100 Meters, 1948

Gold Medal, 4x100-Meter Relay, 1948 and 1952

Gold Medal, 110-Meter Hurdles, 1952

Harrison "Bones" Dillard was perhaps as well-known for a race he never ran as for his four Olympic gold medals. In 1948, he was indisputably the world's greatest hurdler, having won 82 consecutive races and having set a world record of 13.6 in the 110-meter hurdles; yet a

Harrison Dillard in 1984. Photo by Fogarty and Carlson

bad qualifying race in the trials eliminated any chance for him to run his specialty in London. Instead, he won the 100-meter dash in what at the time was considered a major upset.

Four years later, Dillard came back to win the hurdles in Helsinki. In both Games he also ran on the winning 4x100-meter relay teams.

Dillard, who got his start running for Cleveland's East Technical High School, the same school that produced his childhood idol, Jesse Owens, is now Chief of the Business Department for the Cleveland School Board, where he has worked for more than 20 years. Before that he spent 10 years with Bill Veeck and the Cleveland Indians baseball club. Now in his mid-sixties, the quiet, self-assured Dillard still looks as trim as he did a half-century ago when he earned the nickname "Bones" because of his slender build.

If you want to know why there are so few great white sprinters and hurdlers, with my generation you have to go back to Jesse Owens. Young blacks wanted to be like him. He was the cause of a lot of athletes going into sprinting, jumping, and hurdling. I think if Jesse had been a middle- or long-distance runner, many of us might have gone into those events. The fact that Africans are now great distance runners belies the theory that blacks are innately unable to run distances. If you have the ability and lung capacity, all you have to do is work. There are world-class white sprinters in other parts of the world, so what we are really talking about is America.

Our white athletes elect to play football, baseball, tennis or golf. If more of them would try sprinting, you'd find that Bobby Morrow or Mel Patton. I also think that when the word gets out that you can make anywhere from $150,000 to half a million dollars a year running, you're going to find that some of these guys will stop playing football.

I first saw Jesse Owens when he came back to Cleveland for a parade following his Berlin victories. That parade passed within a mile of where we lived, so a bunch of us got permission from our parents to go. We stood there on the curb at 65th and Central Avenue and saw Jesse come by, sitting on top of the back seat of this open convertible. I remember exactly what he was wearing. He had on a navy blue suit with a pinstripe, a white shirt, and a dark tie. When his car passed us, Jesse looked down, winked, and said, "How are you doing?" or words to that effect. Of course, we thought this was the greatest thing in the world. Our idol had actually spoken to us. Back then we had three idols: Jesse, Joe Louis, and Henry Armstrong. At that time, black history wasn't taught in the North, so we naturally took our heroes from sports.

After Jesse and the parade passed, I ran all the way back home and burst into the kitchen. I almost tore the door off the hinges. I told my mom, "I just saw Jesse Owens, and I'm going to be just like him." She said, "Yes, son, I'm sure you will." She passed it off just that lightly, but ever since, when people ask when I began thinking about the Olympics, I always point to that one incident with Jesse.

The following year I met him briefly when he had a job at a recreational center that was directly across from Cannard Junior High School where I was a student. He worked there a very short time, and I got some tips from him before he was forced out because of some kind of political problem. Even before that we used to take the seats out of abandoned cars in our neighborhood, burn off the fabric, and then use the springs for our hurdles.

At the time, East Technical High was rated one of the best three or four high schools in the country for technical training. You had to apply, and I did, mostly because Jesse Owens had gone there. Ivan Green was the coach, and he asked me to come after I finished second in the hurdles in the junior high city tournament. I also knew that everyone who graduated from East Tech got a job if he wanted one.

In the 10th grade, Coach Green asked Jesse Owens and Dave Albritton, the 1936 bronze medal winner in the high jump, to talk to our track team. I still have pictures of that day in 1939. They encouraged us by telling us we had the talent to win the state championship. I think I got third in both the high and low hurdles in the state that year. I did the same the next year. In my senior year, I won the state championship in both hurdles, running the highs in 14.4.

During that senior year I signed a letter that I would go to Ohio State. Jesse had gone there, and Larry Snyder was still the coach. But at the time, 140 miles seemed like such a long distance from home. Two of my high school teammates, Harold Lane and George Clark, were going to Baldwin Wallace along with another friend, Curtis Smith, who was a basketball player. Eddie Finnegan was the track coach. At the last minute I changed my mind and decided to go 18 miles down the road to Berea. Frankly, I never regretted the decision.

I was in the army reserve at Baldwin Wallace, and I was called to active duty about a week before my sophomore year ended. There were about eight of us who were called to active duty. We all got a three-day pass from basic training to run and give Baldwin Wallace its first Ohio Conference championship. That was in 1943, and I think I won four events that day.

I didn't run in 1944 because I was in Italy with the 92nd Infantry Division. All the troops were black, although the high-ranking officers were white. We were in three campaigns and fought initially next to the 442nd Infantry Regiment, which was made up of Japanese-Americans. They incurred the highest casualty rate of any American group in World War II. I recall vividly seeing them walking through fire on the lowlands below. They were over there dying while their relatives were back home in detention camps.

I can also remember the 99th Pursuit Squadron flying over us in Italy. Those were black pilots. When we saw them go over, we knew that we could get out of our foxholes and wander around because there was going to be no action or incoming artillery fire as long as they were in the air.

When the war ended in Europe in May of 1945, a sergeant came around asking if anyone wanted to participate in sports. His name was Roscoe Browne, and he was later to become a famous movie actor. I can still remember our first meeting. He was, of course, very articulate and fluent not only in English but I think also in French, Italian, Spanish, and even somewhat in German. The first thing he said to me was, "I understand you run excellent hurdles." I told him that I did run the hurdles, so I got to try out for the division track team, and we subsequently became very good friends.

This later became the Fifth Army Team. We went to Frankfurt to compete for the Mediterranean Theatre against the European Theatre in what was called the GI Olympics. I won four gold medals. General Patton was there with his shiny helmet liner and his pearl-handled pistols. After I won my fourth medal, I heard him say, "He's the best goddamn athlete I've ever seen." I felt pretty good about that because Patton himself had been in the Olympics back in 1912.

After the war I returned to Baldwin Wallace in 1946 and was actually given an extra year of eligibility, so I competed through 1948. In addition to running the high and low hurdles, I would run both sprints and sometimes the relays if we needed the points. I ran at least four events in every track meet and sometimes six. But I never ran the sprints in national competition because the sprints and the hurdles were back-to-back events, and that made it a little too tough.

However, in the 1948 trials in Evanston, Illinois, I elected to try to make the Olympic team in three events: the 110-meter hurdles, the 100-meter dash, and the 4x100-meter relay. And I had made up my mind to enter the 100-meter dash even before I failed to make the team in the hurdles.

I actually ran the sprint qualifier on Friday evening and finished third behind Barney Ewell and Mel Patton. Patton and I got lousy starts. The hurdles came the next day. So when I stumbled in the hurdles, I was already on the team. It is a better story the other way around, and the reporters always told it that way. Actually, if I had been running for any other country, one bad race would not have knocked me off the team, but in America you either qualify in the trials or not at all.

I was the underdog in the 100 meters at London in the minds of most people, although there was one Swedish writer who predicted I might win. In 1947, I had run several sprint races in

Sweden, and he wrote that if I elected to run the 100 meters in the Games I would have to be given a chance. I had run a 10.3 in Stockholm, which was one-tenth of a second off the world record. On the basis of that and some of the relay races I had run, I knew that I could run with any sprinters in the world on a given day.

Barney Ewell was one of my roommates in London, and I remember telling him after the qualifying heats, "Barney, I'm going to beat you in the finals on Saturday." He just laughed it off. Barney was a great competitor and thought I was just trying to psych him. We'd tease each other and play around. But I envisioned myself running that race and winning it.

The race was close. Barney thought he had won. He went through the tape relaxed, knowing that he was in front of everybody he could see. He was in lane two and couldn't really see me in lane six. I actually led him all the way. I could see out of the corner of my eye that someone was there, but I didn't know who. When the race ended, Barney started jumping up and down, thinking he was the winner. Lloyd La Beach of Panama was between us in lane three, and he said to Barney, "No, mon, you not win. Bones, he win."

I guess that I really won the race by 12 or 15 inches, but we were so far apart in our lanes that a photo officially decided it. I won the race, and Barney, being the good friend and competitor that he was, was the very first to come over and congratulate me.

I had been called "Bones" since I was eight or nine years old. I was so little and frail. I think I weighed 49 pounds when I was 10 years old. In high school I began to fill out a bit, but even when I graduated I weighed 148. When I won in London I was back down to 148, although by that time I normally weighed 153. I had worked so hard for that race, especially on my starts because all of those other guys were tremendous finishers, that I had lost 5 pounds.

It was great to see how magnificently the people of London had rebounded from the war. The city had been cleaned up, but a lot of the rubble still stood in piles where it had been left. In fact, the track itself was made from ground-up rubble from the destroyed buildings. They ground the brick into a powder and mixed it with whatever adhesives and chemicals they needed to give it the right consistency. It was kind of the color some of these synthetic tracks are today. Even our Olympic Village had been a Royal Air Force base.

We got along very well with the British, as we did four years later with the people in Helsinki. Many of us were very mature. For example, Mal Whitfield, Andy Stanfield, and I were all up in our 20s, and that kind of maturity helps not only in competition but in relating to the people around you. You're viewed more as a person instead of just an athlete.

I finished school in January of 1949, and the college put me to work recruiting students. I did that for three or four months until I received a phone call from Bill Veeck, owner of the Cleveland Indians. He offered me a job for what was then a tremendous salary of $125 a week, which was considerably more than I would have made teaching school. I did a little writing and made a lot of appearances. I recall making more than 100 appearances around the state between October and April during one off-season.

Bill Veeck was a real down-to-earth guy. He'd often sit in the stands with the fans. He was very colorful and energetic but, above all, very human. He loved people. He was also very competitive. He wanted to win, but he believed that until you win you do all the other things to make the fan's life enjoyable.

I stayed with that job for 10 years, and I kept running. By 1952, Bill Veeck was gone, and Hank Greenberg was the general manager. I told him that I wanted to go to California for a month to train and compete in preparation for the Helsinki Games. He told me to go ahead and that he would send me my checks. That was illegal under the amateur code of that time, but no one said anything. I entered three major meets out there, and I don't think I won any of them. I remember Gordon Gobbledick, the sportswriter for the *Cleveland Plain Dealer*, asking me whether or not I thought I could win the Olympics. I told him that I was going to win both the nationals and the Olympic trials and then win the Olympics after that. And that's just the way it turned out.

I knew that once I was in shape I could beat the competition. Jack Davis was tough. Jack was six feet, 195 pounds, and a real power runner. He closed on me at the end of those races, but I was able to hold him off. I don't know how many times I raced against him, but as I recall he beat me once indoors in a national championship and perhaps once outdoors.

In Helsinki, we ran a close race, but it came out just as I thought it would. About halfway down the track I saw that big foot and leg coming, and each succeeding hurdle I could see more and more of Jack. I can remember going over the final hurdle. Jack was still behind me, and we both knew that if I was ahead coming off the last hurdle there was no way he could catch me on the flat. I had won my Olympic hurdles, and I can remember saying to myself, "Good things come to those who wait." I was 29 at the time.

The Russians were there for the first time in 1952, at least the first time since the revolution. They had not been eligible for London in 1948 because they weren't a member of the International Olympic Committee. In 1952 they were ready. No question about it. They fielded an excellent team. They even had a hurdler who got to the finals and finished fourth. In the unofficial point totals they were ahead of us until the final day, when our boxers pushed us ahead in the final count.

It would be interesting to be able to run against the great hurdlers of today. I would love to run against Skeets Nehemiah, Roger Kingdom, or Greg Foster, or even going back to Hayes Jones and the guys who immediately followed me. We would all have to be in our prime. It would be a hell of a race, I know that. The methods of training have changed more than the actual techniques.

There were a couple of things that I was maybe the first to do that everybody does now. For instance, the start. When sprinters today get on their marks, their heads are looking down at the ground. As far as I know, I was the first one to do that. If you start with your head up and then stand up, you find that you are looking up at the sky. Looking up also causes tenseness in the back of the head and in the shoulders. I just naturally let my head drop and relaxed.

One of the other things I did was an extremely high action with the trail knee going over the hurdle. Many athletes do this today. The knee is slightly higher than the ankle. It used to be that it was flat when you dragged it across the hurdle. Now the knee is up, and it's whipped over. It seemed like a natural motion for me. This also forced the lead leg down a little more rapidly, and it got that trail leg out front so you could get it on the ground more quickly. In other words, you resume your running action that fraction of a second sooner.

I was extremely competitive. As a youngster, growing up scrawny and skinny, I was naturally picked on by the other kids, so I had to prove myself by fighting back. Later, I accepted my losses gracefully, but I certainly did like to win, and I couldn't wait for my next chance. I remember when Bill Porter beat me in a low hurdles race in California, which I thought nobody should ever do. I couldn't wait until two weeks later in Salt Lake City, when I beat him by what must have been four or five yards in world record time.

I always appeared calm. As a matter of fact, before the 100-meter finals in 1948, I fell asleep in the locker room. Other guys would get very nervous. Mel Patton, for example, would actually throw up. Barney Ewell would get very jittery. Nobody could talk to him. He'd snap your head off if you said anything. My nature was totally different. But I still planned on winning.

Bob Mathias in 1986. Photo by Fogarty and Carlson

ROBERT BRUCE MATHIAS

Gold Medal, Decathlon, 1948 and 1952

One of America's most popular athletes, Bob Mathias was only 17 when in 1948 he became the youngest Olympian ever to win a track and field event. Four years later he repeated his decathlon win by the largest margin in Olympic history; in fact, Mathias was never defeated in the decathlon.

In addition to his four AAU titles, Mathias won the the 1948 Sullivan Award as America's finest amateur athlete, starred as a halfback for Stanford University, and is a charter member of the U.S. Olympic Hall of Fame.

Off the field, Mathias's contributions have been equally remarkable. An international goodwill ambassador for the State Department, a four-term congressman, and the first Director of the United States Olympic Training Center, Mathias has spent most of his adult life in the public service of his country.

During my senior year at Tulare High School, my track coach, Virgil Jackson, came up to me and said, "I've just heard about some event called the decathlon that will be included in a meet in Los Angeles about a week after you graduate. It'll give you something to do after you get out of school." He wasn't even sure what 10 events were included, but he looked them up. That was May of 1948. Three months later I was standing on the victory stand in London.

I started throwing the shot and discus as a freshman because my older brother, Gene, had done it. The next year I began the hurdles simply because they were fun. It went on from there, and by the time I was a senior I had added the high jump and the relays. I even long-jumped in one meet when the regular guy was sick. So in high school I had already tried several events that were a combination of throwing, jumping, and running. I did have to learn the javelin and the pole vault, and I had never run the 400 or 1,500 meters. Of course, it was a 16-pound shot instead of a 12, and the hurdles were 42 inches high instead of 39. My dad had to buy me a javelin because the school didn't have one, and Coach Jackson got the school's wood shop to make some three-inch extensions for the hurdles.

The week after I graduated from high school, Coach Jackson and I went to the Pasadena Games in Los Angeles for my first decathlon competition—and I won, which surprised everybody. I went back home to Tulare, thinking that was it, but three or four days later Coach Jackson came by the house to tell me about the nationals in Bloomfield, New Jersey, which were also going to be the Olympic trials. I thought that was great, but I knew I couldn't afford to go until he told me that the AAU would pay our expenses. Three weeks later we were off to New Jersey.

I won the nationals, and three weeks after that I was in London for the '48 Games, where I won again. I was just too young in London to be intimidated. I was only 17. I really didn't understand what the Olympics were all about. I knew that it was a really big competition, but I really didn't know much beyond that. Don't forget, there had been no Games for 12 years, and there was no television then. Somebody asked me what I was going to do to celebrate and I said, "I'll start shaving, I guess."

My times in the longer races were terrible. I think I ran the 1,500 meters in 5.11. Even in 1952 my time was only 4.50. That was my worst event, but at the time the philosophy was to work on the first nine events and then just gut it out in the 1,500 meters. Everybody did it that way because the conventional wisdom was that if you trained for the distances, you would hurt yourself in the other nine events. The coaches felt the same way about weight-lifting, so you were not allowed to touch them because they would make you musclebound.

After a year at Kiski Prep in Pennsylvania, where I made up a couple of high school courses, I was admitted to Stanford in the fall of 1949. I wanted to play football because that had been my best high school sport, but I couldn't that first year because I was so busy traveling and making public appearances. I did start as a running back my sophomore and junior years before taking off my final season to get ready for the '52 Games.

We didn't have the decathlon in any of the regular college meets, but Jack Weierhauser and Ray Dean, who were my track coaches, helped me prepare for the only meet that included the decathlon, the national AAU championships. In the meantime, I ran the hurdles and threw the shot and discus for Stanford, and sometimes in the dual meets I would high jump and run the relays.

I really worked hard on the decathlon only after school was out in June. That gave me about a month to get ready for the nationals, which were usually in July. It was a terrible way to do it, but that's the way I had to train for each of my four AAU championships.

At Helsinki, I broke my own world record in the decathlon with 7,887 points. The competition was better, but I beat second-place Milt Campbell by 800 points, and you just don't see that kind of a spread in the decathlon. I had improved my marks in all 10 events from '48. On the first day, I ran the 100 meters in 10.9; long-jumped 22 feet, 1 inch; put the shot 50 feet, 1¼ inches; high-

Photo courtesy of Bob Mathias

Bob Mathias on the victory stand at Helsinki in 1952.

jumped 6 feet, 3 inches; and ran the 400 meters in 50.2. The second day I ran the hurdles in 14.7; threw the discus 153 feet, 8 inches; pole-vaulted 13 feet, 1 inch; threw the javelin 184 feet, 1¾ inches; and finished with a 4:50.8 in the 1,500 meters to break the world record I had set the same year in our nationals.

I graduated from Stanford in 1953, and the following year I went into the Marines. I had retired from track and field, but in my second year I was talked into competing in the All-Service Meet. I hadn't worked out in two years, but I got in shape and won the decathlon without having to run the 1,500 meters. That was my 10th and final decathlon, and I won every one of them. Now, as I look back, and if I had it all to do over again, I think I would train harder and differently. I would also have tried out for the '56 Games. I wanted to do it then, but I had already been declared a professional.

Shortly before I went into the Marines, I made a motion picture called *The Bob Mathias Story.* Jim Fallon was a promoter in Los Angeles who convinced me that we had to do something to capitalize on my fame. In those days you couldn't do anything as an amateur, so the movie made me a professional, and unfortunately it did not do all that well at the box office.

I also did a bunch of commercials. I did one for Vitalis, one for an exercise machine, and one for men's slacks. I received a flat fee with no residuals. I think I got $10,000 to do the exercise machine commercial, which was good money in those days.

I got out of the Marines in 1956 and went to work for John Wayne's Batjac Productions. He was a super guy, and it was great fun to hang around him and his friends. The television hit "Gunsmoke" was then in the planning stage, and the producers wanted the Duke for the lead. He told them he was a movie star and didn't do television, but that his one contract player, Jim Arness, might be interested. He was, and I replaced Jim at Batjac. I got a weekly salary for about two years, and I made one film. It was a war picture called *China Doll* in which I played Victor Mature's copilot.

It was also during this time that I began making goodwill trips for the State Department. The department wanted to extend its foreign contacts beyond those made with government officials. The way we did it was to have our local embassy or consulate make contact with the Minister of Education, who would then book me into various towns and villages to talk to school kids and give clinics and demonstrations. I was the first athlete to do this, and then the Harlem Globe Trotters started doing it as well. I really enjoyed the traveling and the contacts I made around the world.

After a couple of years at Batjac I somehow knew that I was never going to become another Jim Arness. I did, however, play Keenan Wynn's sidekick in a 26-episode television series called "The Troubleshooters." Then, in 1960, I went over to Italy to star in *Theseus and the Minotaur*. This was the era of the epic films, and I played Theseus. I was the only American actor, so they dubbed my voice. I went next to Greece to costar in a film with Jayne Mansfield called *It Happened in Athens*. It was about Spiridon Loues, the Greek shepherd who won the marathon in the first modern Olympic Games back in Athens in 1896. I played the American coach.

I finally got back to L.A. and sat around for about nine months. The agents were no longer calling, so in 1962 I decided to call it quits with acting and do something I had always wanted to do, which was to open a boys' camp. It became the biggest camp on the West Coast. I kept it for 16 years and eventually opened a girls' camp as well.

In 1965, some Tulare friends approached me about running for Congress. What really made me interested was all the traveling I had done for the State Department. I knew somebody from just about every country in the world. I didn't immediately announce my candidacy, but I gave all sorts of sports talks, which allowed me to work in my thoughts on foreign policy. My opponent didn't have equal time because I wasn't officially running until six months before the election. I won and spent the next eight years in Washington.

I was a Republican in a district that was about 60-40 Democratic. The first two years I was on the Agriculture Committee because my district was largely rural. Then I got on the Foreign Affairs Committee and stayed there until I was defeated in the 1974 elections.

I stayed on in Washington for a couple of years, a brief time as Deputy Director of the Selective Service, and then as one of President Ford's fund-raisers. After Ford's defeat in 1976, I didn't want to become a lobbyist or run again for office, so I came back to California to settle down and run my camp. But as soon as I got back, the United States Olympic Committee called about my becoming Director of the Olympic Training Center. Over the years I had always kept up my ties with the USOC, giving talks and helping them raise money, so I sold the camp and moved to Colorado Springs, where I served as director until 1983.

The training center was created after the '76 Games because we were winning fewer and fewer medals. We were looking for a solution, but within our political and athletic systems. The idea was to have a facility available for the 37 Olympic sports where the national governing bodies themselves would select and subsidize the athletes and coaches who would then train in Colorado Springs. The problem is that most of the athletes come in for just a couple of weeks, and that's not nearly long enough to make them world class. And those who already are at the top, such as Edwin Moses and Carl Lewis, have their own training facilities and don't need the center.

Our Olympic athletes need financial help. We can't pay amateurs for performing, but we can subsidize them. Traditionally, we have developed our athletes through our schools. The government doesn't help, and I don't think it should. We just don't have the federal funds available to set up a national program. If we were to do it like the European countries, especially the Communist ones, we'd have government control at all levels. We would have to have a Minister of Sports, and the coaches would be government employees. That's just not our system. Our way is to raise money through the Olympic Committee and through the individual sports themselves.

The other problem we have in this country is pro sports. When you get a good all-around athlete and he has an option of signing a million-dollar contract to play football, basketball, or baseball, he will certainly do that rather than try out for something like the decathlon. A decathlete such as England's Daley Thompson is subsidized by various sports organizations, and he does get appearance money in the big meets. But unlike most other track and field events, you can't do the decathlon every week.

The five of us American decathlon gold medalists—Milt Campbell, Rafer Johnson, Bill Toomey, Bruce Jenner, and I—are working on something called the U.S. Decathlon Association. Last year we had two decathletes train under us, and if we get the financing we'll add a couple more. This means training the year around with good coaches, a good sports medicine program, lots of clinics, and the necessary meets. In other words, we want to subsidize them completely. If we don't do something like this, I'm not very optimistic that we'll ever again be able to produce world-class decathletes.

Vicky and Lyle Draves in 1986. Photo by Fogarty and Carlson

VICTORIA DRAVES

Gold Medal, Springboard Diving, 1948
Gold Medal, Platform Diving, 1948

Born Victoria Manalo to a Philippine father and an English mother, Vicky Draves was forced to use her mother's maiden name to gain admittance into the racially restrictive pools of San Francisco.

Finding adequate coaching was also a problem until she met, and later married, her coach, Lyle Draves, who was to produce numerous national and Olympic champions. Now, 40 years later, after having raised four divers of their own, they remain active in the world of swimming.

My parents never talked much about their childhood, but I do know that my mother emigrated from England to be with a sister, and my father came over from the Philippines with a string band. They met and married in San Francisco, and that's where I grew up.

I always loved to do anything with acrobatics, and I was blessed with coordination, but I didn't start diving until I was 16. Our family was far too poor for lessons, but a good girlfriend of mine was a diver, and through her I met other divers. I had a crush on one of the fellows, and he encouraged me to start diving. He introduced me to Phil Patterson, who at the time was running the Fairmont Hotel's swimming and diving team, and he agreed to take me on as a member. In recent years, the Fairmont has become well-known to television audiences because ABC's "Hotel" is shot there.

There was a lot of prejudice in those days, or maybe it was just Phil Patterson, but without telling me, he had gone to my mother and told her that it would be better if I used her maiden name of Taylor when I started diving for the Fairmont Hotel. As a matter of fact, he didn't make me a member of the Fairmont Hotel Swimming Club; instead, I became a member of the Patterson School of Swimming and Diving, which was a separate small organization where he gave lessons. It was just a thing with him, I guess, but he set me apart in the beginning, and that doesn't do much for your confidence.

Later, there were other incidents. Once I was invited to dive at the Olympic Club in San Francisco, which was a very posh and exclusive men's club. In fact, it was something for them even to allow a woman to give an exhibition. My father went there to see me, and, without anyone saying a word to me, they weren't going to let him in. My coach had to persuade the officers to let him in. If I had known that at the time, I would never have dived for them.

The way Phil Patterson taught me my first dives was really something. I went to my first workout, and I asked him what I was supposed to do. He pointed to one of the other divers and said, "You just do everything she does." And that's how I learned my first set of dives.

I was developing quite well until World War II broke out. Phil Patterson went into service, and I had no coach. I was still diving only in local competitions, so I kind of resigned myself to the fact that my diving was probably over. About a year later, I saw a picture in the paper of Joan Pringle, one of the divers who trained at the Fairmont, and I thought, I really do want to dive, and I can be as good as she is.

I joined Charley Sava's swimming team at the Crystal Plunge in San Francisco. It was a big old indoor pool that had salt water. Charley contacted Jimmy Hughes and asked him to coach me. But it was during the war, there was gas rationing, and my family still could not afford to pay for lessons. It was asking a lot of Hughes to give up his time without any compensation. It was also hard on me. I graduated from high school in 1942 and took a temporary civil service position so I could help my family financially. Of course, this meant that I had to do all my diving after work and on the weekends.

It got to be too much for Hughes, so I was again without a coach. I talked to Charley Sava about whether or not I should just quit again, but he suggested I go see Lyle Draves, who was coaching at the Athens Athletic Club in Oakland.

Lyle was raised on an Iowa farm, where he learned to dive in the proverbial swimming hole. In 1933, he met Fred Cady, the USC coach, at a swimming meet in Iowa, and when Fred invited him to come to California, Lyle packed his bags. In Los Angeles, Lyle took a job coaching at the Lido Club of the Ambassador Hotel, where his best-known student was Zoë Ann Olsen. He had started her as a youngster, and she became his protégée. By the time I met Lyle, they had moved to the Athens Athletic Club, which is where Zoë Ann met Jackie Jensen, whom she later married and who played ball for the Boston Red Sox.

I really didn't want to go see Lyle at first. I told Sava, "Oh, Charley, he's got Zoë Ann. What does he want with another diver? He won't pay any attention to me." But Charley told me to at least talk to Lyle. I did, and he took me on. Two years later we were married, and now, 40 years after that, we're still together.

It was a little difficult at times, but Lyle is a very fair man, and when he's coaching a group of divers you're just one of them—rather than his special person. He just treated everybody the same, and if you understood that, you had no problems. Zoë Ann's mother Norma got a little upset with the attention she felt I was getting, so Lyle had a parting of the ways with them and the Athens Club. Norma was a dear heart, but she was kind of the Hollywood type. Zoë Ann was a fine gal, and I think if her mother had let her alone, she would have been a lot better off. After Lyle left her, her father took over her coaching, but her diving didn't really progress that much.

Zoë Ann did get a lot of publicity, but that never bothered me. I was always interested to read about her, but I never took it personally that she got more attention than I did. I didn't even like to read articles about myself, especially when I was about to dive in a meet. I tended to get a little nervous anyway, so I figured I didn't need any extra pressure. In order to dive well, I had to concentrate all my attention on what I was trying to do and not worry about who was watching or writing about me.

Photo courtesy of Vicky and Lyle Draves

Newlyweds Victoria and Lyle Draves on their honeymoon in 1946.

Lyle's coaching made all the difference in my career. I just couldn't believe the wisdom he had about diving. He told me things that I had never even thought about. All this time I had been diving on just sheer guts and whatever natural ability I had. Nobody had explained to me how to walk on the board, where to place my arms, how to lift up into a dive, and the reasons behind all this. He tried to treat me like I had never dived before. He started me over completely, making me begin with very simple dives. At first, he didn't even allow me to compete, but within two years I was a national champion. I just wish I had had his coaching from the beginning. I think I would have been a far different diver.

At the Olympic trials in 1948, Zoë Ann won the springboard and I won the platform. Fred Cady was the Olympic diving coach, but he was very ill. There were times when he couldn't make the practices and had to ask Lyle to fill in for him. But Lyle got in trouble with Elsie Vietz Jennings for doing it. Elsie was one of our Olympic officials, and she did know her swimming, having produced some good teams for the New York Women's Swimming Association, but she was also a typical Brooklynite, very opinionated and abrasive, and she and Lyle did not get along. In fact, we were fortunate to get Lyle to London. The Olympic Committee wouldn't help, not even with a reservation on the same ship or anything else. They told us that they felt it was better if we didn't have our relatives along. I thought, Relatives? This is the man who brought me to this point. The officials in those days seemed to be more interested in their own image than in the coaching and welfare of the athletes. Even in our nationals we were not supposed to have our coaches around once the competition started, but I noticed that the European divers all had their coaches and that they talked to them between dives.

So Lyle was not on the deck with me in London. Actually, the way he got into the pool was as an official timer for the swimming events. We were not even allowed to stay together. He was at the Cumberland Hotel, where he roomed with Zoë Ann's father, Art, and I stayed at Southlands College with the other swimmers and divers.

Lyle was not the only American coach who was not allowed to get too close to his protégé in London. Bill Smith, who won the 400 meters, was from Hawaii, and his coach was Suchi Sakamota, who later produced many fine swimmers for the University of Hawaii. Sakamota was, of course, of Japanese heritage, and our officials made it very clear that he was not welcome anywhere near the swimming deck while we were in London.

I did become the first woman to win both diving events in the same Olympics, but it was a struggle. In the springboard it wasn't until my last dive that I nosed out Zoë Ann for the gold. Competition was always hard for me. Zoë Ann thrived on it. She could look like limp spaghetti in a workout, but once the meet started she was an entirely different person.

Sammy Lee, who won the men's platform, was very supportive. I was very worried about that last dive, which was a back one-and-a-half layout, because I had not been hitting it at all in practice. I said to him, "Oh, Sam, what am I going to do? This is the dive I have to get." He told me, "Come on. You didn't come all this way just to say, 'I can't do it.' You've got to get up there and hit it."

I had met Sammy at some meet, and he had taken an interest in me. In fact, because my father had passed away in 1945, it was Sammy who gave me away at my wedding to Lyle. He was always so positive and encouraging to everyone. He was just fantastic—

and he hasn't changed one bit to this very day.

I did hit that last dive, but as I look back, I wish I could have done better, especially in the platform. I wasn't at my best, and I was particularly disappointed in my swan dive. But it was so different from the diving I was used to. In the women's competition they did not do the difficult dives, and we had only 8 dives from the springboard and 6 from the platform. In our nationals it was 10 and 8. I was also used to flights that qualified you for the finals, where you would again repeat your dives. In London, they ran all the divers at once and just spread the competition over a period of days. This meant you had to keep your competitive edge over a longer period of time.

I turned professional right after the London Games. Lyle and I went with Larry Crosby's Rhapsody in Swimtime. Then we joined Buster Crabbe's Aquaparades and toured Europe and the United States for the next two years. It was a wonderful experience; in fact, all my diving has been my education.

In 1950, Buster's show went broke. He went back into the movies, and I pretty much retired to raise four boys, all of whom became good divers in their own right. We never pushed them because we had seen too many negative results from that very thing. Now I sometimes wish we had pushed them just a little harder. We were probably too much the other way. I never said much to them about being a two-time gold medalist. We tried to keep everything low-key because it's hard for children of champions to follow in the same sport. Everybody just expects too much of them. But they have certainly had fun with their own kind of diving. They do trick and fancy diving at such places as Magic Mountain, Sea World, and Marineland. They do springboard, platform, and the high ladder. They specialize in trick dives from 90 to 100 feet, dives that I certainly would never have attempted. They've even dived off the cliffs of Acapulco, which made me very nervous.

Lyle is still teaching and coaching diving. Over the years he's tutored several divers who have won Olympic medals, including Pat McCormick, Sue Gossick, and Paula Jean Myers. He's now also beginning to work with a producer on a movie about my life.

So I've been very fortunate to have Lyle and others who cared enough to take an interest in a little girl from the wrong side of the tracks in San Francisco and who was too poor to give them any financial compensation for all their help. I believe that God has a plan for people, and His plan for me has been so very, very good.

Alex Groza in 1986. Photo by Fogarty and Carlson

ALEX GROZA

Gold Medal, Basketball, 1948

Everyone knew the Groza family in Martins Ferry, Ohio. Father Groza was a 340-pound amateur baseball player who owned the local tavern. His four sons were almost as big, equally rough, and all great athletes. Lou was an all-pro tackle and place kicker for the old Cleveland Browns, and Alex was a three-time All-American basketball player at Kentucky and voted college player of the year in 1948 and 1949.

After a two-year professional career with the Indianapolis Olympians, Groza coached for seven seasons at Bellarmine College in Louisville. He later served as business manager of the Kentucky Colonels and general manager of the San Diego Conquistadors. He now lives in San Diego, where he is the Regional Sales Manager of the Chemical Division of the Reynolds Metals Company.

Five of us from our NCAA champion Kentucky Wildcats made the Olympic team, but one of my best friends in London was Don Barksdale, who was the first black American to play Olympic basketball. Don had been an All-American at UCLA but was then playing for an AAU team because professional basketball was still holding the color line. Don was a smooth, finesse-type player. He could run, jump, and shoot with anyone. What few people realized was that he probably could have qualified for the Olympics in either the triple jump or the high jump. He had won the AAU triple jump in 1944 and had gone six feet, eight inches in the high jump. We were sitting together watching the high-jump finals at Wembley Stadium, and I leaned over and asked him if he could have beaten the Australian who won it at six feet, six inches. Don was very modest, but he said that had he trained seriously for it, he could have beaten him. After watching him leap on the basketball court, I think he could have made it without much training.

Don was highly motivated, just like so many of the black kids playing basketball today. So it's no mystery to me why so many of the great ball players today are black. I'll tell you a story. When I played pro basketball for the Indianapolis Olympians, I signed a promotional contract with Pennsylvania Basketball, which paid me a couple of hundred dollars a year to put my name on its balls. They also sent me a case of basketballs. One night after practice I was driving through a black part of Indianapolis, and I saw two kids shooting baskets. It was already dark, but there they were, two youngsters really going at it. I stopped and watched them. They were playing with a ratty old basketball, so I gave them one of my new ones. Then I asked them why on a Friday night they weren't at a movie or something. They told me, "Our family can't afford something like that, so we're out here doing what we really like, playing basketball." That's how it is. Black kids are hungrier than most white kids today. They just want it more. They were kept down for so long, and now they're coming on more aggressively. I think it was like that for us Grozas when I was growing up.

My father and mother came from Hungary in the late 19th century. They settled in Martins Ferry, Ohio, where my dad worked in the coal mines. When things got bad in the mines, he bought a tavern. My brother Lou and I were born upstairs. All of us Grozas were good athletes, and all of us were big. Dad was six-foot-four, weighed 340 pounds, and played sandlot baseball.

Mother was 6 feet tall and weighed 220. My brothers John and Frank were as tall as my dad but weighed 100 pounds less. Lou was the runt of the litter at six-foot-three but ended up playing tackle and place kicking for the old Cleveland Browns. I was the youngest and finally blossomed out at six-foot-seven. So the genes were there for the Grozas to be a big and stout people.

We were always playing some kind of ball, and my brothers were rough—but no rougher than my father. I can remember one football game when Lou got kneed and my father came out of the stands and chased the kid who did it, all the way to the locker room. Another time during a basketball game one of the kids on the other team kept calling Lou and me stupid Hunkies. Lou stopped the game and told the referee he better tell the kid to shut up or he would take care of him. After the game that kid came over to fight Lou, but there stood Mom, Dad, and the whole Groza clan. Lou just knocked him out with one punch.

I was all-state for two years and led the state in scoring my senior year with something like 24 points a game. I was hoping for a scholarship to Ohio State because Lou had gone there, but for some reason they didn't want me. Floyd Baker was my high school coach, and he was a good friend of Adolph Rupp's, so Kentucky invited me down for a tryout. At the time that was legal, so I went down to Lexington for a weekend, knowing that if I was good enough I would get a scholarship. There were 25 or 30 kids there from all over the Midwest, but only two of us were offered scholarships. As I recall, several other coaches did a lot of their recruiting right in Lexington, waiting for Rupp's rejects. I guess they figured if a kid was good enough to be invited for a tryout at Kentucky, he was probably good enough to play at their school.

I started at Kentucky in the fall of 1944 and played until January 15, when I was inducted into the army. I spent 21 months in the service and started school again in September of '46. I think those years right after the war really marked a Golden Era for college sports. We were a little older, and there was a tremendous amount of talent coming back from the service. Wah-Wah Jones, Cliff Barker, Kenny Rollins, Ralph Beard, and I started for Kentucky, and the press labeled us the "Fabulous Five." That first year we had two All-Americans sitting on our bench. So we had plenty of talent, but it took Coach Rupp to mold it all together.

Rupp had already forgotten more about basketball than most coaches knew. His practices weren't long, but they were very well organized, and not a moment was wasted. From the time you walked into that old Alumni Gym, you kept your mouth shut. You said nothing to your teammates. You didn't tell any funny jokes. You didn't even say hello. You got dressed, shot around for 15 or 20 minutes, and at 3:00 sharp the whistle blew and you started practice. There was none of this clapping, cheering, or hollering. Adolph was a very funny man, but if he said something humorous you didn't dare laugh. He didn't allow it. If you wanted to laugh, you waited until you got out of the gym because those two hours belonged to him. He was very intense, but he didn't scream, and he was a stickler for fundamentals. Every drill we ran was part of his offense. And he had eyes in the back of his head. We'd run a play, and it seemed perfect; the guy would go in and make the basket, but he'd blow his whistle and say to someone well out of the play, "You were six feet out of position," and he was always right.

He taught us that the easiest way to get a basket was to outrun our opponents so we always ran the break, and we always played man-to-man defense. I can still hear him saying, "Well, if they run a zone defense against us, the hell with them. We'll just run our man-to-man-offense. They can't stop us anyhow."

By today's standards, at six-foot-seven, I would be a lost ball in the tall weeds, but even then most of the centers were much taller than I. We had a six-foot lane, and goaltending was legal, so most coaches tried to station their big guy three feet from the basket. I compensated by taking my man away from the basket, and I was quick and mobile enough so that I could fake and move around him for easy baskets. On defense I would use my quickness to outmaneuver my opponent from the side. I had learned how to block out, so I got my share of rebounds, and because I was faster than most big guys, I could outrun them on the fast break.

I really think we had sounder coaching in those days, especially on the high school level. I am absolutely amazed by pros today who lack basic fundamentals they should have learned even before they went to college. Some of the pro stars are terrible passers and rebounders, and a lot of them do not know the basics of defense. They can put the ball in the hoop, and they do make a lot of money, but they are not well-rounded ball players.

Of course, it's more difficult coaching many of the kids today. My high school coach was really tough. If I made a mistake, he'd slap me upside the head. And if I went home and told my dad—well, I didn't dare tell him because he'd hit me even harder. If the

The 1948 U.S. Olympic basketball team. Standing (left to right): W. Jones, R. Pitts, D. Barksdale, B. Kurland, L. Wilkie (general manager), A. Groza, L. Carpenter, V. Borlya, C. Rennick. Kneeling (left to right): R. Browning (Oiler's coach), R. Beard, J. Robinson, C. Barker, R. Lumpp, K. Rollins, L. Beck, A. Rupp (coach). Photo courtesy of Alex Groza

coach said you made a mistake, you made a mistake. Today if a coach slaps a kid, the dad calls a lawyer. Our coaches didn't really hurt us. They just did it so we would learn to play the game the way it is supposed to be played.

There are still some coaches like that, and Bobby Knight is one of them. And there are still some parents who want their kids to play for coaches like Bobby. Lots of coaches have more talent than he does, but no one gets more out of his players. His kids are so fundamentally sound, and they play with such intensity. That's the way I was taught, and I loved it.

Before the '84 Games, Bobby asked me to come down and talk to his Olympic team. He introduced me by saying I was kind of the Michael Jordan of my day. He told them that I had been the leading scorer and most valuable player in the country and all that. I pulled my gold medal out of my back pocket and told the kids, "Fellows, I don't know how many of you have seen one of these, but this is my gold medal. You heard Coach Knight tell you that I made All-American for three years and all those other honors. Well, those awards were voted on by people. This medal I earned myself. And you are in the same situation today as I was 36 years ago. No sportswriter is going to vote you one of these. You have to go out and do it yourself. This is my own blood and sweat, and it's more valuable than any other possession I have. I earned it, and I hope you guys do the same thing. I'll run across you somewhere in your pro careers, and I'm going to ask you, 'Was it worth it?' If you answer 'yes,' you'll understand what I'm talking about now."

Don Barksdale in 1986. Photo by Fogarty and Carlson

DONALD ARGEE BARKSDALE

Gold Medal, Basketball, 1948

A great all-around athlete, UCLA's Don Barksdale considered trying to qualify in both the high jump and the decathlon in 1948 before becoming the first black man to play on the U.S. Olympic basketball team.

In 1951, when the NBA finally opened its doors to blacks, Barksdale joined the Baltimore Bullets. Two years later he became the first black athlete to play in an NBA All-Star game.

Although now retired from his radio, nightclub, and real estate interests, Barksdale remains active as the President of Save High School Sports, an organization pledged to make competitive sports available to all kids in the San Francisco Bay area.

Not many of us from my day could play in the pros today. The kids now are so much bigger, more mobile, and shoot so much better than we did. But Alex Groza could have made it in any era. He was only six-foot-seven, but he played much larger. He was as strong as an ox, had great moves, could get out and run, and if he got the ball with you on his backside, it was all over. He had about 10 different moves to the basket, and on each of them he'd keep his body between you and the ball. He was also one of the nicest guys you could ever meet. Friendly, warm, and modest describe Alex, but he could also be tough. I can remember when I first got on the Olympic team, some of the other guys wanted to show me just how rough they were. Alex would look over at me, laugh a little, and say, "Go get 'em, Barks. Show 'em how it's done." He was a small-town boy from Ohio, and I was from Oakland. He was white, and I was black. And I was a couple of years older than he. There were those kinds of superficial differences, but we were just good friends.

My parents were from Mississippi, but I grew up in Oakland and went to Berkeley High School. For three years I went out for basketball and never made the team. You have to remember that back then racism was still overt, and my high school coach had a quota of one black, and that was it. The kid who made the team was my best friend, Em Chapman. He was a better player than I, but there were a lot of other kids on the team who were not.

I started playing organized basketball at Marin Junior College, where I did well enough to win a scholarship to UCLA. Some other schools were interested, but I chose UCLA because of Jackie Robinson and Kenny Washington. I had met them at a high school football game and was so excited that I decided right then and there that somehow I was going to UCLA. Most blacks in California pulled for the Bruins because athletes like Robinson and Washington were allowed to play at a time when many schools played only whites. For example, when I was young you never read about a black athlete at USC.

My first year at UCLA was 1943, and I played seven games before the army inducted me. I returned after the war, and in 1947 I made All-American. Playing in Madison Square Garden and having the New York sportswriters select me as the best player to play in the Garden that year helped give me the publicity that any athlete needs to make All-American.

Of course, that didn't help me get a professional contract, because pro ball was still lily white. Instead, I played for the Oakland Bittners, an AAU team, and it was as a member of the Bittners that I qualified for our 1948 Olympic team.

The Olympic basketball team was picked much differently in those days. Five players were taken from the winning college team, which was Kentucky; five were taken from the national AAU champion, the Phillips 66ers; two were picked at large from the college ranks and two more from the other AAU teams.

I originally thought of trying to make the '48 Olympic team in either the high jump or the decathlon. I had pretty good marks in six or seven of the 10 events. Back in 1944 I had won the national AAU triple jump, and I had gone 6 feet, 8 inches in the high jump and 25 feet in the long jump, but when I found out in June that I had made the basketball team, I forgot about track and field.

The U.S. was so far ahead of anybody else in basketball that we had only one tough game, and that was against Brazil. England, for example, probably had the worst basketball team ever fielded. One game we would start the Kentucky five, and the next game it would be the Phillips 66 players. Bud Browning and Adolph Rupp were the coaches. We used to call Adolph "Silver Tongue." He just had an answer for everything. He was quite a guy, and I really learned to love him. We had such a close relationship that when we docked in New York, he told me, "Don, I have so enjoyed you both as a man and as a ball player that when I get back home I am going to look for a colored ball player, and if I find the right one I'm going to bring him to Kentucky." Several years later he did break the color line in the SEC with Tom Payne.

Rupp was a genius. He had us working on things that you didn't see elsewhere in basketball until 10 years later. He approached the players in a way that made you want to run through a wall for him. It wasn't a rah-rah approach. There was just something about the way he presented things that made you feel like a champion who couldn't be beaten.

Even after winning a gold medal there was no chance for me to go into the pros. I remember getting one letter from Ben Kerner. I think he had a team in Moline, Illinois, at the time. He wrote something to the effect of, "Gee, if you just weren't colored." And you have to remember, this was well after Jackie Robinson had integrated professional baseball.

It was not until 1951 that Red Auerbach signed Chuck Cooper out of Duquesne to be the first black in professional basketball. Soon after that Sweetwater Clifton went to the Knicks, Earl Lloyd signed with Syracuse, and I went with Baltimore. I wasn't at the end of my career, but it would have been a lot better if I had been there five years earlier.

In 1953 I became the first black to make the NBA All-Star team. That was a special honor. The following year I played for Auerbach and the Boston Celtics. Auerbach was one of the finest guys you'd ever met. He never believed in having 25 or 30 guys trying out for his team. Usually he would start with 15, and after he trimmed those guys down to the limit he'd say, "OK, you're my team. As long as you give 100 percent, you don't have to worry about anything." And he lived up to that. He never traded anybody. You started reading about Boston trades after the team was sold and he was no longer in control.

We had a good team in Boston. We were right behind Minneapolis. The only reason they beat us was because George Mikan was so strong that you couldn't move him out of those six-foot lanes. He also had some very good players with him, like Vern Mikkelson and Jim Pollard. Pollard was another of the very few players from that era who would probably be a star today. A lot of the rest of us could probably play today, but we'd have a tough time.

I quit basketball when I still had a contract in my pocket. I was 34 or 35 and was working as a disc jockey in Oakland during the off-season. I had promised myself that if I ever could make two-thirds of my basketball salary doing radio, I would give up the game before it gave up on me. I was paid $20,000 my best year in the pros, and that was pretty good money then. I think George Mikan was the highest-paid, and he made $25,000.

So in 1955 I decided not to go back east. I worked in radio, and I did some scouting for Boston. I wrote Auerbach about a young fellow at the University of San Francisco who I said couldn't hit the broad side of a barn with his shooting but who was the best shot blocker and rebounder I had ever seen. Auerbach traded Ed

McCauley and the rights to Walter Hagen for this budding superstar—and the Bill Russell era began.

I worked as a disc jockey for 12 years. I also bought a couple of nightclubs. The Sportsman was kind of a hangout for athletes, and the Show Case was mostly for entertainment. I had made up my mind I was going to bring big names into Oakland—big names to blacks, that is. I'm talking about people such as B. B. King, Ike and Tina Turner, Lou Rawls, Redd Foxx, and Richard Pryor, most of whom were unknown to white audiences until radio and television opened up.

I also had other interests. At UCLA I majored in business administration and minored in art. I had done a senior thesis on real estate in which I concluded that one should always buy properties and never rent and that one should sell as seldom as possible. Years later, when I was in a position to buy, I kept that in mind. I never rented anything. If I couldn't buy it, I didn't touch it. So I ended up with quite a bit of real estate in the Oakland area and was able to retire when I was only 58 years old.

That's why I now can devote my energies to a program called Save High School Sports. The idea came to me in 1981 as I lay in a hospital a very sick man. I had something called pancreatitis, and it was touch and go for awhile. I happened to read that 20 percent of California's 809 secondary school districts were charging their kids anywhere from $38 to $85 to compete in each sport. I couldn't believe that. I knew that if my dad would have had to pay ten dollars for me to compete, there's no way I ever could have. So I decided that if and when I got out of the hospital I would look into this.

I did, and four or five of us started an organization called Save High School Sports in California. At the moment we've limited ourselves to six Bay Area counties, but we're hoping that if we can show enough success, we can go state and even nationwide. We don't receive grants from anybody, and we don't give money directly to the the schools. We try to work with booster clubs, parent organizations, and the schools themselves to show them how to raise money. We do insist that the money be divided equally between men's and women's sports. Even with Proposition 13, we hope to see the day when free and creative activities such as music, art, and sports will be as much a part of the school program as are English, history, and math. To me, they are just as important because they make school fun for kids. We've also talked to many business executives who agree that a kid who participated in sports has a slight competitive edge over one who has not. You don't have to be great—and we include intramural sports as well—you don't even have to be good; you just have to compete.

This program has been great for me. If I wasn't involved in it, I don't know what I'd be doing. I'd probably be sitting around doing a whole lot of nothing.

8
HELSINKI, 1952

Helsinki was granted the 1940 Games after the International Olympic Committee took them away from Tokyo because of the Sino-Japanese War, but World War II forced Helsinki to wait until 1952 before she was ready to host what Lord Killanin, a former president of the IOC, called "the happiest Games [and the ones] conducted closest to the Olympic ideals."

However, several political disputes had to be resolved by the IOC before the 1952 Games began. Relatively minor in nature, they nevertheless served as precursors of more serious trouble ahead. East Germany applied for membership in the IOC as a separate entity, but the IOC rejected the application and continued to recognize only West Germany. Both Nationalist China and the People's Republic of China belonged to several international athletic federations, but the IOC failed to act on the application of the People's Republic until just before the Helsinki Games were to begin, when it was accepted. Nationalist China immediately withdrew, but the People's Republic of China, evidently feeling their invitation came too late to prepare adequately, did not send a team.

For the first time in 40 years, Russia participated in the Olympic Games. Beginning in 1946, the USSR began to send athletic delegations to various international competitions in both Eastern and Western Europe and even to some in the United States. It may have felt that its athletes were unprepared for the world-class competition at the London Games, but it did send a team to Helsinki, and that team was ready.

The Soviets offended some officials even before the Games began when they refused to allow the Olympic flame to pass through Estonia on its journey from the Temple of Zeus in Greece to Helsinki. No reason was given, but this meant a detour of hundreds of miles before relay runners brought the torch into the Olympic Stadium, where the incomparable Paavo Nurmi carried it around the track and lit the fire in front of the peristyle. He then handed it to Hannes Kolehmainen, the triple winner of the 1912 distance races and the first of the Flying Finns, who climbed the steps to the top of the tower and lit the second Olympic flame.

The Russians further annoyed officials when they insisted on their own Olympic Village for their athletes and those of Hungary, Poland, Bulgaria, Romania, and Czechoslovakia. It was increasingly clear that for the Soviets these would be political as well as athletic contests. The Soviets had spent great sums of money to develop a national sports program, and they made no secret of their intentions to use athletics as a propaganda tool against the West.

When it appeared during the competition that the Russians were going to top the unofficial point title, they had a large scoreboard erected to show off the respective national standings, but when the U.S. came on strong at the end with 5 gold medals in boxing, the Soviet officials quickly took down the scoreboard, but not before an American reporter witnessed the dismantling and sent out a story under the headline, "Russians Caught with their Points Down." When the Games ended, the U.S. had 40 gold medals to the Russians' 22, but the Soviets had garnered 30 silver and 19 bronze medals compared to the U.S. totals of 19 and 17.

As in London, the 10,000-meter race was held on the first day of competition, and again Emil Zatopek won it, cutting almost 43 seconds off the Olympic record he set in London. The bronze medalist was Aleksandr Anoufriev, who thus became the first Russian medal winner in the history of the Games. Zatopek also won the 5,000 meters and the marathon, each in Olympic record time, for an amazing sweep of the distance races. A short time after the 5,000-meter race ended, Zatopek's wife, Dana, won a gold medal in the women's javelin throw and set her own Olympic record. When shortly before the marathon Emil was asked if he wasn't too tired to enter the 26-mile race, he replied, "At present the score in the Zapotek family is 2–1. This result is too close. To restore prestige I will try to improve on it in the marathon."

The 100-meter final was run on the second day of the track and field events, and for the first time in an Olympiad, there was no American favorite in the race. Jim Goliday of Northwestern University, one of the best 100-meter runners in the world, had suffered pulled muscles in training and didn't make the Olympic team. Andy Stanfield had also been plagued with muscle trouble and passed up the 100 meters for the 200-meter event. Much to everyone's surprise, including his own, the final was won by Lindy Remigino, a relay runner on Manhattan College's sprint relay team.

In the 3,000-meter steeplechase, Vladimir Kazantsev, the world record holder, was given the best chance to win, but he slipped and broke his stride at the water jump. Horace Ashenfelter, a 29-year-old FBI agent, passed Kazantsev at that point and won, setting both an Olympic record and a world record.

Harrison Dillard won his specialty, the 110-meter hurdles; Mal Whitfield tied his '48 time in winning the 800 meters; and Bob Mathias again won the decathlon. The "Vaulting Vicar," Reverend Bob Richards, won the pole vault, and Parry O'Brien took the shot put. O'Brien and Richards repeated their wins in 1956 in Melbourne.

Dave Browning led an American sweep of the springboard diving competition, and, at the ripe old age of 32, Dr. Sammy Lee repeated his 1948 win in the platform. Pat McCormick won both the women's springboard and platform events, a double she would repeat in 1956.

Best among the five American boxers who won their gold medals on the last day of competition was a seventeen-year-old middleweight from Brooklyn named Floyd Patterson. "Patterson," wrote New York reporter Red Smith, "has faster paws than a subway pickpocket, and they cause more suffering."

The closing ceremonies were held on August 1, and two weeks later J. Sigfrid Edstrom stepped down as President of the International Olympic Committee. The vice president, Avery Brundage, longtime controversial chairman of the U.S. Olympic Committee, assumed the duties of president.

Dr. Sammy Lee in 1986. Photo by Fogarty and Carlson

SAMUEL LEE

Gold Medal, Platform Diving, 1948 and 1952
Bronze Medal, Springboard Diving, 1948

Irreverent, witty, outspoken, and talented all describe Dr. Sammy Lee, who remains one of America's most popular Olympians.

Lee credits his Korean-born father with teaching him to take pride in his ancestry and to put as much effort into his studies as into his diving. But Sammy Lee needed little prodding. He won his first AAU title in 1942, retired to complete his medical studies at USC, then came back in 1946 to win the AAU. Lee was a lieutenant in the U.S. Army Medical Corps when he won his first gold medal in 1948. Four years later, at age 32, he became the oldest athlete ever to win an Olympic diving title.

A specialist in diseases of the ear, Dr. Lee is equally talented when telling stories of his colorful career.

My father emigrated from Korea to California in 1905. He was sponsored by the American Railroad Workers. He was a Buddhist when he arrived, but after attending Occidental College he became a Christian. He originally planned to return to his homeland, but after the Japanese invaded Korea in 1910, he decided to stay, so he sent for my mother. They wanted their children to be born as free Americans.

We were too poor to go to the 1932 Games in Los Angeles, but when my father told me what the Olympics were all about, I told him that I wanted to be an Olympic champion. He laughed and asked, "Well, in what sport?" I told him, "Gee, I don't know, Pop, but some day I'll find it." It was a lucky thing that no one threw me a basketball.

Not long after that I discovered that I could do things off the diving board that other kids couldn't do. All day I would just turn somersaults off the board in the municipal pool in Los Angeles. One day a black kid named Hart Crum, who was a great athlete himself, asked me, "Hey, Sammy, how come you only do one somersault?" He then double-bounced me off the board so I could get higher, and as a result I did my first one-and-a-half somersault. That was the greatest thrill of my life. I ran home and told my dad, "Papa, I've found my sport. I'm going to be an Olympic diver." He didn't really know what diving was, but he came to the pool to watch me. Afterward he said, "Son, I don't care if you want to be an Olympic champion, but remember, exercise your mind as well as your body, and don't forget, I want you to be a doctor." So at an early age I had my dual purpose in life.

Two things happened during the '36 Games that really inspired me. First, Kitei Son won the marathon. He was competing for Japan, but my father told me that his real name was Sohn Kee Chung and that he was Korean. On the victory stand, he tore off his Japanese emblem and announced to the world, "I'm Korean, not Japanese." The Japanese put him under house arrest, but he is still a national hero in Korea. The second thing was listening on the radio to Jesse Owens taking one victory after another. Somehow I kind of projected that this was happening to me, and 12 years later, when I was standing on the victory stand, it was as though I were still sitting by that radio alongside of Jesse.

We were the only Orientals in the Highland Park area of Los Angeles while I was growing up, and, except for my sisters, I was the only Oriental in my high school. There was a Japanese fellow who had graduated about three years ahead of me, and he told me the places I couldn't go. So I knew, for example, when my classmates would suggest that we go to the Pasadena Civic to a dance, that I couldn't get in. I'd just say that I had to work because I didn't want to embarrass them. They were fine. It was their parents who were the problem. When I visited their homes, I could feel it. It was a traumatic experience. There I was, the student body president and covaledictorian of my class, but I wasn't welcome.

I can remember one party that never started because I was there. I finally had to go home because the girl's parents wouldn't let the party start with me in the house. I went home crying, and I asked my dad: "Papa, why wasn't I born white?" He said, "Son, if you had been born in Korea under the Japanese, you wouldn't have the opportunity for success that you have here." And then he said, "I'll tell you something else. If you are ashamed of your Korean ancestry and how you look, how in the world will your fellow Americans respect you? If you're not a good Korean, you'll never be a good American."

I never forgot that. He never showed anger. When someone would slam the door in our faces, he would never say, "See what those goddamn whites are doing?" Instead, he'd say, "See, son, that's why you have to become educated. Through education you'll show these ignorant people what kind of person you are."

My father decided that I was to become a doctor because he believed that the community would need me regardless of my color or my race. He never talked to me about money. I can remember I wanted to interrupt my medical studies to join the service in 1943, but he told me that even if I were to become a famous war hero, in the eyes of the West I would always be an Oriental, and as such they would soon forget any heroics. But as a doctor I could always serve the community. The following week he suffered a stroke and died.

Sometimes I forgot that prejudice can cut two ways. During the war every Chinese- and Korean-American wore a huge button with the American flag on it and then something like "I'm Chinese, not a Jap." Mine, of course, said, "I'm Korean, not a Jap." These buttons were supposed to protect us from whites who thought we should be in the concentration camps. I was wearing my button on a cross-country train going to the 1942 outdoor national championships when I ran into one of the Japanese-

Americans who had swum for the Hawaiian swim team and who was then in what was to become the famous 442nd Japanese-American Nisei Division. There I was wearing my big "I'm Not a Jap" button. I immediately said, "Geez, I'm sorry I got this button on." He said that he understood, but I took it off and never wore it again.

I was 18 when I got my first big break in diving. I was already pretty good, but I'd hear remarks like, "Gee, that Sammy Lee could really be good, but he's not white, so they're not going to let him into some of the private clubs." So I was pretty much training on my own. On Mondays I could swim at Pasadena's Brookside Park because that was so-called International Day, when non-whites were allowed in the pool. Afterward the custodians supposedly drained the pool so the honkies could use it the next day. Even the YMCA didn't want me to train there. The officials said something about my having to have a chest x-ray and clearance from a doctor. My father had a lot of pride, and that bothered him. He told me, "We don't have to take that. Don't worry, something will work out."

You see, most coaches didn't believe that Orientals could become great athletes, but I knew better. I knew about the Chinese acrobats, but I also knew that I needed coaching if I was to get any better. One Monday I was practicing with Dick Smith, the great diver from USC. We were diving at the Los Angeles Swim Stadium, where they held the swimming events in the 1932 Olympic Games. We were doing our dives when I noticed a great big hulk of a man standing at the other end of the pool talking to Duke Kahanamoku, the legendary Hawaiian who had won gold medals in the 1912 and 1920 Games. His name was Jim Ryan, and he had on a green suit that made him look like the Jolly Green Giant—but he wasn't jolly. He was a tough, foul-mouthed Irishman who stood six-feet-four and weighed about 275 pounds. We didn't hit it off at all at first, but he was to become the diving coach I so desperately needed.

The first thing Ryan said to me was, "Hey, kid, do you like to dive?" I told him I was nuts about it. He said, "OK, let's see you do a front dive." So I did, and I thought it was pretty damn good, and I expected him to tell me the same thing. Instead, he said, "Who taught you that dive?" I pointed to Hart Crum, who was standing over by the side of the pool. He said, "Go over there and kick him right in the ass. That's the worse goddamn dive I ever saw." After every dive I did that day, he'd say, "You stupid damn Chinaman." I finally told him, "I'm not Chinese. I'm Korean." Then he'd say, "You stupid damn Jap." I finally told Dick Smith, "I'm going to get that big son-of-a-bitch. I'm going to dive in, jump up, and hit that bastard right in the mouth and then get the hell out of here." But Dick told me to swallow my pride because Ryan was the answer to my prayers.

Fortunately, I overheard Ryan telling Kahanamoku, "See that little Chink over there? I'm going to make him the world's greatest diver, or I'm going to kill him." I went up to him, grabbed hold of his belt buckle, and said, "Sir, I told you I'm not a Chink or a Jap. I'm a Korean." He looked down, spun me around, kicked me right in the ass, and said, "I don't give a shit what you are. Get back on that diving board."

Ryan had been the Pacific Coast diving champion, and he really knew the fundamentals of diving. He had married a wealthy woman and was financially independent. He also was not affiliated with any organization, so he didn't care about any social restrictions. He had coached Farid Simaika, the great Egyptian diver who then lived in this country. One day Simaika explained to me just why Ryan was so tough on me. We were practicing diving into a sand pile in Ryan's backyard, and when I would screw up, Ryan would make me bend over and grab my ankles, and then he'd hit me with a damn shovel handle. And he'd never call me Sammy. He'd always scream, "You goddamn Mongoloid idiot." I'd be washing all that sand off me, and I'd get so goddamn mad. Well, one day Simaika, who was helping Ryan coach, came up to me and said, "Hey, Black Meat." That's what he always called me—"Black Meat." "I know how you feel, but I want to tell you why he's so tough on you. You know I won the platform in the 1928 Games, but three days later they reversed the decision. We had to go through the victory ceremony again, and I had to turn over my gold medal to Pete Desjardins. Jim Ryan was so mad that he threw a couple of officials in the pool in Amsterdam." Then Simaika said, "Sam, with your black meat they're not going to give you the championship. You cannot be just as good as the next man. You've got to be so much better that they have to give you that medal."

It's an ironic thing. Simaika was killed in the war—fighting for this country! When I won my medal in 1948, several Egyptians came up to me and told me that I had vindicated Farid Simaika's honor.

So Simaika and Ryan convinced me that I had to impress the world that I was superhuman, and I really started to work hard on my diving. By 1939 they were calling me the "Yellow Peril" because I was doing dives never done before in competition, such as forward three-and-a-half somersaults and reverse and inward two-and-a-half somersaults.

Another fellow who had an influence on me was Miller Anderson, who was a great Olympic diver for us. I once said to him, "Hey, Miller, are you Swedish?" He told me, "Sam, you never call a Norwegian a Swede." So I told him, "Well, Miller, you don't ever call a Korean Japanese either." We shook hands, and that started a lifetime friendship. The two of us were diving at the nationals in 1942, and we talked about what would happen to us after the war. Miller said, "I'll tell you what, Sam. Let's make a vow that if we both survive, we'll come back and be Olympic champions."

In 1945 I got a letter from Miller saying that he had been shot down in his 113th mission over Italy. He had broken his leg, but he reminded me of our pledge to make the next Olympic team. We both did, but he had to do it with a six-inch plate in his leg.

Miller came in second in the springboard in London, missing a dive he had never missed before. Afterward he came up to me and said, "Sam, I let you down. Now don't you let me down." Well, I was already nervous. There I was going for something that I had been working toward for 16 years. I was 28 years old, already finished with medical school, and a lieutenant in the Army Medical Corps. I always had to get angry to do well, and during the finals Miller told me that his wife was sitting near the judge's stand and had overheard Larry Johnson, the President of our AAU Swimming Federation, say to the judges, "I hope you don't favor that Korean."

That was all I needed. I really started diving. I came to my last dive, the forward three-and-a-half somersault that I had put in the record book, knowing that all I had to do was to hit it to win the gold. I thought to myself, Geez, I feel like a pregnant woman. This is my baby. If it comes out assbackwards, I've certainly screwed up everything. All I can remember is hitting the water and it tingled all over—like when you take a belly flop. I thought, My God, what did I do? I came to the surface, and I saw 10, 9½, 9½, 9, and a 7. I knew it was all over, and for the second time in history a man walked on water.

There was another American at London whose story is worth telling. She was born Vicky Manalo, which means "Double Victory." Her father was Filipino and her mother English. When she started diving, she had to take her mother's maiden name of Taylor because they wouldn't allow her in the San Francisco Fairmont Hotel Pool with a name like Manalo. I used to tell her, "Some day your father is going to die, and you'll regret that you did not carry his name." She finally went public that she was not Polynesian, a nationality romanticized at the time. When her father did die, she asked me to give her away at her marriage to her diving coach, Lyle Draves.

By 1948, she was competing as Vicky Draves. I wanted to build up her confidence, so I told her, "I've got the map of the Orient on my face, and I'm going to make it whether I'm ugly or not, but you're so beautiful you're going to make it without any trouble." And she did win her "Double Victory" in the diving. She was the first half Asian-American to win a gold medal for the United States, and I was the first full-blooded Asian to do so. And to this day it gripes me when I see an Olympic poster with only a white and a black athlete on it. I believe that our country's posters should represent all races: white, black, brown, and Asian.

All the years I was coming up, no one knew what a Korean was. It took the Korean War for most Americans to find out. It was 1952, and I was a doctor in the army's residency program at Letterman Army Hospital in San Francisco, when the Olympic diving coach, Mike Peppe, asked me to make a comeback. I asked General Leonard Heaton, my commanding officer, who incidentally later became Eisenhower's personal physician, if it was morally right for me to ask for time to train for the Olympics while we were at war. He told me, "Sam, we've got lots of doctors who can heal the wounded, but we've got only one guy who can win the Olympic medal in diving." He transferred me to San Pedro's Fort MacArthur's Hospital so I could train afternoons at the Los Angeles Swim Stadium. I didn't make the team in the springboard, but I did in the platform. I became the first diver to win successive gold medals, and the oldest ever to win, and I did it on my 32nd birthday. When I hit the bottom of the pool after my final dive, I knew I had won, and I said to myself, "Happy birthday, you son-of-a-bitch! You did it again."

The determination that made me an Olympic champion also drove me to become a medical doctor. It was never easy. At college, where I was known as the "Oriental from Occidental," my undergraduate advisor told me that he wouldn't recommend me for medical school because I was trying too hard to win the Olympic medal. He told me that I didn't have a Chinaman's chance to do both. But I told him, "You're not God. How do you know how much I want to be a doctor—and an Olympic champion?" No one can predict how much drive a man has. I had earlier applied for a scholarship at UCLA, and they asked me what I would do if I didn't win the Olympic diving championship, much less become a doctor of medicine. I told them that I didn't plan on failing. They looked at each other as if to say, "Who does this Yellow Peril think he is?" and gave the scholarship to some other kid.

I got into USC's medical school by the skin of my teeth and then nearly flunked out. Because of the wartime need for doctors, USC had dropped its discriminatory admissions policy. There were one Chinese, two Koreans, and about six Jewish kids in my class. That was unheard of at USC at that time. I didn't apply myself the first 12 weeks, and it began to look as if my Occidental advisor was correct. I was failing just about everything, when Dr. Scott, the assistant dean of the medical school, called me in and told me he wanted me to quit until I was ready to devote my entire attention to my studies. I came home, and my mother was crying. Already the Korean community knew that I was flunking out. I told her that no way was I going to quit. The next morning I went back and told Dr. Scott that I had never quit in my life and that he would have to flunk me out. I was the only boy in my family, and I just couldn't let them down. If I hadn't been a competitor, I never would have made it through medical school. In both athletics and your profession you have to make a commitment to excellence. If I didn't think I could do a certain kind of surgery as well as or better than anyone else, I would never do it.

I'll tell you a story about Greg Louganis, whom I finally ended up coaching. I first saw him dive when he was 10 years old. He was trying to do dives he wasn't quite strong enough to do, but you could already see his greatness in the way he sprang off the board, his grace, and how he could line up with the water. His talent was just indescribable. He was poetry in motion. Everything looked so easy. I said to my son, who was also 10 at the time, "There's the greatest prospect in the history of diving if he gets the right coach." A little later my son says to me, "Hey, Dad, who would you rather have as a son—that kid out there who can dive like that or me?" That was pressure, but I said, "Son, I'd rather have you—you're ugly just like your old man, and I'd rather have somebody who looks like me." He just kind of shook his head and said, "Geez Dad, I wish you wouldn't look so pissed off."

Charles Adkins in 1986.

CHARLES ADKINS

Gold Medal, Light-Welterweight Boxing, 1952

At Helsinki the Soviets participated in the Olympics for the first time since 1912, and most of their athletes were of world-class caliber. It even appeared that they would win the unofficial team championship—that is, until the American boxers came on to win five gold medals.

One of America's winning boxers was Charles Adkins, a collegian from San Jose State University. Adkins, who would go on to a brief professional career before taking a permanent supervisory position with the Chicago Park District, remembers the tremendous pressure he felt when he met his Russian opponent for the championship.

Once the boxing started we went practically around the clock. There were that many bouts. You had a number and they would call it out when it was time for you to fight. Then your next match might come 12 or 26 hours later. I fought five bouts in six days.

When I fought the Russian in the finals, it was not Charles Adkins versus Victor Mednov; it was the United States against the Soviet Union. There was so much hype going on I couldn't even rest the day before the finals. So many reporters and photographers were camped in front of our quarters, you could hardly get in the door.

I did feel the pressure. I knew if I allowed this man to beat me, I couldn't go back home. It felt like I had the world on my shoulders. I guess the Russian felt the same way. He couldn't speak any English. He gave me a little smile and looked at me like a big bear, and I guess I looked at him like I wanted to tear that bear apart.

It wasn't until the second round that I realized that I could take him. I hit him in the stomach, and it was just like sticking a pin in a balloon. All the air just rushed out. Then I knocked him down. In the third round I handled him easily. I didn't think there was any doubt that I had won, but it was a split decision. The English and Canadian officials voted for me, but the Polish judge gave it to Mednov. There was really no way he could have done so, but he did. After the decision, Mednov told one of the American officials that it was the toughest fight he had ever had and that I was a true champion. On the victory stand he gave me a hug, and that's the last I ever saw of him.

Helsinki was one of the finest places in the world. We were there for about three weeks, and that entire time there was no night. You had to sleep with blinders on. The people were very loving. They were so appreciative of having us there, and they made me feel so important. You just couldn't find better folks. If we could have brought some of that love back to America and given it to our own people, it would have been wonderful.

I got into boxing really because I wanted my father to be proud of me. He was a hard-working man who loved sports; unfortunately, he never lived to seem me box a single time even though I started boxing when I was only thirteen.

I worked my way through the Golden Gloves and then won a boxing scholarship to San Jose State. DeWitt Portel was my coach, and he was like a father to me. I really loved him. When I arrived, I didn't know a soul. He picked me up at the train station and took me to his home, where I stayed. They made me feel like I was part of his family. They gave me a warmness I will never forget.

I had roughly 50 fights in college and didn't lose any. I learned then that boxing was an art as well as a sport. I also learned that you get no more from boxing than you put into it. Some of the kids today think they're just going to go in there, knock somebody out, and make a million dollars. But that's not what boxing is about. You have to pay your dues. You need to learn how smart you can

Charles Adkins in 1952.
Photo courtesy of Charles Adkins

be, not how many guys you can knock out. You don't want to hurt somebody, but outsmart him. You need to learn respect for yourself and your opponents.

I majored in criminology and accounting at San Jose State because I wanted to go into the FBI, but after I won the gold medal I turned professional and never did get my degree. That was probably a mistake, but there were a lot of people pulling at me from different directions. It's a funny thing, but my daughter now has her master's in accounting so I feel she's doing what I wanted to do. Somehow it has all worked out; in fact, in the 1970s I did go to Ohio State University to finally get that degree.

Parry O'Brien in 1986. Photo by Fogarty and Carlson

WILLIAM PARRY O'BRIEN

Gold Medal, Shot Put, 1952 and 1956
Silver Medal, Shot Put, 1960

A fierce competitor who once won 116 consecutive competitions, Parry O'Brien is generally recognized as the greatest shot-putter of all time. After perfecting a revolutionary style, O'Brien won 2 Olympic golds and a silver and 17 AAU titles and officially broke the world record on 10 occasions.

O'Brien has enjoyed great longevity. In 1966, at age 34, and two years after coming in fourth in the Tokyo Games, he set a career best of 64 feet, 7¼ inches. Even more remarkable was his determination at age 50 to attempt a comeback in masters' competition. After devoting two years to intensive training, O'Brien set age-

group world records in both the shot and the discus with marks that would have beaten the best at Helsinki in 1952 when he won his first gold medal.

I competed in the masters' competition for those of us over 50 in 1984 and 1985. Over the years I had remained active physically, but working out and throwing the shot or discus are two very different things. My experience is living testimony to that. I decided that I would devote two years to making a comeback and try to set my age-group record in the discus and the shot. Seniors' competition is really kind of a step down. It's a picnic-type atmosphere rather than one calling for killer bees. Al Oerter, who continued to compete against world-class athletes thoughout his 40s, has a different attitude than I do. He is not terribly concerned if he finishes 9th or 19th. I shudder at the thought of finishing at those levels because my ego would not permit it.

So I approached the masters' competition differently than most. I didn't go out just to have a day at the park—to get whatever I could out of my body and win some sort of medal or other. I was definitely out for blood, and I was determined to get the maximum out of my body in order to achieve the goals I had set. My whole personality is geared toward achievement, and the only way I can do that is to become totally immersed in what I am doing, devoting total concentration and then throwing to kill. Of course, it was myself that I almost killed trying to do this.

In order to train for the masters', I had to give up a lot of other things I enjoyed. I didn't play golf for two years. I spent a lot of time with ice packs and whirlpools, but I never really got my muscles back to where I wanted them. I don't know that it's possible in the throwing events. In the discus or the shot there is a compact explosion of the muscles. And the recuperative power was just not there. I was not the same guy, but my mind kept saying that I could be if I just worked a little harder. I paid for that kind of thinking. I'd be dragging around the office like I was 100 years old. I found great solace in a refrigerated pool followed by the whirlpool. I would do this several times a day. I also went into massages, which I had never done before. I slept 12 hours a day and ate all the right foods. I had been like a man possessed when I was competing, and I was trying to attack the masters' with the same ferocity. I was successful mentally, but my body did not always back me up.

It was an interesting experience. I thought it would take me about three months to get where I wanted to be, but it was more like six, and then it was unpredictable whether or not I could hold my form, technique, and body strength. I ended up setting age-group records in both events. I threw the shot 58 feet, 1½ inches, and the discus 185 feet, 11 inches. My discus distance would have won the gold medal in 1956, and my shot exceeded my winning throw in 1952.

I became interested in the shot put quite by chance when I was about 14. My parents had taken me on an extensive summer trip to Canada while I was recuperating from mononucleosis. As the trip progressed I was feeling stronger. I was getting a little bored, so I amused myself by going down to a nearby riverbed, selecting some large rocks that had been well-rounded by the action of the river, and started throwing them around. I didn't even know what a shot put was at that point, but I became interested in how far I could throw those stones.

In high school my major sport was football and then basketball, but it was mandatory that the varsity football players turn out for track. It was kind of, "You big guys go over to the shot put ring, and you thinner guys start sprinting." By the time I was a senior, I was Southern Section California Interscholastic Champion. I threw the 12-pound shot 57 feet, 9½ inches, which by today's standards would not pick up a medal in anybody's meet.

In 1950, I went to USC on a football scholarship, but after my freshman year I asked that it be changed to track. I grew considerably in both height and weight that freshman year and set a national freshman collegiate record of 53 feet, 10 inches with the 16-pound ball.

The following year I won the national AAU and NCAA championships, beating the then world record holder, Jim Fuchs. As a result, I was invited on an AAU tour of Europe. We had a small team, and I was throwing the shot and the discus and running the first leg of the 4x100 relay. I was a pretty good sprinter and actually clocked a 10.8 in the 100 meters that summer.

About a month into the tour I was getting fatigued. We were competing three or four days a week, and I was looking for an easier way to throw the shot. So instead of the conventional side-saddle hop, in which you sort of straddled across the side of the ring, I was looking for an easier but just as effective alternative. Little by little, degree by degree, I turned around with my back to the throwing area.

I brought this idea back with me in late 1951 and started working hard on it. I met with a great deal of skepticism on the part of the so-called experts of the day, who claimed that with an Olympic year approaching I was crazy to defy principles that had been proven over the years. But I fully believed that I was on the right track—at least for me—to contribute something to the sport while at the same time approaching world-class standards. I stuck with it, but to have a new technique accepted you have to be the Olympic champion, which I became in 1952, or break the world record, and that I did in 1953.

The Soviets entered Olympic competition for the first time in 1952, but they had a separate camp away from the rest of us. We were very curious as to what kind of athletes they were. Their facilities were closed, but we sneaked in and took a look at them. As it turned out, my main competition came not from them but from my two teammates, Darrel Hooper, who won the silver, and Jim Fuchs, who finished third, although he then held the world record.

The Russians did serve notice in 1952 that four years hence in Melbourne they would be a formidable power in all events. It was their declared intention to promote communism through sports. They wanted to prove that their system could produce better athletes than could our democratic system. We sort of listened and said, "Well, we'll believe that when we see it." But they did become formidable, and they have continued to use sports as a political tool.

I was a fierce competitor. Between 1952 and 1956, I won 116 consecutive shot put events and extended the world record several times. I worked very hard on my physical conditioning and on the development of the "O'Brien technique" of putting the shot. I didn't like to lose, and whenever I did I wanted to do something about it as soon as possible. I remember one time in 1956 I was beaten by Ken Bantum in the national AAU championships when I had a case of the flu and shouldn't have competed. I was so upset by the loss that I literally drove myself into a competitive frenzy. The next week at the Olympic trials in Los Angeles I surpassed the world record by a good margin, with the first throw over 63 feet.

At Melbourne, I peaked a little early, but I won with a throw of 60 feet, 11 inches. Bill Nieder came in second, and then he beat me in Rome in 1960. I came in fourth in Tokyo in 1964 and continued to compete actively until 1966, when, at age 34, I managed a personal best of 64 feet, 7¼ inches.

Shot-put medalists (left to right): Darrow Hooper, silver; Parry O'Brien, gold; Jim Fuchs, bronze. Photo courtesy of *Track and Field News*

It depends on the event how long you can remain world-class. There are also economic considerations. When you're out of school and presumably have a job and family, you don't have the same opportunity or commitment to train that you had earlier. And when all these things don't come together, it's really difficult to maintain that international competitive edge. You can continue to compete on a local level, but I could stay with it only as long as it was rewarding and I was able to improve.

When I was competing regularly, I didn't do a lot of conscious psyching out of my opponents. I would, however, psych myself up to a very high degree, and that often seemed to affect my competitors. I always wore two sweatsuits, which I would gradually peel off during my warm-ups. If I immediately threw long, my opponents would think, My God, how can I beat him when he's throwing it that far with two sweatsuits on? I would also stand at the side of the circle and do standing throws well over the last line in the competition. This was not true distance, but it would kick up chalk at that far distance, and there would be a lot of ohs and ahs from the stands. That also demoralized the competition if they were spending too much time watching what I was doing.

Then there was the little white plastic jar I always took with me into competition. No one knew what was in it, but I always made it quite visible to the others when I'd swig on it. All it was was clover honey cut with water, but when someone would ask me what it was, I'd always say, "It's an energy-giving substance." I didn't say anything else, and I always offered it to anybody who wanted to test it. They were all afraid to try it because they thought it must be something very high-powered. From a physical standpoint, the potential energy of the honey, if there was any, would never have had time to be assimilated into my body during the actual competition, but it gave me a tremendous psychological advantage over those who were paying too much attention to what O'Brien was doing instead of worrying about their own performances.

Steroids were legal while I was competing, and, coming from California where bodybuilding was so popular, I had certainly heard about them. But nobody understood the side effects. There were rumors about possible damage to kidneys, the urinary tract, and even sexual organs. So I stayed away from them. I saw some of the claimed results on several of the weightlifters, but I was not interested in being a chemical guinea pig for anybody.

If someone were to experiment with steroids, he would have to do it under a doctor's care, and in our day there was no such thing as a sports physician. This is a whole specialized field today, and it is a field where we are well behind the Eastern Bloc countries. Rumor now has it that the Czechoslovakians and East Germans have developed an anabolic steroid that is undetectable. They have made sports medicine into a complete and distinct science. They can heal injuries 50 to 60 percent quicker than we can. They also deal with the philosophy of sports medicine. It's amazing what they've been able to do with their athletes, and it's very unlikely that they will share this information.

When you have a free society, you get into the question "Is there any money in it for me?" In the state-controlled countries money is no object. So aside from a small cadre of sports physicians, we Americans have not expended the time and money needed for advanced research in sports medicine.

I know what I'd be worth if I were competing today as a world record holder. I don't know if I would be as large a draw as an Edwin Moses or a Carl Lewis, because the weight events usually do not enjoy that same kind of glamor, but I certainly would have been in there somewhere. One of the reasons I say this is because I always had good relations with the press. I gave the reporters as much insight as possible into what I was trying to accomplish. Some said I was giving too much away and sowing the seeds for my eventual defeat. I never felt that way. I knew I was going to be defeated someday, and, in the meantime, if I could teach somebody to compete on my level, it would just serve to make my performance that much better.

Photo by Fogarty and Carlson

Norbert Schemansky in 1986.

NORBERT SCHEMANSKY

Gold Medal, Weightlifting Middle-Heavyweight, 1952

Silver Medal, Weightlifting, Heavyweight, 1948

Bronze Medal, Weightlifting, Heavyweight, 1960 and 1964

Norb Schemansky started weightlifting in a friend's Detroit garage in 1938 when he was 14. In spite of interruptions for war, crippling injuries, and severe fi-

nancial hardship, he lifted competitively until 1965, winning a gold, a silver, and two bronzes, and became the only Olympic lifter in history to win four medals. He also won 10 AAU championships and was a three-time world champion in the heavyweight division.

Now in his 60s, and still working six days a week, Schemansky talks with considerable bitterness about the state of his sport and all the sacrifices he had to make to become America's most successful lifter.

It cost me a lot of money to go to the national meets because in the early days I had to pay my own way. There were no sponsors then. I worked, but it cost me a lot of jobs because I always had to take time off to go to the meets. I'd probably be way ahead of the eight ball today if I had never lifted.

I worked in factories, breweries, and all kinds of places. I was working for Briggs Manufacturing when I won my first Olympic medal in 1948. When it came time for the 1952 Games, I asked for some time off. They said they'd give me all the time off I wanted. They'd fire me. So I just left. I won the gold in 1952 but didn't compete in 1956 because I had a ruptured disc and two operations on my back. Then I got a job working at Strohs Brewery. I won the bronze in 1960 while at Strohs, but when it came time to start working for the 1964 Games, instead of giving me a better job, they gave me a worse one. And when I tried to get a job with them as a salesman, they told me they weren't hiring athletes, but a few months later they hired a football player. So I quit Stroh's.

I once looked up the early Olympic contributors, and what I found was that some of these big companies that are now kicking in millions because of the advertising value were then giving donations of $200 or $300. Today, everything is sold to the highest bidder. The Games are a money-grabbing spectacle, and that includes the athletes. Now everyone gets paid. Everyone thinks that Ueberroth did such a tremendous job, but all he did was make the Games more commercial than ever.

When I was lifting, I used to drink a lot of beer and eat lots of pizza and hamburgers. At the time everyone thought that was terrible. Today I would make thousands in commercials. I was just born 30 years too soon.

I ate anything and everything. I used to tell those guys who were on a steak diet or whatever, "If you've got to have a special diet,

I've got you beat already." If the guy didn't get his special food, he started worrying more about his diet than his training and his competition.

There was no such thing as steroids when I started out. You thought you were doing something bad if you took a couple of aspirins and a Coke. Some people thought that would stir you up. Today everybody is taking some kind of drugs. If they aren't taking synthetic steroids, they're taking goat hormones, which can't be detected. Sure it helps their performance. It took me 10 years to gain about 50 pounds. If a guy goes on steroids, he can go up that much in three or four months. Years ago if you had a 5- or 10-pound lifting lead on a guy, you had him beat for a year because it would take him that long to catch up to you naturally. But once steroids came in, these guys were jumping up 50, 75, 100 pounds a meet. This was one of the reasons I was forced to quit—because guys I used to beat were sailing right by me.

The first time I really noticed all this was in the early 1960s. We had a guy who went from being an average lifter to world caliber in a matter of a year or so. A couple of times we asked him, "Are you still taking those things?" He said, "Hell, yes." I asked him, "Did you ever stop?" He answered, "Yup, once, and all my lifts went down, so I've never been off them since."

Is this dangerous? They really haven't proven anything yet. There have to be thousands of kids—even girls—taking this stuff now. How many are dying from it?

I don't know about the Russians. When I competed against them, we just figured they had better training methods and more time to practice. I would be getting canned from some job because I had to train and compete, but they would just go to school or into the army, where they had all the time they needed to train.

Our overall weightlifting program is very poorly run. We have some of the same people in there now that we had in 1952. I'm not one of their favorites. I always tell them that they should be coaching our ski team because ever since they came in everything has been downhill. If you tell them the truth, you're out. But the record speaks for itself. Since 1960 we've won only one gold medal in Olympic weightlifting.

These guys even have a Weightlifting Hall of Fame. That's the biggest joke there is. A Hall of Fame should be for our world champions and world record holders. They've got 30 or 40 lifters in there, which isn't too bad, but they've got another section for contributors. This takes care of all the officials, and they've got as many of them in the Hall as they do lifters. I'm in it, but I don't take any pride in that. There are some lifters who are world champions and some who set world records but are not yet in. If someone doesn't sponsor you, you don't get in.

All the Olympic federations got money from the 1984 Games. Even the poor cousins got at least $1 million. But we're not using the wrestling money to develop young lifters. We are so far behind that I don't even know if we can catch up. Hell, I could even have made the team in 1972, and I was 48 years old at the time. I knew I wouldn't have placed better than tenth in the competition in Munich, and in 27 years I had never done worse than third. I thought it would have been embarrassing, but most of our present lifters just go along for the ride.

We need more numbers in this country and more training. If you get only one champion out of 1,000 lifters, you have to make sure that you've got 100,000 training. I think that we now have only 2,000 or 3,000 lifters in serious training.

For several years I tried to be a coach for the national team, but it's an old buddy system. They've got a whole bunch of hangers-on. Some of them are just towel carriers and stuff like that. And when it comes time to pick coaches for the Olympic year, they vote for one another. These guys make all kinds of trips around the world to international competitions and meetings to learn coaching techniques, but when they come back they can't transmit it to the kids because they didn't know what they were talking about in the first place.

I got into weightlifting because my brother was a national-caliber lifter, and I used to tag along with him. There were a group of guys on the east side of Detroit who formed a club of their own in a garage. They put heat and showers in it. I used to hang around with them, and while they were showering I'd fool around with the weights. I was about 14 at the time, but in a few months I was doing more than most of the guys in there.

I wasn't all that big for my age. When I was 16 or 17, I was still about 155 pounds, but I was already serious about weightlifting. I always had to do it on my own, although there are now lots of people who are willing to take credit for my successes. If they hung around you for a few months, they thought they coached you. But there was no real coaching then.

I was 24 years old in my first Games in 1948 when I won the

Norbert Schemansky in 1952. Photo courtesy of Norbert Schemansky

silver as a middle-heavyweight. I was still the same weight in 1952 when I won the gold and set a world record. I set another world record in the 198-pound class in 1953, although my back was already bothering me. In 1954 I got up to 220 pounds, took the world championship, and set three world records. In 1956 I had my ruptured disc. Paul Anderson won the gold, but I think I could have beaten him, even though he weighed 100 pounds more than I did. In 1960 I had a bad knee, but I finished third in the heavyweight division and took another bronze in 1964 when I was 40 years old.

The only thing anyone was doing for me in those years was, when I got on a plane to go to a big meet, they'd give me an AAU emblem and tell me to put it where it belonged—over my heart. I'd tell them that I'd put it where it belonged—in my back pocket.

Bob Huffman of the York, Pennsylvania, Club used to pick up the tab for the trips, but you would get to go only if you at least had a chance to get one of the top three places. Sometimes they wouldn't even pay unless you were going to be the winner. When I won the world championship in Vienna in 1954, I came across the border, and they wanted to know how much money I had. I told them, "Nothing." They pulled me aside. They thought I was joking. I told them, "I don't have any money. I'm broke." They couldn't believe that I could be a world champion and not have any money. I had traveled all the way to Europe with empty pockets.

I now wonder why in the hell I did it, training for all those Olympics and losing all those jobs and money. I was just hooked on lifting, and I did like to win. I always liked the challenge of somebody telling me I couldn't beat some guy or other.

I now work for an engineering company as a construction inspector. Hey, I have to work until I fall over because I lost all that money when I was competing. I still work six days a week, and, although I'm 62, I do work out occasionally. I do bench presses and a few leg squats to keep myself toned up. I don't believe in masters' competition for weightlifters. Some of those guys are taking more steroids than the young kids. I know some of them from years back, and they're doing almost as well now as when they were younger. Some are also falling over with bad hearts and everything else. To walk out there with big varicose veins, huffing and puffing, is kind of silly. I can see guys staying in shape, but forget the competition.

I'd tell a young kid who wants to be a world-class lifter to go to school and take up football or baseball. Even if he makes it to the Olympics, what is he going to get compared to other sports? So what if I was once the greatest lifter in the world? When I get on the bus, the driver still wants his 50¢.

9
MELBOURNE, 1956

The Melbourne Games were the first to be held in the Southern Hemisphere, where, because of the reversed seasons, they lasted from November 22 through December 8.

For the first three years after the Helsinki Games there was considerable doubt that Melbourne would actually host the Games. All sorts of bickering and infighting occurred during that time, even between Australia's two most prominent political figures, Robert G. Menzies, the Prime Minister, and John Cain, the Premier of Victoria and a leader of the opposition Labor Party.

Some of the conflict was the result of the Australian penchant for nonconformity and individualism, but more important was the question of whether the Commonwealth or the Victorian government would pay for the construction of new facilities and for the renovation of the old. After an uneasy settlement, a series of labor strikes put construction so far behind schedule that International Olympic Committee President Avery Brundage seriously considered moving the Games to Rome, where the work for the 1960 Games was much further advanced. In the spring of 1955 Brundage traveled to Australia and issued a clear warning: "I hope the Games don't have to be taken away but . . . today more than ever the world thinks we made a mistake in giving the Games to Melbourne." His words seemed to galvanize the Aussies into action, and by the end of 1955 it was clear to even the most skeptical that Melbourne would be ready after all.

By the end of October 1956, 74 nations had agreed to compete in Australia, despite the long traveling distance for many of them. But within the next several days the Hungarians rebelled against Russian control of their country, a rebellion the Russians brutally crushed with tanks and guns on November 4. Then Israel attacked Egypt in the Gaza strip, and Britain and France moved into the Suez Canal zone. Part of the Hungarian Olympic team was already en route to Melbourne aboard a Russian merchant ship. The rest of the team was waiting in Czechoslovakia to board a plane for Melbourne. After considering their options, they reluctantly decided to continue their journey.

Egypt, Iraq, and Lebanon withdrew from the Games in protest over the Israeli invasion, and Spain, the Netherlands, and Switzerland withdrew to protest the brutality of the Russian action in Hungary, although the Swiss later changed their minds after Otto Mayer, a member of the IOC, pointed out to his countrymen that the Games had to be kept above politics. The People's Republic of China also withdrew because Nationalist China was allowed to compete.

Despite the ominous events of early November, the Games opened on schedule. The facilities were excellent and the sports-loving Australians enthusiastic hosts. From the beginning the Australians made it clear that there would be no separate accommodations for any country, so the Russians stayed in the Olympic Village and fraternized with the other athletes.

Another kind of East-West fraternization also occurred in the Olympic Village. Harold Connolly, the American champion hammer thrower, and Olga Fikotova, the gold medalist discus thrower from Czechoslovakia, began a well-publicized romance. A year later they were married in Czechoslovakia after several U.S. officials, including the Secretary of State, intervened to permit them to live in the United States after the ceremony. The Connollys, now divorced, raised a family in Santa Monica, and later Olga wrote *Rings of Destiny*, a book about the events of their courtship and marriage.

Every competition pairing the Russians and the Hungarians inspired an obvious reaction on the part of the large number of former Hungarian émigrés then living in Australia, who booed the Russians right from the opening ceremony. Such tensions also affected the athletes. On the first day the Russian Vladimir Kuts won the 10,000-meter run, but there was no congratulatory handshake from the second-place winner, Joseph Kovacs of Hungary. Things turned particularly unpleasant in the water polo match when a Hungarian swimmer emerged from the water with blood over his face after being slugged by one of the Russians. The match was immediately terminated and the victory granted to the Hungarians. After the Games ended, many in the Hungarian delegation, including several journalists, decided not to return home. Clearly forgotten in all this was the quote of Baron de Coubertin's that had flashed on the giant scoreboard on opening day: "The Olympic movement tends to bring together in a radiant union all the qualities which guide mankind to perfection."

Among the athletes making an Olympic reappearance at Melbourne were Emil and Dana Zatopek, but this time Emil's best showing was a sixth place in the marathon and Dana's a fourth in the women's javelin throw. Among the American athletes at Melbourne was Bobby Morrow, who won the 100- and 200-meter dashes and anchored the winning 4x100 relay team. Tom Courtney overtook Britain's Derek Johnson in the final 25 yards to take the 800-meter title. In the 110-meter hurdles Lee Calhoun and teammate Jack Davis had the same time of 13.5, but Calhoun was declared the winner by a few inches. This was the second Olympics in a row in which Davis was edged out of a gold though given the same time as the winner. In Helsinki, Harrison Dillard had beaten Davis at the tape, although they shared a record time of 13.7. Glenn Davis comfortably won the 400-meter hurdles, a feat he duplicated four years later in Rome. Greg Bell of Indiana University won the long jump, and in the shot-put competition Parry O'Brien beat his '52 Olympic score with a throw of 60 feet, 11 inches. Pat McCormick repeated her double Helsinki victories in the women's springboard and platform diving events and thus became the first diver, male or female, to win consecutive Olympic gold medals in both events.

James Boyd took the light-heavyweight title, and Pete Rademacher won the heavyweight division for the United States' only two boxing titles. Rademacher was invited by the team to carry the flag in the closing ceremonies, and later he became the first fighter in history to move directly from the amateur ranks to a title match for the heavyweight championship of the world.

Olympic regulations forbade any official scoring along national lines, but employing the 10-5-4-3-2-1 system favored by the American press, the Soviets convincingly outpointed the Americans 722 to 593. They took 37 gold medals to the U.S.'s 32 and led 99 to 74 in total medals. Naturally, all this did not set well with American reporters, some of whom pointed out that if the women's scores were not counted, America still reigned supreme.

The closing ceremonies broke with Olympic tradition in two ways. In the past the ceremonies had included the Prix des Nations equestrian jumping events, the most colorful competition in the Games. But because of Australia's strict quarantine laws for horses, the equestrian events were held the previous June in Stockholm. Also, instead of a parade of athletes marching behind their country's flag, the athletes at Melbourne formed a single line without regard for any order, national or otherwise. Some saw this mingling of uniforms as a hopeful sign of international friendship.

GREG BELL

Gold Medal, Long Jump, 1956

Truly a renaissance man, Greg Bell is much more than a gold medal–winning long-jumper. He is a successful dentist, as well as a poet and sculptor; above all, he is a student of the human condition.

Born one of nine children in racially segregated southern Indiana, the young Bell had no thoughts of doing anything beyond "getting a job" after becoming the first member of his family to graduate from high school. A series of circumstances changed all that, but not without considerable struggle.

Warm, generous, and gregarious, Dr. Bell is today an accomplished motivational speaker who uses his own life as an example of someone who rose above the circumstances of a humble birth. He is also a man who speaks his mind on controversial issues.

I was one of the few people in this area who spoke out against our 1980 Olympic boycott. It was so sad that this great opportunity for the promotion of goodwill and understanding was thwarted by the stroke of a pen by one man who simply had no concept of the

Greg Bell in 1986. Photo by Fogarty and Carlson

consequences of what he was doing. How dare anyone make a unilateral decision that so adversely affected the lives of so many young people and negated the sacrifices of not only the participants themselves but their families as well? It takes years of sacrifice to pursue that elusive gold medal, and to have this jerked out from under you is unconscionable. I think of Sugar Ray Leonard, who would have been just another black kid in the ghetto had it not been for his Olympic exposure.

I know that members of the U.S. Olympic Committee were coerced into voting for the boycott. The administration threatened to take away the committee's tax-exempt status and to ask some 50 major corporations to withdraw their financial support if its members didn't support the boycott. It is really tragic that we who are constantly holding ourselves up to the world as a model turn around and do the very thing that we condemn. It is certainly not what the Olympic Games are all about.

I grew up on a small truck farm outside of Terre Haute, Indiana. My father, whose family was descended from North Carolina slaves, cleared the land and built the house where I was born in 1930. He was 5-foot-7 and never weighed more than 140 in his life, but I've never seen a stronger man for his size or one more confident of his own ability. When he was past 65, he was still racing around the neighborhood with the kids, jumping fences and playing games. I think I got some of my competitiveness from him.

Our first house burned down when I was an infant, so nine of us kids literally grew up in a chickenhouse with not much more room than my present living room. When I was about 12, the government bought our farm to build a defense plant, and we had to move to town. My father was then about 60 and had no marketable skills, so we grew up very poor. At the time, I was the only one in the family to graduate from high school, although a sister later did. I couldn't even go to the baccalaureate services because I couldn't afford to rent the gown.

It wasn't until my sophomore year at Garfield High School that I went out for track. I wasn't big enough to play football or tall enough to play basketball, but I could outrun most of the kids in the neighborhood. I ran the dashes and high-jumped, but what I really wanted to do was pole-vault. I got up to about 11 feet with that old bamboo pole, but after I hurt my back, the principal, Jim Conover, suggested that because of my speed and spring I should try broad jumping, as it was then called.

We had a couple of jumpers on the team, so I watched them, and then I tried it. The first jump I ever took beat the best Garfield had, so I had found my event. I got up to where I was jumping 20 feet consistently and went through my entire high school career undefeated until the Indiana State meet in 1948, when a young fellow named Russ Smith from Anderson beat me by three inches on his last jump.

I never dreamed of going to college. I just started looking for a job. I had no background in math or the sciences. I was in a general curriculum, and I was interested only in getting out of school, not in studying. I thought if I could ever get a job where I could have $100 cash in my hand at one time, I would be a howling success.

I graduated in 1948, and jobs were hard to find. I did various things for about three years before I went to Chicago to work in a packing company shaking the salt out of hides. My hands became so demolished by that salt that I couldn't put them in my pocket. I could always get a seat on the streetcar because no one wanted to get within three blocks of me. You just couldn't wash that smell off. One week was enough. I figured that anything was better than that. I drove a semi for a while, but then I got my first permanent job—I was drafted into the army.

I was in the service for 23 months. While I was stationed in France, I heard that there was going to be a track meet in Bordeaux. I scrounged up some shoes, ran around the company area for four days, and went to it. I won the long jump and the pole vault and took second in the 100 meters. Two weeks later I won the long jump at the European Armed Forces Championship in Nuremberg, Germany.

My best jump in high school had been about 22 feet, 2 inches, and much to my surprise I had got up to 23 feet, 5 inches without any real training. Apparently the latent ability was there, but I was slow in maturing. That encouraged me, but I had no grandiose notions about any future in track.

When I got discharged in 1954, I decided to enter some Indiana State AAU meets. I found a pair of cheap track shoes and gym shorts and got my first 24-foot jump, breaking the state AAU record. I also got a job at the Allis-Chamblers Manufacturing Plant in Terre Haute. I worked my way up to $1.59 an hour, but that was only because I was working the night shift.

I was married by this time, and one night at work it suddenly dawned on me that I had gone as far as I was ever going to go. I knew that there had to be something more out there. I owe a good deal of credit to a good friend of mine, Dr. William Bannon, who is probably the world's greatest sports fan. I first met him when physicians were still making house calls. I had been discharged from the service and was living at home in a small black neighborhood in Terre Haute. I had a bad case of tonsillitis, so my mother called him. When he came in the house, he saw a couple of track and field trophies on the mantel. He asked my mother whose they were. She told him. He came into the bedroom, and the first words he spoke to me were, "Get your ass out of that bed and go to school." He wanted to know why I was wasting my time working in a factory. He hounded me for years. He took me to various track meets while I was trying to decide whether or not I was going to do something. On three separate occasions he took me to Indiana University and introduced me to Coach Gordon Fisher.

Fisher was one of the nicest men I've ever known. He was an anachronism among coaches because he believed that you should go to school to get an education—even if you were a world-class athlete. So he also helped convince me that it was time to do something with my life, and I enrolled at IU in the fall of 1954.

I was also very fortunate that my wife was educationally oriented. She married me when I was a nobody, so everything I now am I really owe to her pushing me. Her father worked in a foundry, but he was an intelligent man who stressed education. My family could have cared less whether or not I went to school. As a matter of fact, when I did start at IU, they thought I was being foolish. Everyone else had good jobs, and we were down there starving—and we were—with a new baby, at that.

Those were rough times. My wife had just finished her nurse's training, so she got a job on campus that supplied us with food. My track scholarship paid my tuition. I got to rent my books for a quarter of their cost, and the GI Bill paid for our housing. My father had died, so we also had to send my mom a couple of bucks to help her out. I worked nights in a snack bar, and I can still remember taking slices of cheese home to help make ends meet. My wife used to wait up nights for me to come home because we were allowed to clean out the empty cartons of ice cream. She loved butter pecan, and I would always bring some home for her.

I think all this makes me impatient with young athletes today. I don't condemn them entirely, because this is a completely different society. But when I hear some of the excuses that they use for abusing their bodies with drugs or alcohol, I want to vomit. They say, "Well, I couldn't stand the pressure." You're making $300,000 a year, and you want to tell me about pressure? Try supporting your family on 75¢ an hour while taking 20 hours of classes, including courses in science for which you have no background. That's *real* pressure.

I'll never forget the first chemistry class I went to at IU. The professor told us to balance this equation. I thought to myself, "Equation? What the hell is an equation?" I had to take trigonometry and algebra, and I really don't know how I caught up and struggled through. I was fortunate to have some sensitive instructors. I can remember my first math instructor believed that we should be graded primarily on progress. Well, I knew nothing when I walked in there, so I had nowhere to go but up. Surprisingly enough, by the end of my freshman year I had made the dean's list.

I wasn't in school for fun and games, and athletics were simply a means to an end. I had to be dedicated enough to develop my full potential, but athletics were never of paramount importance in my life. I can remember one time when I was taking myself and my jumping a little too seriously. We were living in a little 20-foot-long trailer. Hell, I could jump farther than that trailer was long, and I had not been defeated in about two years. Well, I came home and said something that indicated that I was pretty pleased with myself. Now, I'm talking to the woman who washes my dirty socks, not to some adoring fan. She looked me in the eye and said, "So you can jump farther than anyone else in the world. So what?" I got insulted and went outside to sulk, but finally my brain started working, and I thought, You know, that lady is right. Who really gives a damn that I can jump farther than anyone else? That doesn't make me a better person, and it certainly doesn't make me a great man.

I started looking around at all the people who had other talents—people who could paint or play some musical instrument or were great scientists. I just happened to be fortunate enough to be able to do one thing better than anyone else. Fortunately, that one night was all it took for me to realize what it was all about. Never again did I go around with an inordinate sense of pride. I was proud of what I was able to accomplish, but no longer was I disdainful of people whose talents were different from my own.

I was 26 years old at Melbourne, and it was certainly one of the most exciting experiences of my life. I did feel some apprehension because I knew that Australia was a lily-white country with restrictive immigration laws against people of color. My competition was over after the second day, so I had time to get to know the people, and they couldn't have been nicer. In restaurants I had people invite me over to their tables for drinks; young ladies offered to escort me any place I might want to go; in fact, I had three proposals of marriage while I was there. One couple took me into their home for a few days and made me part of their family. They showed me their country and its culture. It was a great education for a young man from Terre Haute, Indiana.

I also became friendly with the other athletes, a couple of whom were Russians. This made me realize what a magnificent opportunity the Games are for the kind of understanding that transcends color, language, and politics. All my life I had carried an image in my mind of Russians being some kind of alien entity, so it was a very pleasant surprise to find out that they are the same kind of people one finds everywhere. They can be nice or nasty, beautiful or ugly, hard or soft, just like all the rest of us. So when someone

Greg Bell in 1956. Photo courtesy of *Track and Field News*

asks me what I think of Russian athletes, my answer is usually, "I don't know any Russian athletes. There are athletes, some of whom live in Russia."

On the practice track we'd help each other any way we could.

We'd signal one another how far our steps were off and things like that. These were supposed to be our hated enemies, but they really weren't. Since then I've mentioned several times how nice it would be if the United Nations could take a leaf from my Olympic experiences. I spent approximately a month in the Olympic Village in Melbourne, and never did I hear a negative word about race or nationality.

In the competition itself I almost made a cardinal mistake. Never had I been guilty of being overconfident upon entering a meet. In my practice jumps I was bouncing over 25 feet and feeling fantastic. I was just so sure that there was no one who could beat me. Then I got in the stadium for our preliminary jumps, and the real world came crashing down around me. I was the only one in the first round to jump under 24 feet. I completely fouled up my approach, and I was a real wreck.

I told myself that I better get my act together, or I would be going back home with nothing. So I came back with a good jump and qualified for the finals. My first jump in the finals was all right, but nothing outstanding. On my second try I went 25 feet, 8¼ inches, which was better, but I still wasn't satisfied. On my next attempt I got a terrible leg cramp coming down the runway. I thought I had done something terrible to my leg. I kind of collapsed on the infield, but someone said to have the trainer look at it. I was in the trainer's room when something happened about which I still get nightmares. Someone rushed in and said that I was going to be disqualified for leaving the competition without checking with the officials. No one had told me this. I rushed out, lay down on the grass like I had never left, and tried to massage the cramp out of my leg. I never really recovered, but, fortunately, I didn't need another jump. I still wake up in a cold sweat thinking about what would have happened if I had been disqualified.

I grew up in an era when there was still a lot of discrimination and hostility directed toward minority people. After having been turned away from root beer stands and denied access to hotels and restaurants, I guess maybe I felt some bitterness toward this country I call home. But when I stood on the top step of that podium, half a world away, and saw the Stars and Stripes being raised and listened to "The Star-Spangled Banner" being played, this old skeptic got a lump in his throat. It was then that I realized that, although we've got a lot wrong with this country, I can at least voice my displeasure with the things that are wrong and work to change them. So it was in Melbourne that most of my bitterness melted away.

I don't knock the athletes today for making money from commercials or whatever. If someone offered me $100,000 for doing something, I would take it, but what I do find so disappointing is that they feel that once they've won the Olympic medal, that's it. They feel no sense of obligation to utilize their good fortune to try to improve the world they live in. As proud as I am of that Olympic medal, I feel it would be so disappointing if that is all I had to represent 56 years of life. You can't sell it for much. You can't eat it. It doesn't make you a superior person.

I don't want any kid to be Greg Bell. In the first place, they can't. I didn't attempt to be anybody else. I admired Jesse Owens. I didn't really know anything about him except that here was a man who could outrun a horse. As I look back on it now, I think how terrible it was that he had to do such things. I was too young then to understand. I subsequently came to know Jesse and what a great man he was.

There is no way I could have endured some of the things that Jesse did. My wife had to tell me, "You're forgetting that when you were competing you were working toward a doctorate in a profession that you knew was going to earn you a living. The only thing Jesse had to sell was his own image, which was not a very marketable commodity at the time."

There are lots of people I admire. I recently toured the biomedical research lab at Purdue University and met Dr. Leslie Geddies. I admire him tremendously. He does things that I could never dream of doing, but I don't want to be Leslie Geddies. I couldn't be. So my point is that it is fine for a kid to use me for a role model to the extent that I am living proof that all things are possible. Don't be Greg Bell. But have a dream that will let you accomplish significant things in your own lives.

I have loved poetry all my life. I've memorized about an hour's worth of Paul Laurence Dunbar's poetry, which I present at programs—primarily his dialect pieces. They are entertaining and delightful insights into the black culture. I got so engrossed with Dunbar that I decided to write my own poetry. I have about 52 pieces copyrighted now.

One of my poems is about Martin Luther King, Jr. When I was younger, I didn't realize that you could have so much dedication that you could passively resist and not retaliate. I am not that way by nature. I have to attempt to overcome immediately, but I have great admiration for those who have succeeded in the face of an adversity under which I am not sure I could have stood up.

However, as you get older, you learn to use different approaches to confront racial attitudes. It takes a lot of maturity and confidence in your own ability to use something like humor to deal with such a situation. I treat mental patients in my dental practice, and they don't hold anything back. I was starting to work on one such patient when he indicated that he didn't want these black hands in his mouth. So I told him, "Don't worry. I've had this stuff on over 50 years, and it doesn't rub off." If we can laugh at ridiculous situations, it can help, but I still don't like being ostracized for something that I had no choice in—my color—although I wouldn't change it now if I could.

While in California for the 1984 Games I was reunited with a lot of old friends and got to mingle with some of the greats of all sports. We were at some kind of press conference, and my daughter Shari said, "Gee, Dad, you sure know a lot of important people." She thought about that for a moment, and then she said, "And you're one of them." I'll never forget the expression on her face. Of course, she had grown up knowing that her dad had won the Olympic gold medal, but I don't think it really hit home to her until that very moment. Sometimes I still forget that I'm one of them because I look at these people and I think, What fantastic individuals these are, and to be numbered among them is an honor that transcends description.

HAROLD CONNOLLY

Gold Medal, Hammer, 1956

Hal Connolly emerged as the media star of the Melbourne Games, in part because he defeated his Soviet rival, Mikhail Krivonosov, in the hammer, but primarily because of his love affair with Olga Fikotova, the Czech gold medalist in the discus.

It was the height of the Cold War, and their romance became a political soap opera eagerly followed by people everywhere. Not to be denied, Hal and Olga married, moved to the States, and continued to compete on Amer-

ican Olympic teams, Hal through the 1968 Games and Olga through 1972. After 16 years of marriage and four children, their storybook romance ended with a divorce in 1973.

Often overlooked were the athletic talents of Hal himself. A nine-time national champion who broke the world hammer record seven times, Harold Connolly did it all with a left arm that had been withered since birth.

When I was born, I weighed 13 pounds, and the doctor told my father that he couldn't save both my mother and me. My father told him to try but not to let his wife die. Fortunately, we were both saved, but at the cost of my left arm, which was badly damaged. All the nerves in my shoulder were torn. I had an operation when I was three months old, but the doctor couldn't find all the injured nerves. In those days microsurgery wasn't being done. Throughout my childhood I was in a brace and had to go regularly to the Children's Hospital in Boston for physiotherapy. It was very embarrassing to have to leave school with my mother for those trips to the hospital. When I was 13, I decided that I wouldn't do it anymore.

I just didn't want to be with the handicapped kids, most of whom were polio victims. So I started exercising myself. I discovered a weight training magazine called *Strength and Health* and decided that I needed to develop not only my left arm but all of my body. I wanted to prove myself as an athlete because I came from a family of athletes, mostly boxers.

I became an overachiever in sports. Because of my left arm, I could not become a boxer, but in high school I did run the hurdles, throw the shot, and play a very aggressive tackle on the football team. I just wanted to show everybody I could do it.

I went to Boston College, as did most good local Irish Catholic boys. Realizing that football was not going to be my sport, I continued with the shot put, but you need your left arm to pull you through the motion, and mine didn't work that way. I never really thought about throwing the hammer because it is a two-handed event, but our coach, William Gilligan, lived not far from my house, and I used to wait around after practice to get a ride home with him. The last athletes he coached each day were the hammer throwers, and, to speed things up, I would get in the outfield and throw the hammers back. Before long I was throwing them back

Hal Connolly in 1986. Photo by Fogarty and Carlson

over their heads, so I had found my event. Strangely enough, my left arm did not handicap me in the hammer as much as it did in the shot put. I adapted by switching the emphasis to my legs, with my arms functioning as a whip.

In the summer of 1954, Bob Backus, a 1952 U.S. Olympic hammer thrower, and I paid our way over to Germany. We wanted to learn from the Germans because there really were no great hammer coaches in this country. One night we were doing a little drinking with a German hammer thrower named Hugo Ziermann, who told me that I would be lucky if I ever threw 180 feet. That upset me, and a couple of days later I not only beat him for the first time, but I threw the hammer 180 feet, 3 inches. I was sitting in a pub that night with Sepp Christmann, one of the greatest and most renowned hammer coaches in the world, when we heard over the radio that the Russian, Krivonosov, had just set a new world record of 209 feet. That seemed an impossible throw to match, but Sepp told me, "If you really want to, you can win the Olympics in 1956."

I don't know whether he was just trying to encourage me after Ziermann's remark or whether he really did see something, but that was all I needed to hear. Christmann had revolutionized the hammer throw by getting his athletes to turn on their heels and toes rather than toe-turning and jumping around in the circle. He told me how to train, and I went home and worked like a man possessed all through 1955.

I can't really distinguish the mental from the physical in throwing. Looking back to when I began throwing, I now know that if the mind is willing, the possibilities for what you can accomplish are almost unlimited. In 1955 I went over 200 feet for the first time and then pushed the American record to 209, although the world record was still about 7 feet beyond that.

I was the favorite in our Olympic trials in 1956, but I finished a very disappointed third; however, I changed that attitude very quickly because of Ernie Shelton, a friend and high-jumper with whom I was staying during the trials in Los Angeles. He was the world's best, having cleared 6 feet, 11 inches some 20 times, and he was planning to become the first to clear 7 feet. In his home he had a crossbar set at 7 feet right across the foot of his bed. I began to focus on his quest, and that made both of us nervous. After coming in third and barely making the team, I felt disgusted and sorry for myself until I saw Ernie weeping in the Coliseum dressing room. Not only had he failed to make the team, but the 19-year-old Charles Dumas had won and become the first ever to clear 7 feet. I stopped feeling sorry for myself and became determined not to blow my chance at the Games.

The Russian, Mikhail Krivonosov, was clearly the favorite in Melbourne, but by this time he had heard of me. We had exchanged the world record a number of times, pushing it over 220 feet. Through an American distance runner he met in Belgrade, Krivonosov sent me a card saying, "See you in Melbourne." So I got a picture of him and put it on the visor of my car. Every day I could look up at him and say, "See *you* in Melbourne!"

I guess that was the beginning of our psychological battle. The first day of practice I waited for him to arrive before starting to throw. It quickly became a contest to see who could throw the farthest. After that, the Russians took him away, and he didn't train anymore in the Village. He simply disappeared. I went looking for him and found out that he was training at Melbourne University. My teammate Al Hall and I went over to watch him. He wasn't there, but the groundskeeper told us that we didn't have a chance because Krivonosov and his teammates were breaking the world record on every throw. We did see their divots in the grass, and they were out there a long way. We threw for a while, but we weren't even close to the Russian marks. We knew that wouldn't do, so we stood in front of the ring in order to beat them. Then we stuck an American flag in the farthest hole and told the groundskeeper to tell the Russians that the Americans had been there.

It must have worked. Before the finals I was sitting across from Krivonosov in the holding room, and when I looked at him his head went down. So I got up, walked over, and shook hands with him. I just wanted to show him that I wasn't nervous. When I shook his hand, it felt cold and wet. That made me feel more confident.

I should have won on my first throw because it was to be my best and far beyond the Olympic record, but it was a slight foul. I was trying to put the pressure on everyone else with that first throw, but now it was on me, and I began to get nervous. Going into the fifth round, Krivonosov was leading. I had a lot at stake because the day before Olga had won the women's discus, and I knew if I didn't win I'd never be able to face seeing her again. It was an ego thing, I guess. On the fifth throw I beat him by about 6 inches with a throw of just over 207 feet. But he still had his final throw. I watched him take off his sweats, step into the circle, and look at the hammer and sickle on his shirt. He just stared at the symbol and girded himself for his effort. I was thinking, My God, what if he does it? But he had made himself so tight that he never even let go of the hammer.

I felt tremendously relieved but also a little embarrassed because the winning throw was so short. It was windy, and the pollen was making my hay fever act up, but mostly it was the tension that had affected all of us.

On the victory stand I stood transfixed by the whole experience. Tom Courtney had just come from behind to win the 800 meters, and the entire stadium was electric. There were 100,000 shouting people. I stood there wondering where Olga was and forgetting what I was supposed to do. They started playing "The Star-Spangled Banner" and raising the flags of the place winners. The two Russians on the stand turned to face the flag, but I remained staring off into space. Finally, I felt Krivonosov's hands on my hips, turning me to face the American flag.

I had met Olga a week or so before the finals. We had accidentally bumped into each other in an equipment shed where she was getting a discus and I a hammer. I wanted to get to know her better, and she mentioned that her birthday was coming up. So I got our press book and had all our athletes sign it for a birthday present. She was a very attractive woman with a warm, outgoing personality. We went out on a few dates, and one thing just led to another. Looking back, I have to say that it was the romance of the whole situation. It's difficult to talk about now because we are divorced and lead different lives. But at the time it was extremely exciting. I guess we fell in love in the sense that we were totally enraptured and caught up in the events surrounding our lives.

No American officials put any pressure on me, although they did tell me I would never see her again after she returned to Czechoslovakia. I can remember Reverend Bob Richards, the Olympic pole vault champion who had a lot of international experience, telling me, "You better get her to stay, or it's good-bye." But I didn't even try to get her to defect. She was an only child, and she felt that she had to share her Olympic victory with her parents. She also wanted to complete her medical studies in Prague. She had her whole life there, and we both needed to find out what we really wanted.

Before the end of the Games, the Czech officials, obviously fearing she was going to defect, spirited her out of the Village and then sent the entire Czech team back to the Soviet Union on a Russian ship.

I didn't know where she was for those weeks she was aboard the ship to Vladivostok and then on a train across Siberia to Moscow. I wrote to her in Prague, but the letters never reached her. I was going frantic thinking they had really cut us off, and I was determined to see her again.

At the time, our State Department was sending American athletes abroad as goodwill ambassadors, so when I was asked if I wanted to go to Europe, I naturally jumped at the chance. After receiving my itinerary, I asked the State Department representative if afterward I was free to go wherever I pleased. He asked, "You mean like Czechoslovakia?" I nodded and was told, "You've got a ticket to come home that's good for a year."

After many difficulties, I got a visa through the Yugoslavs and arrived in Prague the end of February. Emil Zatopek and his wife Dana put me up and were very supportive once Olga and I decided that we really did want to marry. My visa expired before the government granted its approval, and I had to leave the country. But through political pressure I was once more able to return. I think all the publicity of the free press helped because the Czech government didn't want to look foolish by preventing a marriage that the whole world insisted on having. A *New York Times* editorial summed up how people felt:

> The H-Bomb overhangs us like a cloud of doom. The subway during rush hours is almost impossible to endure. The common cold is still with us. But Olga and Harold are in love and the world does not say no to them. Cynicism sweeps drearily across the landscapes of the earth, but Olga and Harold love each other in the way that began in the dawn of time. . . .
>
> Harold could have married any girl who was willing and able to marry him. Secretary Dulles said so. But Olga couldn't marry Harold unless the Czechoslovak Government said she could. The Czechoslovak Government now says yes. We say yes. The hearts of all who have ever known romance say yes.

With the Zatopeks standing up for us, we had three marriage ceremonies in Prague. There was nothing in the newspapers about any of them because the government tried to keep everything a secret. We got married on a Wednesday, but 40,000 well-wishers showed up for the civil ceremony. People were just everywhere. Afterward we were supposed to go by car to the Catholic church, but we couldn't move, so we just walked through the crowds. When we arrived, there were already 5,000 people inside of the church. After that we moved on to Olga's Protestant church, and again the people just followed us. The whole thing lasted from about eight in the morning until midafternoon. It was just unbelievable.

When we arrived in the States, it was another kind of struggle. We had 35¢ in our pockets. Olga had nothing but the clothes she was wearing and a few things she brought from her home. I had no prospects of a job except as a high school social studies and English teacher in Boston.

In New York a refugee furrier wanted to give Olga a fur coat if she would wear it to some of the public events to which we were invited. She refused. We also had all kinds of offers to come to Las Vegas. Bob Hope's agent was after us, but we weren't impressed by that whole Hollywood scene. Olga was very suspicious of capitalists. She had been told by the president of Czechoslovakia that she would have her head turned by the money interests and would become a disgrace to her country.

We even had religious problems. On the ship I had received a telegram from Archbishop Cushing of Boston telling me to speak to no one about my marriage until I had talked to him in his office. Later, he suggested that I had committed some public scandal in Catholic Boston by marrying outside the church. He didn't know that the Vatican had approved the marriage and that I had a document of permission from the Archbishop of Czechoslovakia.

We settled in a very inexpensive apartment in Boston, and I went into the insurance business, hoping to make more money than I could teaching school. The company thought I could use my fame to sell insurance, but it bothered me to sell people more insurance than they could really use or afford. The company showed me statistics to prove that the last thing an economically troubled family gives up is its insurance policy, but I just couldn't make money that way. I told Olga I had to go back into teaching, and in 1958 we moved out to Santa Monica, California, where I have been in high school teaching and administration ever since.

As the years went by, Olga wanted to assert her individuality and achieve something on her own, and she felt that in the eyes of the public we were always Harold and Olga. She felt trapped by that, and she wanted to be an independent person. The women's movement was also becoming more popular, and she had to prove to herself and maybe to others that she could accomplish things totally on her own. Maybe she believed that the last time she accomplished anything by herself was when she won the gold medal in Melbourne. She had the courage to make the break, and it wasn't easy for her to do that with all the world expecting us to stay happily together for all eternity.

I have no regrets. I've gone on with my life and have a new family, a wonderful wife, who as Pat Winslow was a U.S. pentathlete in 1960, 1964, and 1968, and two more children, Adam and Shannon. As I look back to when Olga and I married, I think we were in love, but we were not as compatible as we needed to be to have it last a lifetime. But we had 16 years together, and we have four beautiful children. That beats most marriages.

Hal Connolly winding up, 1956. Photo courtesy of *Track and Field News*

I competed in the '60, '64, and '68 Games but failed to win a medal. In 1968, because I was in my fourth Olympiad, I was invited to carry the flag in the opening ceremonies. The officials told the press that I was going to do so, but after thinking it over I refused. I was and am philosophically opposed to the fact that we don't dip our flag when we march past the reviewing stand. Now, because we won't, the Russians won't either. Our refusal goes back to the 1908 London Games when Martin Sheridan, one of the so-called New York Irish Whales, refused to dip the flag to the English king as a demonstration against British rule in Ireland. It was political then, and it still is, and I consider it arrogant not to dip the flag. When I told our officials this, they just went crazy. But, if the Olympic Games are supposed to signify friendship among nations, you don't show this kind of disrespect.

I'm also somewhat of a maverick on the subject of performance-enhancing drugs. I used steroids for the first time in the early 1960s. After the Rome Games I heard that the Russian weightlifters were taking something that made them superior to anyone else. They even looked different. I came back to the States and asked my doctor about it. He did a little research and concluded that the only thing that could build lean muscle and tissue mass was anabolic steroids. I told him I wanted to try them. He put me on one or two a day, but after six or eight weeks nothing had happened. At that time, I didn't think to increase the dosage.

You have to remember that steroids were not a prohibited drug until 1968. I can remember American weightlifters taking injections of testosterone and other steroids at the '64 Games. So after '64 I got into a controlled experiment where I was put on Anavar. I took 20 milligrams a day and went right up there in strength, but it did not really improve my performance that much. I think I was just spending too much time getting strong and not enough time improving speed and technique. In 1965 I threw the hammer 233 feet, but that was only one foot farther than I had thrown it in 1962.

I am still unconvinced that anabolic steroids are dangerous if used under careful medical supervision. The real tragedy is that most athletes are not monitoring their intake, and the unmonitored use of any drug—even aspirin—becomes extremely dangerous. I've seen athletes who have taken too many Motrins and got stomach ulcers. Unfortunately, many athletes are taking anabolic steroids on their own, and this is far more dangerous than in a number of other countries where such things are carefully controlled.

The anabolic steroid problem is a long way from being solved, and I don't think that testing is the final solution. Certainly we have to protect the health of our athletes, and American doctors feel that testing is the best way to do this. But athletes are very cynical about the whole process because they do not think that testing and suspensions are imposed impartially. I know of a number of athletes who have tested positive for steroids but have not been suspended.

Since the 1960s, scientific and technological innovations in international sports have been as real as in nuclear or space competition. The fact that we have not been able to get international agreements on nuclear testing, an area that directly affects the very lives of everyone on this planet, would seem to indicate that it is naive to believe that all nations are fairly and equally observing the Olympic rules about the use of performance-enhancing drugs.

As long as international sports are flaunted as prestigious for national image and are exploited as avenues to inordinate wealth, many nations and individuals will continue to invest scientific expertise into ways to circumvent the consequences of testing.

Carefully controlled research to confirm or dismiss the purported health dangers of such substances accompanied by an extensive educational campaign, similar to what has been done with tobacco, would effectively lead to a solution to the great dilemma: avoid using performance-enhancing substances and be at a significant disadvantage or use them and risk significant health injury. History has proven that strict prohibitions alone do not work.

OLGA FIKOTOVA CONNOLLY

Gold Medal, Discus, 1956
(competed for Czechoslovakia)

Olga Fikotova was a medical student in her native Czechoslovakia when she set a new Olympic discus record at Melbourne in 1956. Though she is a great natural athlete who also played basketball and handball for Czech national teams, it was her widely publicized romance with Harold Connolly, the winning American hammer thrower, that brought her worldwide recognition.

After marrying Hal, moving to the States, and becoming an American citizen, Olga won five national AAU titles and competed for her new country in four Olympiads.

In 1972, as a 39-year-old mother of four, she set a new American discus record of 185 feet, 3 inches. It was the best throw of her career, but in Munich a controversy over athletes' rights, the Israeli massacre, and her determination to reestablish the Olympics as a forum for peace occupied her attention, and she did not do well in the competition. She was, however, honored by her teammates, who selected her to be their flagbearer during the opening ceremonies.

Although she did not win any medals for the United States, and by definition should not be included in a book of America's gold medal winners, Olga provides a fascinating perspective as an athlete who competed for, and against, the United States. Her efforts to restore and preserve the apolitical integrity of the Games are worthy of mention in a volume devoted to heroes and heroines.

On the street where I grew up in Prague, I was one of only two girls my age. The rest were boys. We played soccer with them in the middle of the road because cars were a rarity in that neighborhood. Not being as quick or strong as the boys, my friend played defense, and I tended goal. This did not thrill my parents, who wanted me to concentrate on the violin. They planned for me to become a teacher, and for this I needed some knowledge of a musical instrument. But I preferred sports, and by the time I graduated from the Gymnasium I had represented Czechoslovakia in team handball and had played basketball in the top league.

After entering the School of Medicine at the Charles University of Prague, I found that being tied to team practices was not compatible with my studies. I also had philosophical differences with my coaches over game strategies and the reorganization of the sports club system. Because I refused to apologize for talking back to them, I was suspended for six months. So I turned to individual sports, looking for something I had not tried before, and I found it in the discus.

My father had also experienced troubles with the authorities. He had been one of the Legionnaires who fought during World War I alongside the Allies. When Czechoslovakia was created in 1918, he was selected for the Presidential Guard. He served at the Prague Castle next to Tomás Garrigue Masaryk until the new country's beloved leader drew his last breath. My father was not a political man, but the distinction of his army position placed him among the suspects detained by the Nazis. Then, after World War II, when the people voted in the communists, my father was again incarcerated, and this nearly cost me my chance to go to the university. Trying to resolve my situation, I chose to apply for a "people's job," and I worked in a machine shop for more than a year, awkwardly proving that I was free of my "bourgeois past." Of course, being a skilled athlete helped when trying to establish my "political reliability," and I was eventually accepted into the university.

Olga Connolly in 1986. Photo by Fogarty and Carlson

Quality Czech athletes usually joined special teams representing the military in order to obtain needed time to train, eat, and rest. I did not want to give up medical school, so I had to improvise on my own. But no one can claim total credit for himself. Among those many who cheered me along the way was "Father" Jandera, a former excellent hurdler whose dreams had abruptly perished in a Nazi concentration camp. After the war he coached juniors at a police athletic club not far from my house. About 70 at the time, restless and filled with ideas on how to embellish the art of coaching, he presented the discus throw to me as a dance step and let me practice to the sounds of "The Blue Danube" played over the public address system.

I competed in my first track meet in 1955 when I was 22 years old. I really didn't know much about competing, but I placed second and was nominated to my third national team. Then I began to receive a monthly subsidy from the state, which approximated the monthly salary my mother earned as a stockroom clerk. As an athlete I was allowed to use this money only to purchase extra food, in order to have a better diet than did most Czechs and thus gain nutritional equality with athletes coming from Western countries with a higher standard of living.

In 1955 I competed in the Progressive Youth Festival in Warsaw, Poland. It was only my third meet, and I had a terrible day. The shiny new discus kept slipping out of my hand, and I finished last. It was a dismal performance, but "Father" Jandera had taught us not to make value judgments based on whether we won or lost but, rather, to analyze our performance with a degree of academic detachment in order to improve the next time.

Later that evening, I walked back to the stadium, sat next to the throwing ring, and started thinking about what I did and didn't do, what I should have done, and what I would do the next time. Suddenly, out of the darkness emerged a group of Soviet athletes walking around the track. You have to remember that at the time there was considerable tension and resentment toward the Russians among many of the Czech athletes. The Soviets tended to stay separate from everyone else, clammed into a kind of silence. You had to come to them; they would not move halfway. But to my surprise, a woman detached herself from the group and walked straight toward me. It was Nina Ponomareva, who had won the discus at Helsinki in 1952. She asked me how I had done, and I told her. "No wonder," she commented. "You are so skinny. You're too thin to throw the discus." She told me to meet her the following morning, and she would coach me. When I told my teammates, they scoffed at the idea that a Russian would share knowledge with anyone. In many sports, they had learned from us, but it was a one-way street. Yet the next day, Ponomareva spent two intensive hours with me. She genuinely tried to pump everything into me about her training and conditioning that she considered important. As we were parting, she said, "So long, until Melbourne." We shook hands, and that was it.

Our Czech technique for throwing the discus was outstanding, and many other nations, including the Soviets, learned from us. But when the Soviets decided to enter the 1952 Games, they chose to emphasize women's sports, and they mastered a tremendously well-researched conditioning program for women. This is what Nina Ponomareva taught me, and those methods remain superior to most others to this very day.

In Melbourne, I did not see Ponomareva until I beat her in the competition. She was upset and didn't really talk to me on the victory stand; we just shook hands. I didn't see her again until on the way home, when the Czech team traveled with the Soviets on their ship, the *Gruzia*. We had flown to Melbourne on a French plane, but during the Olympics rumors were circulated that some kind of sabotage might be directed at us, so we and some other Eastern Bloc countries traveled home by ship. The truth of the matter seemed to be that the Soviets wanted to show off their Olympians via a big tour across the outposts in Siberia with a final celebration of their team victory in Moscow. None of us wanted to go by ship, but our officials accepted for us—without asking.

On board our existence was pathetic and vaguely amusing at the same time. The ship was dangerously overcrowded, with people sleeping on makeshift bunks even in cargo areas. Some 500 passengers were on a ship whose capacity was 350.

But there was the comical side. The ship ran out of toilet paper and fresh water for showering. And there were battles with the cook, who proudly served us cold jellied borscht, which we decided to boycott. We'd send it back to the kitchen, and he would send it out again. This went on at least a half-dozen times. People were growling at one another, trying to find someone to blame for the sorry state of affairs.

Finally, the inquisitiveness of Emil Zatopek improved the situation. A running legend, Emil would work out whether aboard a ship, in the back of a plane, on a train, or in place when expected to stand still. It was while running around the two decks that he discovered that the Soviet athletes also resented being aboard. He found Vladimir Kuts, the 5,000- and 10,000-meter gold medalist, who was in the midst of a three-day drunk strike because he had been promised to go home by plane. The officials called Kuts in for a self-criticism session, but he appeared at his hearing so drunk that two comrades had to support him upright. Zatopek's telling of the Kuts story revived the Slavic sense of humor, and we all got along much better after that. I tried to hang around with Zatopek because he was so open-minded, and I suspected that whatever he did had to be all right.

Dressed for Australian summer, we arrived in Vladivostok in the middle of Siberian winter. I caught a terrible cold and was so ill at the start of the train passage across Siberia that I could not leave my compartment. Nina Ponomareva heard about it and brought me some kind of liquor, which tasted so bitter that after you took it you either got instantly well or expired on the spot. Fortunately, I got well after two treatments, and Nina and I became friends.

What one learns from such experiences is that, in spite of all the differences and divisions that separate people, there is this marvelous humanity that we all possess in common. It is a physical, intellectual, emotional, and deeply spiritual commonality. This realization made me very impatient with the barriers that stand between people and nations.

I competed in five Olympic Games, and Melbourne was probably the last time in which you could find that easy familiarity among the participants. Although the pain of the revolt in Hungary and its aftermath touched us all, there was a friendliness among the participants that knew no ranks, regardless whether one was a "winner" or one of "the other" competitors. That everyone was a champion from somewhere was understood and honored. In the subsequent Olympics the "Who's Who" divisiveness became much more apparent.

The American athletes appeared to be so free and open. Their modesty and the apparent lack of pressure to have to prove anything to anybody magically attracted me to them. The Czech teams were used to being constantly on guard, and we were expected to watch one another's moves. I never went along with such nonsense. I told the team officials that I would never check or tell on my teammates if they, for example, fraternized with persons who had previously escaped from Czechoslovakia and were then living in Australia. Only if I judged something to be really dangerous would I tell the officials. My attitude was disquieting to the officials, and, as a result, I would always find myself assigned to a room with or near a policewoman. In Melbourne her name was Maria. The Americans didn't seem to have problems like that. They seemed to do whatever they pleased, whether their officials liked it or not. I felt I was more like them, and it was a refreshing feeling.

After my marriage to Harold and my emigration to the United States, I too became a U.S. athlete. As a member of four U.S. Olympic teams, I found out that not everything was as I originally thought. Sure, we could freely discuss political issues, but in other ways we were treated more like unthinking bodies than as mature, self-disciplined representatives and champions of the United States. For example, at the 1960 Games in Rome I wore the track shorts in which I had won four years before. The women's team manager called me in and told me they were indecent. She also strongly suggested that women wear girdles.

I was also surprised by the near obsession of the officials with eliminating any alcoholic beverages. I don't particularly enjoy or tolerate alcohol, but I don't appreciate being told that as an athlete I may not have a glass of wine with my dinner. That decision belonged to me. No less a star than Emil Zatopek always packed a good supply of Pilsener Urquell when traveling to make certain that he did not miss his daily "medicinal" bottle of beer, which he believed would replenish his body fluids after he worked out.

On our way to Rome we had a stopover in Dublin, so I ordered an Irish coffee in the airport. Immediately an official turned up next to me. "Don't touch that. You'll be sent home!" What? I thought. Why should I be sent home? Then somebody told me the Eleanor Holm story. Such actions offended my sense of dignity and maturity. And it's certainly a bit incongruous that today Olympic and amateur sports officials seek manufacturers of alcoholic beverages to become sponsors of athletic events. I wonder if anyone has offered belated apologies to Eleanor Holm and returned her to her rightful place on our 1936 Olympic swimming team.

A far more troublesome incident occurred during the preparation for my final Olympiad in Munich in 1972. After Tommie Smith and John Carlos raised their black-gloved fists on the victory stand in Mexico City in 1968, our Olympic officials began to act very paranoid. They would simply not tolerate any discussion of their decision-making process. I felt that it was a question of our civil rights being abrogated. We were told that any interview or written piece that contained the words *Olympic* or *Olympics* had first to be approved by the Olympic Committee and that all interviews would be prearranged and supervised. In short, the team managers told us, "There will be no talking to the press."

This was as threatening as any censorship I had known in Czechoslovakia. Responsible but free journalistic inquiry is essential to a living democracy and a just society. The right to speak to the news media was not to be withdrawn from the Olympic team members, and I discussed this passionately with the journalists. Of course, I had to accept the risk of being sent home should the officials' punitive threat be upheld.

I found nothing amusing about the situation then or today. And you can imagine how happy I was to see a man show up in his running shorts at the Olympic headquarters and realize it was my California Senator, Alan Cranston. I had filed an urgent plea with his office to review the constitutionality of the ruling, and I was really pleased that he arrived personally to resolve the conflict.

In 1972, there was also the Vietnam question. I was strongly

Olga Connolly, 1956. Photo courtesy of Olga Connolly

opposed to our involvement because from my studies I understood that it was a futile way to try to solve the complex problems in Indochina. I was "Another Mother for Peace," and my belief was then, as it is today, that our fragile planet Earth cannot bear any more vast destruction and that the protection of living things is especially entrusted to women.

An athlete should go to the Olympics with single-minded purpose, thoroughly concentrating on the demands of his or her event. But I arrived in Munich heavily burdened by what I felt were my responsibilities to humanity. It was also my first Games in which Harold was not on the team. My well-publicized marriage was headed for a divorce, and that, too, was a matter of crushing importance. The murder of the kidnapped Israeli athletes and the accompanying suicide of their Palestinian captors showed that the Olympics have not been greater or better than life, but have become to a great degree a tool of the very interests I have always believed they had the power to counteract.

I felt that some gesture should be made that would go beyond placing a wreath in front of the Israeli team headquarters. Because any effort to organize a meeting of athletes in the Olympic Village was nearly impossible, I drafted a letter addressed to the then Secretary General of the United Nations, Kurt Waldheim. We also thought it was important to have the letter signed by interested Soviet athletes. I walked over to the Soviet headquarters and asked for help with the translation and for the use of a Russian-alphabet typewriter. But they refused. Then the German official in charge of the Olympic Village refused to allow the letter to be posted in front of the dining rooms where all the athletes could read and sign it. I was told that the letter was mixing politics into the Olympics. I read and reread the letter and found it to be reconciliatory rather than political:

> We the undersigned, the athletes and Olympic officials assembled in Munich, Germany, . . . appeal earnestly to all nations and people on Earth to apply their brilliant and sensitive minds towards a settlement of old disputes through genuine dialogue rather than through violence.
>
> Only if all nations consider their ancient hostilities with reason divorced from stubborn emotion, will the Family of Man be able to break through the vicious circle of mistrust, friction, conquest, and revenge, and be able to focus its attention on the cooperation desperately needed for solving the problems of poverty, lack of medical care, lack of education and communication, and the ever more threatening environmental destruction that affects us all.
>
> Brothers and sisters that we are, we beg all nations to halt further accumulation of weapons of mass destruction, and to cast away the racial, religious, social and economic prejudices that have traditionally and painfully separated us.

Now, 15 years later, I feel as seriously about the needs spelled out in that letter as I felt then, and I do not understand why it was dismissed as political.

So in Munich I went through one skirmish after another, none having to do with throwing the discus and none of which I had really anticipated. By the time I had to compete, throwing the discus had become a duty rather than an expression of artistic perfection, and I performed poorly. Yet my participation in the '72 Games equaled, if not surpassed, the thrill that I experienced in Melbourne. In Munich, I was elected by individual U.S. teams to be the flagbearer for the American delegation. This meant that I led our team into the stadium as America's chosen representative among the athletes and nations of the world. To be appointed to such an honor would have been breathtaking, but to be elected by one's peers doubled the honor, and I was overwhelmed. In 1960, I had become a naturalized American citizen, and then 12 years later to have my citizenship so gloriously confirmed was for me the very essence of the Olympic dream.

PETER RADEMACHER

Gold Medal, Boxing, Heavyweight, 1956

Many Olympic boxers have gone on to successful professional careers, but only Pete Rademacher started at the top. His first professional fight was against Floyd Patterson for the heavyweight championship of the world. Rademacher planned his "dream bout" even before he fought for the Olympic title.

Rademacher was a born promoter. Warm, intelligent, and an extrovert, he pretty much coached himself to his Olympic victory. And during his professional career he often served as his own matchmaker, publicist, and financier.

He is currently President of Kiefer McNeil, a manufacturer of pool chemicals and swimming equipment. He also gives sales seminars, does public service speaking, and referees pro and amateur boxing matches in the Cleveland area.

Photo by Fogarty and Carlson

Pete Rademacher in 1986.

I grew up on a 30-acre apple farm in the Upper Yakima Valley, but when I was 16 my father sent my brother and me to Castle Heights Military Academy in Lebanon, Tennessee. He was a great follower of Bernarr MacFadden, and the MacFadden Foundation ran the school. Because my father was a frustrated general and because he was a great athlete himself, he wanted us to have four things: good health, good exercise, military science, and a good education. We hated the school at first, but it was a great experience. Before we went, we had never been out of our backyard. We got on that train in Yakima and got off four days later in Nashville, totally lost, befuddled, and scared to death. But the school officials took care of us, put us right into their regimentation program, and within six weeks we were adjusted and loved the place.

The first year there I made the boxing team, but I got rheumatic fever in January and spent four months in the hospital. When I returned to school, I was not allowed to do anything—no drill or exercise, just go to class. I did learn to play the trombone, and I marched in the school band. By spring, an examination showed no heart damage, and they let me play baseball. I went back the next fall and played football and baseball, and I boxed. I won three letters and the outstanding athlete award.

I graduated in 1948 and was supposed to start classes at Yakima Junior College, but I really didn't want to go to school anymore. I figured I was educated enough and knew everything there was to know. But, thank God, my father forced me to go on. He told me either to show him my registration receipt for classes or get the hell out of his house. I can really appreciate that today!

After two years in junior college, where I played football, baseball, and basketball and boxed, I begged Forrest Evashevski for a chance to play football for him at Washington State. He did our sports banquet, and I told him what a great player I was, but I didn't even get a nod. He was the coldest personality I ever met. Everybody was scared to death of him. I went to Washington State anyway, and he let me try out. One practice I was competing against his two biggest tackles, Randy James and Gordy Larson. Larson was six-foot-eight and weighed 245, and James was something like six-foot-three and weighed 285. I weighed about 200, but I was quicker, and I made them look like a couple of saps. I went over them, through them, and under them, and for the next two years I was Evashevski's first-string guard.

I couldn't box for Washington State because I had already boxed in the Golden Gloves, and the West Coast Athletic Conference had a rule against that, but I wore the school colors and unofficially represented the school all through my Golden Glove boxing.

I won eight Golden Glove tournaments in the Washington area, and then, in 1953, I won the national AAU championship in Boston. I mostly coached myself, but I did have some help from Jack Hurley and George Chemeres, who had trained several good professionals. I met them in 1950 when I was in Tacoma for a Golden Gloves tournament. I was sitting alone eating dinner about eight o'clock, and I was supposed to fight about nine. Of course, I didn't know anything about training or proper diet. The guy next to me looked kind of familiar, and I asked him if he knew anything about boxing. He said, "Yes, I work with some of the pros." This was George Chemeres, so I asked him if he would give me a few pointers. He asked if I knew anything about boxing, and I told him, "Yea, you stick your left hand out a couple of times, and then you whack them with the right, and they fall down."

He taught me several things in just a few minutes. First he told me that it was kind of silly to eat when I was going to fight in an hour. I told him that nobody hits me in the belly. But more importantly, he taught me a stance, how to feint, how to move my feet, and how to jab. I learned to move my feet to maintain a 45-degree angle to my opponent, no matter where I was in the ring, and how to pivot on my left heel and right toe when I turned to the left. When you do that, your head moves three or four inches. He told me not to try to tear the guy's head off when I jabbed but to move that shortest distance between two points, which, of course, is a straight line.

He taught me to fight with my feet and my head. "Once I teach you these things," he said, "all you have to do is feint, step over, and the guy will jab where you were, and you counterjab over his hand or feint another little bit and draw the right hand and pull back; he'll miss, and you'll be set to turn and throw your right hand as a counter before he recovers." I went in the ring that night and knocked out three guys in a total of about three minutes and won the Golden Boy award as the best fighter in the tournament.

George Chemeres is a fantastic trainer, and he had learned from Jack Hurley, the old "Deacon of Swat." Jack also used to take me in the back room of the Cherry Street Gym. We'd put the gloves on but never lace them up. He'd position my feet and body. I would jab into his open hand, and he would jab into mine. On the third count he would make me execute one of the basic moves of boxing. So it would be bang, bang, and then do the move. He'd put me in front of a mirror and make me execute those things, and then I would do it on the bag until everything became instinctive. My hands were always low because he wanted me to look as if I were vulnerable. "I want you to beg for disaster with your chin and body," he'd tell me. "The whole theory of this game is to follow these rules and mechanics, and it's impossible to get hit."

So you walk right up to where the danger is, beg for disaster, move your feet when you've made him come after you. For a guy to hit you he has to change the position and weight on his legs. You'll sense that. You'll sense movement in the shoulders and in the hands. Don't look at his eyes. That's the worst thing you can do. You make these feinting moves and build up your opponent's confidence until he's really punching hard. You let him hit your hand or touch your forehead once in a while. He's fat and happy because he's hitting something. Soon he'll begin punching harder and harder. Then you make the second move and knock him on his ass. And it always worked.

I became so confident that I would go to Seattle from Pullman, get an hour lesson from George, go visit my future wife, Margaret Sutton, who was then a student at the University of Washington, and go back to college, argue with the boxing coach, Ike Dieter, about my style, and then work over his fighters, one after the other.

That shifty style, with my hands down in front of me, was a bit like the style of Jersey Joe Walcott. Archie Moore also did some of these things very well. The net result was that boxing was fun, and I never hated working out.

In 1953 I graduated in animal husbandry, won the national AAU heavyweight title, and married Margaret with the promise that I would never again go back into the ring. She liked boxing, but she was afraid that I was going to get hurt. I went into the army the following year with a second lieutenant's commission and was sent to Fort Benning, Georgia, where I was put in charge of the boxing program. I also began training again in secret, but one night at the Officers' Club, someone said to Margaret in a loud voice, "Isn't it wonderful that Peter is going to the Olympics?"

Well, it really hit the fan! It took about three days for things to quiet down. But I finally convinced her that I could do it, and then I really started to train in earnest. I didn't fight until 1956, when I took my Fort Benning team down to Coral Gables for a Golden Gloves tournament. I entered as a heavyweight and won my first bout handily. I won the first two rounds of my second bout, but in the third round I got hit on the button. I went down to my knees, got up, but lost a split decision.

I went home to a whole barrage of everything. My wife called me an old man and told me that I had no business fighting anymore because it was a kid's game. But I survived my battle on the home front. My next bout was in the Montgomery Golden Gloves. Alabama was segregated in those days. They had a white tournament and a black tournament. All my fighters but two were black, so we had to split up our team. The bouts were all held in the same arena, but the seating was also segregated.

I think all of my guys won. The black guys automatically advanced to Chicago. The white guys had to go to the southern tournament in Nashville. I had taken my team there the year before, and at the time I had told Ray Johnson, the sports editor of the *Tennessean*, that I was going to come up there the next year and bounce his humpty-dumpties around. He laughed and told me that at 26 I wouldn't be able to do that. But I did. I think I flattened three guys, each in the first round. I just had a heyday. It was one of those beautiful things; I would make those moves and they just didn't understand what I was doing.

We went from there to Chicago. That had to be in March of 1956. Again I had three bouts and knocked everybody out, including Billy Ray Smith, who was to become an all-pro tackle for the Baltimore Colts.

Those were the quarterfinals. In two weeks we went back for the semis. There were 380 fighters in that tournament. The second guy I fought was a black guy from Alabama named Soloman McTear. I'm doing a job on him, but in the third round I get hit on the chin and go down to one knee just as I had at Coral Gables, and I lose another split decision. So I went home to another battle, and this one was really a beaut! Margaret was just furious. But I knew that the Olympics in the fall was my final chance, and I finally convinced her and the rest of my family that I could still do it.

This meant I had to earn the chance through the Armed Forces tournaments. The toughest fight I ever had in my whole life was beating the only other heavyweight at Fort Benning. He was inept, inexperienced, and couldn't punch; yet, on the way to fight this guy, I got sick to my stomach and threw up. I went on to flatten him in one round, so it was just the nervousness and stress I had put on myself to get by this first elimination bout.

I went on to the Third Army and then the All-Army Tournament. At the All-Army I won my first two bouts easily, and then in the third one I was fighting a guy named Johnny Johnson who was the reigning army champion. This guy was built like an Adonis. He had a huge neck and shoulders, with a waist of maybe 28 inches and a 52-inch chest. He was a hulk of a man. One of my good lieutenant friends was in his corner, and he later told me that he had told Johnson that the only way he could possibly beat me was to "go out there and hit Rademacher right in the balls." He did, and he knocked me unconscious. As I was coming to, I was on a stretcher, heading for the hospital, and the referee was holding up my hand.

After that, I was the All-Army champion. I next won the inter-service title, and then it was on to the Olympic trials at the Cow Palace in San Francisco.

In one of the preliminary tournaments I had torn some muscles, and I couldn't straighten out my right arm. At the trials I could get my arm only partway down. I had four guys to beat, including Johnny Johnson, who had flattened me with the low shot. He had qualified through a Golden Gloves tournament. I had to do it all with my left hand, but I did it and then ended up again in the hospital the next day. They packed the arm in ice for six days while periodically putting heat on it. On the 12th day they let me out, but one of the coaches, Dubby Holt, said to take someone else to the Olympics. Don Miller, who was the other boxing coach and a major in the army, insisted that I had earned my place, and he prevailed.

In Melbourne, we had about three days to get acclimated before we started our bouts. My first opponent was a Czechoslovakian who was a big, good-looking orthodox fighter, but he made mistakes. He turned his body, and I hit him in the kidney. The referee started to warn me, but the Czech got up. I feinted, and he turned his back again. I hit him, and down he went. The referee counted him out, but again he started to foul me out. It was just so fast and slick that he couldn't get out of the way of the punch.

Then I met a South African who was a southpaw. I didn't know he was a left-hander until he walked out there and turned sideways to me. I just automatically clicked into gear for a southpaw, and everything went perfectly except that I forgot to step over. I awakened at the count of six. I was flush on my puss with my hands lying there beside my hips, so I had gone down face first, and I couldn't move a thing. I was absolutely numb. My brother had flown to Australia to see the Games, and he ran up to ringside and yelled, "You can't win a gold medal lying on your belly!" That kind of jarred me out of it, and I just beat the count. The guy came in to finish me off. I was a bit befuddled, but instinct took over. I went right back into my plan, but this time I executed. I feinted, stepped twice, hit him with my right hand, and down he went—all this in about the first 40 seconds. I had him down again in the first round, twice in the second, and knocked him out in the third. That put me in the finals against the Russian, Lev Moukhine. He was supposed to be very good. He had gone through a seven-foot, 300-pound Bulgarian and a Swede, who after two rounds just walked out of the ring and kept right on going. Then he fought an Italian, whom he hit with about eight perfect low blows. I mean, that Italian had bruises on his thighs. That put the two of us in the ring together.

I wasn't given much of a chance, but Moukhine did everything just like every other guy I had ever met. I just walked up to him, made the feint, and stepped over; he jabbed, and I knocked him down in the first 20 seconds. He went down again in another minute and a half. He was just hanging on the ropes. I got to hit him again with a left hook before the referee stopped the fight. When this guy went down the first time, some of the Russian fans started to leave. After the second time, they just stampeded out of the auditorium. After the final blow, the Hungarian boxing team rushed into the ring and hoisted me onto their shoulders. That was right after the Russians had put down their revolution, and they seized this opportunity to express their feelings.

It was very emotional. I bawled for about 30 minutes, what with the medal and the national anthem and everything. I was just sitting in the dressing room afterward, and I couldn't stop crying. Even today I still get emotional when I think about those moments. They just tear me up. It was just the greatest experience a youngster could have. I had the chance to buy somebody like Olga

Pete Rademacher defeating Lev Mouhkine of the U.S.S.R. for the gold medal in 1956.

Photo courtesy of Pete Rademacher

Fikotova a milk shake, and I met the Russian coach. Both he and Moukhine hugged me. There was no animosity, just friendship and good feelings.

The night I won the gold medal I told George Meyers of the *Seattle Times* that my next bout would be against Floyd Patterson for the heavyweight championship. Meyers thought I had been hit too hard, but I told him I had been thinking about this ever since the trials. I knew that if I could win the gold medal over a Russian, and if Patterson, who was also a former Olympic champion, could beat Archie Moore for the title, we would have a dream bout. I wanted to do something no one had ever done before, something that in all likelihood would never be repeated. I just knew that such a bout would capture everyone's imagination.

I went home to Yakima and enjoyed a full-blown parade and all the excitement and parties and speaking engagements that went with it. I told the local recruiting officer to call Fort Benning and ask if I could get an extra month's leave. I told him I would make two recruiting presentations each day in all the schools of the Yakima Valley. All he had to do was book me. I'd wear my lieutenant's uniform, talk about the value of education and the Olympic Games, and let the uniform speak for itself. The army agreed, and, as it turned out, those initial speaking engagements probably gave me more confidence and help with what I do today than anything I've ever done. During that time, I also told my mother that my next fight would be against Floyd Patterson for the heavyweight title. She gave me the oddest look and said, "Peter, please, why don't you hang them up? I think you've had too much now." I told her, "No, Mom, everything is fine. I'm totally rational. I can still add two and two. I love Margaret, and I love you, and I'm not hurt. I feel good about this, and I'm going to do it if I can pull it off."

I went to New York and met with Cus D'Amato, Patterson's manager, who thought it was a hell of an idea. He looked me in the eye and told me that anybody who could knock out three guys in the Olympics has got to be a threat to anybody in the heavyweight class. He then asked if I had any money. I told him that my backers and I had $150,000. Cus said, "We're going to be ridiculed off the face of the earth, but if you get me $250,000 up front, I'll get you a contract." He later insisted that we put another $50,000 in escrow to guarantee a return match if, as he put it, "the big guy hits Floyd one and knocks him out." He wasn't too sure how good Floyd's chin was.

I went into that fight against Patterson without a sign of a butterfly. The whole thing was to pull it off and become the only guy in history who had ever done it. The fight itself was almost anticlimactic. Just to be in the ring with the heavyweight champion was what I was after, and if I got lucky and knocked him out, so much the better.

In the dressing room before the fight, George Chemeres told me, "Pete, you may not realize it, but you can't go more than six rounds. So let's plan to flatten him in six rounds or suffer the consequences. If it gets too tough in there, I'll watch out for you because I don't want you to get hurt." I walked out there for that first round fully expecting to dump him. I handled him easily in the first round, knocked him down in the second but couldn't finish him, hurt him in the third, started to go down myself in the fourth, got up and beat him in that round, then went down four times in the fifth and twice in the sixth. The fight ended at the end of the sixth with me sitting on my butt with my hands on my knees taking the count. I wasn't hurt. I didn't have a mark on me other than a few blisters on my fanny.

I still look at that fight film and think, My God, if I had had another month to train and had had maybe four or five 10-round experiences during my training, I might not have gotten so dog-gone tired and lost my cool. Mechanically I did things to Floyd that befuddled him and put him into all kinds of traps. I felt absolutely comfortable working with the guy. We figured that he'd jump at me, I'd feint, step back, and knock him dead. But he'd come at me so fast that I'd get hit before I could move.

I ended up winning 17 of my pro fights while losing 6 and drawing 1. As a pro, I learned that competing is only part of the battle. You have to sell yourself. I think back fondly on my third pro fight against Tommy Thompson. I promoted and financed it myself in Columbus, Georgia. I was the self-appointed boxing commissioner. I was the matchmaker. I even set the ring up, including the chairs. I did the publicity and sold the tickets that night at the gate. I introduced the prelim fighters, went back and got dressed, flattened Tommy in the fifth round, showered, paid off the guys, and cleaned up the joint.

Once I even interviewed myself. I was supposed to be on a radio show, but the interviewer didn't show up. So I interviewed myself for about 30 minutes. I even played my manager as well. It was a good show.

My last bout was in Hawaii, where I knocked Bobo Olson all over the ring and then announced my retirement. There I was, 33 years old. I was not the heavyweight champion of the world, nor was I a multimillionaire; but I had all my faculties, and I still had a lot of zip and desire to do something. I just didn't know what, except that I didn't want to go back to farming.

We moved to Medina, Ohio, where I sold real estate for a couple of years while at the same time I helped develop a system called *instinct shooting*, which is a hand-to-eye coordination system for learning to shoot a shotgun with both eyes open. I also developed some products to go along with this instinct shooting. I sold them to the McNeil Corporation and then started working in sales for them. That was 21 years ago. I am now President of the Kiefer McNeil Division, where my job is to manage people, assist in seminars, and develop products. I still do a little refereeing, and I play lots of golf.

So my life in boxing and out has been one of some successes. I learned years ago how to lose gracefully and to use that moment for analyzing my game plan and to move forward again. I'm an up guy; I'm enthusiastic. I think there's nothing in this whole world that you can't get over, around, underneath, or through. Life is my playground, and I've played a pretty good game on it.

10
ROME, 1960

There was something magnificently fitting about the setting of the Olympic Games in Rome. With the Italian flair for the beautiful and the dramatic, the Italian Organizing Committee not only designed the sites of the various Olympic competitions to take full advantage of Rome's splendid ancient ruins; it also redesigned some of Rome itself in the process. Architect Pier Nervi skillfully designed modern, futuristic sports arenas to blend perfectly with their ancient surroundings, and the competitions were held in both new and old sites. Boxing, weightlifting, and some basketball games were held in Nervi's Palazzo della Sport and the smaller Palazetto, while wrestling was presented among the ruins of the Basilica of Maxentius. The Villaggio Olimpico, a series of three-storied buildings, provided housing for the 6,000 athletes, and after the Games ended it became a low-cost housing project for government workers. In order to make Rome ready for the thousands of people expected to attend the Games and to make the sites accessible, the Organizing Committee initiated the construction of a new water supply system, new superhighways around the city and roads through it, and new parks and shopping centers.

The 1960 Games had the further advantage of being held at a

time of relative political stability throughout the world, and international goodwill was at an all-time peak in Rome. Even the Russian and American athletes got along well together, partly because they had gotten to know each other better during the previous two years when each country's national track and field teams competed in meets on the other's soil.

Before leaving for Rome, the U.S. Olympic track and field athletes were heralded as being the best American Olympic team in history. But in Rome the Americans lost 8 of the first 11 events they competed in, including the 100- and 200-meter dashes. Twenty-eight-year-old Otis Davis won the 400-meter run and set a new world and Olympic record of 44.9. Later, along with Jack Yerman, Earl Young, and Glenn Davis, he anchored the team that won the gold medal in the 4x100 relay. The Americans did make a sweep of the hurdling events, and Glenn Davis and Lee Calhoun won their second consecutive pair of Olympic gold medals in those competitions. Discus thrower Al Oerter successfully defended his 1956 Olympic title, and Don Bragg, who dreamed of playing Tarzan in the movies, thumped his chest and gave the Tarzan yell when he cleared 15 feet, 5⅛ inches in the pole vault.

For the sixth consecutive Olympic Games the decathlon championship was won by an American, this time by UCLA's Rafer Johnson, who had finished second in 1956. Going into the final event, the 1,500 meters, Johnson led his UCLA teammate and Taiwanese native C. K. Yang by 67 points. The metric mile was one of Johnson's weakest events, and to win the gold medal he had to finish within ten seconds of Yang. He ran a personal best of 4:49.7 and finished just over a second behind Yang, who became the first athlete from Taiwan to win an Olympic medal. Johnson later became an actor and television sports commentator. He was also a great admirer of Robert Kennedy and was standing next to him when the senator was assassinated.

Perhaps the best American track performance at Rome was turned in by Wilma Rudolph, who prevented a shutout of the U.S. in the women's events. Rudolph won the women's 100- and 200-meter dashes and anchored the 4x100-meter relay team, which consisted entirely of her Tigerbelle classmates from Tennessee State University.

Winning the light-heavyweight boxing title was a young athlete from Louisville whose lips seemed to move as fast as his fists. His name was Cassius Clay. The U.S. won three of the eight divisions in freestyle wrestling, although none of the American winners—

Terry McCann, Doug Blubaugh, and Shelby Wilson—had won his division in the Olympic trials.

In the swimming and diving competitions, the Americans made some gains on the Australians, who had dominated the pool in Melbourne. Jeff Farrell, who qualified in the Olympic trials eight days after having an emergency appendectomy, anchored both the 2x200-meter freestyle relay team and the 4x100-meter medley team, earning a gold medal for each. Bill Mulliken, who vowed he would win a gold medal in Rome after being inspired by a motivational talk given by Olympic pole-vaulting gold medalist Reverend Bob Richards, did just that by taking the 200-meter breaststroke title in an upset.

DONALD GEORGE BRAGG

Gold Medal, Pole Vault, 1960

No one ever vaulted higher with a metal pole or was more colorful than Don "Tarzan" Bragg, who on the victory stand in Rome gave his famous Tarzan yell.

Bragg entertained no inflated childhood notions of becoming an Olympic champion, but he did want to be Lord of the Jungle; in fact, he still does.

To his critics, he was loud, boisterous, and unpredictable, a show-off who just never grew up. Time has little changed him, but underneath the bravado and horseplay lies a serious man who has published a book of poetry and who is now at work on what promises to be a very unusual autobiography.

I was always very perceptive and quick to pick things up that related to the human condition. I was also very sensitive. I used to cry in high school if someone screamed at me. I'd just go to the bathroom and cry. After a while I realized that I had to overcome this. Something Tennessee Williams said changed me. He maintained that you could not be a happy individual without developing the faculty for insensitivity. I thought, Man, that's it. But I added, "Don't destroy that which makes you sensitive—just control and protect it." A lot of people try to destroy the feelings that bring them pain. Mine stay alive, but I control them.

I started regressive hypnosis because I had certain feelings. For

Don and Theresa Bragg, 1986. Photo courtesy of Don Bragg

instance, when we entered Rome for the Olympics, I said, "Hey, I win here." Someone asked, "What do you mean, you win here?" I told him, "Man, I was here before." I didn't know whether I had been there as a gladiator or what the hell it was, but I just knew I had been there. Everyone laughed at me, but it turned out all right when I won the gold medal.

A hypnotist once told me that he thought I put myself into a state of hypnosis when I competed. I could put myself to sleep in Madison Square Garden in front of 15,000 screaming people, and someone would have to call me, "Hey, Don, wake up. Next jump."

I don't know whether it was posthypnotic suggestion or what, but I once went to the library to look up the Scottish Battle of Culloden. I went home that night and put myself under. My wife was there with the tape recorder. For 15 minutes I lay on the bed, my body arched with only the back of my head and my heels touching, shooting stuff out of my nose, and sweat pouring off me. My wife was scared, but I told her, "It's OK. I control this." I talked of my mother's name being really McKay instead of McCoy, and I described various things about the Battle of Culloden that I had never read in any book.

About a month later I started writing poetry. I ended up writing

300 or 400 poems, which I then published myself. I'm not wise in the ways of the literary world. I just did my own thing, capturing some of the thoughts that I had. I wrote a lot of poems in bars on napkins while watching people. I don't like poetry that is just about love and nature. Mine is basically philosophical, although I try to weave in a love of mankind. Here's one of my poems. I call it "Identity."

Am I different? Possibly so
But only by searching do I ever know
The pain and the suffering of that pursuit
Emanate from the basic root
Of all mankind and his consuming goal
To keep immortal his fragile soul.

Poetry was one of the first things in my life that was a passive type of activity for me. But when I had my financial problems, I decided that I wouldn't write again until I cleared up my financial mess. Now, things are going better for me, so I'm considering doing a book about my life. I've toyed with the idea for 15 years.

I'm still a little bit crazy. In 1984, we went on a cruise ship with several other former Olympic athletes: Sam Jones, Wyomia Tyus, Jim Ryun, Don Quarrie from Jamaica, and others. As soon as I got on the ship I told my wife, "Hey, honey, I'm going to dive off the top." She said, "What? We're guests of this company, and you're going to ruin everything." I told her, "OK, but. . . ."

I used to see all those pearl divers going off the top of cliffs or from the masts of ships, so I just had this feeling that I had to dive off that ship. For a couple of days everything was all right. I became good friends with Wyomia Tyus's husband, Dwayne. He was a good guy, and we would drink together after everybody else had faded out. When we pulled into the port of Jamaica, we were warned that there could be trouble in certain bars and, specifically, not to go into Jerky's Place or Big Daddy's Lounge. So naturally that's where the two of us had to go.

We're sitting in Big Daddy's with Rastafarians all around, and in my best Jamaican accent, which I had picked up while making a Tarzan movie there, I asked them, "Hey, mon, how ya doin? What's hoppenin'?" They asked me where I was from, and I told them, "Mon, I'm from Kingston town." They answered, "Ya, we thought you Jamaican, mon." When I later told them that I was actually an American, they told me, "Mon, you can be white-skinned, but your heart is surely as black as ours." They then made a motion toward Dwayne. They thought he was a black Jamaican who had just brought me there. When they asked him, he said, "Say, what? Nah, man, I'm from L.A."

After a few hours of serious activity, we took off for the boat. There was a dock there that was about 10 feet high but with no ladder. There were a group of Jamaicans standing around, so I asked them, "Hey, I'm going to dive off this ship, and I want to know if you will pull me out of this ocean because there is no ladder for me to get out on." They looked at me and said, "Hey, mon, no problem, because you are not going to dive from this ship. Look at how high it is."

When I got on the ship, Dwayne looked at me and said, "Sure, you're going to dive off this ship. Sure." So I took off my sneaks and handed them to him. He just said, "Um-hum. You're not going off that rail." I gave him my T-shirt, and he looked around to see who was watching. By that time I had climbed up on the rail and taken off. He said that I looked like a big white whale sailing through the air.

Later, the ship's bartender told me about this lady who was sitting on the deck reading a book. He yelled at her, "Hey, this guy is going to dive off the side of the ship." She just said, "Uh-huh." So he told her, "Look, he's getting ready to jump." Again she said, "Uh-huh." Then she closed her book and added, "It's probably just my husband. When he gets up, tell him I left." The bartender told me he figured that I must do that kind of stuff all the time.

I'm from the town of Penns Grove in south Jersey. As a youngster I went to a lot of Tarzan movies, and I was always trying to emulate him, swinging through the trees on ropes and diving into gravel pits. I always had a lot of black friends, and they could always outrun and outjump us white kids. We couldn't beat them at too many things, but one day we went down to Weinberg's furniture store and picked up these bamboo poles that they wrapped carpeting around. Then we tried to jump across this ditch. I did it, but the others couldn't. So I said, "Let's jump over the clothesline." They told me I was crazy, but I jumped over it. One other guy tried and almost castrated himself. From that point on I realized that here was something I could do that they couldn't.

I was always going to the woods, where I had a hideaway called Tarzanville. People would ask, "Is Don at home?" My mom would say, "No, he's out in the woods." I'd be out there, swinging through the trees and trying to vault over poles that I'd place between the branches.

In eighth grade I passed the track one day where some athletes were pole-vaulting. I told them, "Hey, that looks like what I do in Tarzanville." Somebody said, "Oh, yeah? Let's see you try it." So I ran down the runway, went up about 11 feet, and fell straight backward onto my back. A pole-vaulter named Bill Cochren was watching. He took me aside and said, "Hey, listen. You're holding the pole for 11 feet. Hold it down here for 8 feet, which is where the crossbar is; take a little longer run, and maybe you can make it." If he hadn't done this, I might never have become a pole-vaulter.

When I was a sophomore at Penn Grove High, my father took me to the *Philadelphia Inquirer* Charities Meet. I met Bob Richards and told him that I wanted to pole-vault. I remember Bob said, "If you want to do it, son, you can." I think he definitely influenced me. Little did he know that I would be competing against him the week after I graduated from high school. It was the national outdoor championship, and everybody was there. Richards won it, but I came in third with a vault of 13 feet, 9½ inches.

Jumbo Elliot sold me a bill of goods to come to Villanova. I was all set to go to Penn State when Jumbo came to the house and told my father, "You know, we have an indoor board track where he can train even during the winter." When I came home, my dad told me what Jumbo had said, so I told him, "Okay, let's go to Villanova."

Charley Jenkins, who was to win the 400 meters at Melbourne in 1956, and I were freshmen together at Villanova. We went down to the field house, and I said to Jake Nevins, the famous Villanova trainer who just passed away, "Hey, buddy, where's the indoor board track?" He said, "It's outside on the football field. Now don't bother me." I told him, "No, the new indoor board track that Jumbo told my father about." He said, "Look, kid, you're new here. The indoor track is outside on the football field. Now get out of here." We went outside, and there it was.

Jumbo used to make me run around that track. I weighed 200 pounds, and when I ran it was thump, thump, thump, so Jumbo started calling me "Horse." He was a great coach. We know that, but he was also much more than just a coach. He wanted you to maintain a certain behavior. Once, we were going down to Baltimore, and I'm on a train for the first time in my life. We were eating in the dining car, and I'm cutting my meat into little pieces.

He looked over at me and shook his head. When you were doing something he didn't like, he'd just make this no-no movement with his head. So I asked the other guys what I had done and went back to cutting my meat. Jumbo looked over and again made that funny movement with his head, so I went over to him and asked, "Jumbo, what have I done?" He told me, "You only cut one piece of meat at a time."

To some extent, I didn't like Jumbo. I did a lot of crazy things at Villanova, like diving out of the rafters into the swimming pool. When Jumbo felt my ego was getting too big, he would bang down on me. He would grab me by the cheeks and say in that pompous way of his, "Look me in the face when I'm talking to you." I'd tell him, "Hey, Jumbo, if I look at your face, I'll laugh." He'd smack me in the mouth. He was tough.

He didn't know that much about pole-vaulting, but he did improve my speed, which was tremendously important. He used to let me run in some of the meets. Without knowing how to start, I once ran a 9.8 100 on a cinder track. Jumbo would sit up in the stands with the other coaches, laughing and saying, "Look at that big son-of-a-bitch. No start. Look at him come. If I could train him, he could run the 220."

I loved football better than pole vaulting. I loved to catch the ball, and I could have had a football scholarship to West Virginia as an end. When I got to Villanova, I asked Jumbo if I could go out for the team. He said, "Horse, are you here on a track or a football scholarship?" I said, "Track." He said, "That's what you're running, and that's all you're running." So I used to sneak out and play semipro in South Jersey under the name of Joe Dominick. One game I scored three touchdowns and was written up in the papers. Everyone wanted to know who Joe Dominick was. A couple of days later I go down to the track, and Jumbo says, "Come here." He grabbed my cheeks and says, "Who's this guy Joe Dominick? I'm hearing stories. You tell Joe Dominick that if I catch his ass playing any more football, he can pack up and hit the pike." Then he added, "Why didn't you ask me if you wanted to play football?" I told him that I had, and he said, "That's right, and you're not playing."

When I graduated from Villanova, I didn't like Jumbo, but after a couple of years I thought, Hey, he wasn't so bad. About five years out of school, I thought, Humm, he was all right. Then after another five years, I admitted to myself that the dude was a genius. He knew how to handle men, even those of us who were unusual.

We didn't receive too many special privileges at Villanova. In fact, my freshman year I flunked economics. I figured that Jumbo was going to help me—you know, talk to the professor or something like that. But it was just the opposite. He came to me and said, "If you need a tutor, fine. I have some professors who will teach you. But you better pass those courses. If not, pack your bags and hit the pike."

I'll never forget how I missed making the 1956 Olympic team. I had ripped a leg muscle and had my leg shot full of novocaine—six shots. I cleared the qualifying height, and as my pole was coming down an attendant grabbed it and knocked the bar off. Jumbo came flying out of the stands and went a little crazy. I went into the infield and started crying. We looked at the film, and it showed that I had cleared the bar and that the attendant in grabbing the pole had knocked off the bar. But the officials just said, "Sorry." Some of those officials were from the University of Southern California and had two or three of their boys in the competition. But I remember Jumbo defending me, and I was really proud of him for doing that.

I don't think there were any other pole-vaulters who had my physique. I was a freak. There were others who were as tall as my six-foot-three, but no one had my upper body strength. For seven years, I ate only one meal a day because when I exceeded 200 pounds the poles would just break. I had to live on 1,200 calories a day—lots of salad and steak. Finally, they made a pole that would hold me, but it was so stiff that it would tear my shoulder out every time I used it. About 1959, I received a new pole that I could use without hurting my shoulder, and with it I broke the indoor record that year and the outdoor in 1960.

I think psyching is a bunch of shit. I think everyone magnifies how well it is supposed to work. If you don't beat a guy's butt, you're not going to psych him out. But if you beat him 7 out of 10 times in meets, he's got a psych on himself. I did do something once against Bob Gutowski at a national indoor championship in Madison Square Garden. We were always jumping against each other. We each made 15 feet, 1 inch and then failed at 15 feet, 3 inches, so they lowered the bar back to 15 feet, 1 inch. We each made it, and they raised it back up, and we missed again. It went back and forth this way for about an hour. We were getting exhausted. It's about midnight. I cleared 15 feet, 1 inch again, went back, put my pole in its case, taped it up, took off my spikes, and started walking out of the Garden. Everybody said, "Hey, Don, where are you going? Gutowski's got another jump." I told them, "It's all over. He's too tired. He's exhausted. He's just flown in from California, and he can't last this long. The meet's over. I've won it." I grabbed my pole and walked out. Gutowski was looking around, trying to figure it all out. As soon as I got outside the exit, I peeked around the corner and saw him hit the crossbar going up. Then I came running back in.

The Californians would always try to psych me out at their home meets. They'd put a comic book cover on my locker with Tarzan and a chimpanzee on it. The chimp would be saying, "Me Bragg, you Tarzan." They didn't know that they were creating a monster.

Rome was purgatory for me. Some guys were happy just to be there, but I was there to win the Olympics. A lot of guys took their wives. My girlfriend wanted me to take her, but I told her that I wasn't going there to party or to worry about her. Most of the guys who took their wives or girlfriends did not come up to par. You have to have complete concentration. I was also worried because I had hurt a leg muscle about two or three weeks before. Our officials wanted to pick up some expense money, so they made several of us compete in a meet in Berne, Switzerland, just five or so days before the Olympics. I told them I couldn't jump, but I had to go along anyway. After the meet, they put us on a train for 10 hours without food, water, or air conditioning. When we arrived in Rome, at least one-third of the team was dehydrated and sick. Those officials hurt a lot of us because of that trip.

I really felt the pressure in Rome. I remember missing one jump at 14 feet, 4 inches or whatever, and the crowd stood up and booed. I asked the guy next to me, "Who are they booing?" He told me, "They're booing you." It was like, "Don Bragg, you no miss. You champion."

A day or so before the finals we were practicing, and East Germany's Manfred Preussger went down the runway and with one hand vaulted over 12 feet. Eeles Landstrom from Finland came running over and screamed, "Don, you see dat? Mit one hand, he yump ofer 12 feet. Wat you dink?" I told him, "He's probably the greatest one-armed pole-vaulter I've ever seen, but this sport requires two arms, and I'm the world's best two-armed pole-vaulter." In the finals, Preussger couldn't adjust to the wind

Don Bragg in 1960. Photo courtesy of *Track and Field News*

and failed to make 14 feet, 6 inches and didn't finish among the top eight.

Ronnie Morris and I were the only ones to clear 15 feet, 1 inch in the finals. So I'm thinking, Ronnie is a little technician who can sneak out an inch at a time, but if we jump the crossbar up 4 or 5 inches, he'll be vulnerable. I helped him out of the pit after he cleared 15 feet, 1 inch and said to him, "Hey, Ronnie, great, we just beat the Russians and the Germans and everyone. Let's go for my world record—let's go for 15 feet, 10½ inches." He said, "15 feet, 10 inches? I don't know. How far did I clear that last one?" I told him, "Man, Ronnie, that was the greatest jump I've ever seen you make. You cleared it by a foot. Let's go for 16."

I finally got him to raise the bar to 15 feet, 5 inches. At the end of the runway, I said to myself, Your leg is bothering you, but what in the hell are you saving it for? This is it! Go get the son-of-a-bitch. Never mind settling for second or for a tie for first. Take it. It's there. Now, I don't want to call anyone dumb, but we had T-shirts that were made of wool, and the numbers were like a foot big. When you were sweaty, these numbers would hang down when you jumped. So I cleared 15 feet, 5 inches by a good 5 inches, but coming down my baggy shirt touched the crossbar. It stayed on, but I thought, I could have missed this jump and the gold medal because of this damn shirt. John Thomas had the same problem when he was high-jumping. How stupid can you get, just because the shirts were donated by some sporting goods company or other?

Anyway, I made 15 feet, 5 inches, and Ronnie says quietly, "Good jump, Don." He gets ready to jump, and I say, "Come on, Ronnie, we just beat the Russians and everyone. This is the Olympics, man. We missed in '56, but now we're taking 'em all. Come on. You can make it. Make sure your standards are right. Watch the wind. It's changing a bit. Make sure you have it right. Come on, Ronnie, you can do it." He started to get ready, and I yelled, "After this we're going to 16. Come on. You can make it—I think."

Ronnie gave it a very nice try. His second attempt wasn't too good, and on his third he went under the bar. But the only reason that my psyching worked is because I had already beaten him 7 out of 10 times.

I told the officials to shove the bar up to the world's record of 15 feet, 11 inches. I cleared it, but I just grazed the bar with that stupid shirt. Everyone in the stands was yelling because they thought they had seen a new world record, but as I started to get up out of the pit, the crossbar fell off and hit me in the head. Ever since, I've maintained that they screamed it off.

Of course, on the victory stand I let out my Tarzan yell. It echoed through the stands, and everybody went crazy. The pressure was off. The gods had messed with me in 1956 when I didn't make the team, but they did me a favor when they waited until 1961 to bring out the fiberglass pole. It was a better pole by far than the aluminum ones. If that pole had been perfected one year sooner, I would not have been the gold medal winner, and I would not be in this book.

I made a Tarzan film, but it was never released. That's the craziest story of all. I was supposed to be Tarzan. Sy Weintraub had the exclusive rights from the Edgar Rice Burroughs estate to make Tarzan films. When I came back from Rome, he was wrapped up in litigation. He kept saying that he was not free to start filming but that I was his first choice to play Tarzan. Finally,

I became fed up and went into his office and said, "Hey, Sy, are we going to make the film or not?" I was getting tired of hanging around Hollywood. I had passed up a couple of other parts. I would tell them, "I'm not an actor. I'm Tarzan."

So I left Hollywood, returned home, and a couple of days later I stepped on a broken bottle and had to have 19 stitches in my foot. The next day, Sy called to tell me that he had clearance and was ready to shoot *Tarzan Goes to India.* He even told me I didn't have to have the nose job he had insisted I have when he first considered me for the role. I had to tell him that I couldn't because I was on crutches. So he moved Jock Mahoney up to Tarzan.

That was 1961 or '62. About a year or two later a guy called me and said, "Don, my name is Sandy Howard, and I want to screen-test you for Tarzan." I asked, "Is this Sy Weintraub?" He said, "No, this is Sandy Howard. We're going to do the six stories on which the copyrights have expired, and we want to interview you for the role."

I won the role, and we went off to Jamaica to start shooting. It was great. I was doing most of my own stunt work, swinging through the trees and jumping off cliffs into tiny creeks. Hell, even the stuntmen wouldn't do some of that stuff. Then one day these two attorneys came on the set and handed Sandy an injunction to stop filming. They finally impounded the film, which would have been the first Tarzan movie in color. Sandy went broke and disappeared until he popped up with *A Man Called Horse* and several other successful films.

I was afraid to return home. When I left Trenton, everyone had a big party for me because I was going to be a big movie star. I stayed in Jamaica for three or four days, and that's when I started drinking.

I returned home, and the next thing I know is I get a call: "Don, Sy Weintraub. Can you fly in 24 hours to South America?" But just a few days before I had done something to my back. The doctor thought I had a ruptured disk and wanted to operate immediately. I told him to hold off. In the meantime, Sy calls back to tell me that the film was to be called *Tarzan and the Imposter* and that I was to play the imposter. I told him, "Sy, I don't want to do anything like that. I'm Tarzan." He promised that I would get to play Tarzan in the television series, but I had my spine operation instead, and that was that. A cut foot, litigation, and then my aching back destroyed my Tarzan career.

I started a summer camp for boys with some money I borrowed from my mother-in-law. My father-in-law helped with the construction. We almost went under that first year, and everyone said, "Look at him. What a dumb ass. Everything he tries fails." But the second year it caught on. Then everybody called me a genius. We sold the camp about six years ago, and with the money I made I kept buying land and more land. I owned about 700 acres that at the time was valued around $3 million. Then the state environmental commission came in and told me that the land could not be developed. I think they drew their goddamn restrictive lines wherever I owned land. There were a lot of things that could have been done, but they said no to everything. It cost me a million-dollar construction project. I ended up selling the land back to the state for conservation purposes for one-tenth of its original cost.

I went into bankruptcy for three years. I'm just now getting on my feet again. When I lost everything, I was so upset that I was going to call a bunch of reporters and take my gold medal and throw it off the Mullica River Bridge because I didn't want it. I didn't want anything to do with America. I had never been given anything. Nobody gave me my money. And all of a sudden some legislators can sign a few papers, and I'm broke. I really didn't want to be an American. It disturbed the hell out of me. You represent your country, work like a dog, and someone comes in and says, "My, my, look at the tree frogs. Don't mess with the rattlesnakes."

What do I see in the future for me now? I still want to be a fireman or a policeman when I grow up. Who the hell knows what he wants to do? I told my wife when I got to be 44 or 45 that I was going through male menopause. She asked me, "How long is this going to take?" But something has happened to me. I'm getting more mellow. I still have a bit of a temper, and I want to lash out at things, but I don't know whether the energy force has died or what, but it just takes too much energy to start hollering and screaming like I used to do.

I love it when someone asks these kids today, "What's your goal? What do you want to do?" Goddamn! I don't know, and I'm 51. I know I want to have fun. I want to try to eliminate the economic pressures that I have. I want my bread and butter, but I no longer want a Rolls Royce or a big house. We had a big house on a lake with 300 acres, but I had to sell it to settle my bankruptcy. My wife doesn't like it because I don't dress properly, but I enjoy it around here because there are a lot of clammers and pineys. I won't say lower-class people, but they are not running to be great accomplishers. We hang around the bars and bullshit and drink some Captain Morgan's Spicy Rum. Once in a while I'll go to a track meet and greet some of the achievers. But I don't want a steady diet of the big life. I don't need it, and I don't want it.

GLENN DAVIS

Gold Medal, 400-Meter Hurdles, 1956 and 1960
Gold Medal, 4x400-Meter Relay, 1960

Glenn Davis was runner and hurdler nonpareil in the late 1950s. At one time he held five different individual world records. But perhaps his greatest achievement—greater even than his three Olympic gold medals—was leading his Barberton, Ohio, track team to the state high school championship in 1954. What made this victory so remarkable was that he was his team's only member.

Davis played two years of football for the Detroit Lions and was a successful track coach at Cornell University before returning as a teacher to the same Barberton High where a quarter of a century earlier he had begun his journey to athletic immortality.

Both my parents died the same day when I was 15. My father died of cancer at six o'clock in the morning; my mother went into a coma and died at six that evening. She just didn't want to live. I also suffered several other family tragedies. One brother was killed in the military, and another one flipped his race car and was killed. Then a sister died in an automobile accident. It was just one horrible thing after another. I could have ended up a mess. What helped me overcome all of this was my brother Ed. He made me into a competitor. He kept telling me that I had to make something of myself. He had gone on to school, and he wanted me to go. I just kind of listened to him and behaved myself.

I think most white kids today just have it too easy. When I grew up as one of 10 children, I had a rough way to go. We were very, very poor. I also had a little Indian blood in me. Maybe that made

Glenn Davis in 1986. Photo by Fogarty and Carlson

a difference. In any case, I didn't have the so-called white man's disease. I could run, and I could compete. Blacks being the competitors that they are—being hungrier—just have wanted it more than most white kids. And that's the way I was.

I grew up on a farm near Bethany, West Virginia, where I used to spend my days running around, throwing apples at pigs, and playing all sports. In seventh grade we had something called Junior High Field Day, and I won four events, one right after the other. I went 19 feet in the long jump and about 5 feet, 11 inches in the high jump. I won the 50- and 200-yard dashes. It wasn't that I matured so early. It was just kind of a natural thing. The maturing came later.

In the 10th grade, I got a second in the low hurdles in the state meet and a fourth in the highs. I was hurt my junior year and took a third in the lows—or maybe it was the long jump. Then in my senior year I scored all 20 of Barberton's points, and that was enough to defeat Mansfield and Springfield for the state championship. I was the only athlete to qualify from Barberton. I came in fourth in the 100-yard dash, which I should have won. I won the 220 and the 180-yard low hurdles and the long jump. Doing it all alone had never been done before, and I don't think it has ever been done since.

Woody Hayes offered me a football scholarship, but a fear of injury and not getting a chance to compete in the Olympics made me decide to take a track scholarship at Ohio State instead. I had already started thinking about the Olympics in high school. I had pictures of such Ohio greats as Jesse Owens and Harrison Dillard on my wall, but the event I didn't pay much attention to was the one I won. I didn't even know that the 400-meter hurdles existed in the Olympics. But as soon as my Ohio State coach, Larry Snyder, saw me run the 440-yard dash, he decided that I was going to be a 400-meter hurdler. A lot of people didn't like to run the event because they would fall so often on the last two or three hurdles. I actually ran the 400-meter hurdles only about five times before the 1956 Games. It wasn't run in regular college meets, just in some of the big relays. When I broke the 50-second barrier, the event started to get some publicity.

Snyder was a different kind of coach from most. He would instill confidence in his athletes by patting them on the back and explaining things. He made you feel like there wasn't anyone in the world who could come near beating you. He'd say, "Hey, you've worked so hard, so just do it." If I was having a little trouble with my steps, he'd just sit back and watch and then tell me what was wrong. In fact, at Melbourne before the '56 Games I was having problems. I was kind of in a slump, and I had shinsplints. Larry stopped by on his way back from India. He took one look at the track on which I was practicing and took me immediately away to a grass track. He worked with me for three or four days. That was all I needed to restore the snap in my legs. When I hit that cinder track in the stadium, it was heaven. It was fast, the pain was gone, and I won rather easily.

Ohio State was kind of touch-and-go for me at first. I wasn't a good student when I got there, and I was a little worried about making it. My brother Ed moved down to Columbus and took a job, and that helped a lot. We'd go places together, and we'd talk. Sometimes he'd even fly to the big meets.

I ran just about every event at Ohio State. I even threw the javelin, the shot put, and the discus. In 1959 I started working toward the decathlon. I was bound and determined that I was going to win it in 1960. I had an excellent chance, but I twisted my lower back and couldn't throw the javelin. This also weakened me in the shot and the discus. I was close to the world record in six of the events. I ran the 100 meters in 10.3; I long-jumped over 26 feet; I high-jumped over 6 feet, 8 inches; I pole-vaulted around 14 feet; and I held the world record in the 400 meters; in fact, I held five world records at that time. I weighed only 165, but I had very good upper body strength. I could bench-press 310 pounds.

I lost only once in the 400-meter hurdles. A kid named Richard Howard defeated me in an AAU meet in 1956. I was running a fever of 102 degrees at the time, and I was completely exhausted by the last hurdle, when he passed me and went on to win. The next day he said something in the paper about being the greatest and that no one was ever going to beat him again. I cut that article out and put it on my mirror for about a week until I met him again, and this time I beat him pretty good. I didn't say anything to him. I just didn't talk to my competitors. I doubt that I spoke 10 words to Eddie Southern or Cliff Cushman, who were my toughest competitors in the late 1950s.

I was like that even in high school. I can remember the state finals in 1954. There were seven black kids and I in the dashes. One of them walked up and said, "We're going to whip your butt." I told him, "It wouldn't be the first time, my friend; go ahead and try." That's all I said. Three of them did beat me in the 100, so they said the same thing before the 220. But I told them, "I don't think so." And I got them.

I had a different style from most of the 400-meter hurdlers back then. I would run 15 strides, and then the last two hurdles I would go to 13. But I did best when I had stiff competition. I believed that I could always run fast enough to win—whatever it might take.

I just wish I had had the opportunity to compete against Edwin Moses. I would give anything to have run against him. There are going to be a lot better hurdlers, but you have to give him credit. He's a great athlete and a great competitor. I tried 13 steps between hurdles, but no one really has worked on it like he has. I wish I had, but I was so comfortable with 15, and no one could catch me, so why go to 13? I think I had better flat-out speed than Moses. Don't forget, I had run the 100 meters in 10.3, the 220 in 20.3, and the 440 in 45.7. I also think I was stronger than Moses because I had run a 1.52 half. Don't forget, he runs on all-weather

Glenn Davis in 1960. Photo courtesy of *Track and Field News*

tracks, whereas I had to run on cinders. I just wish I could have run against him.

Rome in 1960 was a bit easier for me because by that time I was positive that I wouldn't make any mistakes. I was nervous, but that's good. All I wanted to do was get nervous. The confidence and conditioning were there. I knew that I could win. I had just come off a barnstorming trip through Europe and Russia, and I was peaking perfectly just a couple of weeks before the Games, and I knew that I could hold my peak for one or two months.

I didn't play around much in my most competitive days. I spent a good deal of time with my friend, Rafer Johnson. We ran around together, and we talked about poetry. I liked to read poetry, and he wrote his own. We had a lot of common interests. I really got to know him. Talk about respecting a person: he had everything going for him, both as an athlete and as a person. I used to work out with him and help him prepare for the decathlon. I don't think I've ever said that I could have beaten him, but I think I could have.

I graduated from college in 1958 in education. I started coaching in the off-season in 1959 in junior high in Clinton, Ohio. After I came back from the Games in 1960, I tried out for the Detroit Lions. I played for them for a couple of seasons. I was the smallest guy in pro football when I got there. I weighed only 170. They teased me to death about coming from track, but I was tough. They knocked me around a lot, but they could never hurt me. I was determined to make the team, but I didn't know whether I had the ability. I didn't play much my rookie year, but in my second year I understood the game much better. I was catching the ball and thinking more like a football player. When we lost our first four games that second year, George Wilson put in a new offense, which he called the Zephyr Offense. My teammate, Joe Schmitt, labeled me the Zephyr, because I was put in as a starting wide receiver and was supposed to be the deep threat in Wilson's wide-open passing attack.

In the first game with the new offense I caught like seven passes. Every time I would catch a pass, Alex Karras would say, "Hey, Zephyr, you're OK with me." That meant that Alex had accepted me. We won nine straight games with that offense. I was a starter, and I was really proud of it. In training camp my third year I dislocated my left shoulder. I came back in four weeks, but I popped my shoulder out again. That was going to be my last year in football anyway, and that just speeded up the process.

I already had the position of track coach at Cornell University. I coached there five years. When I got there we were always last, but we moved up to first or second for the five years I was there. Then I decided that that was not what I wanted to do. I really wanted the job at Ohio State, but they gave it to somebody else. It was too easy at Cornell; in fact, that was one of the reasons I left. I liked the kids. They were great to work with, and they would do anything you asked of them. You would explain something to them one time, and they would almost have it. You'd explain it a second time, and they *would* have it.

I've been back here at Barberton High School for 20 years. At first I was teaching, coaching football and track, and running several restaurants that I opened in the area. Coaching high school was different, but partly because of my reputation the kids here also listened to me.

About six years ago I gave up the restaurant business, and I no longer coach full-time. I still do go over after school and help with the hurdlers. During the day I teach mechanical drawing to kids who have no idea that I competed in the Olympics. That was 26 years ago, and that's a long time.

I don't know that winning the gold was so important to me. I would say that setting my first world record meant more. Or perhaps it was just competing. Because of the way I grew up, my chances of making it were very, very slim, so just having a chance to compete and living up to the Olympic ideals were probably more important than winning the gold medals.

SHELBY WILSON

Gold Medal, Wrestling, Lightweight Freestyle, 1960

Shelby Wilson's victory in the lightweight wrestling competition in Rome culminated a high school and college athletic career more notable for its near wins than for its victories. In high school Wilson was undefeated for three years in the regular season, only to lose in the state championship finals. At Oklahoma State Wilson's most noteworthy wrestling triumphs came in his junior and senior years, when he won the Big Eight championship and took second in the NCAA both seasons.

After the Olympics Wilson gave up wrestling to coach and work with various Christian youth organizations such as the YMCA and the Athletes for Action branch of Campus Crusade. While in Texas from 1961 to 1968 he took graduate courses at Southwestern Seminary and became a minister. He coached wrestling at the University of Colorado from 1968 to 1974, when he resigned to devote his time to working with the Stronghold Youth Foundation, an organization he and his wife founded in Boulder in 1973.

Wilson moved to Indiana in 1983 and now coaches at Owen Valley High School in Spencer, at the same time continuing his work with young people and adults.

Getting into wrestling was the greatest thing that ever happened to me. I was a shy little farm kid whom nobody paid much attention to. I had an inferiority complex and all the things that went along with that. But wrestling gave me an identity, not just as a wrestler but as a person. I became a somebody. Even the other kids quit picking on me: bully kids don't pick on wrestlers.

I grew up on a farm near Ponca City, Oklahoma, and although I was strong because of all the farm work I did, like lifting bales of hay, I was very small and very shy. I was the kind of kid who didn't say much, and some of the other kids kind of pushed me around a little bit. Sometimes on the school bus they'd take my lunch from me and do things like that.

There were two brothers who were coaches in my junior high school, Loren and Don Smith. Loren was the head coach and also my industrial arts teacher, and Don was the physical education teacher. One day soon after I first got to Ponca City Junior High, Don Smith rolled out a wrestling mat and had his seventh-grade PE kids do some impromptu wrestling. I'd never seen a wrestling match in my life; in fact, I'd never even seen a wrestling mat. Maybe Don thought I might have some potential, or perhaps he just thought I was strong, but afterward he suggested I go out for wrestling. I had never thought about going out for anything, and I really had no desire to, but Don was the kind of guy you didn't want to say no to. He was a World War II veteran and used to tell his seventh-grade kids a lot of shoot-'em-up war stories. And he looked and acted like a sergeant, you know, with a clipboard under one arm and a kid under the other. You felt more like saluting him than arguing with him. So I went out for wrestling.

That was about 1949, and you just couldn't believe how naive I was when I first started wrestling! I didn't know anything. When the coach told me to get a jockstrap, I had no idea what that was or where to get one. And I remember one kid said to me, "I hear you're going out for wrestling? Hey, man, you might get a letter." Well, to me a letter was something that showed up in the mailbox, and guess what? I waited two weeks for this wrestling letter to come. Can you believe it? That's how naive I was.

Every match I had in junior high I won. More importantly for me, I developed an identity, a sense of who I was. I don't mean that I just thought of myself as Shelby Wilson the wrestler; I thought of myself as Shelby Wilson the person.

In my last year in junior high, in the 9th grade, my coach was Grady Peninger. Just recently he retired as coach at Michigan State University. Loren Smith had been my 7th- and 8th-grade coach, but he was retiring, and they brought in Grady, who was just out of college, where he was an AAU champion. The head high school coach was Marvin Clodfelter. He had wrestled in the '32

Shelby Wilson in 1985.
Photo courtesy of Shelby Wilson

Olympics. Clodfelter retired that year, and Grady Peninger moved up to the high school, so I had him as coach from the 9th through the 12th grade. He stayed there about nine years, then he went to MSU. My brothers also had him as a coach. Both of them, Steve and Doug, were state champions in Oklahoma. Incidentally, each of their sons was also a state champion. I'm the only one in the family who didn't win a state title.

I guess in high school I gave Grady a combination of joys and disappointments. Three years in a row I was undefeated, ranked number one, and lost one match. It was common practice then to wrestle in your normal weight division, then shed pounds to pull down the next weight. Every year that I wrestled in my regular weight class I was undefeated and ranked number one, but then I would always pull down the next weight, and I never enjoyed it. I didn't feel good, and I hated going to practice, and I never did my best that way. I think it's good discipline to have to do a certain amount of that, but most often it's ridiculous.

As I said earlier, wrestling gave me a real identity, but it didn't give me all that I needed because it was an identity on the outside. I still felt a kind of emptiness inside. I was still shy and still didn't feel very confident with people. I felt a whole lot better than I had before I started wrestling, but there still seemed something missing inside. When I lost that match in my last year in high school, I really had to think seriously about what was going on. I began to realize that if wrestling was the only thing in my life, if it was my purpose for being, then if I lost, I'd have no purpose, and there was no happiness in that. For me, to simply lose a match was not just an unhappy event; it was devastating. And when I lost during my last year, I had to do a lot of soul-searching and thinking about life and what it was really about. I know it sounds kind of crazy that losing a match could cause that kind of reaction, but it did. It took losing a wrestling match for me to say, God, what's it all about?

I began to hang around with the guys who looked like they had their lives together. I began to go to church and to listen, and I found Jesus Christ, and He gave me a purpose and a hope for eternity. I was 18 years old, and my life changed at that point. Gradually I became smarter in my wrestling and more self-confident and outgoing as a person. Now this didn't happen suddenly in one day but evolved over a period of time. When I found and accepted Christ, I had a purpose, and that has continued throughout my life.

I think a lot of athletes have that kind of emptiness inside. Perhaps that's why they take dope or other chemicals—to obtain a little better performance. They think that a better performance will give them a reason or purpose for what they do. But they'll never find it that way.

I was recruited heavily: I say that with tongue in cheek. In those days there wasn't a lot of wining and dining. Actually, the only recruiting that took place was that Port Robinson at Oklahoma University had me come down and look over the school. I have a lot of respect for Port, but I never had any desire to go wrestle for Oklahoma U. I was a farm kid, and I always wanted to wrestle for Oklahoma State, which was Oklahoma A & M at that time. All my coaches were State graduates, and that's all we ever heard; wrestlers went to Oklahoma State. The coaches used to take us there to watch the State wrestlers, and I always wanted to wear their orange and black colors. But I had lost in the finals in my senior year, and I figured that loss meant I wouldn't have a chance of going to State. They didn't take losers: they didn't want secondplacers. That's what I thought then. Little did I know that many of the guys who were recruited by Art Griffith, the wrestling coach, were second- and third-placers. He was a genius at picking people who could wrestle.

One day Art Griffith showed up at the farmhouse unannounced. I don't remember that he even called. He just showed up one day and talked to me for a few minutes. It wasn't a formal interview or anything like it. He asked if I'd like to go to Oklahoma State and wrestle. He gave me an application right then. We didn't sit down and negotiate a scholarship or a contract or anything. He said that if I could get into the school he'd give me a full scholarship, and we shook hands and that was it; no papers were drawn up, and no lawyers were there to look them over. We just shook hands. I got into the school and had a scholarship every year, and I never signed a contract at any time, as far as I can remember. I figured that if I did my job, Griffith would do his and I'd have my scholarship, and that's the way it worked out.

As far as I'm concerned, Art Griffith was the greatest wrestling coach who ever lived. He coached me during my freshman year and part of my sophomore year before he retired and Myron Roderick took over. Loren and Don Smith, my high school coaches, were fine at teaching the basics, which was what I needed at that time, but Griffith was extraordinary. He taught me more about wrestling and thinking wrestling than all the other coaches I've had combined. Art Griffith was a thinking man. He taught me several moves, sure, but it was his philosophy of wrestling—the way he taught me to think about wrestling—that really helped me develop as a wrestler and as a wrestling coach. He's gone now, but I still have a lot of respect for that man. I seriously doubt that I could have won the Olympics if it hadn't been for him.

I was at Oklahoma State for about five years, 1955 to 1960. You know what they say: all athletes cram four years into five—or six or seven. As a junior I won the finals of the Big Eight, but Paul Aubrey, the fella I beat there, beat me out for the national title. The next year I beat Paul again in the Big Eight finals, but I lost the nationals to another wrestler.

In 1960, my last year of college, I was supposed to be eligible because of an injury at the beginning of my sophomore year. However, the NCAA ruled that I was ineligible, though the Big Eight allowed it. Since the NCAA ruled against me, I dropped out of wrestling and just helped coach that year.

Myron Roderick suggested that I try out for the 1960 Olympic team. I hadn't even thought about that. The only time I had wrestled freestyle was in April of 1959, when the national AAU was held at Oklahoma State. Of course, we all entered because we were there and it was there, but I knew nothing at all about freestyle. All I did was take a guy down, let him go, then take him down again. Every time I did that I was penalized because it was against the rules, and I'd get a draw. I ended up with three draws—six black marks—so I was out of the tournament. I said, The heck with this; I'm not interested in this kind of wrestling.

After Myron suggested I try out for the Olympics I started practicing with some of the people at State who had some freestyle experience. They were from back east, where freestyle was more common. At that time I didn't really have making the Olympic team as my goal, though that was my goal later. In the beginning I was just trying to get some knowledge about freestyle wrestling.

I was always good on my feet, and I was known as a takedown artist. Olympic wrestling at that time wasn't structured in such a way as to give the takedown artist an edge, but it could give him an opportunity to win, if he played his cards right. Olympic matches were 12 minutes long, and if you could get three points ahead by the end of the first 6-minute period, you had the choice in the second period to wrestle either on your feet or to take parterre, which meant one man was underneath for 2 minutes, then the other man was down for the next 2 minutes, and then both were on their feet for the last 2 minutes. Well, my plan was to get ahead by three points in the first 6 minutes, then take that straight through, on my feet, for the next 6. If I did it right, that meant I could wrestle on my feet for the entire match.

I practiced defensive moves on the bottom parterre position so that if I did get underneath I could defend myself and not be scored on. I also worked on perfecting my takedowns. I didn't work at all at becoming good on the top position because I felt that wouldn't matter if I was really good in the others. Also, I just didn't have time to learn and practice all the moves I would need to know to be good on top.

In the national qualifying tournament I got into the finals and wrestled Frank Bettucci, who had been on the Olympic team in '56 but did not compete due to an injury. I got a draw with him, and that meant I could go to the training camp, which was open to the top three wrestlers in the qualifying tournament. Bettucci won first place, I won second, and a guy from Iowa State, Veryl Long, won third. Jim Burke from Colorado came in fourth, and he got to go to the camp also, but as a hardship case.

After the freestyle matches at the qualifying tournament, I waited around to enter the Greco-Roman matches. I figured one way or another I was going to go to Rome—if not in freestyle, then in Greco. Anyway, I placed second in freestyle and third in Greco. I went to the training camp and made the Greco team first and then the freestyle. I chose to wrestle freestyle in Rome, and that meant that the man I beat in Greco for third was able to get on the team.

When I arrived at the training camp at Norman, Oklahoma, I was sick and spent the first three days in the infirmary. When I got out I had just two days to practice and the next day went right into the Greco-Roman trials. Becoming sick forced me to rest, and I think that was probably very good for me at that time. The same thing happened in Rome. I was training very hard the first few days there, then I got some bug and was really sick. When I got over that a couple of days later, I felt great. I had two or three days of good practice and then began my matches. I really think that my getting sick those two times was a kind of blessing from God; knowing that I didn't have sense enough to slow down and rest, He forced me to do that by allowing me to get sick.

I was supposed to have six matches at the Olympics, but I got a bye on one, so I had only five. One of those was against the Japanese wrestler, Kazno Abe. He and the Russian, Vladimir Sinyavski, who was a two-time world champion and the number-one contender for the Olympic gold medal at that time, were big rivals. They had wrestled in '59, just before the World Games. Abe beat Sinyavski in Japan and lost to him in Russia, so they figured that one or the other of them was going to win the gold medal. The Japanese were very innovative in their wrestling, and they had just introduced what we call the "high crotch" series, which is a deep move to the outside, like a duck-under. Abe was very good at using that move, and few wrestlers from other countries had ever seen it.

As I was going up the steps to the mat for my match with Abe, Sinyavski was coming down after beating his opponent. He looked me straight in the eye and made a kind of slight wrestling gesture like the high crotch move that Abe used so well. He was warning me to watch out for that move. I guess he thought that, if I could

Shelby Wilson in 1960.
Photo courtesy of Shelby Wilson

accidentally beat Abe, then he, Sinyavski, would have a chance at me, and I'm sure that he didn't see me as any threat. As it turned out, Abe was the only wrestler I met in my matches who was not a defensive wrestler. Abe came out there to wrestle, and that was just what I wanted because I had come to wrestle, too. All the others I wrestled, including the Russian, wanted to win at any cost. They used the rules to try to get that win. They'd try to get off the mat, to get to the edge and put their heads off before they got pinned or before the time was up. Not Abe. He came after me, and I loved it. I took him down eight times because of his aggressiveness, and I felt good in that he was a world-class wrestler. I had never been in an international meet before. The only people I'd wrestled were other Americans, and at that point Abe was only my third opponent.

Sinyavski watched the match, and he was surprised. Everybody was. I had beaten Abe 10–2. Later Terry McCann and Doug Blubaugh told me that I had the Russian psyched out. Sinyavski had never heard of me, some greenhorn farm kid, and here I had beaten the guy who was ranked up there close to him.

My match with Sinyavski was the next day. I thought, Maybe I can psych him out a little more. For the first time in my life I did something cocky. I was stretching and doing my thing at my end of the mat, while at the other end he was going through his warm-ups and was watching me. I kind of jumped up and puffed out my chest and breathed hard a few times, slapped my hands together, and began a dynamic loosening-up routine. I think it worked, because in the match Sinyavski never did figure out my moves. I took him down five times in the first period, while he spent his time clawing and crawling to the edge of the mat to get his head out, which he managed to do three times. In U.S. collegiate style, those five takedowns would have been clean two-pointers each. I could never wrestle the way he did. I wrestled in the middle of the mat, not on the edges. But he dragged me to the edge three times and then stood up. To try to win like that is beyond me. Wrestling should be done in an honorable way. You go out there and give it your best shot. If you lose after doing your best, you shake hands with your opponent and still feel proud of yourself because of your performance. Anyway, I ended up beating Sinyavski 4–0 or something like that. I did it by following my earlier plan.

On the final day of the competition I beat the Iranian, Mostaf Tajiki, pretty easily, and that put him out of the tournament. That was my last match, but it might not have been. It all depended on the next match, between Won Bong Chang of Korea and Emio Dimov of Bulgaria. If that match had ended in a fall, I would have had to wrestle the winner. If it had ended in anything else, such as a draw or a win, they were out of the tournament, and I would be the Olympic champion. Earlier, on the bus going to the tournament, Chang sat across from me. Because he didn't speak much English, in a few words I told him to win; to beat the Bulgarian, to pin him. If I had to wrestle one of them, I'd rather it be Chang. We had never met before, and he looked right at me, held up one finger, and said, "You number one," meaning he thought I was going to win. I was really surprised that he had that much confidence in me. I appreciated that. Chang had little chance of beating Dimov, but he had managed to get up among the top five wrestlers at that point.

After I beat Tajiki I didn't want to watch Chang and Dimov, so I went back to the dressing room and lay down and waited for the guys to come in and tell me what had happened. They said that you would have had to have a calculator to keep track of the points the Bulgarian was scoring on Chang. He really beat him up. He had Chang on his back the whole 12 minutes, but every time the referee was about to call a fall Chang would bridge; he'd rise off his back, and he'd come back. That went on for 12 minutes, and Dimov couldn't pin him. I don't remember the score, but it was high, much higher than would be allowed today. If that match had been played today, and the points reached 15, they would have stopped the match and given Dimov the win. But Chang held on. I wanted to ask him what was going through his mind concerning the relationship between that match and me. I know that Chang knew he couldn't win. He was behind, yet he kept fighting and kept getting beat up. I honestly believe he had a purpose, not for himself, but for me. You can't wrestle like that without a purpose. He wanted me to get the gold medal automatically, without having to wrestle Dimov.

After the Olympics I decided to stop wrestling. In those days you had to give up a lot to wrestle. There just wasn't any real financial help to keep you going. Doug Blubaugh came out of college and joined the army for four years for just one reason: so he could wrestle for four years and prepare for the '60 Olympics. Terry McCann moved from Illinois to Tulsa, Oklahoma, and trained for eight years. We had the AAU, but that wasn't much help. You still often had to hitchhike to get to a tournament. Nowadays things are better. USA Wrestling, the national governing body for wrestling, does a lot. They help pay for trips and run clinics and tournaments. Today you can also be an assistant coach somewhere. In my time, if you got anything, it caused you to lose your amateur standing. I remember that a jewelry store in our town gave Blubaugh and me each a watch. It didn't affect my status because I had decided to give up wrestling, but it threatened to get Blubaugh banned. He still had a couple of weeks to go to finish up his time in the service, and he wasn't sure yet whether he was going to continue wrestling.

A short time later Blubaugh and I were invited to be on the old TV program "I've Got a Secret." Well, the Olympic Committee decided to intervene for us. You got some kind of prizes when you were on that show, so the TV people contacted the Olympic Committee and said they wanted to play by the rules and not do anything to get us in trouble. They wanted us because we both won Olympic gold medals in the same Olympics and we were both from the same town. That was to be our secret. The Olympic Committee told the TV producer that they would agree to let us go on the program in return for a donation to the Committee. I don't know exactly how much that was, probably about $300 for each of us. The Olympic Committee never acknowledged that to us. They never said boo to us. We learned about it from the people connected with the program, and they thought that making such a donation was standard procedure. Procedure, baloney! The Olympic Committee didn't have any procedures. It wasn't any of their concern to intervene for us, and besides, I wasn't even an amateur wrestler anymore. We ended up with a toothbrush and toothpaste or something like that. The Olympic Committee just took the money and ran. We never even got a note of thanks for the donation we made through that program.

Grady Peninger had left his coaching job at Ponca City High School for the coaching job at Michigan State University, and I replaced him as the high school coach. I stayed there a year and then moved to Fort Worth at the invitation of a friend. In Fort Worth I took graduate courses at Southwestern Seminary and then got involved in full-time Christian youth work. Meantime I also worked at the YMCA.

In 1968 I moved to Boulder, Colorado. Athletes in Action, a branch of Campus Crusade, asked me to coach the first wrestling team they had. About the same time the University of Colorado contacted me about a coaching job there, and after praying and thinking about it, my wife and I moved to Boulder. I stayed there from 1968 to 1974, when I resigned to work full-time with the Stronghold Youth Foundation. That is a nonprofit organization that we founded in Boulder in 1973. It was organized to help kids who needed a place to stay while they were trying to get through some difficult period in their lives. Off and on we had kept kids in our home in Texas, and after we started the Stronghold Youth Foundation we realized that if the Lord wanted us to do this, and we believed He did, then we'd better do it full-time.

In 1983 we moved to Bloomington, Indiana, to help Doug Blubaugh with a sports camp he had here. We helped him for two years and at the same time continued our work through the Stronghold Youth Foundation. We decided at the end of two years to remain in Indiana instead of returning to Colorado. We felt that since God had taken us to Indiana, we would stay until we feel it is time to move on, if ever.

When I see all the terrible things that have happened at the Olympic Games in recent years, things like murders, boycotts, and demonstrations, it seems to me that the 1960 Olympics was probably the last "pure" Olympic Games. Of course there had been many problems and disputes and bad feelings in past Games, but these didn't seem as uncontrollable as they have become in the Games after 1960. In the 1960 Olympics the idea that the best athletes from all over the world could come together and compete in a spirit of mutual respect still seemed to be possible. But in most Olympic Games since then, it seems that international political disputes have become so strong that the old Olympic idea of peaceful athletic competition open to all amateurs seems to have died, and it's very sad to see that happen.

WILLIAM MULLIKEN

Gold Medal, 200-Meter Breaststroke, 1960

Bill Mulliken was not favored to win the 200-meter breaststroke in Rome; in fact, he surprised many when he made the American team. Two weeks before the Olympic trials, he had finished fifth in the nationals, but he upset everyone at the trials, and in Rome he improved his best time in the 200-meter breaststroke by almost four seconds.

Now a practicing attorney in Chicago, Mulliken is also active in masters' swimming. In 1985 he again swam against Yoshihiko Osaki, the Japanese swimmer he had upset in Rome a quarter of a century before.

If you believe that the Olympics can encourage understanding among nations, boycotts are always counterproductive. I was even opposed to leaving South Africa out in 1964, and I was certainly against every boycott thereafter. If the Germans were able to name a street in West Berlin Jesse Owens Avenue, anything good can happen. In my race in 1960, the man who came in second was Japan's Yoshihiko Osaki. My father fought in the Pacific during

Bill Mulliken in 1981.
Photo courtesy of Bill Mulliken

World War II, perhaps against his father. My mom once said she thought it wonderful that although my dad won medals in a war against the Japanese, I won mine in athletic competition.

A quarter of a century later, I again swam against Osaki, this time in a masters' competition in Japan. His wife also swam and defeated Australia's Dawn Fraser, who had won gold medals in three different Olympiads. Even his mother and father competed. Osaki told me that his oldest daughter had made the Japanese Olympic team in 1980 but didn't get to go because of the boycott. So his family represented three generations of swimmers, but because of war and politics only he got the chance to swim in the Olympics.

The interesting thing about our masters' competition was that this time he finished ahead of me—but neither of us won the race. A West German really took us apart. He had not been able to compete in 1960 because he was then living in East Germany and, as I understand it, was in some kind of trouble with the authorities.

It would have been nice if the media had covered our "rematch," but they seldom do justice to the sport of swimming. Every four years they try to learn a little about the sport when we need the medals for the count. I can remember in Rome being interviewed by a reporter from *Time*. He asked me, "Oh, by the way, which stroke is the breaststroke?" Even a small-town sportswriter would know the difference between the butterfly and the breaststroke!

The two of us talked for quite a while. He liked the fact that I was from downstate Illinois, which to him meant I was kind of a country boy, although at the time I had already been accepted into Harvard's law school. I finally asked him, "Are you a sportswriter?" He laughed and answered, "No, I cover the Middle East, but I was the closest guy to Rome, so they sent me here." Four days later, I was walking along, and this same reporter stops and asks me, "Hey, kid, do you know which one is Mike Troy?" Mike had just won the 200-meter butterfly. I thought to myself, That really puts it all in proper perspective. It's the Andy Warhol thing. I had gotten my 15 minutes of fame, and now it was all over.

There was a lot of pressure on us in Rome to do well in the swimming competition, especially after Lance Larson lost the opening 100-meter freestyle to Australia's John Devitt in the most controversial decision of the Games. You really couldn't tell who had finished first. Larson probably did win, but I don't think there was anything malicious about the decision against him. It was not as if we were favored to win everything. Both the Australians and the Japanese had done much better than we had in 1956; in fact, our only gold medal in Tokyo was Bill Yorzyk's in the 200-meter butterfly. So if there had been any prejudice, it should have been the other way around. It was not like some of the stories you hear about diving from 1952 and 1956, when everyone was just so tired of the U.S. always winning. But it became the big swimming story, and people knew much more about it than Bill Mulliken and Mike Troy's victories. I even told Lance that at the time.

The coaches used the whole Larson controversy to convince the rest of us that we would have to win decisively because any close decisions would go against us. Of course, they didn't take my chances all that seriously, and from our first day in Rome they certainly did little to build up my confidence.

I was feeling pretty good when we landed in Rome. Sam Hall, the diver who was to win the silver in the springboard and who in 1986 got picked up on espionage charges in Nicaragua, and I decided to room together. We had been good friends for years. We were getting unpacked, and our swimming coach, Gus Steger, walked in and asked Sammy what he was doing there. Sammy told him that the two of us wanted to room together. Gus said, "Well, we're going to room all of you guys who have a chance to win a gold medal in singles, so Sammy, you come with me, and, Bill, you wait here, and I'll send you another roommate." And he did.

I was always the kind of kid who struggled along and kind of made the team. I always made the cut, but I was never top dog. I was the outsider who had a chance but was never the favorite. There have to be hundreds of stories like that. There have to be many more Bill Mullikens than Mark Spitzes.

Too often the hero of the Olympics is someone like Spitz, the athlete who was supposed to do great things. But I wasn't supposed to win. I wasn't even expected to make the team. Two weeks before the Olympic trials I was fifth at the nationals, and that year they announced that they were going to take only the winner of the breaststroke to the Games rather than the first two finishers. I really went through some soul searching before the trials because I was so desperate. I even thought of taking benzedrine. It was not illegal at the time, and there were those who thought it would pump you up physically. But I really didn't trust it; instead, I decided just to relax and be positive. I went into what we now call a *relaxation response mode.* I did practice my strokes and turns, but I spent a lot of time thinking about specific race strategy. Above all, I learned just to remain calm.

Of course, no one thought I would make the semifinals or the finals in Rome. Even my dad was not too sure about my chances, although he did tell me at least to try and beat "just one Russian."

The top Russian breaststroker was in my first preliminary heat. I stayed with him for the first 100 meters or so. I was feeling good, so I took off on the guy and won easily. I had beaten a Russian for Dad, but I had also swum two or three seconds faster than I had ever gone in my life. That heat ended up being the fastest one in the prelims, and by this point Steger was putting bricks on me trying to calm me down.

In my semifinal heat I drew Osaki. I figured, What the hell? This guy's never lost to an American. Now would be a good time for a first. I came off the turn at the 150 mark, and I was right with him. I had never had that kind of control. While I was under water I thought of George Breen, who had set two world records in the 1956 Games and had not won a gold medal because he used everything up in the heats. So I thought, Well, I don't want to break a world record, but I do want to beat this guy. I moved a little bit ahead of him and stayed right there. I think I probably won the Olympics on that final turn. Osaki had never had that done to him. He had always been the one doing that sort of thing to other people. That was the best race I ever swam. I think I could have broken the world record, but winning is always more important than breaking records, and I wanted something left for the next day.

I still had my doubts about beating Osaki in the finals, but an interview with several Japanese reporters helped build my confidence. Contrary to their American counterparts, they were incredibly knowledgeable about swimming. They asked me if I realized how unusual it was to have one's best performance in the Olympics. I told them that I thought one always gave his best performance in the Games. One of them then told me that the Japanese swimmers had found it almost impossible to achieve their best times under the pressure of the Olympics. I thought, Gee, I've never had anybody help me that much. And I did win the finals, although it was not as satisfying an effort as in the semifinals.

I did get a kick out of watching the Russian swim team in Rome. They trained right after we did. The swimmers themselves were warm and friendly, but their officials were humorless types who

Bill Mulliken in 1960.
Photo courtesy of Bill Mulliken

wore those stereotypical trench coats and hats. We always called them the KGB. They really looked like seconds out of an anticommunist B-movie. They'd ask us what we'd done for workouts, and we'd tell them the most outrageous stuff, but all they had to do was watch us, and they did. Four years later, a Russian woman won the 200-meter breaststroke in Tokyo, and Raymond Ray, who was my college coach, said to me, "If you want to see what your stroke looks like, watch her." What they had done was to copy everything we did, but they didn't realize that Chet Jastremski had revolutionized breaststroking in the United States, and so they were still a generation behind. The year after I won the Olympics, the world record in the 200-meter breaststroke was broken by nine seconds; in fact, the first seven places in the U.S. nationals broke the old record. But the Russians, like everyone else, caught on soon enough.

I grew up in Champaign and trained with the University of Illinois team. I was coached by guys who were getting their graduate degrees under Tom Cureton, so I was blessed with incredible coaching. We did the kind of experimenting that is necessary for breakthroughs in any sport. Most people don't think of it this way, but Bannister and Landy really revolutionized more than just running when they broke through the four-minute barrier in the mile. That led to a generation of kids who destroyed all the records in swimming. I think when Ovett and Coe let us know what they do for training, we'll go through another revolution. Those guys can't be doing what everybody else is and achieve what they have over such a long period of time.

Even something like the Salk vaccine had a dramatic effect on our training. Before the vaccine our parents wouldn't allow us to work out during the dog days of summer. The conventional wisdom then was that if you became too fatigued you were susceptible to polio. No one really knew what caused the dread disease, but my parents used to send me to northern Wisconsin in August just to be on the safe side.

But today many of our athletes are pushing themselves too far. For young kids to be swimming 12,000 to 16,000 meters a day is just insane. The whole thing seems to be to reach your point of athletic failure. And that's when you hurt yourself, both mentally and physically.

I'm very conscious of this now because I train with swimmers who are 15 to 20 years younger than I am. Now I always have some kind of hurt or other. I don't remember having that when I was in college. I just did my workouts and tried to beat the hell out of whoever was there. My teammates helped by taking turns trying to wear me down.

The mindset when I was young was that after you graduated you were dead as an athlete. There was no masters' competition. I had never seen anybody of my father's generation swimming. To them, exercise was golf once or twice a week. Nobody jogged. Nobody even played tennis. A few of the older oddballs on college campuses might do something physical, but it was not part of our culture the way it is now.

I expected that it would be the same for me. I did some training with the team while I was in law school at Harvard, and after graduation I played several years of water polo for the Illinois Athletic Club. I enjoyed that, but I surely didn't expect to be doing anything athletic after I hit 30. But I remembered the warning of a high school coach. He didn't know much about swimming, but after watching me work out he told me I would be dead of a heart attack by the time I was 45. There's a good chance he might have been right if I had not gone back into swimming. My blood pressure is borderline high, and I monitor it pretty closely. I've got a high-tension job, and it's considered very unsportsmanlike to reach across the table and hit somebody in the mouth when you're angry with him. So I use swimming as my stress release.

At the end of the day, I can just feel the tension drain out of my body when I get into that pool. And I still love to swim. That's why I was good at it in the first place. I like the feeling of being in the water. It's an incredibly sensuous experience.

When I was young, I dug it deep. Now I'm trying to dig it long. I'm 47 years old, and I don't put the time into it that I did when I was young. I do train an hour a day, six or seven times a week, because I want to learn just how much the human body can withstand as it goes through the aging process.

Recently, I studied the top five places in the 100- and 500-yard freestyle for each age group. I found out that you slow down at the rate of half a second a year for each 100 yards. That's 1 percent. But that's not really accurate because you're comparing the guys who are 25 against the guys who are now 50. And the one thing we know is that by the time those 25-year-olds are 50, their times are going to be faster. So we still don't have the right kind of control group, but when we find it, we will certainly prove that we can hold out physically much longer than earlier generations ever thought possible.

We simply put too much emphasis on always winning. Everyone who knows about my 1986 trip to Japan to race Osaki always asks if I won again. I lost, but I didn't really lose. I swam faster at age 46 than I did the first time I placed in the nationals when I was 19. That's not losing. Someone just swam faster than I did.

Don't mistake what I'm saying. I love to compete. My idea of heaven is at the three-quarter mark to see somebody there because I know that's going to bring out the best last quarter in me. There is something inside that makes most of us afraid to lose, and we'll do anything to avoid it. And when I do lose, I go into a blue funk just like everybody else, but I also realize that those guys I'm competing against want to win just as badly as I do. I've also come to realize that you do learn a lot more about life through losing than through being constantly victorious. I've actively participated in political campaigns where we've lost, and I've done acquisitions and mergers that were utter disasters. In each case, defeat was bitter, but there was also much to be learned in the process. You can always savor a victory, but you have to analyze a loss!

LEE QUENCY CALHOUN

Gold Medal, 110-Meter Hurdles, 1956 and 1960

Lee Calhoun is the only person to have won two Olympic gold medals in the 110-meter hurdles. In 1956 and 1957 he held the AAU indoor and outdoor titles as well as those of the NAIA and the NCAA.

In 1958 Calhoun lost his amateur standing for a year because he married and received gifts on the television program "Bride and Groom." He came back in 1959 to win the AAU outdoor championship and to take a second in the Pan-American Games title.

While in the service in Korea in 1965, Calhoun created and coached a military team that beat the Japanese national team at the site of the '64 Games in Tokyo. After his graduation from North Carolina Central University, he coached at Grambling and later at Yale. He left Yale in 1980 and since then has been coaching at Western Illinois University.

I grew up in Mississippi on a farm about eight miles from Laurel. That's the same town that Leontyne Price and Ralph Boston are from. I was born on February 23, 1933, but my birth certificate got lost before it was registered. Later when the army came looking for people, like an idiot I declared that I existed, and sure enough, they took me.

My parents moved to Indiana when I was nine. I enrolled in Roosevelt School in Gary. That was what they called a consolidated school in those days: you started in kindergarten and graduated in the 12th grade. As a result, the coaches got to know what talent there was in the whole school.

I guess I'd have to say that Roosevelt was a prejudiced high school. If your family stock had not proven itself in the system, you didn't get much of a shot at making the respective school teams. It was like horse racing: you needed a pedigree. So the coaches were very selective in choosing members of the team, and I never bothered to try out for the track team, even though I was the second-best hurdler and high-jumper in the school. Anyway, I always had jobs after school. I liked to hear the jingle of change in my pocket, and we weren't a well-to-do family, so I'd always have some kind of job to go to.

One day when I was in the 11th grade, I was walking down the hall, and one of the high school coaches, Bo Mallard, was standing outside his office. Most of the coaches in those days stood around the hallways or by the gym door, slapping the side of their legs with a paddle, what we called "the persuader." At that time corporal punishment was legal, so to speak. Well, Bo called me over and said, "We need a high-jumper this year." I told him that I'd give it some thought. He kept tapping his leg with that paddle, and it didn't take me long to make up my mind because I knew that if I didn't go out for the team my next two years in physical education were going to be real physical.

I decided right then to go out. After all, what was seven steps and a jump? It was the easiest job on the whole track squad. Well, I made it to the regionals, but I didn't qualify for the state meet that year. The next year, 1951, I began to learn more about how to do things. In our first meet I was pulled over by the coach and asked to fill in in the hurdles. So with no training at all I almost won the race, coming in just behind the city champion and beating my two teammates. I thought nothing of it, but at practice on the following Monday, I was doing the high jump and minding my own business when Bo called me over and told me that the three members of the

Lee Calhoun in 1986.
Photo courtesy of Western Illinois University

hurdling squad wanted to challenge me for position: they wanted their positions back. I told Bo, "Fine. They can have their positions back. I don't want them; I'm a high-jumper." I was keeping in mind "seven steps and jump." That's all a high-jumper has to do.

But Bo told me I had to do it; I had to let them challenge me. We discussed things for a while, and the more we talked, the angrier I got, because I was being subjected to something that wasn't necessary. Why take me, the number-one high-jumper, and make me mess around with hurdles and all the extra training that would mean? But Bo lined us up, and by that time my blood was boiling, and I beat all three of them. Then I said, "OK, coach, they can have their positions back. I'm going back to the high jump." "No," he said. "That's not the way it works. Each one of them has to challenge you."

Each time I ran against one of them I got angrier, and I widened the margin between us. I could easily have loped along and lost, but I was the type of athlete who, regardless of whether I was in a neighborhood game or a serious meet, had to do my best.

After I beat each one of them in the three separate races, Bo said, "You're it."

"It what?" I asked.

"You're my new hurdler," he answered. That meant that one of them had to drop off the team, and I felt very bad about that.

I was almost undefeated that season in both high jump and hurdles until we got to the state meet. I was seeded either first or second in both events. At the state meet the weather was awful—rain, snow, sleet, and hail. I never cleared a height in the high jump, and after coming out of the blocks in the hurdles I hit the first five of them, the first time I hit one all year. By the time I started clearing them, the field had gotten ahead of me, and I finished fifth. I got just one point, but that helped the school get its first state championship in track and field. I was very proud of that, and I got my letter sweater.

There was a man sitting in the stands at the state meet, Dr. Leroy Walker. He recruited me to North Carolina Central University in Durham, the only offer I got. I later asked him why, with all the hurdlers at that meet, he chose me. He answered, "Because of the determination I saw in you. You are not the type of person who would quit, even if you got off to a bad start, and that's the kind of person I want." Later he was the head coach and I was the assistant coach of the '76 Olympic team.

So I agreed to go to North Carolina, sight unseen. That was in 1951. Dr. Walker picked up several of us, and we traveled to North Carolina in his car. What a shock I had when I got there! There were new buildings and half-built buildings all over, and no sidewalks anywhere, just wooden planks to walk on. It rained the whole first month I was there. It was awful being so far from home, and I stayed wet and miserable that first month.

I was conference champion for the first two years before I went into the army. I also ran a few races against Harrison Dillard and Jack Davis during that time. I wasn't last in those races, but you'll find my name somewhere in the lower brackets.

Uncle Sam decided to take me in 1953. After basic training at Fort Leonard Wood, Missouri, they sent me to Camp Chaffee in Fort Smith, Arkansas, to motor mechanic's school, something I had no talent for and no interest in. I was sent to Korea, and because there was a surplus of drivers and mechanics, I ended up at the 111th Evacuation Hospital and eventually was put in charge of special services at the hospital.

In the spring of 1954, with scrapbooks under my arm, I went to Special Services Headquarters to see about starting a military track team in Korea. I got permission, and we put together a team of army and air force personnel, which became the 8th Army Track Team. The following year we had a meet against the Japanese National Team at the site of the '64 Games in Tokyo, and we beat them. They couldn't believe that an army team could beat their national team, but that was how strong we were. A lot of those athletes returned to the States and to their education and made names for themselves.

After my army time I returned to college in 1955, a little wiser and a little stronger. We had a small team: 20 men was as many as we would ever carry. Walker picked his team very carefully, and he always chose multitalented individuals who could do more than one thing.

That winter I ran what was called the winter circuit, and I won every meet except one, doing a world best in the 60-, 70-, and 80-yard indoor hurdles. Jack Davis was also on that circuit. He had come in second to Harrison Dillard at the '52 Games, and he was expected to be the number-one hurdler in the world at the '56 Games. I beat him that indoor season.

I had a good outdoor season in the spring of 1956, but I noticed in the paper that the times in the West Coast meets were much better than those on the East Coast, perhaps because the West Coast had better weather and better tracks. I had finally worked my time down to 14-flat when I went to a meet at Quantico, Virginia. Jack Davis came east for it, and I figured that, although his times were better than mine, this would be a good opportunity for me to lower my times if I could stay with him. He was quick out of the blocks, though not as fast as I was, but he had good staying power. The gun went off, and Davis ran a 13.7, I think, and I ran 13.8, the first time I'd ever been under 14.

We never met again until school was out. I went to California for the month of June and lost to Davis in several meets, but each time I closed the gap a little bit.

At the Olympic trials in Los Angeles, Jack and I ran a dead heat. Joe Shankle, who was from Duke and whom I used to train with secretly in Durham, was third, Milt Campbell was fourth, and Harrison Dillard fifth. So I was on the Olympic team, but I was reluctant to go because the Games in Melbourne were going to be in November and December. I had already taken two years out of my college work while I was in the army, and I was apprehensive about missing another semester of school. When I told my coach that I wasn't going, he thought I was crazy. The president of the college talked to me and told me that I could be the first Olympian the school had ever had. They let me stay in school, but I had to work out a study plan with each professor and then take the finals when I got back. That's what I did, and I passed my courses with flying colors.

At Melbourne I qualified in my heat, Jack Davis in his, and Joe Shankle in his. Our only threat was a young upcoming hurdler from West Germany, Martin Lauer, who later held the world record.

When the gun went off for the finals, the only thing in my mind was to lead Jack. If I could beat him out of the blocks and then hold him off, I knew I had a chance to win. But I also had to be strong from the sixth hurdle on to the finish line, because that was where Davis's power was. He'd get into that rhythm and just overtake you. Well, he never caught me. By the barest of margins I got there first. We waited for 15 or 20 minutes before they announced the decision. I don't know what I was thinking during that time. I don't remember whether I was hoping I had won or whether I was just glad it was over. When the names flashed on the board, Davis's name came on first in the second position, and I thought, Oh, I lost. But then above his name my name appeared in the first position, and we both had the same time. Shankle was third, Lauer fourth. I had won by leaning into the tape.

That was a happy day for me. Television was pretty new then, but my parents, relatives, the people where I was born, and the kids at college had watched the race.

Word had gotten out to most of the athletes at Melbourne that there was a rivalry between Jack Davis and me. After I ran against him at Quantico, Jack had said that I was just a flash in the pan, that I was a good indoor hurdler, but I didn't have the strength to go the longer outdoor distance. Well, that remark just fueled me up to train harder. On the airplane on the way back from Melbourne, Parry O'Brien hushed everybody up and asked Jack, "What were those statements you made back in the spring about a young hurdler from North Carolina who was a flash in the pan? How bright is that flame burning now?"

After college I got married on a TV program called "Bride and Groom." The contestants were chosen on the basis of the love story that the girl wrote. The TV people didn't know me. Well, the AAU got involved. A friend of mine called me and said, "What's this about your being banned?"

"Banned for what?" I asked.

"Haven't you read the papers?"

I hadn't, so he read to me from the local Indianapolis paper that if I went through with the wedding on television I would be banned for life from amateur sports. I was going to New York anyway, so I made an appointment to talk to the AAU.

I met with Dan Ferris, head of the AAU, and their lawyer. At the time, the AAU was trying to buy that old house on Fifth Avenue. We met for about 45 minutes and discussed the whole thing. It seemed that it didn't matter where I got married, just so long as it wasn't on national television. I could even have received the same kinds of gifts I would get on TV if I would get married anywhere else, even in a corn field. Their rationale was that the AAU bylaws state that capitalizing on athletic fame was forbidden. I explained that everyone has a chance to be on that program, not just athletes. They would pick a couple on the basis of the woman's story, assign a date, and that's the date you got married. It had nothing to do with anything I had or hadn't done. But the AAU wouldn't relent, and I had made up my mind. I told them what they could do, and they told me what I could do, so we parted with that.

After I got married I went to work for John Nagye, who was chairman of the AAU Lake Erie Association in Cleveland. Harrison Dillard helped me get the job, which was in the Cleveland Recreation Department. That November the national AAU asked the local associations to help raise money. All the associations got busy on fund-raising projects. John and our association raised between $35,000 and $40,000, but at the national convention, before he would give the national AAU the money, he wanted them to dispose of my case once and for all. A recess was called, and the AAU officials came back and announced they had decided I would be banned for one year from the date of the infraction. Well, that gave me a year of rest.

NBC had their lawyers ready and was going to sue the AAU over its decision to ban me for appearing on that program, but I asked them not to. That was probably a mistake. I can't help wondering what would have happened if that had gone to litigation. We might have found out how much power those AAU officials really did have.

Some years later I met Dan Ferris at a convention. I guess I kind of shocked him. He was getting older and I think had suffered several strokes. He was using a cane, but his mind was still sharp. I walked up to him, began talking to him, and introduced my wife.

I said, "Oh, by the way, Dan, I want you to meet my wife. We're still together, although 20 years ago you suspended me for marrying her." A short time later Ferris passed away, and a good friend of his asked me if I would like to donate to his memorial. I told him no, I didn't think I would.

I never stopped training during the time I was suspended. I was still working in Cleveland, but I was starving to death. I was making about $3,800 a year, and my wife was also making very little as a typist. I realized that, with the GI Bill and some kind of job that would pay $150 to $200 a month, I could go to graduate school and have the same income as I did working, and that's what I did. We moved back to Durham, and I lived in a dormitory. My wife, who was pregnant, went to live with her folks, about 70 miles away. I went to graduate school at night, trained in the afternoon, and worked during the rest of the day.

I went back into training for Rome. Hayes Jones was coming on the scene, and I lost every indoor meet that season to Hayes, but I was determined to make a comeback and beat him. Even during the outdoor season I wound up chasing him. Hayes also beat me in the Russian-American Dual Meet in 1959. I continued to lose right up until the Olympic trials, when I finally beat him. I ran 13.4 for a new American record. Then just before the Games in Rome, I tied Martin Lauer's world record of 13.2 in Berne, Switzerland. But world records are always beaten, and that wasn't my main goal. I was interested in one thing: becoming the first person ever to win back-to-back Olympics in the 110-meter hurdles.

I figured that the only thing I needed to work on was speed. Everything else was pretty much where I wanted it. I had worked out a system to run a 13.1. In Berne it had worked out to be 13.2, but I felt sure it would come at the Olympic Games. Well, it didn't happen. The wind was always in our faces, and it rained. The track was new and became soft, and my final time was only 13.8, which was $\frac{3}{10}$ of a second slower than my time at Melbourne.

Again it was a photo finish. I dove for the tape at the last instant. My good friend, Willie May, was second, Hayes Jones was third, and once more Lauer was fourth.

Winning the gold medal at Melbourne meant a lot to me, of course. But winning it a second time in Rome was a special achievement since no one else had ever won consecutive Olympic gold medals in the high hurdles. I was out to prove I could do it, and what with going through that suspension hassle, it gave me an especially good feeling.

11
TOKYO, 1964

Tokyo is one of the most densely populated major cities on earth, and nothing short of a massive redesign and reconstruction of much of the city was required to prepare it for the '64 Olympic Games. At a staggering cost of $2.8 billion, the Japanese, working with feverish intensity while enduring major inconveniences and dislocations, completed the work just in time for the opening ceremonies on October 10. Exactly one year earlier, the efficient Japanese staged an International Sports Week in Tokyo, which served primarily as a rehearsal for the Olympics. The Japanese left nothing to chance. They had even sent a large delegation to Rome to observe and take notes on every aspect of those Games, from the competitions to the food served in the dinning halls. Nothing escaped their attention. For the Japanese, losing face is unforgivable, and they were determined that nothing would mar the Tokyo festival.

So thorough were they that one week before the Games began they staged another rehearsal, this time of the opening and closing ceremonies. To do this, they used 70,000 schoolchildren, 8,000 of them acting as stand-ins for every person who would be in the National Stadium during the real events ahead. The rest of the children played the spectators.

The only political problem that could have caused the Japanese Olympic officials some concern occurred when 11 Indonesian and 6 North Korean athletes were not accepted as contestants at Tokyo. In 1963, these athletes had participated in the Games of the New Emerging Forces, an Indonesian-sponsored all-Asian mini-Olympics. The international governing bodies of swimming and track and field declared this an outlawed meet and said any of their amateur athletes competing in it would be automatically suspended, which would make them ineligible to take part in the Tokyo Olympic Games. North Korea and Indonesia withdrew and sent their delegations in Tokyo back home.

By the time the opening ceremonies began, the success of Tokyo's preparation efforts was apparent. A new expressway between the airport and the city proper provided visitors easy access to both. A new high-rise hotel had been constructed, and new stadiums had been built, including the swimming arena, perhaps the finest in the world. And everywhere, athletes and visitors alike were made to feel welcome. Avery Brundage, the president of the IOC, was moved to comment, "The entire nation, from newsboy to industrial tycoon, adopted the Games as his own project and went out of his way to please the visitors."

The Games were opened by Emperor Hirohito on Saturday, and the competitions began the next day. It would be difficult to single out the performance of any one athlete at the Tokyo Games for special mention, as that Olympics produced several astonishing achievements. Peter Snell of New Zealand had burst onto the Olympic stage as a 21-year-old unknown in Rome to win the 800-meter race. By 1964, Snell had set world records in the 800-meter, the 880-yard, and one-mile runs and was the hands-down favorite in the 800 and 1,500 meters. He won the 800 in the Olympic record time of 1:45.1, and he took the 1,500 meters in 3:38.1, running the final quarter in 52.9, the equivalent of a 3:55 mile.

The Americans recaptured the 100- and 200-meter titles they had lost in Rome when Bob Hayes, a football player at Florida A & M, set a world record of 10 flat in the 100, and Henry Carr of Arizona State set an Olympic record in the 200 meters. Later, while anchoring the 4x100-meter relay team to a world record 39.0, Hayes ran his 100 meters in an impossible 8.6 seconds.

It was in the distance races that the results were really unexpected. The longer races had always been the weak events for Americans, but that changed in Tokyo. Bob Schul became the first

U.S. athlete to win the 5,000-meter run. The 10,000-meter race had all the trappings of a movie scenario. The race was packed with star performers: Ron Clarke of Australia, Pyotr Bolotnikov of the USSR, Murray Halberg of New Zealand, and Ron Hill of Great Britain, all holders of various world distance records. The only American contender was thought to be Gerry Lindgren, who had defeated the Russians in the Russian-American Dual Meet earlier that summer. The least likely winner was Billy Mills, an orphaned, part-Sioux Indian Marine. Running on a muddy track, Mills did the impossible and won the race in the Olympic record time of 28:24.4. His life and surprising victory are chronicled in the 1983 movie *Running Brave.*

An Ethiopian palace guard named Abebe Bikila had amazed everyone in Rome when he won the marathon running barefoot. In Tokyo he repeated his victory, this time wearing shoes but only five weeks after undergoing an emergency appendectomy. Five years later Bikila was so badly injured in an automobile accident that he never walked again. Of his misfortune, he said, "Men of success meet with tragedy. It was the will of God that I won the Olympics, and it was the will of God that I met with my accident. I was overjoyed when I won the marathon twice. But I accepted those victories as I accept this tragedy. I have no choice. I have to accept both circumstances as facts of life and live happily."

The American triumphs in track and field also had their equivalents in the swimming and diving competitions. Don Schollander won gold medals in the 100- and 400-meter freestyles and as anchor in the 4x100- and 2x200-meter relay events and set three world records. He also set a personal record: he became the first swimmer to win four gold medals in one Olympics. Cathy Ferguson set world and Olympic records in the women's 100-meter backstroke and 4x100 medley relay.

In the 1900 and 1904 Olympics, the winning American eight-oared rowing crew came from the Vesper Boat Club of Philadelphia. In the Games from 1920 through 1960, the winning American crews were from one of the collegiate rowing powerhouses such as California, Yale, or Harvard. In 1964, a noncollegiate eight from Vesper again took the gold. Since Tokyo, American eight-oared crews have been picked at large, rather than simply selecting the winning college or boat club team from the trials. Whether coincidence or not, since then Americans have lost their dominance in this event.

The basketball competition came down to a battle between the U.S. and the USSR teams for the fourth consecutive Olympics. The captain of the winning U.S. team was Princeton's Bill Bradley, a Rhodes scholar who later played with the New York Knicks and eventually was elected to Congress as U.S. senator from New Jersey.

The closing ceremonies in Tokyo were held at sunset. As part of the ritual, hundreds of schoolgirls ringed the track in the darkness. Then each lit a torch. The scoreboard flashed "Sayonara," and the XVIIIth Olympiad became a memory.

WILLIAM "BILLY" MILLS

Gold Medal, 10,000 Meters, 1964

In one of the most spectacular races in track history, Billy Mills won this country's first and only Olympic gold medal in the 10,000 meters at Tokyo in 1964. As a matter of fact, Mills, who is part Sioux Indian, is one of only two Americans ever to win any kind of medal in the 10,000 meter run. Ironically, the other medalist was also an Indian, Lewis Tewanima, who won the silver medal at the 1912 Games, the first year that race appeared as an Olympic event. Mills also ran in the marathon at Tokyo, placing a respectable 14th.

Mills's track career was rather undistinguished before the Tokyo Games, but in 1965 he set a world 6-mile record at the AAU championships and a U.S. record in the 10,000 meters. He also won the U.S. indoor 3-mile championship.

Billy Mills, who was orphaned when he was 12, grew up on the Sioux reservation at Pine Ridge, South Dakota. He attended Haskell Indian School at Lawrence, Kansas, and graduated from the University of Kansas.

In 1983 Robbie Benson starred in Running Brave, *a film about the life of Billy Mills and his quest for identity and athletic greatness. Today, with his wife, Pat, Mills is involved in various business enterprises and is particularly active in promoting Indian self-awareness and education.*

Billy Mills in 1985. Photo courtesy of Billy Mills

I was born in a small village on the Oglala Sioux Indian reservation in South Dakota. Society calls us the Sioux, but we go by the name Lakota. My mom died when I was 7, and my dad died when I was 12, but including my mom and dad, there were 15 of us in the family.

I was very close to my dad. When he was younger, he used to box and wrestle, and he used to encourage me to participate in sports and said that sports was a vehicle through which to compete with the white man. He used to say, "Compete in sports, take care of your body, believe in a creator, and learn to live with the white society." He said that if I competed with the white man—with the dominant society—in sports, I could have fun at the same time. At the time I didn't really understand all the implications of what he said, but in retrospect I believe that he was trying to prepare me to live in that society as well as in the Indian society.

I started out with boxing, but I was pretty weak in the shoulders, and the other guys hit a lot harder than I could. I continued to box, but I knew that boxing wasn't for me. I attempted basketball, too, but I never really played very well. I tried rodeo. Almost every person, Indian or non-Indian, growing up on a reservation tries rodeo.

There were quite a few white people living on the reservation; probably 1,000 of the 8,000 people there were white. At that time not many Indians were going off to college, so most of the educators were white people. And the whites controlled the economic base of the reservation. They operated the stores and, of course, ran the Bureau of Indian Affairs. Also, there was always the anthropologist who was working on his or her doctorate degree. They would come and study us for a summer and then go back and have a book published. We always resented being studied like some kind of insect.

Today the Indians are almost an invisible people. There's some indescribable history there, but it's not being taught, and it's not being learned. There's probably not a high school in this nation where even one of the treaties an Indian tribe has with the U.S. government is studied. And yet every right that an Indian person has today in America is not a right that has been given to them; it's a right that has been retained for them by their ancestors through a treaty.

But as I said, the Indians are almost an invisible people. There is a museum at the University of Kansas, and in it is Custer's stuffed horse, Comanche. I was one of five Indian students on campus, and I went to the museum and saw that at the stuffed horse there was a sign that said, "The Sole Survivor of the Battle of Little Bighorn." When I saw it, I thought, Hey, what about the winners? What about the people who won? But, see, the dominant society didn't understand that there were more survivors of that battle than a white man's horse. That was one of those little things that I had to deal with, and those things bothered me.

As I tried various sports I soon found that I liked running. I felt an incredible tranquillity when running, an incredible peace of mind. While I was training for boxing I'd go on four- and five-mile road runs, just jogging, and I really enjoyed having my feet pound against the earth.

I went to high school at Haskell Indian School in Lawrence, Kansas. It was a boarding school, like Carlisle Indian School in Pennsylvania, where Jim Thorpe and Frank Mt. Pleasants and many other great Indian athletes went to school. I ran my first race at Haskell in a very slow time, but I won. That was the half-mile, and I also won a mile race. I was boxing, too, but I lost many more fights than I won. In basketball and in football I was always on the B team. I never started. But in track I won, and that showed me there was something I could do.

In my sophomore year I finished fifth in my first cross-country race, third in my second cross-country, and I won my third race. That year I finished first in the state in cross-country. I came out of high school undefeated in cross-country after my sophomore year and was the fifth or sixth best miler in the nation. I was offered 18 scholarships—me, an orphan who grew up in poverty. The significance of that didn't hit me until much later in life.

I knew that it was going to be a major transition for me, going from the predominantly Indian culture at Haskell, a boarding school of 1,000 Indians from all over the nation, to the predominantly white environment of a university. The Indian coach at Haskell, Tony Coffin, had become like a second father to me.

I considered several colleges and finally decided on the University of Kansas, partly because it was a good school and had a fine track program. Wes Santee, the great distance runner, and Al Frame, who had won the NCAA cross-country when I was coming out of high school, were at Kansas.

I thought that since the university was also in Lawrence, I'd have less trouble making the adjustment in a familiar area. In retrospect, however, that was probably a mistake. I think going to the University of Oklahoma would have caused a less severe transition. Going to school at the University of Kansas was a very cruel experience for me. I'm 48 years old, and I'm just now learning to understand and to have the compassion to put things in perspective.

At the school on the reservation and at Haskell, I was taught to be gentle, to respect the elders, to listen. Nothing prepared me for how the white society was going to treat me. I was one of the top high school athletes in the state, and when I got to the university I began to be rushed by the fraternities, and then found I wasn't allowed to join because I was Indian. When I started to date a few girls at Kansas, their parents became very upset when they learned I was an Indian. In retrospect, I can understand now that some of that might have been not because I was an Indian, but because here I was, an orphan, raised in poverty, and the prospect that their daughter might have some security with me was very slim. But at the time, I understood that they didn't want their daughter to have anything to do with an Indian, even a part Indian.

I had a very difficult time making the transition, and I took out a lot of my frustration and resentment on my coach at Kansas, Bill Easton. Easton was a quality coach. He was tenacious and dogmatic, but he knew how to coach track. However, he didn't understand me and my background. He assumed it was an easy transition for me, and I was holding in most of my anger and frustration, yet focusing it on him. Easton saw some incredible potential in me. He felt I could become a great distance runner, even an Olympic runner. In a sense he was asking me to trust him, to do things his way. I had a love-hate relationship with Easton. I wanted to please him, but I wanted to do things my way, the way I knew was best for me. And the hostility that grew out of all the blatant and subtle rejections that society was throwing at me I took out on him, and he really had no idea I was doing that. I was trying to find answers to questions I couldn't even express, and my coach was not a sociologist or a psychologist. He couldn't determine where I was coming from. So during my years at Kansas my track career languished. Once I entered a race and got so angry that I quit and walked off the track. That happened in my senior year at the NCAA championships.

It was a very hot day, and I was running in the back of the pack. As I came by Easton he said, "Billy, get up where you belong; get up in front." Another lap went by, and I heard him say, or I thought I heard him say, "Get up where you belong or get off the track." And I thought, You know, there's a third way to do this, and it's my way. I'm a senior in college. I can do it my way, which is to run in the back and come up slowly. When Easton said that again, I walked off the track. He sent for me and said, "Why did you quit?" I answered, "Coach, I didn't quit. You said to get up in front or get off the track. I got off the track." "You quit," he said. All the pressures I was feeling I took out on this man who was really trying to help me. By walking off the track I may have appeared to be protesting against my coach, but in reality I was protesting against society. I don't think he ever understood that.

Then it started eating at me. I did quit. If I really believed strongly enough in myself, I would have ignored his command to get up in front and done it my way. Had I done that, I might have finished first or second. The best I had ever done in NCAA track was fifth.

I learned something very important from that experience. By being able to recognize that I did quit, I learned that I had matured to the point where I could deal with it. I came to the realization that the height of competition is not for me to compete against another or for him to compete against me, but for me to compete against myself. That's the real competition. In retrospect, I think that was part of what my father was trying to tell me.

Later, in the '70s, I found out I was allergic to a multitude of foods and that those allergies would sometimes cause hypoglycemic symptoms, which in turn compounded my other problems in running. Even though I didn't realize my full potential in track at Kansas, I made the first team All-American two years in a row in cross-country and the second team once. I finished third two years in a row in the AAU cross-country and was the first American to finish. So I had a fairly successful college track career, but my real potential languished. Yet I knew the ability was there, and I was determined to try to make the Olympic team in 1964.

I graduated from Kansas in 1962 with a degree in physical education and a teaching certificate for elementary and secondary schools. Pat and I were married when I was a senior, and I had signed up for the officer's candidate program. After I graduated I took 12 weeks of training and was commissioned a second lieutenant in the marines.

I ran several one-, two-, and three-mile races while in the service, and in 1963 I ran the 10,000-meter at an intermilitary meet in Belgium. Meanwhile I kept a training book in which I kept track of my times and my workout program. At Belgium I ran a 30.08 race, and at that point I knew I could make the team and maybe win a medal. I kept increasing my practice distances and reducing my times. While at Camp Pendleton I ran in the Culver City marathon and came in second. That qualified me for the Olympic team in the marathon. Ten days later I broke the American record in the 6-mile race, and a few weeks after that I made the Olympic team in the 10K with a 29.10. For the next six weeks before the Olympics I switched from my distance running and concentrated on preparing for the 10K. I was still going to run the marathon and see what happened, but my training was for the other race.

Pat was with me in Tokyo, but I had to pretty much avoid her. I was keyed up for the race, and any little thing would set me off. So I just hung around the Village and continued my practice runs. I knew I was going to win. That was something I had wanted to do since I was a sophomore in high school—to make the Olympic team and win a medal at the Games. In retrospect, I know that I was running not just to win a medal but to have a better understanding of who I was as a person.

There were a lot of great distance runners in that race. Ron Clarke of Australia held several world distance records. Pyotr Bolotnikov of Russia held the official record in the 10K, and there was Murray Halberg of New Zealand, Ron Hill of England, Mohamed Gammoudi of Tunisia, and Mamo Wolde of Ethiopia. The reporters from all over the world were always stopping these people and asking them questions, but no one asked me even one question. It was like I was invisible. Yet I knew that if I stayed up with the leaders and put on a good final kick I would win. What the reporters didn't know was that in my speed training a few days earlier I had run a 220 in 23.6.

Well, the race began, and Ron Clarke nearly broke me at the 5,000-meter mark. I was within one second of my fastest 5,000 meters ever; actually, my fastest 3-mile ever, because I was going by the 3-mile times and not really considering the difference between meters and miles. In my mind I was converting my 5,000-meter time back to 3 miles because 5 didn't mean much to me: I had run only four 10,000-meter races in my life. Clarke and I crossed the 5,000-meter mark at 14.06, and my best 5K had been 13.57. But I was within one second of my fastest individual 3-mile, and at that point I was thinking that I couldn't continue at this pace. I had taken the lead at the 5,000, but I dropped right back to fourth, and the leaders started pulling away from me. I thought that I might just as well let them go.

I started trying to understand the 5,000 because meters were still pretty new to me. Then I thought, Hey, wait a minute—13.52, 14.06; I have an 11-second leeway: I can slow up 11 seconds and still hold it. So I started fighting back, slowly coming up on them. At one point I was going to go one more lap, take the lead, and go one more. That way, if I did have to quit, it would be while I was winning. I kept thinking that if I had to quit I wasn't going to do it in front of where Pat was sitting; I'd do it at the other end of the field.

Gradually I worked past that bad spell where I thought I might have to quit. From that point on, it was "I'm here to stay." With two laps to go, Bolotnikov fell off, Wolde fell off, and there were three of us left. I was in second place, and Clarke looked back. I saw him look back, and I thought, My God! He's worried. It was just so clear in my mind: he looked back, saw Gammoudi and me, and was worried. From that point on I stayed with him.

Going into the bell lap I moved into Clarke's shoulder and took a slight lead. We were coming up on one of the lapped runners, Temu. He was a barefoot runner from Kenya and won a gold medal at the next Olympics in Mexico City. We were closing on him fast, and I had Clarke perfectly boxed in. When I ran Clarke into Temu's back, I was going to start my kick. We were coming off the first curve with another curve to go, about 375 yards from the finish, when Clarke saw that I had boxed him in, and he gave me a little nudge. I nudged him back, and then he leaned into me a little, and I leaned into him. Then he lifted me up and pushed me into the third lane. I thought I was going to fall, and my legs started to buckle. But I recovered and started to close back on Clarke's shoulder. Just then Gammoudi broke between Clarke and me, knocking Clarke to the inside and me to the outside, but neither of us really stumbled. Gammoudi pulled probably 12 to 15 yards ahead, and I'm 3 or 4 yards behind Clarke. All I could think of was that we had about 250 yards to go.

There were probably 75,000 screaming people in the stadium, but all I could hear was the throbbing of my heart. In my mind, in a kind of self-hypnosis, I was reliving my training sessions at Camp Pendleton. I'm on Clarke's shoulder, and the previous year he broke the world record in the 10K. Every day of my training, in my mind, I went by Clarke just a second before the finish, and I'd win. But this was real. Gammoudi was leading, and Clarke took off after him. I kept thinking, One more try. One more try. We came off the last curve, and I could see the tape stretched across the finish line. Then I thought, I can win. I can win. My mind was racing. With about 80 yards to go they were 5 or 6 yards ahead of me, and I thought, I may never be this close again. Drive! Drive! At 60 yards to go they were still ahead of me, and I couldn't hear anything except my heart pounding. And I knew I had won. I knew I might not get to the tape first, but I knew that at that stage I was the fastest man on the track, and if I had enough time I would go past them. At 40 yards out I realized with every stride that I would win. Then I felt the tape break across my chest. I came to a stop, and a Japanese official came running up to me and said, "Who are you? Who are you?" I panicked. I thought, Oh my God, do I have one more lap to go? But the race was over, and I was being led off to a press conference.

But they wouldn't allow me to take a victory lap. Within a few minutes they had brought Pat down from the stands, and we stood there waiting for the press conference to begin. I wanted to express myself with a victory lap, but they wouldn't permit it. I wanted to extend that one fleeting moment when I was the best in the world because I knew the moment would be gone forever. They wouldn't let me take that lap because there were still some runners on the field finishing the race, and it would be too complicated.

After I caught my breath and calmed down, I had this very powerful feeling come over me that my dad knows—he knows I'm an athlete.

Over the years since then I watched many races, and I watched the winners take their victory laps. I always felt incomplete in my victory: I didn't get my victory lap. But in 1984 Bud Greenspan was making another one of his great films on the Olympics, and he invited Pat and me to Tokyo. We went out to the National Stadium to set up the filming. The Japanese showed me the plaque listing the names of the gold medalists who had won their medals in that stadium, and I could see my name on it. It was raining, but I knew what I wanted, and Pat knew what I was going to do. I went down onto the track and jogged and walked up one way, then came back and jogged and walked the other way. I went on around, taking that victory lap I so desperately needed. At the same time, in my mind, I was reliving that race. I could feel Clarke push me, and I could sense people in the stadium. Toward the end of my lap, I heard one person clapping; it was Pat, clapping for me. I started crying. I needed that victory lap so badly, I started crying, and rather than let the group see me cry, I lifted my face up to the rain, walked up the track a way to get my composure, then finished my lap.

WILLIAM WARREN BRADLEY

Gold Medal, Basketball, 1964

Excellence and success have characterized Bill Bradley's entire public career, from his All-American basketball days at Princeton through his studies at Oxford as a Rhodes scholar and his 11-year career with the New York Knicks to his present career as a U.S. senator from New Jersey.

Senator Bradley has written extensively on the reforms he believes are badly needed if the Olympics are to survive as a positive force for international goodwill and understanding and as an athletic celebration worthy of the memory of Baron de Coubertin. The following comments were excerpted from published materials sent to the authors by the senator's Washington office.

The Olympic Games first began in Greece 2,600 years ago and continued at regular intervals for nearly 12 centuries without a major interruption. Held in honor of Zeus, the Games were more than athletic competitions. They were Panhellenic festivals, with contests in dance and choral poetry held on the plain of Olympia. In those ancient times, the Games continued even when participating states were at war with one another. In fact, athletes from warring states were granted safe passage when going to and from the site of the Olympics.

The modern Olympic Games began in 1896 and, like the ancient contests, were intended to promote the ideal of a sound mind in a

Bill Bradley in 1986.
Photo courtesy of Senator Bill Bradley

sound body and to foster competition among people in athletics instead of conflict among states.

Unfortunately, in practice the modern Games have been unable to emulate the ancients' ability to honor sport by subordinating war and politics. Nor have they been successful in encouraging a sense of oneness and mutual understanding among the world's people. Over the past 50 years, the Games have been marred, time and time again, by nationalistic displays and buffeted by international politics. There were the "Nazi Olympics" of 1936, the withdrawal of the Swiss and the Dutch in 1956 in condemnation of the Soviet invasion of Hungary, the events of 1968 and the assassinations of 1972, the withdrawal of 28 Third World countries from the Montreal Games in 1976, and the boycotts of 1980 and 1984. I remember, when I participated in the 1964 Games in Tokyo, waking up in the middle of the night to a commotion in the next dormitory. It was the North Koreans pulling out of the Games. Such conduct makes it clear that the Olympics as constituted today are far from the ideal that their founders intended.

Many people have called for the abolition of the Olympics, claiming that they have become too expensive, too political, and too dangerous. I believe that the Olympics should be continued, but only with drastic modification.

First, we need to have one uniform standard of eligibility, making skill the only criterion for competition and abandoning the ridiculous notion of amateurism in a world of differing social and economic systems.

My personal experience in 1964 illustrates why ability should be the sole criterion for eligibility. In the finals, we played the Soviet Union. We won. Two years later, while studying at Oxford, I was playing a couple of times a month for an Italian meatpacking firm. We played the Soviet team in the European Cup finals, and, man for man, that team was the same one that played in the Olympics of 1964, except now they were called the Soviet Army Club Team. The army paid them to play basketball, but according to the rules of international competition they were still considered amateurs. In reality, they were professionals, if viewed from the standpoint of compensation and how much time they spent playing the game.

The traditional amateurism of an Avery Brundage eliminated the lower and middle classes of capitalist countries from competition. Without some form of subsidy they could not afford to compete against wealthier athletes. Since compensation for athletic services violated Olympic rules, officials often found less obvious ways to reward poorer participants. As a result, many athletes had to be dishonest about their compensation. It is time for the hypocrisy to cease and the rules to be modified by allowing open competition.

I think we need to abandon team sports in the Olympics because they too easily simulate war games. One has only to look at the Hungarian-Soviet water polo game in 1956, or the Czech-Soviet ice hockey match in 1968, or any time the Indians and the Pakistanis play field hockey, to recognize that these contests go well beyond friendly competition.

We should continue to recognize individual achievements. I will never forget that moment standing on the platform after beating the Soviets in the finals, watching the flag being raised and listening to the national anthem being played. It gave enduring meaning to the years of personal sacrifice.

But we also need to champion individuals other than just the fastest, the strongest, and the most agile among us. Why not extend the Olympics to two months and also recognize creative, intellectual, and artistic ability? A film festival, poetry readings, concerts, cultural shows, and athletic events might even run simultaneously at an expanded Olympics. The whole person should be the theme of the festival. The emphasis would not be on the rewards to be taken home but on the experience of living for two months in a microcosm of the world.

The Olympics should be much more participant-oriented. Too often, the years of grueling training and individual discipline are overshadowed by extraneous events. In many cases, the athlete has gotten lost amid the gigantic construction projects, the television cameras, and the hordes of tourists that flock from one site to another. If the purpose of the Games is to promote mutual understanding and brotherhood, the way to do that is by enhancing the experience of the athlete who lives in the Olympic Village and meets and interacts with people from all over the world. That was the most enjoyable and memorable aspect of my experience.

I remember the athletes with whom I shared those weeks, and I remember the sense of pride and achievement we all felt. In the final ceremony I walked into the stadium with a New Zealander, a Nigerian, a Pole, and, I think, an athlete from Ireland. These were people whom I'd gotten to know in the Village dining halls and

Photo courtesy of Sports Information, Princeton University

Bill Bradley in 1964.

recreation areas, and we became friends. It was a vivid demonstration of unity that you don't always have in a world that is fractured by national aspirations.

The Games should be permanently located in their ancient birthplace, the country of Greece. This permanent home would come to be identified with the Olympics as an institution, and the Games would no longer be identified with the nationalistic displays of temporary hosts. The way it now is, too often the host country attempts to produce a gigantic display of nationalism. This also encourages a situation where the Olympics infringe on the domestic politics of the host country, as happened in Mexico City and Montreal.

In 1980, when the U.S. boycotted the Moscow Olympics, the Greeks proposed a 1,250-acre site near ancient Olympia, but the idea was opposed by the International Olympic Committee. Construction costs for facilities in Greece would have been paid by the participating nations. It would be a matter of spending $10 billion once rather than spending that amount or more every four years.

Putting the summer Olympics permanently in Greece and the winter games in their own home would help the Olympics become a strong institution rather than short-lived competitions vulnerable to political or economic exploitation by temporary host countries and other nations. If the Games had had a permanent home in a neutral country, it is probable that neither the United States in 1980 nor the Soviets in 1984 would have withdrawn from the Games. Given a stable, enduring setting, the Games could take on a special identity of their own, much like the celebrations of old, and they could provide the basis for the beginnings of understanding among nations.

To initiate a permanent site with Games that are true to their original goals will require bold planning and a willingness to share the financial burden by hundreds of nations. It will also require a revision of the rules and the personnel who govern the Olympic movement. And it will demand a strong belief on the part of all of us that peace can prevail.

ROBERT KEYSER SCHUL

Gold Medal, 5,000 Meters, 1964

Americans have won only three Olympic medals in the 5,000 meters, and two of them came in 1964 when Bob Schul took the gold and Bill Dellinger earned the bronze. Ralph Hill won the silver in 1932, but since 1964 the best American finish has been Steve Prefontaine's fourth in 1972.

Perhaps the rigorous training and extreme physical sacrifices have discouraged many would-be distance runners, but not Bob Schul, who learned his art from Mihaly Igloi, the demanding Hungarian coach who in 1956 defected to the United States.

I started training under Mihaly Igoli while I was in the Air Force, and he made me into a runner. I had had some success in high school and at Miami University at Oxford, but certainly not enough for any national recognition.

It was in the spring of 1961 while I was stationed at Oxnard, California, that I got a chance to spend a couple of weeks with Igloi in San Jose. That was a real eye-opener for me. The first day he would only let me watch, but I couldn't believe what he had his runners doing. I didn't think the human body could take that kind of strain, and I surely had serious doubts whether mine could. But I had always had the psychological strength to do anything my coaches asked of me in training, and I never questioned them.

I started the next morning, and it was unbelievable. Igloi had taken the British system of running repeats of a specific distance and modified it. For example, the British might run five times 220 yards at 30 seconds each. Igloi didn't worry about the watch. He put us into different effort modes. He called them "fresh," "good," "hard," and "all-out." He would mix these up as well as the distances. That first morning we did 5 miles of 100-yard repeats. We'd sprint 100 yards, walk the turns, and then sprint again on the other side. We'd do this for 5 miles, while constantly changing speeds.

Igloi had perhaps 30 people in training, and I have never seen a

Bob Schul in 1986.
Photo by Fogarty and Carlson

more dedicated group of athletes. Many of them took jobs below their educational level just to have the chance to train with him. He would be at the track from 5:30 to 8:00 in the morning and then again in the evenings from 5:00 to 8:00. In between he would fill out the logs on his top athletes. He was then with the Santa Clara Valley Youth Organization, a nonprofit group that was probably paying him about $400 a month.

When the funding for the SCVYO stopped in the spring of 1961, Igloi was without any income, but later in the year two businessmen paid him $500 a month to come down to LA and start the Los Angeles Track Club. That was great for me because I was stationed only 60 miles away. We set up a training schedule where I would train with him on Friday evening, all day Saturday and Sunday, and at 5:30 Monday morning before I had to go back to the base for my regular duties at 8:00. Then I'd go back Monday after work and train that evening and early Tuesday morning. He'd give me workouts for Wednesday, Thursday, and Friday morning, which I could do at the base. It was a tiring schedule, and I don't know how I did it because I was making only $78 a month and out of that I had to pay my driving expenses and part of the rent for a tiny apartment in LA that several of us were sharing.

Nobody in this country has really given Igloi the credit he deserves, but there's no arguing with his success. In the years before he defected to the U.S., his Hungarian athletes held every world record from 1,500 through 10,000 meters. And after he got here, Jim Beatty, Max Truex, and I started breaking all the American records. But because of politics and petty jealousies, Igloi was never offered a university coaching position in this country, and in the early 1970s he became the national coach of Greece, a position he held until his retirement in 1986.

I was born in West Milton, Ohio, on a 100-acre farm. I was an asthmatic and suffered from hay fever, and because of that I didn't do much as a youngster. I just couldn't. I can remember standing around the playgrounds in the fall watching the other kids until the first heavy frost would allow me to be active again. In the spring I would play baseball until the hay fever season started about mid-July; then I had to pretty much stay in the house to keep away from the pollen and dust. I really had it bad. I almost died two or three times when I was very young. I'd turn blue, and my folks would have to rush me to the hospital.

The doctors warned my parents not to let me run, but, thankfully, they decided they couldn't keep me indoors forever. When I did get out, I soon discovered no one could catch me in any game that involved running longer distances. Finally, in the seventh grade, I went out for track and slowly developed until in high school I managed a fifth-place finish in the state tournament and a best time of 4:34.

There were no college recruiters knocking on my door, so I decided to work for a year before I started school at Miami University in the fall of 1956. I spent two years there before poor grades and a lack of money made me decide to go into the Air Force. I did manage to set the school record of 4:12 in the mile as a sophomore, but that certainly did not put me at the top of the collegiate runners, who were running around 4:06 at the time.

I returned to Miami in 1963, and by this time I was nationally ranked in the steeplechase and the distance races. I probably should have stayed in the Los Angeles area and gone to USC, but I really loved Miami, and I had some bad memories of USC. When I was a freshman at Miami and without a scholarship, I wrote Dean Cromwell and asked him if USC would like to have a miler. He wrote back and thanked me for my letter, but advised me to stay where I was. He told me, "Your time isn't too bad, but you really couldn't run for us."

When I returned in 1963, Miami paid my $100 tuition and gave me used books from the Athletic Department's pool but nothing else. There were also some problems with the coaching staff. I told them I had my own schedule and I couldn't run in the dual meets because my primary objective was to make the 1964 Olympic team.

Bob Epscamp was the coach, and he agreed. He told me he wanted to train me. I told him, "Bob, I don't know if you can." He was only three or four years older than I, and, truthfully, I knew more than he did, but we tried it for a while. I'd train at 6:00 in the morning, and our agreement was that he was to be there for every workout. He made the first two or three, but then it went downhill fast. Pretty soon he was skipping more than he was making. So I walked into his office one day and told him that it was time that I started training myself.

He tried to make me back down, but I knew it wasn't going to work. From that time on I rarely saw the team and never worked out with anybody. I was by myself. It was tough. After being used to training with guys who were so dedicated and whose energy I absorbed, I now found my days to be very tough psychologically.

In nice weather I trained on a grass field behind the girls' gymnasium, and in winter, when ice and snow covered the fields, I worked out under the football stadium on a 70-yard dirt straightaway. That was tough. The winter of 1963–4 was cold, and many days the temperature hovered around zero. When it got too cold, I'd go in the morning to a small ancient gym that had a small running track that was kind of suspended from the rafters. It was about 5 feet wide, unbanked, with four square turns, and it swayed when you ran. I'd run my 20 yards, slow down for the turn, and then speed up again for 20 yards. It was boring, but I'd spend an hour and 15 minutes at 6:00 A.M. trying to get my body in its best possible condition.

The indoor circuit of 1963–4 established just how far my conditioning had taken me. I had written to all the major meet directors, and for the first time most of them had answered. At my first indoor race in Boston I broke the American record for three miles. I couldn't believe how easy it was. I went on to win all my indoor races, except those I ran against Bruce Kidd, the fine runner from Canada. We split eight races, and neither of us ever won by more than a foot. It was just a great series, with each victory determined by whoever got the good jump on the final lap.

That winter I beat Australia's Ron Clarke a couple of times. He was on his way up and already being touted as the possible Olympic winner in the 5,000 and 10,000 meters because back in Australia he had just set the world record for the 10,000.

I still didn't get much recognition from the press until I won the 5,000 meters at the Compton Relays in the spring of 1964. It was billed as the best 5,000-meter race ever run in the U.S. because the promoters had pulled together every distance star they could find. And no one was disappointed. I broke the American record with a 13:38 clocking, beating Bill Bailey, Kidd, Beatty, and Gerry Lindgren, a high school kid from the state of Washington who had recently given Clarke a great race. Because it was the fastest time in the world that year, the press began to write that maybe I did have a chance at a medal if I continued to improve.

I also won the U.S. nationals in New York and the first of two Olympic trials just four days later in New Jersey. In truth, the Olympic officials scheduled two trials because they were hoping to raise more money. Because I won the first, I was supposed to be assured of being on the team if I "maintained my conditioning," but nobody explained to me what that meant.

Next we defeated the Russians in a dual meet in which we won every distance event. Lindgren won the 10,000, George Young the steeplechase, and I took the 5,000. We had never swept them before. A few weeks later I set a world record of 8:26.4 in the 2 miles, and the following week I broke 4 minutes in the mile for the second time in my career. All this convinced me that my training was producing the kind of speed and endurance that I would need for the Olympics, and I started thinking of winning not just a medal but the gold medal itself.

At the second Olympic trials in Los Angeles I didn't have a care in the world. I was confident, and I knew I was in great shape. Bill Dellinger and I decided before the race that we would come in together if no one was pushing us. No one did, but as we ran side by side down the homestretch, we heard some of the Coliseum fans booing. I thought to myself, Don't these people understand what's happening here? For the first time in Olympic history we finally have the potential to win the 5,000 meters, and they're booing us.

On the first day of the competition in Tokyo, Billy Mills won the 10,000. I had picked him to do well, though I didn't think he could beat Clarke. But he did when Clarke ran a stupid race. That put pressure on me because the odds were so great against two Americans winning events that we had never won before. I had also hurt both my Achilles tendons on the first day in Tokyo because of an uneven surface on which I trained. And, to put even more pressure on myself, back in Los Angeles I had brashly promised the press that I was going to win the gold.

The day of the finals I loosened up at 6:00 A.M., had breakfast about 10:00, and then read and watched television. But watching the other athletes just made me more nervous. I went upstairs to lie down, but I couldn't do that either. I was like a cat on a hot tin roof. I went over my competitors in some English track and field magazines. About an hour and a half before the race I left for the stadium. It was about a 20-minute bus ride, and I noticed how hard it was raining. When I arrived, I went into the U.S. dressing room, and the first person I talked to was Willie Davenport. He was the top hurdler in the world, but he had not made the finals because he had slipped in a trial heat because of the muddy track. That got me to thinking, What if after all my work something like that happens to me?

During the Olympic 5,000-meter race; Schul is wearing number 719.
Photo courtesy of *Track and Field News*

I pushed those thoughts aside and started warming up under the stadium. The two Russians in the finals were there, and whatever I did they followed right behind me. I jumped off to the side and stretched a bit, but when I started jogging, they were there again right beside me. They were just trying to unnerve me.

Twenty minutes before the race we went into the starting room. Everything was deathly silent in there. Even the television set had the sound turned off. Twenty minutes is a long time to sit with your own thoughts. The atmosphere was so heavy you could cut it with a knife. About a minute before the race they released us onto the track. When that cold rain hit us, we just froze. I think it was 52 degrees, which meant that it takes longer to warm up, but we had time for only one run up the track before they called us to the line. As we got ready to start, all my nervousness left me, and I knew I was ready to run.

We got off to a very slow first quarter, in part because everyone was so cold that our muscles took a while to loosen up. No one wanted to take the lead until about the third lap when Clarke finally did. France's Michel Jazy went with him. I was back in sixth or seventh place. All of a sudden the Englishman in front of me catches Dellinger's heel, and down on his face he goes. I jumped over him to the outside, but that could have been disastrous for me.

From then on it was a cat and mouse game. Clarke would speed up to a very fast pace, and positions would change behind him. When he would go, I'd speed up a little bit but not as fast as he would. I wasn't worried, because I was feeling so good. I knew he couldn't keep up that tempo. When he'd sprint, he was probably running a four-minute-mile pace. But his strategy lost only a couple of runners, and during the last stages of the race I think he actually gave up. With two laps to go I started moving up slowly until with 500 meters left I moved into third right behind Jazy and Germany's Harald Norpoth. But just as I made my move, there came Dellinger flying past, taking the lead, and I'm thinking to myself, What the hell is he doing? By the time we got to the bell lap, Jazy had repassed Dellinger, and Nikolai Dutov of the Soviet Union had passed me and moved up on Jazy. Jazy was sort of looking back and forth to see where everybody was, and then he started to pick up the pace for the final 400 meters.

I wanted to go after him, but I was boxed in by Kenya's Kip Keino and couldn't get loose. There was Jazy moving away, and I was helpless to do anything about it. Finally, Keino fell back enough to let me by. By then we had about 300 meters to go, and I'm sprinting all-out. I quickly passed Dellinger and a couple of others. Norpoth was still in front of me, and Jazy was about 10 meters in front of him. About halfway down the backstretch I was going as hard as I could, but I wasn't catching Jazy at all—not an inch and I couldn't go any faster. For the first time in the race I'm thinking to myself, You damn fool. Why did you get boxed in on the turn? You've lost it.

At that point I was determined just to sprint as hard as I could and perhaps pass Norpoth for second. I was by him by the middle of the turn, and for the first time I could see I was closing in on Jazy. He was probably no more than 10 meters in front of me. I could also see that he was starting to tie up. His shoulders were tightening, and by the time we had 130 meters to go I knew there was no way I was not going to beat him. Every step closed the gap. With about 100 meters to go he was only a couple of steps in front. I wasn't running faster; he was just slowing down. By 60 meters I was by him, so then I started wondering what was happening behind me. Was somebody catching me as well? I kept running as hard as I could right through the tape. Later I was told that I had run the final 300 meters in 38.7, which was as fast as New Zealand's Peter Snell had closed in his one-sided victory in the 1,500 meters. And all this on a muddy track in a driving rainstorm.

There are only four of us Americans who have won gold medals in the distance races: Horace Ashenfelter won the 3,000 meter steeplechase in 1952; Frank Shorter, the marathon in 1972; and Billy Mills and myself. And I was the only one who was the favorite and ranked number one at the time. I may have been the first American to win the 5,000, but there were those teammates on the Los Angeles Track Club such as Jim Beatty who paved the way when they first brought distance running to a high level in the U.S. What happens is that those of us who win gold medals have learned to go slightly beyond our predecessors. We are not necessarily better athletes. What we've really done is say, "Let's do a little more experimenting. Let's train a little differently than anybody else in the world." And we build on that. You don't see someone go right from running a five-minute mile to doing it in four. It just isn't done. Psychologically you say to yourself, If I train that hard, I'll break down. But you have to convince yourself to train a little harder to see if you actually do break down. And if you don't, you train harder still. Perhaps then you reach your breaking point, but the next guy believes that to beat you he has to do just that much more.

Distance running is the great equalizer in the world. You don't have to have good equipment or expensive tracks to train on, and it doesn't matter whether or not you're the poorest nation or person in the world. As long as you have enough food to eat, you can go out and do your running. So there is probably more widespread competition in distance racing than in any other event.

In the whole scheme of this world, winning a gold medal is not all that important, but it was still a tremendous thrill for me. I'm not sure how much it meant to the country as a whole. There are stories that make you wonder. For instance, in 1984 all the past gold medalists were to go to the Los Angeles Games as guests of one of the Las Vegas casinos. We were supposed to stay overnight in Vegas and then fly into LA, where we would be all decked out in our jackets and slacks and then march in the closing ceremonies. I was told Peter Ueberroth vetoed it. I'm not sure why. We were told the breakdancers had priority. Can you imagine? Between us and breakdancing, someone decided that they were a more deserving group to have the honor of closing the '84 Games!

Photo by Fogarty and Carlson

EMORY CLARK

Gold Medal, Rowing, Eight-Oared Shell, 1964

Emory Clark was raised in eastern Michigan, far away from traditional rowing waters. But his grandfather, father, and brother had been oarsmen, and when he was sent east to school he too became a rowing enthusiast.

At Yale, he captained the 1960 team that lost to Harvard by seven lengths. It was a humiliating defeat, and Clark was determined to atone for that loss and regain his self-respect by making the 1964 Olympic team.

Clark, who is now an attorney, has published many articles on rowing, and his vivid descriptions of the effort and pain it takes to become a world-class oarsman are unforgettable.

I came to Yale as a freshman the year the Yale eight won the gold at Melbourne in 1956. I knew that my senior year would be an Olympic year, and I just automatically assumed that we would repeat, but we got beat by Harvard in our final race by seven lengths. My push to be an Olympic oarsman goes back to those seven lengths. It was not just that we lost. It was that I had rowed a bad race. I didn't like myself. In my mind, I had quit, and I was captain of this Yale crew. This was not going to happen to me again.

When I got to the Games, I found many other guys who were overcoming some physical or psychological failure. So the seeds of my success were sown in that four-mile boat race on the Thames River at New London where for three miles I was cursing myself without being able to do anything about it.

U.S. Olympic victories in the eights were always by collegians until our Vesper boat won in 1964. We were also the last American eight to win and the last boat to be chosen at the trials. Starting in 1968, the boat was picked by a national team coach from a pool of oarsmen from all over the country. Theoretically, this should make for a faster crew, but since 1964 the U.S. men have won only one Olympic gold in rowing, and that was in the double scull.

Our eight was really the brainchild of Jack Kelly. It was 1963, and I was in the Marine Corps, serving in the jungle in the Philippines and still thinking about losing to Harvard by seven lengths. I would wake up, and my palms would be sweating. Finally, I wrote to a friend of mine, Boyce Budd, who was a year behind me at Yale, and we decided that we were going to row in the coxed pair in 1964. We were not going to rest on our failures for the remainder of our lives.

So I wrote a letter to the commandant and told him I was God's gift to rowing. I described all the great rowing I had done for Yale—except for that final race—and that I needed to be transferred.

In midsummer of 1963 I was assigned to the Marine Corps Supply Depot in Philadelphia. I wandered in there with my orders and someone asked, "What are we doing with an infantry lieutenant?"

I told him, "I'm here to row boats."

He said, "Huh?" Nobody knew why I was there. The captain was a jerk, the major was a jerk, but the colonel was a good guy. He told me, "Hey, take whatever time you need. We'll keep you busy down here. Figure on coming to work every day, but if you need an extra half hour in the morning, that's fine." I would also be able to row after work.

Soon after, Boyce arrived, and we started to work out at the

Vesper Boat Club. Kelly wanted to put together an Olympic eight, but at that time we were still determined to row in the pair with coxswain.

Boyce and I rowed six miles in the morning and six miles at night. Three days a week we lifted weights, and the other three days we ran. We rowed through the winter, in the dark, and our shirts would often be sheets of ice where we'd been splashed. We'd sit in our little Germantown apartment and get drunk on one beer and pound the table and say, "Goddamnit, we know we can win." We'd get so excited that we couldn't sleep, even though we had to get up to row at five. We were determined that we were not going to lose the chance to make the Olympic team because we hadn't trained hard enough.

In the spring another pair of guys showed up—two brothers named Tom and Joe Amlong. They had learned their rowing in Germany, and they were animals. Real animals. They were mean buggers, but they were fast, fit, and really good.

But they knew that a club eight never made the Olympic team, so they were not going to row in the Vesper boat. We knew that too, but for the first time they had split the Olympic trials, with the eights and singles in July and the pairs and fours in August. So if you lost in the eight, you hadn't put all your eggs in one basket. Finally we said, "OK, Kel, we'll row in your eight in the afternoon as long as you let us continue to work out in the pair in the morning."

Bill Knecht, who was then 34 with six kids and who had rowed with Kelly in the double scull in Rome, started working out with us. Kelly also got Bill Stowe, our stroke, transferred from running the Officer's Club in Saigon. He was a blithe spirit and a very good oarsman. We also added what we called two college kids, Hugh Foley and Stan Cwiklinski, who were from some other club.

In June, the Amlongs lost a race. The following Monday they were in the eight. Arrogant and vituperative, they demanded to row in the five and six seats where Boyce and I rowed. We didn't care. We wanted them in the boat because we knew they were good. The Amlongs were the kind who would stop in the middle of a race and Tom would hit Joe on the head because he didn't like what Joe was doing. I likened our entire crew to one of Billy Martin's New York Yankee teams. We thrived on strife. You didn't enjoy it, but the boat went fast. Tom had a theory that the more pissed off we were, the faster we would go, and he knew how to get us pissed off.

Al Rosenberg was our coach. He was a little bit of a guy with all kinds of chips on his shoulder. He was like a little terrier, biting at your ankles. However, he was a genius as a coach, and I got to love him before we were done. Our cox was Bobby Zimonyi. He was 48 years old, had defected from Hungary in 1956 at Melbourne, and had come to the U.S. through the auspices of Kelly. He couldn't speak much English, but he had nerves of ice water, and he could get us there in a straight line.

The big crew to beat at the trials was Harvard. They were undefeated. They had been on the cover of *Sports Illustrated*. All this was great for me. I was going to get another crack at them. This was one of Harry Parker's first good crews. He is a wonderful coach who was to beat Yale 18 years in a row and coach many an Olympic crew.

We drew Harvard in the first heat and beat them by two lengths. This sent shock waves through the rowing world. The race was 2,000 meters, about a mile and a quarter. It's a six-minute race, so it's like running a mile plus two minutes. You have to have that kind of endurance. When we trained, we never stopped rowing. We always had our oars moving in the water, from the time we left the dock until we got back. We thought that this helped us breathe. We didn't want to stop at the end of a race in a big puddle of blubber. Psyching is a big part of everything. When we passed the finish line at Orchard Beach, two lengths ahead of Harvard, we kept right on rowing. We turned around and rowed back by them while they were still slumped over their oars; then we rowed by the stands where there must have been 15,000 Harvard supporters. We were a ragtag outfit out of nowhere. Nobody knew who we were or why we were there. We didn't even wear the same jerseys. We went out of our way to look like Joe the Rag-Picker. The Amlongs would spit tobacco on the dock and talk in loud voices about these Harvard pussies. We were definitely not Ivy League.

It was crude stuff, but I didn't care because I had a vicious desire to beat Harvard. But I also knew we couldn't beat the Ratzeburg Crew from Germany. They were the best in the world. So I knew if we went to the Games in the eight we were giving up our chance for a medal in the pair. I didn't care. At that moment, that medal didn't mean anything. Beating Harvard was what was on my mind, and not just on my mind but deep in my guts, where it counted.

The minute we beat Harvard in the first heat we started getting phone calls. Bill Wallace of *The New York Times* and others started asking, "Who are you guys? Who is Allen Rosenberg? Who's in your boat, and where did they go to college?" I'd tell them, "I don't know if anybody went to college." They just couldn't figure it out. In those days, the results of the big college boat races would be on the front page of the sports section of the New York papers. Rowing got a lot more play then than it does now. We had enjoyed our anonymity up to that point, and now it was over; but being the kind of showboats we were, we didn't mind.

We won the finals, and a month later in the nationals Boyce and I beat Conn Findlay and Ed Ferry by a quarter of a boat length in the coxed pair. Findlay had won a gold in 1956 and a bronze in '60, and he and Ferry would win the gold in Tokyo. The Amlongs also won their straight pair race. So our eight had two sets of national champions in it, but by now we were committed to the eight, so we couldn't row the pair in the Games.

The favorites in Tokyo were the Ratzeburg Club of Germany and the Soviets, who had narrowly lost to the Germans in the European championships that year. I didn't think there was any way we could beat either of these crews; in fact, we were given only an outside chance for the bronze.

On the plane to Tokyo I found myself sitting next to a medium-sized black athlete. I thought I had to make conversation, so I asked him what sport he was in. He said, "Boxing." I asked, "What weight?" He said, "Heavyweight." Then I asked him what was really on my mind: "Do you think you're going to win?" He answered, "I don't see any reason why not." That was Joe Frazier. That stuck with me all through the Games. Here was this so-called disadvantaged black athlete from north Philadelphia who's got nothing but his fists. Originally he didn't even make the team. He got beaten by Buster Mathis, but Buster broke his hand and Frazier was the alternate. He probably weighed 190 and was about 5-foot-11. And there he was, a wonderful guy with tremendous confidence. He was very gregarious, and I made friends with him. I watched him fight in the semifinals against a Russian who was a big, tall, blond kid from the Ukraine, so the contrast was stark. The Russian tagged him pretty good in the first round, and Frazier stepped back and bowed. Like, "You got me that time, buddy." The crowd just went bonkers. The Japanese really loved it. In the second round Frazier reached in and decked this guy. He got up, and Joe decked him again. That's when I learned what the

Eight-oared shell gold medalists in 1964 (left to right): Joseph Amlong, Hugh Foley, Stan Cwiklinski, Tom Amlong, Robert Zimonyi, Emory Clark, Boyce Budd, Bill Knecht, Bill Stowe. Photo courtesy of Emory Clark

expression "throwing in the towel" really meant. I had never seen it happen before, but the Russian trainer took the towel off his shoulder and threw it in the ring, and the fight was over.

I didn't get to see Frazier in the finals because I couldn't get tickets, but I heard it on the radio. It was interesting because it was "Frazier with a left, Frazier with a left." There were a bunch of us yelling, "Hit him with your right, Joe, hit him with your right." His opponent was a big German, a half foot taller than Joe. Anyway, Joe won the finals on points. When I saw him in the Village the next day, he had a cast on his right arm. I asked him, "Joe, what did you do?" Big smile. "I broke my hand fighting the Russian, but I didn't tell anyone because I knew they wouldn't let me fight." So here was a guy who won his Olympic gold medal with one hand. I thought, Emory, you sorry bastard, here you are with your Ivy League education and all your sophistication, and down deep in the pit of your stomach you think you're going to lose. I learned something from Joe Frazier.

There were 14 eights in Tokyo, so we had three heats. The

winners went straight to the finals. The losers had to race again to determine the other finalists. We drew the Germans, the Italians, and maybe the French in our first heat.

That first heat was my best effort anywhere, anytime. I came as close to my maximum physical and mental effort as it was possible to do. I had prepared myself mentally, so if we lost, we lost, but I was not going to have to look in the mirror and say, "You could have done more."

The start is in French: "Messieurs, êtes vous prêts?" You try to watch the starter's mouth. When he begins to pucker up his lips to say "Partez," you're gone. In a rowing shell the start is enormously exciting and dangerous because you have to get 1,600 pounds of meat moving from a dead stop to full speed as fast as you can. You take a three-quarter stroke, then a half, another half, three-quarters, three-quarters, and then you're ready to row your race at anywhere from 36 to 40 strokes a minute, but your start may be at 50. So you row as fast as you possibly can for 25 strokes and then you settle in on the 26th stroke.

You really have to concentrate. You can't let your blade hit a puddle and throw the boat off balance. All this clutter is in your head: The flags on the way to the start, the crowd along the shore, the fact that you're in the Olympics and that you're wearing your USA shirt for the first time and it doesn't feel quite right. You don't know whether your stretcher bolts are tight or whether your rigger is going to break or the button on your oar is going to slip. You think about keeping your blade buried all the way through the stroke and getting your hands away quickly so as to hit that second stroke just right. There are a thousand things going through your mind, but you have to forget them all and concentrate on that first stroke. It seems elementary, but you have to do it, or you're going to blow something.

By the 500-meter mark you're back into your own boat, just you and the other eight guys. You don't care what the other crews are doing. You've already forgotten God, country, and the people back home. You like wearing the colors and all that, but you're no longer rowing for the U.S. or worried about the fact that it is the Olympics. You're rowing for your boat.

By the 1,000-mark, the world is reduced to just you and your partner, just you and the friend with whom you trained so many hundreds of miles. The other guys in the boat have faded away. You're hurting; the pain is starting to seep in. The stuff that is normally automatic, like the rollup and keeping your hands at just the right level, become more difficult. You just look at your partner's back and borrow strength and courage from what he's doing. You try to match his puddle, and that is all that matters.

When you finally get into the last 500 meters, it's just you. You're all alone in the world with whatever God you know, a microcosm of the greater universe, just you and your pain.

As you come into the last 250 meters, you wonder if you are still pulling as hard as you can on each stroke. It is certainly less than in the beginning, but it feels like so much more. Your arms are rubber, your legs cement. You cannot breathe, and the finish line never comes. Winning isn't even in your mind. For once in your life you are simply doing your best.

As far as the race itself, two of the crews fall back, but the Germans are ahead. They are ahead at the 1,000, and they are ahead at the 1,500. Zimonyi tells us we are leading with 250 meters to go. I won't look out. I can't see their puddles. I don't believe the little bastard. But I don't care anymore. As we cross the line, I sense that we've lost, but I don't know why.

We did lose by 28⁄100 of a second. This is one time I believe we stopped rowing. I just couldn't move my oar. I have pictures a friend of mine took of the last 15 or 20 strokes, which show my oar is still bending. I am very proud of that because I don't remember those strokes at all. That was as close as I ever have come to rowing the perfect race.

Anyway, we pull into the dock, and the first person I see is Jack Kelly, who tells us what a great race it was. All I know is that we lost. Then I hear Joe Amlong talking in the bow. I thought, You bastard, if you can still talk, you didn't pull as hard as you could have. I wanted to hit him, but I was too tired. I thought I would have to ask Kelly to help me out of the boat, but I managed to crawl out on the deck on my hands and knees. I got my oar out, again without any help. In getting the boat out of the water, I was in the middle, so nobody knew whether I was lifting or not. I wasn't. We got it up, and I looked back out on the water, and the Germans were still sitting there. It took them half an hour to get their boat out.

We showered and got into our sweats, and the strength started to flow back into me, and I began to think, Hey, we can beat these guys. It was then I realized we could win. Of course, we had to row an extra race, through the repechage, to reach the finals.

The finals consisted of the U.S., the Soviet Union, Czechoslovakia, Italy, Germany, and Yugoslavia, and it was a very different kind of race. The night before I slept until about 4:00 in the morning. I figured that's fine, that's enough. When I got out of bed, I looked out the window to see if the wind was blowing. This is usually the first thing an oarsman does when he gets up in the morning. He looks at the trees, flags, puddles on the street—anything to try to figure out what the water is going to be like. It's because of the wind and water conditions that rowing records don't mean much. In that first heat with the Germans they rowed a 5:54.02 to our 5:54.30. In the finals we were 25 seconds slower.

At 4:00 in the morning everything looked nice. I could see Mt. Fuji 70 miles away. But when I got up, there was a wind and the water was bad. The first race went off, but then they called a halt, as the course was not fair with two lanes sheltered. The eight is the premier race, so it is always the last of the day. We waited around with lots of delays all the long afternoon before they finally put us out there at about twilight. The wind had shifted to a straight headwind. It was choppy. We get under way, and it's just a totally different race. I'm not concentrating anything like I did in the first race. Our start was so good that I'm thinking, This is easy, but don't worry, Emory, it'll start hurting soon enough.

At the 1,000-meter mark we're again a fraction of a second behind the Germans, and everybody else is well back. In the third 500 meters we get five seconds on them. There's no explaining it. All of a sudden we're moving. We're not doing anything different. Just rowing. Our times for each 500 were slower than the one before, so essentially the Germans slowed down faster than we did.

It was a sloppy race, at least on my part. I'm looking around, watching those buggers on every stroke. Then in the third 500, my oar hit a wave on the recovery and spun in my hands, so when I got out to the catch my blade was backward. I had never had that happen before. I couldn't put the blade in the water, so I pulled what the Brits call an "air shot" and spun it back to get ready for the next stroke. Boyce later told me he was perfectly aware of what was going on and was praying I wouldn't catch a crab, but I don't think anybody else knew. It didn't matter. We got to the last 500 meters, and it was just a matter of rowing on in. It was so dark that the Japanese shot up flares to light the finish line, but there was no challenge from the Germans. We had won the gold medal.

For years I wondered what happened to the Germans. Their

boat was filled with Olympic and European champions. They had much more experience than we had. They were fabulous oarsmen, but they were also great sports, and they never made any excuses.

But five seconds is open water, so it was a real upset. Fourteen years later, about 3:00 in the morning and after a lot of beer, I asked one of the Germans what had happened. Even then it seemed kind of an impertinent question. He thought about it for a long time, and I figured maybe he was pissed off at me for asking. Finally, he said, "We rowed too hard to the 1,000." That's all. Still no excuses. I actually think it was the first heat that won the medal for us. We pushed them that hard. In the finals, when we were that close at the 1,000-meter mark, everyone in each boat knew it was the crew that was willing to hurt the most that would win.

CATHY JEAN FERGUSON

Gold Medal, 100-Meter Backstroke, 1964
Gold Medal, 4x100-Meter Medley Relay, 1964

Cathy Ferguson was only 16 when she bested five other world record holders in the 100-meter backstroke in Tokyo. She was even stronger in the 200-meter backstroke, but that event was not included until the 1968 Games.

Ferguson started swimming when she was 10 and retired at 19. Mixed in with fond memories of her Tokyo experience is an understanding of how spending five or six hours each day in a swimming pool can affect a teenager psychologically.

Tokyo was the most exciting, loving place that I had ever visited. When I landed, I really felt like I was a special person. I hadn't felt that way before. Perhaps it was because a Japanese girl named Satoka Tanaka was expected to be in the finals that we backstrokers received the extra attention.

There were 23 of us women swimmers, and our average age was just over 16. We stayed in segregated dormitories; in fact, we called them Fort Knox because there were guards every 100 feet. No men were allowed in the dorms, but when you tell that to

Cathy Ferguson in 1986. Photo by Fogarty and Carlson

American women, the first thing they try to do is smuggle in some poor soul so they can violate the rule. Our chaperone was Betty Philcox. She was just like a mom to us and was a super, neat lady. But she lost 30 pounds on that trip, if that tells you anything.

The hardest thing was just waiting to swim. My roommate was Jenny Duenkle, who came in third in the 100-meter backstroke. People would ask how I could spend the whole day with someone against whom I had to compete. But that is the essence of the

Olympic Games: to be able to separate when it's time to work and when it's time to play. We understood this, and sometimes I think our countries would be in a lot better shape if they were run by athletes.

The competition in the backstroke was nerve-racking. In the first preliminary heat Jenny broke the world's record. In the next heat I broke her record, and then Christine Caron of France broke my record. Each of us had set a new world record, but only a fraction of a second separated us. In the finals, that would make the difference between gold and bronze. There was plenty of pressure, but my family never once asked me to win. In fact, no one really came right out and said, "You've got to win." It was always "Do the best you can." The night before the finals my dad met with me and said, "You know, Cathy, you've come farther than we ever dreamed possible—so enjoy this one." But I was thinking to myself, How can I enjoy something that is putting me through so much punishment? Then I was alone again.

On the day of the finals my warm-ups went fairly well. Then it was into the holding area, where all eight finalists sat and waited. Those were tense moments. Finally, a little Japanese girl marched us into the arena before 15,000 people. I don't really remember anything about that trip, but I do remember getting into the water for the start.

I was slow off the mark, but that was not unusual. I was a come-from-behind swimmer. I actually took pride in that. It was like a little game for me. When we came off the turn for the final 50 meters, it was as if I had more strength than anybody could imagine having. I just felt stronger and stronger. If the race had been extended to 200 meters, I could have just kept right on going. It didn't hurt at all. I can remember my dad saying that the best race I'd ever swim would be my easiest. And it really was. I finished, and, being a very religious person, I can remember thinking, Dear God, let this be my best time. I looked up at my dad. He held up one, two, and then three fingers, telling me I had finished first, second, or third. It was that close. I really didn't know how well I had done. I went over to my coach, and he said something about if I ever got a good start they'd never catch me, but just then the announcer interrupted and said, "We'd like to give the results for the women's 100-meter backstroke." Then up on the giant scoreboard went the name Cathy Ferguson, USA, 1:07.7, a new Olympic and world record.

The only thing I could do was just cry. The time was close to half a second better than I dreamed I would ever go. I looked over at my coach, and he said, "My God, Cathy, you really did it." Those words were so very important, and they always will be, because I had always strived so hard to hear them.

I look back and know that winning isn't everything—that there are so many wonderful things to learn—but had I not won, would I have had the opportunity to learn all those wonderful things? It's easy to say winning the gold medal isn't everything, but to those who don't get the gold medal, what are their feelings? How do they detrain or deprogram? I've seen world record holders who did not make the team. What did that do to them after all that training and effort? I'm glad I didn't have to find out.

I think of Shirley Babashoff with her eight Olympic medals and six individual world records. She also set 37 American records. In Munich, she was supposed to win everything, but her only gold was in the relay. The same thing happened four years later in Montreal. Never mind that she won six silver medals along with her two golds in the relays. The media made it sound as if she had somehow failed. They just crucified her. What did that do to her? I can remember walking up to her at the Mission Viejo nationals and saying, "I don't know if you know who I am, but I've been following your career." She said, "Oh, yeah, I know who you are." There were just the two of us sitting in the stands, and finally she looked out over the pool and asked, "What does it all mean?"

I quit competitive swimming right before the '68 Games. People ask me why I didn't go on. But I knew I couldn't win anymore, and when you know you can't win, you can't go on. I was only 19, but I just couldn't get up for the races.

I feel very strongly that we need some kind of detraining program for our former athletes. The East Germans have a program that helps their athletes get ready to move back into a normal life. It was very hard for me to be totally in the world of swimming and then, all of a sudden, to be completely out of it. It's as if you have a whole pie and take a piece out of it, then try to put that piece back in, only to find it doesn't fit.

I felt quite empty when I left swimming. The thing I substituted for that programmed life was my first marriage. I was 19, and my husband was 26. In some ways I was probably 26 as well, but I had missed many of the experiences of being a teenager. Traveling all over the world and meeting important people was a fantastic experience, but I also needed those experiences that help one grow emotionally. When I was swimming, I was pretty much in control, but when I stepped out of that warm, secure cocoon, I didn't control everything in my environment. I couldn't control my husband, and I couldn't control what was happening to me. At the time, I loved him dearly, but there was a needed growth period. Unfortunately, we both used marriage as a kind of sublimation for something else. I didn't quite understand it then, but all I really needed was just to become "normal" again.

Education helped some. My parents always took it for granted that I would go to college, but, on the other hand, it was more important for my brother to go to a university while it would have been all right for me to have gone to a junior college. Actually, my father had put more effort into my career than into my brother's or sister's, but there was still that underlying belief that education was more important for the man. He needed it to prepare for his profession, whereas for me it was something to fall back on. Of course, neither my father nor I really understood that at the time. It took the evolution of women's rights. Now my father would be the first to fight for my rights as a human being.

You need to know why I swam. I didn't want to be just "C-Average Cathy." There was something inside me that said, "I don't want to be like everybody else." I was brought up to believe that one needs to excel and to be willing to work harder than anyone else to achieve that excellence. I simply took on these values so the drive to be the best was there from the time I started serious swimming at age 10.

I was 12 when I started training with Peter Daland at the Los Angeles Athletic Club. He was to be my only coach, and I was the only swimmer that Peter ever had who went from square one to the top. The rest were guys who swam for him in college. It's funny because he's a man's coach, yet it was a little girl who reached the top.

I admired him tremendously. He was a taskmaster, but he was also an educator who possessed an enormous amount of knowledge. I envied that and wanted to be that smart. Later I wrote him a letter and told him how much he had influenced my life at the time. When we would go to national championships, he would take us to historical places. Most of the other coaches just left you back in your hotel room. He always felt that swimming was only temporary but that education went on for a lifetime.

Because I was swimming with people who were several years older than I, I was expected to be an adult. At times it got lonely, and sometimes people seemed to be pulling me in opposite directions, but I don't know that my feelings were any different from a normal teenager's. I always had boyfriends. I can still remember my first kiss and how exciting that was. I have fond memories of all those neat times, but they were all contained within that narrow world of swimming.

It was an isolated environment. A few years ago I attended my high school reunion. My former classmates talked about all the drugs and drinking that went on at that time. I never knew about any of that. I had to be in bed by 9:00, or I didn't function the next day. It's funny, but right after I got married I was staying up until 11:00 because that was a treat. Here I was supposed to be a mature person, and the biggest thing in my life was being able to stay up and watch the late show.

Being an Olympic champion doesn't make life simpler. It opens the door and lets you get your foot in. But if you don't produce after that, you're gone the same as anybody else. I think that the world has this idea that because you're an Olympic champion you're going to be successful in everything you do. But how many failures did that athlete go through before becoming an Olympic champion? People forget how many times you lost on your way there.

Most people also do not understand just how much training takes out of you. It's lonely in that pool. Just think of the countless hours in the water when you scarcely talk to another human being. All you have is that black line. It becomes your best friend. How many people can take that for more than six or seven years? I can remember being so tired at the end of the day that there was no way I had any energy left over to talk to the other kids. Now that I'm coaching, I include breaks within my practices so that my swimmers have structured social time. I don't know of many other coaches who do that, but youngsters must learn how to make decisions and relate to one another if they are going to become functioning human beings.

I believe wholeheartedly that there is some way to coach besides keeping the kids in the water five or six hours a day. That's the way I'm coaching my swimmers, and I'm having success. Can you tell me why I should have to swim hundreds of miles to go one minute and seven seconds in a race? That's illogical. I was always told that I had to work harder and swim farther than anybody else

Cathy Ferguson in 1964.
Photo courtesy of the International Swimming Hall of Fame

to have a chance. Most coaches go for quantity of workouts, not quality. The kids are always willing to try something different, but it's usually the coaches who are afraid to experiment. Often coaches don't like their kids going elsewhere for stroke clinics. My God, they might learn something new! I don't deal with it that way. My own daughter has just decided to swim competitively. She's 12, and she's very good, but I sat down and told her, "You're not going to train like I did. Now, this is the way I think we can do it." It's a gamble, but I do know that 98 percent of success is in the head and the heart.

We are slowly beginning to see older swimmers. Scholarships for women have helped, and we know that there is no physiological reason to stop swimming. Research now shows that women after pregnancy are stronger and probably more emotionally stable than before. Pat McCormick certainly did very well during and after pregnancy. Sandy Neilson, who won three gold medals in

1972, is still a world-class swimmer, and she's over 30. I think that some of the coaches don't like this because they cannot treat someone that age the same way they would a youngster. But I think it's great. If Sandy had come a little earlier, I might have considered going on. I would do things a little differently, but I bet I would still be just as good.

12
MEXICO CITY, 1968

On October 16, four days after the opening of the Olympic Games in Mexico City, three men stood on the victory stand after the finals in the 200-meter dash. The silver medalist, standing at polite attention during the playing of "The Star-Spangled Banner," was Peter Norman of Australia. The other two medalists stood with heads bowed and a black-gloved fist extended into the air above their heads. That gesture by Tommie Smith, the winner, and John Carlos, the bronze medalist, will forever remain the dominant image of these Olympics for most Americans.

That protest had its beginnings at San Jose State College in the fall of 1967. Harry Edwards, a doctoral candidate, had compiled a list of grievances suffered by the college's black athletes and demanded that they be stopped. He then promised that black athletes would boycott the Olympic Games in protest of what he called "the oppression and injustice" inflicted on blacks. One of Edwards's allies in the boycott movement was San Jose's sprinter, Tommie Smith.

In February 1968, the International Olympic Committee announced its plans to lift the ban on South Africa, which had been imposed just before the Tokyo Games. More than 30 African nations threatened to withdraw if the ban was lifted; the USSR made the same threat, and Edwards saw his chance to expand his boycott. The IOC gave in to the pressure while in newspeak fashion denying that it was doing so. A little more than a month before the opening of the Games, Edwards canceled his proposed boycott but suggested that other forms of protest might occur at Mexico City. Smith and Carlos's black power salute was a genuine, even dignified gesture of protest, but it outraged Olympic officials, who themselves had been waffling on the South African issue for more than four years. The president of the U.S. Olympic Committee, saying that the two had violated "the basic standards of good manners and sportsmanship," suspended Smith and Carlos from the team.

The American team was divided over the issue. Many white athletes sided with the protesters, and many blacks, notably the boxers, did not. But some were torn. Lee Evans, a friend and schoolmate of Smith, was particularly distressed. He also wanted to demonstrate in some way, but he and the other black Americans in the 400-meter finals were warned by U.S. Olympic officials that a demonstration would ruin their athletic careers. Evans and his two black teammates, Larry James and Ron Freeman, swept the 400, and on the way to and from the victory stand they staged their own mild protest by wearing berets and waving their ungloved fists at the crowd, smiling happily as they did. During the national anthem, they stood at attention with the berets off.

Other forces that posed an even more dangerous threat to the Games were at work in Mexico City. Over the summer of 1968, groups of college students periodically rioted to protest, among other things, the increasingly desperate plight of Mexico's poor. On October 2, 10 days before the Olympics were to begin, students held a large, peaceful rally in Mexico City. The army and police moved in to break it up, and in the ensuing panic shooting broke out. When it was over, 33 students were dead, many more were injured, and hundreds jailed. Mexican officials convinced the IOC that nothing would disrupt the Games and that all athletes and visitors would be safe.

Before the opening ceremonies on October 12, there had been much discussion about the effects of Mexico City's 7,000-foot altitude on the health and performance of the athletes, but as it turned out, the thin air may have helped rather than hindered them, for in many events the performances were astonishing, though the distance runners faced serious problems.

The ceremonies opening the Games were held in the Estadio Olimpico, with its huge sunken stadium, pre-Columbian architectural style, and new synthetic track surface. A record 110 nations sent more than 6,500 athletes to the Games, including one lone Mongolian. As usual, the ceremonies were spectacular and the crowds enthusiastic, especially when they cheered the Czechoslovakian delegation. The Mexicans clearly were in sympathy with the way the Czechs had stood up to the Russians in their homeland.

In the first race of the Olympics, the 10,000 meters, Kenya, making only its fourth Olympic appearance, earned its first Olympic gold medal. Naftali Temu outsprinted Mamo Wolde of Ethiopia and Mohamed Gammoudi of Tunisia in the stretch to win it in 29:27.4. The altitude clearly got to Ron Clarke of Australia, who finished sixth and collapsed at the finish.

For the Americans, Jim Hines won the 100-meter dash in the world record time of 9.9 seconds. Tommie Smith and Lee Evans took the 200- and 400-meter titles respectively, also in world and Olympic record times. The U.S. relay teams took both of their events, again in record times. In the pole vault, nine men cleared 17 feet, a height never reached in any previous Olympics. Three men cleared the winning height of 17 feet, 8½ inches, and Bob Seagren, a Southern Cal graduate, took the gold on the basis of the fewest misses. In the high jump, Dick Fosbury introduced the "Fosbury Flop," a backward flop over the bar. Fosbury won his event with a jump of 7 feet, 4¼ inches, an Olympic record. Discus thrower Al Oerter won that event and became the first four-time Olympic winner of the same event.

Some experts wondered if the long jump record set in Mexico City would ever be surpassed, and after almost 20 years Bob Beamon's "perfect" jump of 29 feet, 2½ inches remains safely intact. A few doubters tried to credit the rarified air for his miraculous leap, but no other jumper in Mexico City was able to come within 2 feet of his jump.

The American women's track and field team won three gold medals in Mexico City, more golds than any other country. Wyomia Tyus, who, like Wilma Rudolph from the 1960 Games, was a Tigerbelle from Tennessee State, won a gold in the 100-meter dash. She also anchored the 4x100 relay team and in both races set world records.

Before a noisy, often disruptive crowd in the Alberca, the American swim team won 73 of a possible 144 Olympic medals. The greatest number of golds were won by Debbie Meyer, who became the first woman to win three individual gold medals at a single Olympics. There were many more opportunities to win medals in 1968 than in previous Games because the total number of swimming and diving events had increased from 22 to 33, and 6 of those were in women's events. The expected star of the men's team was Mark Spitz, the world record holder in both the 100- and 200-meter butterfly, but his peak occurred four years later at Munich. In Mexico City he won only two golds in the two freestyle relays, a silver in the 100-meter butterfly, and a bronze in the 100-meter freestyle. Two other swimmers who helped the American team win its 73 medals were Mike Burton, who won a pair of golds in the 400 and 1,500 freestyles, and Charles Hickcox, who won the 200 and 400 individual medleys after coming in second in the 100-meter backstroke.

For the third time in a row, the Olympic Games produced a future heavyweight boxing champion. This time it was George Foreman, who began his boxing career as a street fighter in Houston, Texas.

William Steinkraus became the first American to win a gold medal in an individual equestrian event with his victory in grand prix jumping.

Two weeks after they had begun, the 1968 Games came to a spectacular conclusion. The ceremonies included colorful costumes and music from a mariachi band. The IOC thought the massed, unorganized group of athletes that cavorted on the field in Tokyo had presented a rather undignified element of the closing program and therefore decreed that at Mexico City the parade of athletes would consist of a small group of competitors marching behind its country's flag. After the end of the formal proceedings, and following a dazzling fireworks display, thousands of athletes who had been sitting in the stands poured onto the field and created a spontaneous, undisciplined, and joyous parade of their own.

ROBERT LLOYD SEAGREN

Gold Medal, Pole Vault, 1968
Silver Medal, Pole Vault, 1972

A controversial decision at the 1972 Games cost Bob Seagren his chance for a second consecutive gold medal, but between 1967 and 1972 he won six AAU titles and four NCAA titles while officially breaking the indoor and outdoor world record on 15 occasions.

After his disappointment in Munich, Seagren competed on the professional track circuit and also won ABC's first Superstars competition in 1973, a feat that brought him more fame than any of his victories or records in the pole vault.

Seagren's present work as a film and television producer and actor includes a recurring role as a television reporter on "Dynasty."

Living in California, I was influenced by Ron Morris, Bob Gutowski, John Pennel, and Dave Tork, all of whom were fiberglass vaulters. Fiberglass took over in 1962, and we had the first 16-foot

Bob Seagren in 1986. Photo courtesy of Bob Seagren

jump, although there was considerable controversy over whether the pole vault had become an entirely different event.

The fiberglass pole is an amazing instrument. It can store a great deal of energy. A lot of people think the pole bends and then sort of catapults the vaulter over the bar, but that doesn't happen at all. That sensation doesn't even exist because you are not being thrown through the air. Your body initiates all the action. You have to coordinate and work with the pole, but the spring comes from the body, not the pole. If you stop your action midway in the air, the pole does absolutely nothing.

A lot of things take place in those few seconds of a vault. Your body has to change positions much more than with the rigid pole. Less upper body strength is required with the fiberglass pole, but timing, coordination, and speed down the runway are more important.

I didn't start to bend the pole until 1963, which was my junior year in high school. When I did, I went up about 2 feet in height. I made 15 feet my senior year, which was good, but there was a junior in the Los Angeles area named Paul Wilson who jumped something like 16 feet, 6 inches. That was probably good for me because I had always won every track meet, and it was a real shock to my ego to be beaten by a kid who was a year behind me in school. Before then I had never really trained. I had just vaulted because it was fun, but I started working out very seriously after I lost so badly to Wilson.

After graduation, I entered Mount San Antonio Junior College to get my grades up. My coach was Don Ruh, a super guy and a tremendous motivator. He didn't know that much about pole-vaulting, but none of us did. He did know how to get me in shape, and that helped me set my first world record the following year.

I went to USC after junior college as did Paul Wilson. We traded the world record back and forth in 1967, but he suffered a sciatic nerve problem that really ended his career. They thought it was a pulled hamstring problem and never really diagnosed it properly.

There are tremendous mental barriers in vaulting. The first one I experienced was the 17-foot indoor vault. In 1964, Fred Hansen had jumped 17 feet, 4½ inches outdoors for a world record, but nobody had jumped 17 feet indoors. John Pennel and I were going at each other on the indoor circuit over who was going to be the first. Each week we'd come so close. It was finally at the 1967 AAU indoor championship at Albuquerque that I did it. It's amazing how you can try so many times and not make it; then, after you once make it, it becomes easy. The next week I made 17 feet, 1 inch and then 17 feet, 2 inches the week after that. It's just a psychological barrier.

Then it took me five years before I cleared 18 feet. I had so many vaults that were clearly over, but I would knock the crossbar off with a misplaced hand or something. Finally, somebody else made it—I think it was Chris Papanicolaou of Greece. That was the summer of 1969, and I was really discouraged. I wanted to be the first to go 17 indoors and then 18 outside. It obviously had some kind of adverse effect on me, because I didn't jump 18 feet until 1972. I also got married and had knee surgery, but 1970 and '71 were pretty off-years for me.

Everywhere you went in those days the vaulters knew more about vaulting than did the coaches. It was all so new. My track coach at USC was Vern Wolfe, who had been a vaulter himself, but he had never used fiberglass. So we were both learning. He was always on the field with his camera. We were also fortunate because the only real manufacturer of poles was located in Los Angeles. Herb Jenks developed all the early fiberglass poles. He started with the Browning Silaflex, then with George Moore he developed the Cata-Pole and the Pacer. The two of them were always out at USC, filming and talking to us about new concepts. They'd develop new poles, and we'd try them out.

There is a lot of pressure in vaulting because you can be the best in the world but have a bad day and not make our Olympic team. We don't select our athletes on the basis of past performances. You have to make it in one or two specific competitions. In 1968, we were told whoever won the competition in Los Angeles two months before the Olympics was automatically on the team, even though there would be another trial at Lake Tahoe a couple of weeks later. So I felt I had to win the competition in L.A., and I did, even though I never liked vaulting in the Coliseum because the wind often comes from the wrong direction.

I drove to Tahoe to compete in a tune-up meet the week before the final trials began. I arrived on a Friday and went right out on the track to practice. I was very relaxed because I thought I had already made the team. I was warming up when someone announced that L.A. didn't mean a thing—that the decision had been changed and only the first-, second-, and third-place finishers at Tahoe would make the team. At just about that moment, I bent over to touch my toes, and my back popped. You could hear it all over the field. I just shot up in the air like a rubber band and then hit the ground, face down in the grass. The pain was excruciating. I went totally numb from my waist down. An ambulance came and took me to the hospital in South Lake Tahoe. I had a cracked vertebra, so they put me in traction and gave me Demerol every couple of hours. I just lay there and thought, I can't believe this is happening.

I was so depressed. That was Saturday. By Monday I still couldn't move, and I was still in pain, so I called my father to start making arrangements to fly me home. But when I woke up Tuesday, I felt a lot better. I could pull my legs up. It still hurt, but at least I could move my legs. By Wednesday afternoon I was up and walking around, so I told my dad to forget it. I wanted the hospital officials to release me, but they wouldn't. I got in the worst fight with those people and actually had to sneak out of the hospital. They followed me up to our training accommodations, but I refused to go back.

On Thursday I jogged a little bit and didn't feel anything in my back. By Friday I just had to know whether I could vault or not. So I went out, warmed up, and took one vault at about 16 feet. All the other vaulters had their people out there to see what I was going to do. My back didn't bother me, so I put the pole away and went back to my room. The next day I set a world record in winning the competition.

My problems with Olympic officials started in Mexico City during my warm-ups. Adriaan Paulen of the Netherlands was the head pole vault official, and right away he looked at my pole and said, "Your taping job is illegal." Now, the rules of vaulting state that the pole can be any length or diameter and made of any material. You are not allowed handles or attachments that would act as a hand grip, and if you tape your pole you are restricted to two thicknesses of tape. Those are the only rules, except in 1972 when everything changed.

I showed Paulen that my pole had only two layers of tape except where they overlapped. In those days we didn't have double tape, so you would put one layer around your pole; then you would spin and reverse it. He objected to where I had to twist it to turn it around. So I asked him to show me how to tape it. He told me, "That's not my problem; it's yours." So we didn't get along from the very outset.

There was also a rule that you couldn't put anything on the runway. You could put markers to the side but nothing on the runway. During the qualifying round, one of the West Germans spray-painted his markers across the runway. I was standing by one of these markers getting ready to vault when Paulen came over and completely freaked out. He's standing there in the middle of the runway, and I'm telling him to get out of the way because I want to take my last warm-up jump. He wouldn't move. I assume he thought it was my mark, although I told him it wasn't. We were really yelling at each other. He stopped everything and had several custodians come out with soap and water to try to scrub the paint off the track. All this time, the West German never said a thing. The paint wouldn't come off, and that made Paulen even angrier. He finally found out it wasn't my mark, but I think he remembered all this when we had our problems in Munich.

The "War of the Shoes" was also a fascinating part of the Games in Mexico City. Although it was illegal, the different companies tried very hard to get the athletes to wear their particular brand. Even at the trials in Lake Tahoe when the shoe man arrived, it was like the Good Humor truck pulling up. Everyone was there, cutting his deal. I just stayed away from it. I didn't even want to know about it. I guess I thought that to make a deal based on how I would finish in the competition would put undue pressure on me, but everyone was doing it. One day a guy would be wearing one kind of shoes and the next day some other kind. It was unbelievable. It was still highly illegal at that time to get paid for wearing a particular shoe, but it was one way to help meet expenses.

My roommate in Mexico City was Jeff Vanderstock, a 400-meter hurdler and a good friend of mine from USC. In the finals, I watched him go from second to fourth place in a matter of two strides. That was depressing, especially the next morning when he was packing. I was getting ready for the finals of the pole vault when I noticed this pair of red shoes with Velcro closures on his bed. I had never seen them before, and they were made by Puma. We wore the same size, so Jeff told me to take them. I tried them on and just loved them. They had a plate in the front that made you feel like you were running on your toes, so I wore them in the finals.

I won my gold, and the next day Jeff said, "Come on. I'm going over to the Puma people to pick up my 'reward,' and a gold medal is worth a lot more than a fourth place." We went to the hotel where Armin Dassler, the president of Puma, was holding court. I waited outside his room while several athletes went in and out; then I went in. We talked, and he congratulated me on my victory. Finally he looked at me and asked, "OK, what was our deal?" He thought I had already talked to one of his shoe reps. I didn't know what to say. I finally set a figure, and I'll never forget his look. He had on these Ben Franklin half spectacles, and he just looked at me over the top of them. I realized that he knew that I didn't know what the hell I was talking about, but that started a great relationship, and I spent the next 18 years working for Puma.

A lot of us felt that Mexico City was the last of the really festive Olympics. The atmosphere was so open. In the Village you could come and go as you pleased. There were guards there, but they didn't stop anybody. There were no problems. If you wore your uniform downtown and you stuck out your thumb, cars would compete with one another to see who could get there first to give you a ride. The shop owners were so congenial, and you couldn't buy a drink in a bar.

The black-gloved salute didn't bother me all that much. I had traveled all over the world with Tommie Smith and John Carlos, and I knew them as individuals. Those were militant times for many blacks, and you could not help but sympathize with them. They wanted to bring attention to the condition of blacks in America. I do believe that demonstrating during the playing of the national anthem was poor timing, and I think that they would now agree that the victory stand was not the proper place. The U.S. Olympic Committee was supposed to have kicked them out of the Olympic Village, but I don't think they ever did because I don't remember them leaving.

Munich was extremely well organized, but security was much tighter even before the massacre. I'll never forget the shock of that tragedy. I had left the Village with my family the day it happened and had no idea what was going on. We were driving through Italy, and I had these Olympic stickers on the side of our van and my vaulting poles on top. We stopped for gas, and this Italian tried to tell me what was going on, but I couldn't understand him. Finally, we found an English-language newspaper, and I couldn't believe it. I immediately recognized the pictures of three of the slain Israelis because the day before I had played Foosball with them in the Village. The Germans had put on a really fine Olympics, and it was so sad to have it spoiled by such a tragedy.

The Munich Games proved a great disappointment for me because of the scandal with the vaulting poles. It all started back in Eugene, Oregon, when I set a new world record of 18 feet, 5½ inches, using a new pole. Adriaan Paulen heard about it and started talking about banning these new poles. Actually, the biggest change from the old pole was the color. The old ones were always black, and the new ones were green. Mine was also a little heavier. No one ever contacted the manufacturers to find out if they really were new, so I didn't take it very seriously, but as we got closer to the Games I learned that Paulen and the ruling federation were really serious. So I took six of my old poles and three of the new ones with me to Munich.

The day before the vaulting competition I was doing some sightseeing around Munich with my family. I returned to the Village and discovered that the poles I had left in front of my door were gone. I asked about them, and somebody said that the federation had issued an edict that all the vaulting poles had to be in the stadium by five o'clock that day to be checked for legality. Never had anything like this been done before because the rules clearly state that a pole can be any color, size, or length. It was already past five o'clock, but I had several other poles in the basement. I grabbed them and rushed over to the stadium where I found Adriaan Paulen and the West German pole-vaulting coach deciding which poles were legal. So you've got one guy, who has his own athletes competing, and Adriaan Paulen, who has never vaulted in his life and doesn't know a vaulting pole from a broomstick, determining what will be allowed.

I'm watching these two guys strip off the tape, pull out the butt plug, and then try to weigh these poles on a bathroom scale. They told me they were going to disqualify any poles that were too light. I asked to see the criteria they were using to make such a decision. They admitted they had none. I asked them how could they then determine what a pole was supposed to weigh. They couldn't answer my question. They showed me two poles, a black one and a green one, and the green one weighed 50 grams less. I said, "Fine, here's an old-style one, black in color; weigh it." It was 50 grams lighter than the green one they had declared illegal because it was too light. That should have blown their whole theory.

I told them that the poles were all slightly different in weight and that this had nothing to do with the event. Well, Adriaan was turning redder and redder. He was literally foaming at the mouth.

And we were once again yelling at one another. Finally, he got so frustrated that he screamed at me, "If you say one more word, I'm throwing you out of the competition for unsportsmanlike conduct." I realized that he would do it, so I walked out of there saying to myself, Big deal, I've still got my six old-style poles that I can use.

The next day they posted a chart in the stadium with all the competitors' names on it along with the specific bins where their approved poles could be picked up. Across from my name and maybe eight others there was only a blank. We had no poles. I had nothing, not even my six old poles. I couldn't believe what was happening. So I asked, "What are we supposed to use?" Over against the wall was a pile of maybe 15 or 20 vaulting poles, which we were told we could use. There was nothing close to what I was accustomed. The strongest pole was 180 flex and I was used to a 190 or 195, but I took it and walked out onto the field.

So there I was, going into the Olympic Games with a pole that wasn't mine, and I had to qualify with it. I did that without any trouble and then went immediately to my delegate, a guy named Pinky Sober, and told him I wanted a protest filed. In the meantime, George Moore, who made our poles, was trying to explain to the officials that these were all phony issues. There were a lot of us getting screwed. The East and West Germans, the Greeks, and a few others had their own poles, and all of them were judged all right. Sober told me it was my own fault for calling the green poles new in the first place. I realized that he was not going to fight any battles for me so I went to the head of the U.S. Olympic delegation, Colonel Don Hall, who had an office in the Village.

I should have known I would have trouble with Hall because I had recently threatened to bring suit against the AAU concerning some alleged violations of my amateur standing. But I went anyway. Just before I got there I ran into another athlete who told me he had just talked to him, but when I tried to go into his office his secretary stopped me. I told her it was an emergency and that I had to talk to him. She said, "Well, let me see if he's in." She got on the intercom and then told me, "I'm sorry, but he's not in right now." I said, "Bullshit, that other guy just talked to him." But he still wouldn't talk to me.

So I had to compete in the finals with that same borrowed pole. By that time I was so angry that I was determined to win even if they gave me a broomstick. I just tried to plan a strategy and keep my cool. It worked out pretty well. I jumped 17 feet, 8½ inches and ended up with the silver medal.

Paulen was there supervising the whole thing, so afterward I walked over to him and tried to hand him the pole. At first he wouldn't take it. He wouldn't even shake my hand, but the television cameras were there, so he finally had to take the pole. I gave it to him and said, "Here's your pole back. Do with it what you think is appropriate."

Paulen was made president of the International Amateur Athletic Federation a week after the Games. The election is basically controlled by Eastern Bloc countries. Then, three weeks after the election, all of the vaulting poles were declared legal. So our poles were illegal for only a four-week period.

I never received a good explanation for Paulen's actions. His strongest argument was that these poles had not been made available to all athletes six months before the Games. There was no rule requiring this, and, what's more, the manufacturer of the poles had proof that they had been offered to everyone. Wolfgang Nordwig of East Germany insisted that they had not been made available to him, but at a press conference following the competition I confronted him with the fact that they had been. He finally admitted that he had not liked the sizes that were sent to him. Before the Games Nordwig had also complained that the new poles contained carbon fiber. The manufacturer said they didn't, and, in any case, there was nothing in the rules stating that such a material was illegal. The big winners in all this were Nordwig, who won the gold medal, and Paulen, who became president of the IAAF.

I was really discouraged after that. If I hadn't won the gold medal in 1968, I would certainly have made a much bigger stink than I did. I was at a golden age to go on and win a third gold medal. I was only 25 at the time. As it turned out, I was in peak condition in 1976 because I was on the pro track tour and jumping close to 19 feet in competition, but Tadeusz Slusarski of Poland won the '76 gold medal with a vault of just over 18 feet.

You could make money as an amateur in those days. It was all illegal, of course, but the more you traveled, the more you understood what really went on. You had to do it in order to survive. If you took a regular job, you simply didn't have time to train. But all this hypocrisy increasingly annoyed me. It was easy to get paid by the promoters in Europe, but you could also do it in the States, although you always ran the risk of getting caught. You just didn't know whom to trust, but after a while you developed a rapport with certain meet promoters. The AAU tried to bust me a couple of times. They even taped my conversations when I was asking for a measly expense account.

After I got married in 1970, I often took my wife to meets with me, but I would have to pay for all her expenses. That used to upset me. I didn't think it was a big deal to ask somebody to pick up her expenses, but I got into real problems with the AAU when Renaldo Brown, the high-jumper, and I were invited to compete in Japan. The AAU had a rule that there had to be three or more athletes traveling before they had to send a coach or an official to accompany us. But they sent an administrator with us for the sole purpose of making sure that I didn't make any money. The promoters knew if an official was along they didn't have to pay you. So now the promoters are off the hook, and I've got to pay for my wife's airfare and expenses to Japan. We get over there, and this official shows up with his wife. One morning she tells my wife that because the AAU couldn't find anybody to go, they persuaded her husband by offering to pay for her way as well. And what's more, the AAU was going to pay for one week in Hawaii for the two of them on the way home. Well, I'm out of my mind! I'm outraged! Just to keep me from getting my wife's expenses they pay for two people, including a week in Hawaii. I was so angry that I was ready to bust the AAU wide open.

Matters came to a head a couple of months later. I was with my wife in Europe, and we ran out of money. We were really stuck, so I found a couple of meets where I could make enough money to pay for our airfare home. The AAU bans athletes from traveling and competing on their own, but I didn't care. I was disgusted with all their hypocrisy anyway. After we got home, I made a couple of comments to the press about "the old fogies" who were running amateur athletics in this country. A couple of weeks later I get this letter from the Southern Pacific AAU, requesting that I appear at their next meeting to explain why I made these derogatory statements to the press. I was so irritated that I decided not to show up. Then I got another letter stating that unless I appeared at the next meeting I was going to be banned from amateur competition indefinitely. That really infuriated me. So I hired a lawyer and took him with me to the meeting. When they saw him, they panicked. They suggested that they really didn't mean for the letter to sound so strong. They totally backed down on everything.

My lawyer was a former gymnast who had helped the gymnasts start their own federation because they had become tired of how corrupt their governing body was. We also used this opportunity to recommend a trust fund in which the athlete would not get the money, but it would be administered by the AAU. This was 1970, and they thought I was crazy, but that's exactly what has happened.

I competed on the pro track circuit for four years until it finally died a slow death in 1976. The marks we set in the pros were never sanctioned, which was too bad because I had some phenomenal jumps at world record heights, and they were all legitimate. I can still remember the night Brian Oldfield threw the shot 75 feet. No one has yet come close to that mark, and the real track and field people still recognize that throw as the world's best.

Winning the first Superstars competition was great for me. Both amateur and professional athletes competed in 10 selected events but not in their specialties. For me the best thing was that even though I had set 15 world records over an eight-year period and had won a gold and a silver medal in two Olympics, people really didn't know who Bob Seagren was. They may have known the name but not much more. They certainly couldn't recognize me. Then, in March of 1973, over one weekend of fun and games for ABC, I achieved instant recognition. I also won $40,000, which was considerably more than I had ever won in the amateurs or the pros.

WYOMIA TYUS

Gold Medal, 100 Meters, 1964 and 1968
Gold Medal, 4x100-Meter Relay, 1968
Silver Medal, 4x100-Meter Relay, 1964

Although she was a world-record-breaking Olympic sprinter and the only one ever to defend successfully her sprint title in a subsequent Olympiad, Wyomia Tyus has never received the acclaim she deserves. Perhaps it was because she followed the charismatic Wilma Rudolph, who in 1960 captured the headlines with her three gold medals in Rome.

Both Rudolph and Tyus were members of Coach Ed Temple's legendary Tennessee State Tigerbelles, certainly the most successful women's program in the annals of American track and field.

Tyus set her first world record in 1964 with a mark of 11.2 in the 100 meters. Four years later in Mexico City, she lowered her record to 11-flat, a mark that would not be bettered in the Olympics until 1984.

Women's track and field started at Tennessee State under Tom Harris after World War II, but the famous Tigerbelles really didn't come into their own until Ed Temple took over in the early 1950s. Coach Temple has been the most successful women's track coach in the history of this country. He's won 31 AAU and TAC national championships. In 1960 and 1964 he served as our women's Olympic coach, and 40 of his athletes have competed in the Games. He's now in his 37th year of coaching at Tennessee State, where he also is a professor of sociology.

So when I came along in 1964 and 1968 I was just part of a great tradition. Coach Temple got his program started by going to different track meets, not only in Tennessee, but also in Georgia, Alabama, and Mississippi. He would invite the better athletes to his summer camps in Nashville, and if they kept up their grades and their track skills, upon graduation they were offered a work aid scholarship to Tennessee State. That's how I became a Tigerbelle.

I grew up in Griffin, Georgia, where I got into running because of my three older brothers. I ran both to keep up with and away from them. I had to go through the whole thing that girls weren't supposed to do this and that, and I was always being called a tomboy. But I enjoyed the idea of competing and being out in the fresh air, so I never let that bother me. I also had a lot of encouragement from my father, who believed that there was nothing wrong with a girl playing sports.

There were lots of times when my brothers didn't want me tagging along. I had to be extra good just to get the chance to play with them. The first thing other kids would say is that they didn't want a girl on their team. My brothers would always say, "Well, OK, we'll take her," but they knew I could play just as well as anyone else, if not better.

We did have track and basketball for girls in high school, but the encouragement that goes along with such programs was not always there. Some of the girls would come out for sports, but often they wouldn't stick it out because it was not considered ladylike to be an athlete. You were supposed to be spending your time looking out for your social prospects. I wouldn't say that was the furthest thing from my mind, but I felt that sports and my social life could go hand in hand. And what better place to meet the boys than on the athletic field? Some of the guys did not want their girlfriends competing and developing muscles. But I enjoyed sports too much to worry about those kinds of boys. I always felt that whomever I

Wyomia Tyus at the finish line of the 100-meter dash at the 1968 Olympics.
Photo courtesy of Women's Sports Foundation

was dating just didn't have the choice of telling me I couldn't do something.

I first came under Coach Temple's tutelage when I was 14. He saw me compete in a state track meet and invited me to one of his summer camps. I told him, "Oh, yeah, sure," not thinking anything more about it. I was just running because I enjoyed it. But a couple of weeks later I got a letter formally inviting me to come to his camp. I figured it would make for a nice vacation away from home, and my mom thought it would be good for me to start hanging around with girls instead of only with boys. The letter also promised that scholarship if I improved in track and made my grades.

At Tennessee State we not only had to train, but we also had to put in so many hours a day at a job on campus. Athletes today do not have to do that. When I was competing, track and field was an amateur sport in every sense of the word. Nothing over $50. Today the top 10 to 20 track and field athletes can make enough money to live on. When we were competing, that was impossible, and that was one reason we went into such an early retirement. Once I graduated from college, I couldn't continue to run as an amateur because I had to go out and get a job. I was only 23, and that was far too young to quit. That's an age when you only begin to understand your sport and what you want to do with it. Today's athletes can stay with it a lot longer, which is the way it should be.

Going to Tennessee State gave me the opportunity to learn that women can do a lot of things and that you don't have to be embarrassed because you have a talent, even when it's in a sport that most people thought belonged exclusively to men. And we Tigerbelles did something more with our lives than just run track. We got our degrees and became teachers, doctors, lawyers, and many other things. We also got to travel all over the States and Europe. Because we appreciated all this so much and because we wanted so badly to succeed, we had a saying at Tennessee State: "It's so hard to be a Tigerbelle."

Coach Temple was an advisor as well as a coach. My father died when I was only 15, so he became a father figure as well. He was very strict, and he was very tough. He used to say, "If we're going to run, let's run. If we're going to be spectators, then let's get up in the stands where we belong." He also insisted that we train the European way, which to him meant "No play; just hard work." When I look back on it, I sometimes wonder how I made it, but I also know that he was very good for us as women. He was always there to lend a helping hand, but if you needed to be reprimanded, he was also very good at that. And academics always came first with him. We had to have a C average to compete, but he always pushed us to do much better than that. His whole philosophy was that we were not going to be athletes all our lives, so we had to take advantage of this opportunity to get a college education. We did, and he was always so proud of the fact that of the 40 of us who competed in the Olympics, 38 have college degrees.

In the 1964 Olympic trials I came in third in the 100 meters behind Edith McGuire and Marilyn White, so I barely qualified for the team. McGuire was a couple of years ahead of me at Tennessee State and had always beaten me. She came from Atlanta, which was only about 40 miles from Griffin, so we had run against one another even in high school. Coach Temple told me not to worry, that I had done well just to make the team because I was only 19 and that 1968 would be my year.

At first I was delighted just to be on the team, but after I won my trial heats in Tokyo, Coach Temple started telling me that I might even have a chance to win a medal. But I said to myself, A medal? I have a good chance at the gold.

In the finals I got off to a good start and was leading, but I kept thinking to myself, Where's Edith? At 80 or 90 yards she would always pull up and pass me by. But there was no Edith. I remembered that Coach Temple always told me never to look around, so I just kept looking straight ahead.

I don't know when that victory really sank in. Remember, I had never beaten Edith, which meant that I had never won the nationals or any other really big meet that she was in. All I kept thinking was, I won, but I have to go four more years. I really didn't have the opportunity to enjoy the winning of that gold medal because I kept thinking of what lay ahead. I was just starting college, so I saw it as a beginning, not as an end, but I did realize that my gold medal really meant that I would be able to get a college education.

In 1965 and '66 I set several world records, but by the latter half of 1967 I was not doing well. I barely made the Pan-American team, and then in the 200 meters rather than in the 100. I was just burned out. I kept asking myself, Why am I doing all this? I've already won the medal. I've done the things I want to do, and I'm going to graduate. I had suffered an infected spider bite on my leg that kept me out of training for two months. Then I went on a camping trip and got burned. So I started thinking, I really don't want to go to the Olympics. It's not really necessary. Am I just being greedy, trying to go back and win again?

I had to take stock and say, Hey, you only have one more year of school, and you want to go out on top, so you might as well put forth all that energy once more. I had finally convinced myself that it would be great to graduate and to go to the Olympics again in the same year.

By the time of the '68 Games I felt good about myself again. I knew I had an edge in experience over the other runners. Deep down inside I don't think anyone could have told me that I was not going to win that 100 meters. I just felt that confident, even though no Olympian had ever successfully defended a 100-meter title. I won and set a world record of 11 seconds flat, so it was a good way to go out.

It's too bad that Tommie Smith and John Carlos's black-fist salute on the victory stand bothered so many people. I had total respect for the two of them because it took a lot of courage to get up there and show the world how they felt. I could really identify with their wanting to make their stand against what was happening to blacks in America. Perhaps that wasn't the ideal place to do it, but wherever you make your stand is going to be unpopular with somebody, and they did bring needed attention to important issues. Some critics said that the two of them should not have brought politics into the Olympics, but politics has always been a part of the Games. Twelve years later we don't even go to the Games over a political issue.

As I look back and reflect on my gold medals, it never bothered me that I didn't get as much publicity as Wilma Rudolph did. She came first with her three gold medals in 1960, and somebody had to get the media attention; if not me, I was delighted that it was her. I feel that there's enough for everybody out there. It's like a family situation. If you have three or four children, there's always the favorite child, and Wilma became the glamor person of women's track and field, but that certainly did not prevent me from feeling happy and proud of what I had accomplished.

I retired after 1968, and that was it for five years. I married and had my first child. Then in 1973 I got into the newly established professional track. I ran on the circuit for the three years that it lasted. They only had one event for me—the 60-yard dash. The money was terrible. I think it was $600 for a victory, and you could earn a little more if you set a record. It was really nothing, but I believed that athletes should be paid for their talent. I also thought it would bring publicity to track and field and help all athletes financially. But sports fans were not ready for pro track, and we had no television. For some reason track and field has always been considered purely an amateur sport.

I now have two children, but I've never pushed them into athletics; however, I do push them in other directions, especially academics. I want them to learn the good things about sports, and that includes not having to be so competitive. I want them to understand that there can be rewards just from participating. I also work with other kids through the Amateur Athletic Foundation of Los Angeles. We want everyone to feel like winners, which they are if their primary goal is a healthy desire to participate in their favorite sport.

WILLIAM STEINKRAUS

Gold Medal, Equestrian—Show Jumping, 1968

Silver Medal, Equestrian—Team Show Jumping, 1960 and 1972

Bronze Medal, Equestrian—Team Show Jumping, 1952

In 1968 Bill Steinkraus became the first American to win an individual gold medal in an Olympic equestrian event. He made his Olympic debut at Helsinki in 1952, where he won a bronze for the team show-jumping event. Steinkraus competed in five Olympic Games from 1952 through 1972 and won medals in four of them, including two silver medals for team show-jumping, one in 1960 and one in 1972.

In his professional life Bill Steinkraus worked on Wall Street and in book publishing and remains active in the latter field as a freelancer.

I grew up in Westport, Connecticut, in a nonhorsey family. I suppose that I was a somewhat contrary-minded child, and the

Bill Steinkraus in 1984.

fact that nobody in the family was especially enthused about my special passion probably turned me on to horses that much more. Luckily, however, I had a mother who felt that if the children really committed themselves to some particular activity they should be encouraged. She and my father may have thought horse people were kind of dissolute, but they realized that I was serious about horses and made it possible for me to begin and then progress in the sport.

I started riding in summer camp when I was 10 years old, and after I came home in the fall I was fortunate to enter a school that had a modest riding program. Riding soon became my greatest preoccupation, transcending girls, money, food, and everything else, which is the way you have to commit yourself to any activity if you are to excel in it.

When I was about 16, I started to ride in the afternoons with a local horse dealer named Morton W. "Cappy" Smith, who was at that time perhaps the best rider in America. He had a lot of high-class horses, so for those two or three years before I went into the army at 18, I rode in the afternoons with him. Sometimes I'd ride six or eight different horses a day, and in three months or so there would be a whole bunch of new horses. Thus, in a sense, I had the privilege of growing up like a young professional, though I was still an amateur. For this privilege I did all the chores that one has to do around a stable, and that, too, was a good experience.

In fact, I was very lucky to have had ideal teachers at every level of my training, including the Olympic level. There, I was one of the people who urged the U.S. Equestrian Team, Inc., to engage a European horseman who had come up through the European cavalry schools and was familiar with the established European techniques for solving problems that were new to us in this country. International, Olympic-type courses were very different from ours. The only horsemen in this country who had experience with those courses were our army horsemen, and we didn't have very good access to them after 1948 when the army team was disbanded.

So we were lucky enough to find a Hungarian cavalry officer named Bertalan de Nemethy, and Bert, as he soon came to be called, had been through the Hungarian and German cavalry schools. He provided instant access for us to the great European tradition. He was the one who completed my equestrian education because, as wonderful as Cappy was, he had never ridden in Europe, and he had not experienced Olympic conditions at all.

I went into the U.S. Army Cavalry in 1942 at 18. I think I was in the next-to-the-last increment that went through basic training with horses. We took pistol practice on horseback and charged around with lances and all that. It had been thought that horse cavalry could be used in Burma, and we went overseas with all of our mounted equipment with the task of opening up the Burma Road. We eventually did it, but as a dismounted brigade. We did have mules, of course, and without them we would never have gotten where we were going.

After the war I returned to Yale, and I also picked up my riding career. It happened that a former wrestling coach at Yale was a horse enthusiast—"Professor" I. Q. Winters, as we called him. He had been the world's lightweight wrestling champion before World War I, in an era when wrestling was a very serious sport. He had toured the world with Frank Gotch, the great wrestler of that era; they had even gone to Japan and wrestled against the Sumo wrestlers. When I met him, he was retired after some 20-odd years at Yale. He liked horses, and he had some jumpers, so after classes I'd go over to his place and ride and train his jumpers.

The U.S. had a military equestrian team in the Olympic Games in 1948, and, as far as I knew, we had never had anything but a military team in the Games and never would have. But in 1949 it was announced that there would be no more military involvement in international equestrianism. I was still an amateur, and in 1952 I made the Olympic team and all of the teams after that through 1972, after which I retired.

In those early Olympics it was a major undertaking getting the horses to the Games. We used to send them by boat, and, because you couldn't exercise them on board ship, you had to let them down in training long before they left. After a seven- or eight-day trip by freighter, you needed another long time, often a month, to bring them back up to their best condition. Eventually we were able to fly them over, first in DC4s and now in 747s. The DC4s first held 6 horses, then later 8. Today's 747s can carry 30, and the passengers don't even know they're there.

The safest way to send a horse is to build a double stall so that he can't lean against one side and kick the other side out, but it took a while to convince the airlines of that. We had some hairy trips during those early days of flying. We lost one horse because the pilot ordered him destroyed after the horse began to panic and kicked his single stall apart. But those are mostly problems of the past.

The average horse has a six- or eight-year peak, if he doesn't get hurt. I tried to ride Snowbound, the horse I won the gold medal on in 1968, again in 1972, but he was not a very sound horse to begin with. He had tendon problems before he ever became a jumper, and he continued to have them with us; in fact, he had a bit of a problem when he won the gold medal—we had to keep patching him up. He was like a Mickey Mantle or that type of athlete—he was so generous that he would put out a little too much and kept hurting himself. But he would always go as far as he could go. It was our hope that he would hold up for the '72 Games as well. He would have been 13 in 1972. There were two events at that time, the individual and the team jumping events. Snowbound had hurt himself in the individual and the team jumping event in '68 at

Mexico City, the event in which I won the gold medal. As a result, I had to be on the sidelines for the team event. In Munich in '72 I rode him in the individual, hoping he would be sound enough to come through, but he didn't, and I rode a different horse in the team event. That was the only time I rode the same horse in two Games.

Horses tend to reach physical maturity around 5 or 6, but ordinarily they don't have the experience at that age to cope with international courses. If they're lucky, some horses can go on until they're 14 or 15, and some few even beyond. But by and large, they don't have a long peak. The riders, however, can have a long career. Mike Plumb with his seven Olympics and even myself with five are good examples.

Olympic equestrian events can be confusing to watch for those unfamiliar with horse competitions. Basically there are three equestrian events, each of which has two components: an individual competition and a team competition. These events are dressage, Grand Prix jumping, and the three-day event. Dressage is a test of precision riding on the flat that can be compared to the school figures of figure skating. It's a programmed ride. You memorize the Olympic Grand Prix test, which is the highest, most demanding test of a horse and rider's ability to perform difficult movements on the flat. Grand Prix jumping is the most demanding test of the horse and rider's ability to jump a variety of high and wide fences in a stadium. The three-day event starts with a moderately difficult dressage test on the first day, followed by an extremely difficult and demanding second day, consisting of a steeplechase phase, an endurance phase, and a cross-country jumping phase. The second day really wrings horses out, not to mention the riders. On the third day (which sometimes is the fourth day if there are rest days in between, or if the dressage takes two days) you again do stadium jumping, but at a much more moderate level than Grand Prix jumping. The purpose of the third-day program is to demonstrate that the horse, who has done this extremely demanding second day, is still fit and sound and can continue in service on the third day. So, you see, it's possible to lose the gold medal on the third day, but you can't win it on the third day; you have to win it on the second day.

But you have to understand that this all is a little like PGA golf. Nobody wins many golf tournaments in a row, and no one wins all the Grand Prix events. If you win two or three Grands Prix in a row it is quite unusual, and if you win four or five of them in a year, you are likely to be the leading rider that year. There are probably well over a dozen people who can win any given event, and there are another dozen who are not very far out. So our sport is one in which you never achieve a very high winning percentage. Dressage might be the only exception.

The only Games I've missed seeing since 1948 were the Moscow Games in 1980. Frankly, I had a feeling that the Carter Administration had no very sports-minded people in it, and they didn't understand what they were dealing with. They were grasping at straws, and the straws they grasped never had a chance of bearing much weight. It was a shame, because our boycott was doomed to be a futile gesture from the beginning. It was not done maliciously, but I do regret it. We certainly didn't help the Olympic movement. And for us, of all nations, to have tried to use the Games as a political lever was especially regrettable. But even so, it didn't destroy the Olympic movement any more than have the other boycotts. You have to say that the Games are a very durable institution.

I think we have an even greater threat now, for the International Olympic Committee and others are pushing the idea of open Games. I think if they have open Games it will be the end of an era, because professional athletes are so vulnerable to exploitation by others. The Games might then become victims of many of the pressures that have already beset such professional sports as baseball, football, and basketball. And, honestly, I don't think there is much sport left in those activities anymore; I think they are now primarily parts of the entertainment business. If the Olympic movement becomes only a part of the entertainment business too, it's doomed. I don't think that de Coubertin was being unrealistic when he said that the important thing about the Games was participation, even more than winning. I think he really knew exactly what he was saying, because professional sport has always existed, even back at the times of the original Olympic Games. And certainly professional sports existed in the era when the modern Olympic Games were being promulgated, and they were probably no more and no less corrupt than they are today. But when there is so much money involved, there is always temptation involved.

There is no denying that there are a lot of professional amateurs, but the important thing about the Olympic Games is that it is a

Bill Steinkraus riding "Snow Bound" in 1968. Photo courtesy of Bill Steinkraus

rich fabric of many sports that do not really have a professional counterpart. What, for example, is a professional archer? I mean, there are a few fellows working for the industry, I presume, but basically there is no such thing as a professional archer, nor professional rowers, nor javelin throwers, nor biathletes, nor lots of other things. There can't be. But what worries me about the IOC leaning toward open Games is that the minute you invite the professional sports promoter in, who is an entertainment businessman, the first thing he's going to do is say, "Let's forget these minor sports and see what we can do to hype the others more effectively." But this misses the point. The great thing about the present Olympic Games is that they provide a showcase for many sports that are wonderful to do but not necessarily good enough to invite the public to sit by the tube and watch every week. In these sports you see real people—men and women with real jobs sacrificing to maintain some kind of sporting participation for themselves in some activity in which that is still possible. After all, to be an archer you don't have to be seven-foot-two. You do have to be seven-foot-two to be a college basketball center in a good college program, and you have to be a 10-flat sprinter in any kind of good high school track program. You have to weigh over 200 pounds to play in the line in a good high school program and more than that in college. You have to be freakish, in a way, to play most mainstream sports, and they are the ones with a big professional aspect.

But there are a lot of other sports, and riding is one of them, in which, if you are really dedicated and have reasonable intelligence and determination and some talent and can get enough money behind you to work on refining your skills, you can aspire to be an Olympic athlete. There's probably no professional sport that I could have participated in, and I grew up thinking of myself as a nonathletic person. For me, that's the real value of amateur sport, as quite distinct from professional sport. Professional sport is wonderful; it belongs, and I enjoy thoroughly watching these extraordinary human beings. But Willie Mays as a baseball player is one player out of 50 million. It's nice that I have some sporting thing that I can do that doesn't require me to be that unique.

People don't often make this case for amateur sport because the best place to make this case is in the mass media, and the mass media have long since sold their souls to professional sports—and how could it be otherwise? That's the going thing every week, and professional sports in a sense pays the salaries for the sportswriters of the New York dailies or the television sportscasters. So they have very little feeling for amateur sport and practically no comprehension of it. They think the highest praise you can give amateur sport is that it ought to be all professional. They miss the point entirely. If you talk to someone like Darrell Pace, the two-time Olympic archery gold medalist, you realize that the people in the media don't realize that he exists, any more than they realize that I exist. They can think only of the high-profile people who are going to be able to project their Olympic gold medal into hundreds of thousands of dollars because then they become part of their world. Even Juan Antonio Samaranch, president of the IOC, says that there are no amateur athletes anymore. That's nonsense. There are a lot of real amateurs, but you can't see them on television.

Take equestrian sport. We have a problem getting it on television. We got the most coverage for the equestrian events in Los Angeles that we ever got, but I know firsthand what an uphill struggle it is. We had very good exposure, and we got very good public response to what our riders did in Los Angeles. Guess how many times we got on television the following year? Once, and that was in December, and that was because a sponsor said he would like to televise an event in Tampa. We can't get our world championship on the air. We also have a World Cup in our sport, and our riders have won it six of the eight times it's been held. But nobody knows that. Our media are very much the captives of the professional sports establishment, and that's not likely to change. What is likely to change is that Samaranch is likely to sell out the Games, if we can believe what we read, and that would be tragic.

There's a big difference in doing something for an honest day's wage and doing something for its own sake alone. And the concept of amateur sport—the reason it is antiprofessional sport—is not because money is a bad thing, but because if you are doing it for money you are not doing it for the intrinsics.

Again, consider show jumping. It seems to be a ridiculous sport. Why would you build these huge fences in the middle of a field? It's so easy to go around them, yet it's dangerous and extremely expensive to train horses to jump them. It's a pure abstract challenge. It's like sticking an arrow in the middle of a target X number of times perfectly dead center. That is the true nature of sport. You can make a pretty good argument that sport, as distinct from business, is essentially nonutilitarian—in the best sense of the word—and when it starts to become utilitarian it is no longer sport; it is something else. It may be survival; it may be entertainment, or it may be economics. But if it is too utilitarian, it is really not sport. I hope and pray that somehow amateur sport manages to survive the very materialistic environment it exists in today.

13
MUNICH, 1972

For the world, the most memorable image from the Munich Games is not that of Olga Korbut poised on a balance beam, or of Mark Spitz splashing toward his unprecedented seventh gold medal, or of Dave Wottle running alone, far behind the pack, in the 800-meter run. The most haunting image from the '72 Games is that of the hooded terrorist on the balcony of the Israeli apartment complex in the Olympic Village. That grotesque, skull-like mask will forever remain a symbol of that other, darker side of human nature, which is driven by intolerance and hatred. That it appeared in the midst of an ancient ritual celebrating peaceful, exuberant competition among the best young athletes in the world and that it happened in Germany add a tragic irony to the horror.

In the early, predawn hours of September 5, the terrorists climbed over a fence, slipped into the Israeli apartment complex, and began knocking on doors and barging into rooms. During the initial attack, Moshe Weinberg, the wrestling coach, was killed outright, and Yoseph Romano, a weightlifter, was mortally wounded. Some Israelis escaped and raised the alarm, but nine others were captured and held as hostages by the terrorists.

For most of that day the drama unfolded in Munich and

throughout the world, as television provided a worldwide stage. Various groups, including Olympic officials from several Arab nations, attempted to reason with the terrorists, but to no avail. By early evening the Games were suspended, and German officials decided to pretend to agree to the terrorists' demand for safe passage to an Arab nation.

A bus was sent to pick up the terrorists and their hostages and take them to a nearby helicopter pad, where they would be flown to a waiting 727 at a military air base some 15 miles away; however, there was no intention to let the terrorists leave Germany. Several police marksmen were waiting at the air base to shoot the terrorists when they moved from the helicopters to the 727. But the shooting began prematurely, and in the ensuing barrage of exploding hand grenades and gunfire, one policeman, five terrorists, and all nine Israeli hostages were killed. Those who died at the air base were wrestlers Mark Slavin and Eliezer Halfin; weightlifters David Berger and Zeev Freedman; coaches Andre Spitzer, Kehat Shor, and Amizur Shapira; and judge-referees Yoseph Gutfreund and Yaacov Shpringer.

Many expected the Games to be canceled, but four hours after the terrorists invaded the Olympic Village Avery Brundage, the retiring president of the International Olympic Committee, announced that the Games would go on as scheduled. In controlled but eloquent outrage, the dean of American sportswriters, Red Smith, wrote in *The New York Times*: "Walled off in their dream world, appallingly unaware of the realities of life and death, the aging playground directors who conduct the quadrennial muscle dance ruled that a little blood must not be allowed to interrupt play."

Ten hours after the early-morning invasion of the Israeli apartments, the Games were temporarily suspended, and a memorial ceremony was held the next day. Many still felt that the Games should be canceled, not merely suspended for a few hours. Once again Red Smith bitingly reported that sentiment when he wrote,

> "This time surely, some thought, they would cover the sandbox and put the blocks aside. But no. 'The Games must go on,' said Avery Brundage, high priest of the playground, and 80,000 listeners burst into applause. The occasion was yesterday's memorial service for eleven members of Israel's Olympic delegation murdered by Palestinian terrorists. It was more like a pep rally."

In an attempt to make these the best Olympic Games ever, and to help make amends for the 1936 Games, which the Nazis had turned into a propaganda vehicle, the Germans spared themselves no effort and no expense. Munich had cheerfully spent some $700 million to prepare for the Games, making them to date by far the costliest in Olympic history. The Olympic Park consisted of the Olympic Village, a communication center, and the Olympic Stadium, Arena, and Pool, the last three partially covered by a huge steel and plexiglass roof. All the facilities were superb, and only the latest electronic equipment was used to keep track of the times and scores. These included triangular infrared prism rays to provide instant measurements of distances for javelin, discus, and hammer throws and electronic timing devices that enabled the times in track and swimming races to be determined within a thousandth of a second.

Yet for the U.S. Olympic team, these Games were marred by several instances of poor officiating, costly blunders, and simple bad luck. Imagine two of the best sprinters in the world missing their race because of a scheduling foul-up. That happened to Eddie Hart and Rey Robinson. Picture the greatest miler in the world getting knocked down and out of contention in an early heat in the 1,500-meter run. Thus did Jim Ryun's third and final Olympic appearance end, along with his long-held dream of winning an Olympic gold medal. Think of the world's best pole-vaulter not being allowed to use the pole with which he practiced. Bob Seagren was outraged when the international federation reversed itself for the third time on the eve of the competition and banned the new fiberglass pole he had used to set the world record. And then consider the light-middleweight boxer being declared the loser in a fight he clearly won. Reginald Jones's "loss" infuriated the crowd, which then pelted the ring with debris. Imagine a basketball team winning 50–49, only to see that changed to a 50–51 loss during a controversial extra three seconds of play. After 65 consecutive Olympic basketball triumphs, the U.S. basketball team "lost" its first Olympic game.

The American team did have its triumphs in Munich, the most spectacular being Mark Spitz's unprecedented and total domination of the men's swimming events. Spitz was entered in four individual competitions and the three relays and won gold medals in each, setting, or helping to set, world records in every one of them. What made this achievement particularly satisfying for Spitz was that it redeemed his disappointing showing in Mexico

City. In those Games Spitz was expected to win six gold medals but had to settle for two golds, one silver, and a bronze, which for anyone but Mark Spitz would have been a formidable achievement.

In the 400-meter race Vince Matthews and Wayne Collett took first and second, but their disrespectful refusal to stand at attention on the victory stand, supposedly an unplanned protest against the condition of blacks in the U.S., got them banned from further Olympic competition. That meant the U.S. did not have four eligible men to run the 4x400 relay.

Two of the more memorable victories for the Americans came in the 800 meters and the marathon. Coming from far behind the pack in the first third of the 800-meter race, Dave Wottle, wearing his golf cap, put on a dazzling burst of speed in the last 50 meters to inch by the favorite, Yevgeny Arzhanov of the USSR, at the tape. Frank Shorter became the first American to win the marathon since 1908. Shorter's appearance in Munich was something of a homecoming. He was born in Munich in 1947 while his father, a U.S. Army doctor, was stationed there.

Archery reappeared as an Olympic event in Munich, having been out since 1920, and the U.S. won both the men's and women's divisions. Doreen Wilbur, a 42-year-old housewife, won the women's competition, while John Williams, an 18-year-old army private, took the gold in the men's event. In winning the gold medal in the light-welterweight class, Sugar Ray Seales saved the U.S. boxers from the humiliation of taking only three bronze medals home from Munich.

CHARLES AUGUSTUS "SUGAR RAY" SEALES

Gold Medal, Boxing, Light-Welterweight, 1972

The American Olympic boxing team of Duane Bobick, Davie Armstrong, Reggie Jones, Marvin Johnson, and Sugar Ray Seales was expected to do well in Munich in 1972, but Seales was the only American to win an Olympic gold in the event.

Seales was born in St. Croix, U.S. Virgin Islands, in

1952 and moved to Tacoma, Washington, at the age of 12. At 15 he qualified for the '68 Olympic trials, but because of his age he couldn't go. After winning various amateur titles, including North American champion in 1971, he went to the '72 Olympics, where he fought five times, winning all bouts by decisions.

Seales turned pro in 1973 and won his first 20 fights. He lost a fight to Marvin Hagler in 1975 and fought him to a draw a few months later. Seales was on his way to a shot at the middleweight title when he was KOed by Alan Minter in London in 1976.

Seales was forced to retire from boxing in 1983 as the result of detached retinae, and even after seven eye operations he is still legally blind.

Seales in 1986. Photo by Fogarty and Carlson

I was born in St. Croix in the Virgin Islands, and I learned boxing when I was nine years old, mostly from my father, Charles Augustus Seales, Sr. He boxed for three years in the military in the Virgin Islands. I learned boxing from him, but I learned fighting from both him and my mom because they were always fighting.

In the Virgin Islands not many people knew much about boxing; at least, they wouldn't talk about it if they did. So I trained and practiced with my brothers and sisters. Every day at the Charles H. Emanuel Elementary School during recess we'd be boxing by putting up our fists and throwing punches and dodging. The other kids didn't really know what we were doing, but they didn't want any part of it anyway.

When I was 10, my mom got divorced from my dad and moved to the state of Washington. Her brother worked for the Burlington Railroad there, and he was able to help her. That was in 1962, and two years later she had raised enough money so that the rest of us could follow her. I've been living out here since then, since November 1964.

When I got here, I couldn't speak English. I spoke a mixture of broken English and Spanish, but altogether you couldn't understand it. I went to McCarver Junior High School, and I learned some English there. Lots of my friends, who weren't my friends then, used to laugh at me because of the language.

We lived about half a block from the Tacoma Boys Club, which my brothers and I joined. We were hoping we could find someone there who knew about boxing, but there wasn't any boxing there then. In late 1965 a gentleman by the name of Joe Clough came there and started coaching boxing. He had started out to be a boxer himself, but it didn't work out: he didn't like blood. He got his lip busted, and he didn't like that, so he became a coach. In a way it was the four of us Seales brothers and the Tacoma Boys Club that got boxing started in the state of Washington, and Jim Clough was my first coach, except for my dad.

It was at the Tacoma Boys Club that I was given the name "Sugar." I was 12 years old, weighed 78 pounds, and was about six feet tall, all arms and legs. I was a southpaw, and people said I looked like Sugar Ray Robinson. He was a southpaw, but in his day they didn't fight southpaw, so he had to convert to a right-hander. They said I looked like him, and they processed my hair just like Robinson's hair is done. I became Sugar Ray Seales, which sounded to me like the name a great fighter might have. From that time on I carried myself like Sugar Ray Robinson. He was my idol, and pound for pound he was the greatest fighter who ever lived. He had it all: he was a puncher, a boxer, a master. I didn't try to pattern myself after Robinson, but the fact that I now had his name, a name that everyone respected, made me behave like someone worth respecting.

From then on I really worked hard to learn English. I studied and studied. I wanted to have friends in the state of Washington; I didn't want to be left out. I was Sugar Ray, so I worked hard, and I learned, and I became friends with a lot of people.

I boxed from 1965 all the way till 1972 as an amateur fighter. I had 350 amateur fights, and I lost 12 of them. During that time I won 38 major amateur titles, including the AAU nationals and the Golden Gloves senior championship. I wanted to become number one.

In 1968 I qualified for the Olympic trials, but as a fighter you had to be 16 to go. I was only 15, so I couldn't make it. In 1971 I beat Larry Bonds in New Orleans for the national title, and that meant a lot, not only to me but to Tacoma. Later that year I won three fights in Las Vegas, went to Minneapolis, and won five fights there. I won eight fights in eight days. That qualified me for the Olympic trials for the '72 Games.

When we got to Germany, they broke my weight class down into two divisions, and I wound up having to fight all the tough fighters. The first fight was against the German, Ulrich Bayer. I broke a knuckle on my left hand in that fight, and it still looks bad. I never told anybody, because I would have been disqualified. So it was win today, ice bucket tonight, train tomorrow, and fight the next day.

The next fight I had was against a guy from Ireland, Anthony Montague, and the third was against another real tough fighter, a Cuban, Andre Malina. Cuba had one of the strongest boxing teams at the Games. My fourth fight was against Zvonimir Vujin of Yugoslavia, and my fifth was against a Bulgarian, Anghel Angelov. All of them were tough. They were all expected to win gold medals for their countries.

Both my mother and my father were at the Olympics to watch me. See, two months before I'd qualified for the team, I'd told my mother I was going to be in the Olympic Games. She believed me and went out and bought her tickets—two months before the

Games. Down in the Virgin Islands some people raised the money to send my dad so he could see me, too. Having them there really gave me more confidence. We were sort of a team, a family team.

My mother was even on TV. She was in the stands yelling, "Get him, son; get him, son!" Every time she hollered, I'd get a hit. She was part of the team; she was helping me. And that was the first time my dad saw me fight since I left the islands. But he couldn't stand up and holler like my mother. He kept telling her, "Sit down, woman," and she would tell him to shut up. All the time she was hollering at me to get a hit. If I didn't win, she'd win for me. Well, she caused such a commotion that they finally dropped a microphone down from the roof so they could pick up everything she said.

Howard Cosell was narrating or broadcasting the fights, and he couldn't pronounce "TaCOma." All through my first three fights, until it was clear that I would win at least a bronze medal, he would call me "Ray Seales from TAComa, Washington." Nobody had been paying much attention to me. They were all looking at the big white hope, the heavyweight, Duane Bobick. He won his first fight against a very tough Russian, who really beat him up, and then he lost to the Cuban, Teofilo Stevenson. Bobick had only one day to rest between the fights, and that wasn't enough time for him. When I won my third fight, Cosell gave me my full name and learned how to pronounce my hometown: I became "Sugar Ray Seales from TaCOma."

I got back to Tacoma on September 13, and the following January I turned pro. That year I fought 15 times and won all of them. Actually I won my first 21 professional fights. My first loss was to Marvin Hagler in Boston in 1975, and that was an exhibition for the United Way. We fought in a TV studio in front of 200 people. I was the one who was being featured; Marvin was an unknown then. I lost a 10-round decision. Three months later I fought him again in Seattle, and that was a 10-round draw, but I really won that fight. There hadn't been many fights in Seattle, and at that time the judges there didn't know much about how to judge fighters. I felt that Marvin won two or three rounds and that I won six, the rest being draws.

From there I fought all over the country and in Europe. In 1978 I had a three-fight contract that would have given me a shot at the middleweight title. Win the first two, and the third would be against the champion, Carlos Monzon. I won the first one, which was in Rome, Italy, with a fourth-round knockout. From there I went to London for the second fight, which was against Alan Minter. I lost that fight in a fifth-round TKO. That was a hard fight, and controversial, but I didn't complain. Even though I didn't get to fight Monzon, I knew I was still a winning fighter, and I'd get another shot at the title later. So I kept fighting.

The trouble with my eyes began with a fight in Baton Rouge, Louisiana, in 1980. I fought a six-foot-three fighter named Jamie Thomas on the undercard of a closed-circuit fight between Thomas Hearns and Pipino Cuevas. I got thumbed in the right eye, and there was a lot of blood in it. The eye got worse, and later I had surgery to put it back together. After that it was OK, and the doctor said I could fight again if I wanted to, but he advised me not to box anymore. At the time I was on a winning trend and was looking forward to getting a shot at the middleweight title, so I kept going. But that eye got worse, and so did the other one. After that first injury in 1980, my eyes just started going bad slowly. I ended up having four operations on my left eye and three on my right. I retired from boxing in 1983.

In January of 1984 some people got together for a fund-raiser to help me, Sugar Ray Seales, fight my blindness and get the medical bills straightened out. It was held in the Tacoma Dome, and Marvin Hagler, Boom-Boom Mancini, Muhammad Ali, Michael Spinks, and a lot of other guys came to that fund-raiser. Even Sammy Davis, Jr., performed. It was one of the greatest things that ever happened in the state of Washington.

Today I'm seeing about 60 percent or so out of my right eye, and I have some vision in my left eye. I like to say that the Lord is in my left eye, and He's guiding me through that eye. I'm not fighting anymore, but I still love the sport, and I'm still in it. I'm managing a young fighter named Michael Hattersley—"Sir Michael," he's called. We formed this company, Sugar Ray Seales' Boxing Enterprises, Inc. I'm Sir Michael's manager, and William Tuthill is comanager. Eventually we plan to manage fighters in most of the weight divisions. And we're doing other things, too. I recently released an audiotape for young men who want to become boxers. It's called *Winning Strategies in Boxing*. If that works, out we're planning to do some videotapes.

In my total career of 19 years in boxing, I had 430 fights, both amateur and professional, and of those I lost 19. I've had a great life. I came to Washington as a kid who couldn't even speak English, and the other kids made fun of me. But I learned fast. I learned how to speak, I learned how to box, and I learned how to treat people the way I wanted people to treat me. I have the great name, Sugar Ray, and I always tried to live up to that name and to what that name meant.

DAVID JAMES WOTTLE

Gold Medal, 800 Meters, 1972

Dave Wottle broke the four-minute mile in 1970 while a sophomore at Ohio's Bowling Green State University. The following year he was plagued with a series of injuries but began to make a comeback late in the season, and by the end of the year he had won the NCAA mile and the AAU 800-meter titles.

In the 800-meter race in Munich, Wottle came from far behind and, in a photo finish, edged out the favorite in that race, Russia's Yevgeny Arzhanov. On the victory stand Wottle embarrassed himself during the playing of the national anthem when he unintentionally forgot to remove the ubiquitous golf cap which was his running trademark.

In 1973 Dave Wottle again won the NCAA mile, and in February of 1974 he turned professional. After two years he gave up running for coaching and college administration work, first at Walsh College in Canton, Ohio, and later at Bethany College in West Virginia. Wottle ended his coaching career in 1982 and since 1983 has been Dean of Admissions at Rhodes College in Memphis.

I suppose what most people will remember about me as an Olympic athlete is that I was the one who wore a golf cap while running and also that I forgot to take it off on the victory stand. Most people won't recall what event I was in or how I ran the race, but they'll remember that hat.

I was never so embarrassed in my life! I trained in that hat, I ran my race in that hat, and when the results were announced, I simply climbed up on the platform and got my medal. I was so

Photo courtesy of Bowling Green State University Public Relations

Dave Wottle on the victory stand—Munich, 1972.

excited I never even thought about my hat. It's like a man's wallet; it's in your back pocket, but you don't know it's there unless you think about it. Well, my first reaction when I heard "The Star-Spangled Banner" was to stand at attention and put my hand over my heart, just like I did when I was in grade school. I thought everything went well, and I came down off the victory stand and went up to a press conference, still not conscious of the fact that I was wearing my golf cap.

The first question I was asked, and that was by an Australian reporter, I believe, was what I was protesting by putting my hand over the USA patch on my sweats and keeping my hat on during the medal-awarding ceremony. You know, that question just hit me like a blow to the stomach. I was in a state of exhaustion after the race, and I was very excited about having won, and all of a sudden someone slips me a zinger: "What were you protesting?" It caught me totally off guard. I couldn't believe I had had my hat on, and I felt terrible about it. I thought that if a reporter is asking about it, what are the other people thinking? I remember I didn't handle it very well; I shed some private tears. That initial question seemed to overshadow the remainder of the news conference.

I don't mean this in a bitter way, but I wish that reporter had never asked that question, at least not as the first question. It really shattered me. I thought of the incident with Tommie Smith and John Carlos in the '68 Games and all the ill feeling their protest created. Mine was an honest mistake, but what would the American people think? I remember that right after I left the conference I talked to Jim McKay, and of course he asked about the hat. That was on national television. All I could do was apologize to the American public. That episode just dampened my whole Olympic experience. It should have been my happiest day, but it wasn't; I was simply too embarrassed to be totally happy.

Afterward I received lots of letters and telegrams. I was in the Air Force ROTC at the time of the Olympics, and colonels and captains, and even President Nixon, wrote me and said they were proud of me. Agnew wrote and said, "Hats on or off, you're the type of American I respect." I never received any negative mail about the incident. The people who wrote seemed to understand that it was just an honest mistake; I had just forgotten about the hat.

A lot of strange things happened at Munich, and the worst, of course, was the Arab terrorist attack on the Israeli team in the Olympic Village. That happened on September 5, three days after I won the 800-meter race. Before daylight the terrorists climbed over the fence surrounding the Olympic Village and forced their way into the Israeli apartments, which were very close to ours. There was some shooting. Frank Shorter was my roommate, and his wife, Louise, was sleeping out on the balcony. She heard the shots, which we later learned killed an Israeli, but at the time she didn't know what they were. I got up early that morning to take my normal three-mile morning run, not knowing what had happened. I left our apartment complex, went down to the fence surrounding the Village, and there I saw that the gate at the end of our complex was wide open. That gate was always locked and guarded, and I remember I was a little surprised to see it open and nobody around. Anyway, I went out and had my run.

As I was coming back to the Olympic Village, a reporter spotted me. He knew immediately who I was because I had my cap on. He asked me what I thought of the massacre. I had no idea what he was talking about. He then told me that some Arab terrorists broke into the Israeli apartments and that 15 or 20 Israelis and Arabs were killed. He was wrong at that time, but as it turned out later, he was close to being correct.

By the time I got back into the Village the area around the Israeli complex was roped off, and there were police there and more arriving. There were all kinds of rumors going around, but the information was very sketchy. There were very few events on the schedule that day, so most of the athletes stayed around the village. We didn't know whether the Games would be suspended or canceled or what.

The following evening I went out for my evening run. I was still suffering from the tendinitis I had developed in my left knee six weeks earlier, and I wasn't able to really run more than three miles at any one time before it would flare up. As I was coming back to the Village I had to go around a large building complex, and I saw that an area about 10 yards wide had been roped off and was heavily guarded by German guards with machine guns. They were going to walk the terrorists and their Israeli hostages through this roped-off area and put them on a helicopter and take them over to the airport. I could see the entrance to my apartment on the other side of this guarded area, but the guards wouldn't let me get through that way. That meant that I would have to jog or walk about two miles around the Village to get back in. Well, my knee was bothering me, and I was tired, and I didn't want to go the long way around, so I looked around and saw a shortcut. I went back about 10 yards, went down a slope, jumped over a fence, and ran under a bridge. On top, the bridge, too, was roped off because it was part of the route to the helicopter pad. I had just passed under the bridge when I heard a group of guards in back of me saying, "Halt! Halt!" I stopped, and one of the guards said in English, "Oh, it's Wottle." I had my hat on, and I turned around to acknowledge their recognition of me, and I saw several of the guards pointing machine guns at me. My heart sank to my feet, and I thought, Wottle, you are such an idiot to be out here trying to get around these barricades. You're risking your life to save running an extra mile. It was a very, very touchy situation, and I thought how lucky I was to have had my hat on at that time. It may just have saved my life.

Mark Spitz won his seventh gold medal just prior to the terrorist attack, and after the murder of the Israeli athletes some officials thought that Spitz could be in danger. He was an American Jew and won more gold medals than anyone ever had before, and they thought that he might be a likely target. So Spitz left Munich right after the attack, a week or so before the end of the Games.

And there were other strange things that happened at the '72 Olympics, like what happened to Eddie Hart and Rey Robinson. I remember that, just after my prelim in the 800 meters, Lee Evans came running out onto the warm-up track, which was outside the Olympic stadium, ran up to me and said that the quarterfinal heat of the 100-meter dash was about to begin and that he couldn't find Eddie and Rey. He asked me if I had seen them, which I hadn't, so we set out to find them. I checked the warm-up area down in the tunnels leading to the stadium, and Lee checked the track fields. Neither of us found them, and when I got back up from the warm-up area Lee said that we just had to get those guys to their heat right away. We started running back to the Olympic Village, which was a good mile away. We were running down a highway trying to wave down cars, and finally a military truck stopped and gave us a lift partway back to the Village. About 100 yards from the Village my knee started killing me, and I told Lee to go on alone. When he got to the Olympic Village, Hart and Robinson had already left for their heat. They had been watching the coverage on TV and saw their heat being announced. I understand they had been told by their coach, Stan Wright, that they would be running in the evening rather than the late afternoon. When they saw the heats of the 100-meter announced on TV, they jumped into a car and hightailed it over to the stadium, but it was too late; their heat had been run. What a tragic way to end your Olympic experience—all those years of training down the drain because of a scheduling error.

I started track in the eighth grade at Clarendon Grade School in Canton, Ohio. I also began and ended my football career in the eighth grade. I was a halfback on the football team, but I never gained a yard. I'd hit those big guys and bounce back about three yards. I was just horrible in football. I also played basketball in the seventh and eighth grade and baseball in the summer.

I say I started track in the eighth grade, but all I did was start. On the very first day of workouts I ran in a practice relay race around the school and pulled a hamstring muscle. I couldn't walk and was out of school for three days. When I came back, the coach, who was also my homeroom teacher, really chewed me out, right in front of the whole class, for not calling him up and telling him I had injured my leg. For a very shy and introverted eighth-grader, it was a very embarrassing experience. Anyway, I didn't run anymore that year.

I went out for track in high school—Canton Lincoln High, about a mile from my home. I had just finished my first basketball season as the illustrious 14th man on a 15-man squad. I was the last person coming out of the locker room, and I noticed a sign announcing a meeting for people interested in track. I tried to open the door of the meeting room, but it was stuck, or I was too weak to get it opened, so I continued walking down the hall. Then I thought, Hey, Dave, you'll never know if you can do well in track unless you give it a try. But because I was terribly shy, I didn't want to bring attention to myself. I could imagine myself trying that door again and having the coach open it and my kind of falling into the meeting and everyone laughing at me. But I did go back, tried the door again, and sure enough the coach opened it, and everybody laughed, "Oh, it's just Wottle." I walked to the back of the room, sat down, and at the end of the meeting signed up to be a sprinter.

The previous summer, 1963, I had beaten a neighborhood kid named Bunny who I thought was the fastest runner in the world. He was the fastest on my block, anyway. I jump-started him in a downhill race one time, and I beat him, so I thought I was pretty fast, which is why I signed up for the 100-, 200-, and 400-yard races.

At the first workout the coach put me in with the sprinters. There was a kid in the school named John Cosmedes, and he ended up running the 100 yards in 9.65—in high school. He was quick. I remember lining up in the blocks with him, and by the time I had gotten off the blocks he had finished the race. After the first week of workouts, the coach came over, kind of put his arm around my shoulders, and said, "Dave, I'm going to send you where I send everybody else who has no talent. I'm going to put you in with the distance runners." And that's really how I became a distance runner.

I sort of clicked as a distance runner. We didn't have cross-country in our high school, so I alternated between the mile and the half-mile. By the time I was a senior I had pushed my times down quite a bit, but I still hadn't run the mile in less than 4:20. I finally broke 2:00 for the half-mile that year, but the time wasn't fantastic: 1:59.4. My training was haphazard, and I felt I had gone as far as I could on natural ability alone.

I won the mile at the state meet in my senior year. Right after that I got a letter from Jumbo Elliot at Villanova, asking me to consider going there. Well, the following week I ran in what we call the Ohio Classic Meet, where the best milers from all size schools race against one another to prove who is the top miler in Ohio. I got dead last in the race. I had won the state meet in 4:20.2 and ran the Classic in 4:40 or so. A few days later I got another letter from Elliot, saying Villanova was no longer interested in me.

I was not hotly recruited. I wanted to go to Miami of Ohio, but they ran out of athletic grants-in-aid. I registered to go to Mt. Union, a small liberal arts college in Alliance, Ohio, and had been assigned a room and a roommate, but at the last minute I changed my mind and switched to Bowling Green. I began school there on a one-third tuition grant-in-aid.

The coach at Bowling Green was Mel Brodt, who had been a star distance runner at Miami of Ohio. The training at BG was very rigorous, but that was what I needed. I was running indoors and outdoors and cross-country, and running sometimes over 60 miles a week, which was almost triple the weekly mileage I had been doing in high school. It nearly killed me, but my times came down steadily because of that training. I dropped my mile to 4:06 and my half-mile to 1:54.9 by the end of my first year.

I broke the four-minute mile in my sophomore year, which up to that time was the biggest thrill of my athletic career. I ran a 3:59-flat in Bloomington, Indiana, at the Central Collegiate Conference meet, and I got second in the NCAA mile to Marty Liquori. The following year I came down with a series of injuries, including stress fractures to both the left and right fibulas and bursitis in my right knee. I was out of competitive running for about seven months.

I started coming back from the injuries in the summer of '71, the year before the Olympics. I was extremely eager to succeed in track after being out of action for so long. However, while I may have dreamed of winning a gold medal in the Olympics, I wasn't looking to the Games when I started running again; I was just taking it one race at a time. The Olympics were an ultimate goal, but I had many intermediate goals I had to achieve first. I felt I had to beat everyone in this country before I could look to world competition, and by the end of that year I had won the NCAA indoor 880, the NCAA 1,500-meter title, and then the 800 meters in the AAU. Then it was a natural progression to compete in the Olympic trials. At the trials I qualified for the 1,500-meter race and tied the world record in the 800 meters. That was about two months before the Olympics, and it wasn't until then that I could realistically set my sights on getting a gold medal.

I qualified in both the 800- and the 1,500-meter races at the trials, but I really considered myself a miler. The 800-meter race came first at the Olympics, and I really wasn't in the best condition for it. I got married on July 15, went on a brief honeymoon, and didn't run for several days. The Olympic track team assembled in Brunswick, Maine, to go to Norway for some competition. On the first day of training I tried to do a difficult workout to get my conditioning back up to par quickly. It was a stupid thing to do. Without a proper warm-up, I ran a very hard workout and developed tendinitis in my left knee. The injury cut my mileage from 90 miles a week to 20, and I knew I wasn't going to get it back up in the few weeks before the Olympics. A week before the Games I was running about 40 miles a week, using three shorter workouts, instead of the normal two long workouts, to accommodate the injury.

In spite of my less than ideal condition, when I walked onto the track in Munich I really believed I could win a gold medal in the 800 meters. I think you always have to believe you can take first place. When I saw all the athletes I was competing against and realized that every one of them was in peak condition and had been training well right up to the time of the Olympics, I began to have some doubts in the back of my mind. I had not been training well for the past five weeks, and on top of that I was very nervous, much more so than usual. After all, I had reached the pinnacle of my sport. I was competing for a gold medal, a true "once in a lifetime" opportunity.

When the gun went off, I had butterflies in my stomach like I normally do, but this time they didn't go away. The pack went out the first 200 meters in 24.7 seconds, very quick for an 800 back then. I went out in 25.8, a good 10 yards behind. My nervousness, my concerns about my training, and the initial burst of speed of the others all came together and kept me separated from the pack. I suppose one good thing came out of that: anybody could have gotten a good, clear, postcard picture of me all by myself—if they wanted one, that is. I remember looking up at the stands and thinking what a poor showing I was giving. I decided that I had to at least make it look respectable; I had to catch up to the others.

By the time the other runners had reached the 400-meter point, they had slowed down somewhat, and I had caught up to the back of the pack. At that point I wanted to relax a bit because it had taken some effort to catch them. I wanted to see how the field was developing. Yevgeny Arzhanov, the Russian, was sixth at that point and only two spots ahead of me, and I was in range of him. I thought, Fine. He's the favorite, and I'm right where I want to be. I figured that I'd get back to my prerace strategy of trying to stay close to him, believing that I could outkick him at the end. I wasn't absolutely sure of that because he was very, very quick. He could run the 100-yard dash in about 10.2 seconds, and people told me that if I were with him with 100 meters to go, I would lose. But I still felt that I could outkick him if I was with him. Then I relaxed for 100 meters or so.

With 300 meters to go, Arzhanov took off and charged toward the lead. I made a little move, to about the fifth or sixth spot. I didn't want to start my all-out kick just yet, but Arzhanov committed himself, which was unusual for him. He normally waited until there were 150 meters to go before he kicked. I thought it was very risky for him to start such a new strategy, but he was doing it. I waited. Then, with 180 meters to the finish, I thought I had to move. I was in sixth place, I think, but I was outside of lane two, so I was in good position.

When I hit the top of the homestretch I was in fourth place, and I was ready to settle for a bronze medal. I didn't think there was a chance to catch Arzhanov, who by then had a five- to seven-yard lead. At the top of the stretch I was simply going after a bronze medal. As soon as I passed the first Kenyan, Robert Ouku, I quickly reevaluated my goals: I wanted to be a silver medalist. It wasn't until about five meters from the finish line that I thought I had a chance to catch Arzhanhov. He was faltering at that point. I think he noticed me coming up on his shoulder, and he tried to reaccelerate. His upper body was saying yes, but his legs were saying no. They must have been very tight at that stage, and when he tried to reaccelerate by pumping his arms, his legs wouldn't go with him, and he just toppled directly over the finish line. I just kept charging, and I crossed the line and put my arms up because I thought I had won. I had no sense, through my peripheral vision, that anyone was next to me. Arzhanhov had fallen to the ground over the line, and the difference in our times was $^{3}/_{100}$ of a second! My time was 1:45.86, and Arzhanov's was 1:45.89. I think I won by the bill of my cap.

Did you notice my uniform in the pictures from that race? My wife came with me to the Games on an extended honeymoon, and when we first got to Munich I had to find her accommodations, so I got to the Olympic Village late, and all of the equipment and uniforms had already been handed out. All there was left for me was a pair of extra-large trunks and a very large shirt. I couldn't wear the shorts, so Frank Shorter gave me a pair of his Florida Track Club shorts and said, in jest, "If you win the gold medal in the 800-meter run, you can keep the shorts." Well, I kept the shorts—for a while.

In 1978 the National Track and Field Hall of Fame wanted my hat, and I gave it to them. In 1980 they wanted me and my uniform, which included Frank's shorts. I was inducted into the Hall of Fame that year, along with Frank Shorter's shorts. So my hat was in the Hall of Fame two years before I was, and Frank's shorts were in before he was. It sure is a humbling experience to know that the Hall of Fame officials want a piece of your uniform before they want you.

The preliminary heats of the 1,500-meter were run on September 8, and Jim Ryun fell while trying to get through the pack, which put him out of the race. I made it to the semifinals, but I just missed getting the third spot. Tom Hansen of Denmark and I both had the same time, but he edged me out. I really felt bad for Jim. He came so close in '68, and then to be eliminated that way in Munich was sad, and he was devastated. I consider Jim Ryun to be the greatest miler of all time, but he was under a lot of pressure in 1972. A few weeks before the Olympics he ran a 3:52.7 mile in Montreal, the fastest in the world that year. But shortly afterward he ran a 4:19 mile, so he was under pressure to prove himself in Munich. That was too bad. Jim is a super guy.

After the Olympics I went back to Bowling Green and completed my undergraduate degree. I continued running, of course, and had some good races, especially in the mile. I won all the mile races I entered until the spring of 1973, when I came in second to Len Hilton in the Kansas Relays Mile. I went on to win the NCAA mile title in a record 3:57.1. That spring I graduated and was commissioned a second lieutenant in the Air Force.

In the summer of '73 I ran for the Air Force and the Bowling

Green Track Club. In a special race with Steve Prefontaine in Oregon, I became the third-fastest miler ever, with a time of 3:53.3, and defeated five other runners who were under 4 minutes.

I signed a pro contract in the winter of 1974 and ran as a pro for two years. Meantime I began coaching at Walsh College in Canton, and when I ended my professional running career, I became Assistant Director of Admissions at Walsh and continued coaching. Two years later I went to Bethany College in West Virginia as Assistant Director of Admissions and cross-country and track coach. In 1980 I became Director of Admissions and, in 1982, Dean of Admissions. At that time I gave up my coaching duties.

I came to Rhodes College in Memphis as Dean of Admissions in 1983. I must say that I miss coaching, especially the contact with the athletes and getting to know them as individuals. But I have many responsibilities in my job, and I enjoy the work very much.

I enjoy making a name for myself in another area. You know, I couldn't even tell you who the big names in track are today. I don't watch track meets; I never did enjoy being a spectator. I was the type of athlete who needed to be out there doing it—competing—and if I'm not competing, I don't want to watch. I'd much rather be out in the backyard playing a game of one-on-one basketball than sitting around watching a game or a meet, though I do love to watch football.

When I came away from the Olympics in '72, I was not disenchanted. Because of the murders of the Israelis, and because of all the foul-ups that occurred in Munich, many athletes were sour on the Olympics. Maybe I didn't feel that way because I had won a gold medal, but even if I hadn't won a medal, I think I would feel the same way. In spite of all the politics that have marred the Olympic Games over the years, the Olympics are still a tremendous athletic event, a tremendous goal to set for yourself as an athlete.

BENJAMIN LEE PETERSON

Gold Medal, Wrestling, Light-Heavyweight, 1972
Silver Medal, Wrestling, Light-Heavyweight, 1976

In 1972 Ben Peterson won the gold and his older brother, John, the silver; in 1976, they reversed the order, and each time they lost to the same Russian wrestler, Levan Tediashvili.

Born in upstate Wisconsin, Ben went to Iowa State, where he learned much of his wrestling from his teammate Dan Gable, with whom both he and John trained before the Munich Games.

Ben credits his strong religious convictions for his success in life, and he now teaches religion and coaches wrestling at Maranatha Baptist Bible College in Watertown, Wisconsin.

Dan Gable was a junior and captain of the team at Iowa State when I was a freshman, and I learned an immense amount of wrestling from him. During my last two years he was an assistant coach, and he worked me to death. He was much smaller than I,

Ben Petersen in 1972.
Photo courtesy of Ben Petersen

but he always liked to work out with somebody bigger. He was the perfect model for young wrestlers. He wasn't the strongest, quickest, most agile, or best-balanced athlete. But he worked so hard in all of these areas, and he was always in marvelous physical condition. And, of course, no one was ever more intense.

My brother, John, who had graduated from the University of Wisconsin at Stout, came down to Ames in the fall of 1971 to work with Dan and me in preparation for the Olympic trials. At first I think Dan saw in John somebody to train with, but he liked John's tenacity and eventually saw in him a potential champion as well. I was still taking classes, so John and Dan would train in the morning, and then I would join them for the afternoon and evening sessions. We made the team and moved in with Gable's parents in Waterloo for the month before the Games. His folks put us up, so we had nothing to do but train. They wouldn't even let us pay for the food.

Of course, we didn't have much money. Our parents couldn't afford to pay for our training, and the only way we could legally use our wrestling talent to defray expenses was to work at wrestling camps. We had to say we were counselors rather than clinicians or teachers, and the camps were not allowed to use our pictures in any of their advertising.

Wrestling became a way of life for us, and we did it for eight years. We'd save up enough money to go to the Olympics; then we'd come back home flat broke. We'd spend the next two years going to camps and saving our money so we could resume our intensive training for the next Games. We did that three times. It was kind of fun, but I could have done something else with some of that money, especially the money I spent getting ready for 1980 when the boycott eliminated the Games for us.

I was very nervous in Munich in 1972. It was the first time I had been outside the country, and there I was in the Olympic Village with people from almost every nation on earth. I was overwhelmed by the friendliness and peacefulness of it all. I look at the Olympics as every four years the world puts on a great party for its greatest athletes, and the rest of the world gets to watch.

In my first match I wrestled a guy from Poland who practically ripped my head off. I thought he was going to break my neck. I was exhausted when I finished, and my coach was ready to shoot me. He couldn't understand why I was so tired. I was well known for my physical conditioning, and there I was dying on the mat.

The problem was that I was so nervous I didn't know what was happening, and I'm sure I hyperventilated.

I ended up winning the match 7–5, and that broke the ice for me. I won the next couple of matches rather easily. Then I tied the Russian, Gennadi Strakhov. The Soviets were our great rivals, and I was too awed by him. When the match was over, I was surprised that he wasn't tougher. I felt he was very lethargic on the mat and that I could have exerted more control and won the match outright. But I didn't, and that tie meant I had to win my other matches by pins to have any chance at the gold.

So in the finals I wrestled a Bulgarian by the name of Roussi Petrov, knowing that I had to pin him if I wanted the gold. It was a hard-nosed match, but I pinned him halfway through the second period. John was wrestling on another mat a few feet away and had just finished his match to clinch the silver in the middleweight class. The referee was raising his hand just as John looked over to see me pinning the Bulgarian. He ran over and about broke my ribs giving me a bear hug that I'll never forget.

I still had to wait until Strakhov finished his final match. He had to wrestle the Hungarian, Karoly Bajko, and the only way I could win was if Strakhov didn't pin Bajko or could not beat him by at least 10 points. We thought it very possible that they might try to throw the match. All of our coaches alerted the officials, and they watched it closely. I can remember sitting on a stairway just below the mat, watching and wondering what was going to happen. I can also remember telling God that whatever He wanted was now up to Him. I couldn't do anything more. The Russian spoke several times to the Hungarian during the match, which is totally forbidden. The referee told him to stop. Later we were told that he was offering the Hungarian $400 to throw the match. Strakhov won, but the score was 9–1, and that meant that the gold medal was mine.

My other unforgettable memory from Munich was the Israeli massacre. Everything was so nice in the Village. There we were, athletes from all over the world. We could shake hands, talk to one another through interpreters, and exchange gifts. So I began to think that maybe all that I'd heard about the problems of the world just weren't true. I thought that maybe there could be peace on earth. Maybe man could find his own solutions, and just maybe sports could lead the way.

It was a couple of days after our competition. We got up that morning, and Gable had gone out running. He came back to the Village and told us something was wrong. John and I were going out sight-seeing with our folks, and he told us to take our passes. Normally, if we had on our uniforms, they'd just let us come in the back gate. We went down to breakfast, and we were not more than 100 yards from where the whole thing was taking place. But we left the Village that day not knowing that they had the hostages in the building just down from us or that the police had surrounded it. Actually, the people back in the States knew more about what was going on from watching television than did most of us who were right there.

When I found out what had happened, I was jolted back into reality. As the Bible tells us, we are of a sinful nature, and getting together for a friendly competition is not going to change that. This horrible incident made me understand that's how this world is and that it is not going to get any better. I left the Village a few days later realizing how naive I had been when I thought that things could be different. We can have fun once in a while, but we never know when man's nature is going to destroy our fun and games. Life is tough and sometimes disappointing, and we can't control ourselves, let alone the world. So to me the only answer is God.

Growing up, I heard a lot of preaching, but the strongest message I ever heard was from my mom and dad taking me to church every week. To find the church they wanted, they had to drive 21 miles each way on Sunday, and that meant six kids, two parents, and sometimes my grandmother in one car. I can remember different times asking my parents, "Why do we have to go to church so far away?" They would simply answer, "This is the place where you'll hear the Gospel."

The thing that really hit home to me was how important their faith and confidence in the Lord Jesus Christ were to them, and I could see so much that was more appealing in them than what I saw in the parents of other kids. They taught me what was right and wrong, and they held me to it. My dad was not a tyrant in his discipline, but he did point things out to me, and I didn't want to disappoint him.

For a long time I thought that God would like me because He clearly liked my folks, and I also would look at my friends and say, Man, I'm not as bad as they are. But that wasn't enough, and when I was in junior high I began to understand that I personally would be held accountable for what I did with my life. So I accepted Christ as my personal savior, realizing that only He could pay the penalty for my sins.

I began to grow as a Christian. As a high school student, I learned a lot of principles as an athlete that helped me as a Christian, and I learned a lot of principles from God's word that helped me become a better wrestler. The Bible emphasizes discipline, hard work, being moral, and having the courage of your convictions. Those qualities will also make you a better wrestler.

It was through both Christianity and wrestling that I could honor and show my gratitude to those who had helped and motivated me along the way. I could honor the Lord Jesus Christ through living an exemplary Christian life, and I could show my gratitude to my coaches and family for all they had done for me by doing well in my wrestling career.

I also found that the Bible teaches us that our body is the temple of the spirit of God. So I wanted to take care of my body both as a Christian and as a wrestler. We wrestlers often refer to our body as our "wrestling machine." We know we have to keep it properly fueled, rested, and in good repair if it is not going to let us down. And by keeping my body strong and pure I knew that I also served God.

John felt the same way about such matters, and we often talked about what it meant to be an ongoing witness for the Lord. If a bunch of the guys were telling dirty jokes or wanted to go to a party or something, we would simply say, "It's time for us to leave." We knew that Christ would not want us involved with something like that.

At times that led to real frictions with our teammates. Some of them laughed and scoffed at our convictions. These were men whom I respected immensely as athletes and who had helped me learn to be a fine wrestler, but I could not let them interfere with my beliefs. In my first year at Iowa State some of these guys could beat the tar out of me, yet they didn't keep training rules, so occasionally I thought to myself, Hey, maybe I don't have to, either. I even came close to saying, Forget the whole business. I can remember sitting in my dorm room, battling this not only with my own teammates but with my professors as well. Sometimes I would have to set my school books alongside my Bible and then decide which was right.

One of my teammates was kicked out of the university over what he did at a party one night. The last two months before he was kicked out he would come to me and say, "Hey, Ben, we've got a party planned for the weekend. It'll be a great time." I'd always tell him no. He'd ask, "Why not? Oh, that's right; you don't drink. Well, just come along and drink Coke." But I knew God would not want me to go. It's a funny thing, but on Monday and Tuesday he'd always say to me, "Ben, I'm never going to do that again." But when Friday and Saturday would roll around, he'd do it again. He was standing on a fine edge, and finally God said, "That's enough."

This was a guy whom I couldn't beat on the mat. I trained with him, and I learned from him, but I had to say, "You can teach me wrestling, but you will not teach me how to live life." I had to make those kinds of decisions. It was a testing of the decision for Christ I had made back in junior high.

In the 1976 Games, John won the gold, and I took the silver behind Levan Tediashvili, the Russian who had defeated John in 1972. I lost to him 10–5, and as I look back I don't think I did as well against him as I should have. I made him look better than he really was, but I just wasn't sharp. A lot of things were bothering me going into the Games, and I didn't feel as confident or as intense as I had four years earlier.

When I came back home, President B. Myron Cederholm of Maranatha Baptist Bible College offered me the wrestling head coaching job plus a course in architecture. I had majored in architecture at Iowa State and had worked in Madison as an architect for a year and a half. I had even started my master's at Iowa State in architecture, but I became frustrated with the mentality of architects who were trying to teach me that we could solve all of man's problems if we could just design buildings the right way.

I signed my contract at Maranatha with the stipulation that I would also be allowed to take courses in the Bible College. After the 1972 Games I had done a lot of public speaking. I tried to tell people about the religious and athletic challenges in my life, but I was not a very good speaker, and I became very frustrated when I stumbled all over the place when talking about things that were so important to me. So I told President Cederholm that I wanted to learn how to speak and how to teach the word of God. He agreed, and I started taking the courses that would eventually lead to my master's in theology.

My brother John was still competing, but I told him that I was through. But after a year or so of holding out, John convinced me to come back. I did go to a few tournaments and did horribly. I just wasn't around people who could train and push me hard enough. In the summer of 1979, I did go with John to several wrestling camps to earn money for our training, and after the fall semester I moved to Madison to spend the next six months doing nothing but training. I think it was in February that we first heard that we might not get to go to Moscow, but we continued to train anyway. I made the team by the skin of my teeth, but John came in second in the trials and didn't make the team.

That was the last of our wrestling. John is now in Vienna, Austria, where he has lived for the past five years. He went over there originally to coach the Athletes in Action wrestling team, but he now works with a mission group.

In 1984 I finally graduated with my master's degree in theology. I then took a full-time teaching assignment in Maranatha's Bible Department, where I now teach courses in New Testament and personal evangelism. John and I also run a five-week summer wrestling camp in northern Wisconsin.

In some ways I'm glad I'm not competing today. The amateur wrestling of the '70s was fun. It was hard work, and there wasn't always much money. But we did go to two Olympics, and we achieved enough recognition. And what is more important, we retained our integrity. We didn't have to violate our principles or beliefs. Today, I see our athletes coming back from our Olympic training camps with T-shirts for beer commercials. I'm very glad I'm not involved with that. I talk to high school coaches who are very upset about this. They send their best athletes to the training camp at Colorado Springs, and they come back wearing a T-shirt that is not permitted in their gym.

I asked the president of the U.S. Olympic Committee about this practice, and he explained that they were doing it to raise money from the private sector. I think this is dead wrong. I don't agree that the money donated by the beer companies outweighs the harm done. After all, what messages are we trying to convey to our young athletes when we use them to advertise such products?

14
MONTREAL, 1976

For the organizers of the Montreal Olympics almost everything that could go wrong did, both within Canada and without.

Shortly before the opening of the Games, 24 African nations pulled out of Montreal when the International Olympic Committee refused to bow to their demands to ban New Zealand from the competition. When a New Zealand rugby team toured South Africa, the other African countries interpreted this as support for apartheid, despite the fact that the New Zealand government had had nothing to do with the tour. At previous Games the Africans had been successful in having South Africa and Rhodesia banned from the Olympic meets by the IOC.

The "Chinese problem" emerged once again, but with a different twist. The Canadian government recognized only mainland China, the People's Republic, as the government of China and refused to permit Nationalist China to compete under its real and IOC-recognized name, the Republic of China, suggesting instead that it compete under the name Taiwan. It refused and protested to the IOC, which had the authority to force Canada to admit the Republic of China to the Games or face having the Games removed from Montreal. One week before the Games opened, and despite considerable sentiment among members of the IOC to the contrary, Lord Killanin, IOC President, bowed to the Canadians, and the Nationalist Chinese returned to Taiwan.

From the time Montreal was selected as the site for the '76 Games, chaos reigned, and spiraling costs were at the heart of the problem. The initial estimate of the cost of the Games was under $400 million, but expenditures reached almost $1.5 billion, and judging from the condition of the sites when the Games began, it was not well spent. The planned dome for the stadium was never built, nor was the stadium's 18-story tower. Many facilities were temporary or makeshift, including seats and rest rooms. Some of this was the result of poor planning and inadequate supervision, but the major drain on the money was astronomical labor costs, though inflation also took its toll. Labor disputes resulting in strikes and slowdowns erupted with alarming regularity during the construction period. This meant that when construction was under way, the workers had to work double and triple shifts, at double and triple pay, to make up for lost building time. Then, just when Montreal thought the worst was over, the city's taxicab drivers, nurses, and liquor store owners went on strike shortly before the opening of the Games.

The Games themselves were marred by incidences of cheating, attempted collusion, and doping. The most peculiar example of cheating occurred when the Russian pentathlon competitor was removed from the Games when it was discovered that he had a tiny electronic device in the tip of his épée, a blunted fencing sword. This device permitted the Russian to register a hit on the electronic scoreboard without having to touch his opponent.

Doping is the use of illegal substances for the purpose of improving performance, and it is no secret that some athletes take steroids to build muscle mass and use stimulants to increase speed and endurance. But a unique kind of alleged doping was revealed in Montreal. Finland's great distance runner, Lasse Viren, was charged with "blood doping." It was alleged that at some time before his appearance at Montreal Viren had some pints of blood withdrawn from his body, had it frozen, then shortly before his race, thawed it and injected it back into his body. Supposedly, this extra blood would increase one's stamina. Viren heatedly denied the charge, and it was never proven, nor was it ever established that such a procedure was illegal under the existing regulations.

Queen Elizabeth II opened the Games on Saturday, July 17. The queen was also at Montreal to watch her daughter, Princess Anne, compete in the equestrian events as a member of the British team.

The American male swimmers far outshone their track and field teammates in Montreal. The U.S. swept 4 events and took 27 of 35 possible medals, winning golds in all but the 200-meter breaststroke. Brian Goodell won the 400- and 1,500-meter freestyle, both in world and Olympic record times. But the big winner was John Naber, who took four golds and a silver and established three world and Olympic records. The U.S. women's team could do no better than take the 400-meter freestyle relay. The East Germans completely dominated the women's events, losing only two races.

In track and field, the American showing was poor. However, Edwin Moses made his Olympic debut in Montreal by winning the 400-meter hurdles in the record time of 47.64. In addition, the Americans took both of the relays. The U.S. also took first and second in the long jump, and the bearded, brash Mac Wilkins won the discus throw. The media hero of the Games was decathlon winner Bruce Jenner, whose world record win did much to alleviate the American losses in most of the other events.

American shooters won two events: Don Haldeman won the clay pigeon trap, and Lanny Bassham, who had won the silver medal in Munich, took first place in the small-bore rifle, three positions. Bassham's score of 1,162 was tied by silver medalist Margaret Murdock, a nurse from Topeka, Kansas. A tie is broken by considering the last 10 shots in the kneeling position, and Bassham had outscored Murdock on those and was awarded the gold. On the victory stand, Bassham pulled Murdock up on the winner's platform, where they stood together during the playing of the national anthem.

If gymnast Olga Korbut of the USSR was the darling of the Munich Games, then Rumania's Nadia Comaneci took that title in Montreal. She captivated the spectators as no other competitor did. Her performance was virtually perfect. She won a total of seven perfect 10s and won the gold medal in the all-around, the beam, and the bars.

The closing ceremonies in Montreal included Indians representing all the tribes of Canada, and after the Olympic flag was lowered the scoreboard read "Farewell Montreal—'Til We Meet in Moscow." But for the Americans, there would be no meeting in Moscow. In the spring of 1980, the U.S. government declared a boycott of the Moscow Olympics in protest over the Soviet invasion of Afghanistan, and in April the U.S. Olympic Committee voted not to send a team.

JOHN NABER

Gold Medal, 100-Meter Backstroke, 1976
Gold Medal, 200-Meter Backstroke, 1976
Gold Medal, 4x200-Meter Freestyle Relay, 1976
Gold Medal, 4x100-Meter Medley Relay, 1976
Silver Medal, 200-Meter Freestyle, 1976

With four golds and a silver, the six-foot-six John Naber was clearly the swimming star of the 1976 Montreal Games. So dominant was he that his world records in the 100- and 200-meter backstroke lasted for seven years. He also broke the existing world record in the 200-meter freestyle, but Bruce Furniss defeated him by two-tenths of a second for the gold. Both of Naber's winning relay teams also set world records.

Naber works as a television swimming commentator, in public relations for sports marketing firms and as a motivational speaker.

We still dominate swimming when the Soviets and East Germans don't compete. The American public has grown accustomed to watching swimming to see us win and to watching other events to see us try to win. In that sense they have been somewhat spoiled. I don't think it's fair to expect any one country to continually dominate swimming, especially when there is so little money coming into the sport from other than its own efforts. There is no government support, and there is little corporate money donated directly to swimming. It goes to the U.S. Olympic team, and the officials decide how to divvy it up. They've been very generous, but it's not enough.

There are only one or two major swimming meets a year that fans see on television, and those are the ones in which world records are usually set. But when no records are set, the audience feels disappointed and let down. We must make Americans realize that we can no longer win and break world records at will.

We also have to understand that it was inevitable that we would be challenged. Take, for example, East Germany. It has roughly the population of California. So if their swimmers can outscore the entire U.S., it gives them a great deal of credibility on a global

John Naber in 1976. Photo courtesy of John Naber

scale. And they do emphasize the propaganda value of athletic accomplishments. They looked systematically at all the Olympic events and decided to focus their attention on women's sports and on many of the so-called minor events—and they've been very successful. There have been accusations of drug use, but until such accusations have been proven I don't want to make them an issue. I don't want to stand on the starting block and suggest that the other guy has an unfair advantage unless I can prove it.

The East Germans have tried a couple of novel training techniques. In the U.S. we have now established that four hours of training a day is about the upper limit in terms of diminishing returns. You can train more, but you don't get anything out of those extra hours. The body is just too beat up. So we now recommend two hours before school and two after. The East Germans don't have to worry about school schedules so they have tried three blocks of time consisting of an hour and a half each. This allows more time to recuperate in between and thus more intensive workouts. And because their minister of sport is a cabinet position, they have unlimited resources to spend on such things as scientific research and the politics of sport. By politics, I mean who gets on what international committees, which international officials to influence, and which athletes to send to the competitions. They do this very carefully, and as a result they are politically more powerful than we are. In fact, the United States, for all its size and participation, is one of the least powerful countries in international sports politics.

I don't want to see politicians running our programs. I can guarantee if the government gives us a billion dollars a year, we can spend it wisely, but then it will want to put somebody on our board of directors and some congressman will insist on a representative or Olympian from each voting district or something like that.

I don't think you should pay athletes to swim. Track and field athletes are paid by promoters who can fill a stadium with 80,000 paying customers, but you don't have that kind of support for swimming. I don't think we can prevent swimmers from endorsing products or making personal appearances—and this may serve as an incentive—but I would hate to see the athlete's motivation toward excellence come from the almighty dollar. The word *amateur* goes back to the original Latin *amare*, meaning to love. An amateur stamp collector loves to collect stamps. An amateur athlete should love his sport. If he comes to hate swimming but continues to swim because of the money, he is no longer an amateur.

Swimmers tend to be very young because of the need for total mental concentration in a very boring environment. Marathoners can run through the streets of New York or Boston and the scenery changes, but for me to pay the price necessary to be good, I have to work out four hours a day, six days a week, eleven months a year, with nothing to look at but a black tile line on the bottom of a short-course pool. That kind of single-mindedness is for younger kids who have little else to distract them. They aren't worried about the mortgage, jobs, or even academics because they are usually from upper-middle-class white families where all that is taken care of. Then, too, strength is not what makes good swimmers. It's technique, finesse, and loose joints, and the older guys get stiff faster.

I was born in Evanston, Illinois, but our family lived in Europe until I entered the seventh grade. I played a little cricket and soccer, but I didn't get involved in such typical American sports as baseball, football, and basketball. I was also slow to mature physically. My bones grew far quicker than my muscles, so on dry land I was somewhat uncoordinated, and the only sport I could really do well was swimming.

I enjoyed swimming because I was really racing the stopwatch. That meant I could beat the John Naber of yesterday. My daily progress was my reward, and my perpetual goal was to do a personal best by the end of each season. Every year I wanted to be better than I was the year before, and I would always tell myself that if I were not I should quit. Fortunately, I did do a little bit better every year, even the year after the Olympics.

I went to Woodside High School right near Stanford University. In each of my freshman and sophomore years I got the "most improved" award, which tells you how bad I was to start with. My junior year was 1972, and my progress was such that people were picking me to go to the Olympics. But I cracked my collarbone in a diving board accident the day before our first dual meet. I was in a shoulder brace for about eight weeks, got out, trained for three weeks, and then qualified for the trials but missed making the team by six-tenths of a second. I was close, but not quite there. I did, however, realize that I had Olympic potential and decided to go all-out for 1976. From that time on I didn't lose a major backstroke race to an American.

To understand what happened in the '76 Games, I have to go back to the 1974 USA–East German Dual Meet in Concord, California. In the Belgrade world championships the year before, the East German women had really surprised their American counterparts. They had arrived with their skintight suits, broad shoulders, and world records. So in Concord the question became: Could the American men beat the East German men by more than the East German women would trounce our women?

It was a two-day dual meet, and 15,000 seats were sold for each session. There were two swimmers from each country in each event. In the backstroke Roland Matthes had been undefeated for seven years. He was the king, and I had finished third behind him in Belgrade. He had won the 100- and 200-meter backstroke in both the 1968 and '72 Games, and he was my idol. He was the gentleman of swimming. I have seen him win, and I've seen him lose, and I couldn't tell the difference. I wish people could say that about me—but they can't.

So the groundwork was set for our great match and rivalry. Well, in Concord, I beat him three out of three: in the individual 100 and 200 and in the leadoff of the medley relay. But I didn't break his records. He had a bad meet. He had just had some root canal work done and was just miserable, but that set the stage for our meeting in Montreal.

My goal in Montreal was to beat the time that I thought he would be capable of swimming. I thought he would swim about 55.5 in the 100 and 2 minutes in the 200, so those were my standards. My attitude was that, if I beat those times and he was still faster, I had just miscalculated but had not swum poorly myself. So that was it. I had beaten him once, but could I do it again with the gold medal on the line. Naturally, the press played all of this up.

For some strange reason I had also decided that I wanted to swim more than just the backstroke in Montreal. I had been an NCAA record holder in the 500 freestyle, and I knew that the 200-meter freestyle also offered a place on the relay. Usually early in the season I would swim in the "animal lane" to train distance for the 1,500 meters and then taper to the backstroke lane. That year I swam in the middle-distance lane early in the season and then tapered to the backstroke. It worked, as I made the team in the 200 meters and the relay, as well as in the two backstroke events.

Swimming took up the first eight days of the Montreal Games. The first day was the qualifying and semifinals for the 100-meter backstroke. The heats of the 200 freestyle were the next day. The finals of both of these events were that evening. So I had three big swims that second day. I chose not to march in the opening ceremonies because of this, and that's probably my single biggest regret. I should have marched. Peter Ueberroth made up for it a bit when he allowed me to carry the flag in Los Angeles in 1984.

I beat Roland Matthes in the 100 backstroke that second night. Even more important was the fact that I swam a 55.49, so I had achieved both of my objectives. Then I had 45 minutes to recover before the 200 freestyle. I had qualified eighth in a field of eight in a time well under my personal best. I got a rubdown, slept for 10 minutes, woke up, and walked to the starting blocks. Bruce Furniss, whose best time beat mine by a full second, was the favorite, but I swam what I consider to be the single best race of my life, including all of my backstroke swims. My time was better than the existing world record, but it was two-tenths of a second behind Bruce's winning time of 1:50.29. He won the gold, and I got the silver, but I had become the first swimmer to win medals in two individual events in one day. I was very proud of that, even though the next day East Germany's Kornelia Ender won the first two of her four golds. She outdid me, but I was the first.

Then I had two days' rest, after which I swam the third leg of the 800-meter freestyle relay, followed by the medley relay the next day, a day off, and then the 200-meter backstroke, which was my fifth and final event. I ended up with four golds and that silver in the 200-meter free.

The body takes only 20 minutes to recover after swimming the shorter distances; it's the mind that has the problem coming back. I had to go into what I called my "mind dump." That means you have to forget everything that has gone before; whether you've swum well or not doesn't matter, and the more events you have to swim, the faster you have to put everything behind you. Fortunately, I have a very effective "mind dump." For example, when the lights go out at night, it takes me about 10 or 15 seconds to fall asleep. I just say to myself, "OK, let's race," and I'm gone.

That's what Mark Spitz was able to do. His greatest accomplishment was mentally psyching up for a seventh gold medal when he could have quit after six and been a god for life; yet, he went for a seventh with the risk of not making it, and he did it with that calm Mark Spitz assurance.

I retired from swimming in April of 1977. My obligation to USC for my four-year scholarship was completed, and I had no other goals. I didn't want to go on just to break world records. I had my world records, and they lasted for some seven years. I didn't feel the need to prove anything else. I didn't need to defeat Matthes again. He had retired. There were only two things I did not do in my career. One was a world championship gold medal; the other was making the Pan-American team, and I didn't try out for either of those teams in 1974 and '75.

I never once kidded myself that swimming would be my entire

life. That's why swimmers generally have the highest grade point average of any collegiate athletes. They realize that they have to go on and earn a living after they're done swimming. Among my teammates were engineers, scientists, business entrepreneurs, and all sorts of other professionals.

At USC I majored in public relations and psychology, with the idea that I would be a marketing consultant. I now work out of my own office in Glendale, where for the past seven years I have been self-employed. I do some work as a television commentator for water sports, I do motivational speaking, and I am a public relations representative to corporate sports marketing interests. My assignments seem to come in waves. Between 1976 and 1980 I was a current name, and because we boycotted the 1980 Games, I retained my name recognition. Since the '84 Games things have slowed down a bit.

It's not that the media want only the most recent winners; it's the short American attention span. So my role as a sports commentator is no longer to provide expert analysis or insight—that's something that comes out of the younger kids—but to do the play-by-play description of what is going on in the water so that the viewer who doesn't swim might want his kids to try it.

In my announcing, I've found that executive producers don't care so much what kind of job you do; all they really care about is how many people stay tuned to the program because that is what their bosses want. It's strictly viewership numbers for advertising dollars. I really want to do a good job, and I prepare, but when you are forced to condense a four-day swimming meet into a 20-minute network broadcast, there is no time to elaborate on the specific details that are important to a swimmer but not to that armchair quarterback who wants to get back to his Indy 500 race. ESPN does more justice to the sport when it allows full coverage, but the common market wisdom is "I want it fast, I want it brief, I want it good, and I want it now."

Twenty years from now I can only guess what I'll be doing. My goal throughout college was to get an education that would earn me a job. My goal in swimming was to do a 55.5 in the 100-meter backstroke. My present priority is to make sure that my daughter Christina grows up to be a wonderful young woman. Twenty years from now I'll probably be walking down the aisle with her on my arm. That would be my biggest thrill. Professionally, I don't have such clear-cut goals. I want to continue to serve my sport and the

Olympic movement as I have in the past. I think that there is a real need for corporate America to fund amateur sports, and as long as there is a need for that, there is going to be a need for spokespeople. If I can do that job better than the next guy, I will continue to do so. And the moment I can't—the moment I can no longer compete with the Mary Lou Rettons—I'll quit and find what my friends call "a real job."

LANNY ROBERT BASSHAM

Gold Medal, Small-Bore Rifle, Three Positions, 1976

Silver Medal, Small-Bore Rifle, Three Positions, 1972

Not all Olympic champions are born with innate athletic skills. Some, such as Lanny Bassham, have had to overcome limited natural ability to achieve their greatness. His youthful athletic failures only made Bassham more determined to excel, especially after he discovered that shooting did not demand strength, size, or agility.

Bassham insists he missed the gold medal in 1972 because he was not mentally tough enough. Since then he has developed what he calls "Principles of Mental Management," and these have helped him win 22 national and two world championships, as well as the gold medal in 1976, and achieve considerable success in the business world.

From childhood on, I always wanted to be a winner. I'd run in all the races, but I'd always lose. No matter how hard I tried and no matter how early I showed up for practice, I never was able to do much. At the same time I was infatuated with the Olympics. I read all the books about the Games, and I pictured myself being an Olympic athlete of some sort. It wasn't important which event—just to be in the Games was the thing.

Unfortunately, I was slow, short, and clumsy. I also had no natural ability. I tried out for baseball and got alternate right fielder. In basketball I sat on the far end of the bench. And I was

Lanny Bassham in 1986. Photo courtesy of Lanny Bassham

just too small for football. I finally told my father, "Dad, I'm just no good." He told me, "No, that's not true. There's nothing wrong with you. You just haven't found something you're good at."

One day, a friend of mine told me that he was on a rifle team and that it was an Olympic event. So I said, "Hmmm, rifle shooting; tell me about that. How tall do you have to be?"

He said, "You don't have to be tall. Short people do it."

I said, "Oh, and how strong do you have to be?"

He answered, "You don't have to be very strong. Girls do real well at it, too."

So I said, "OK, how fast do you have to be?"

He said, "You don't understand. In rifle shooting all you have to do is sit still."

I asked, "They give a gold medal in the Olympics for sitting still? That's got to be my sport!"

I started shooting at a junior NRA Club in Baltimore when I was about 12, and from the very beginning my father realized that I needed something to build my self-image. I didn't have any brothers or sisters, so this was also a great time for the two of us to be together. He bought us two rifles, shooting coats, and accessories, and we'd head off to the range together. He was a captain in the army at the time and became so interested in shooting that he eventually became coach of the All-Army Team at Fort Benning, Georgia.

That first year I started shooting a service rifle because that's what my dad was shooting, and they let me be a kind of team mascot. I was about 14 at the time. The significant thing is that I was shooting with the best in the country, and that made a big difference. I may have been shooting poorly compared to these army experts, but what I didn't know was that I was shooting very well compared to all the other juniors in the country.

Juniors were up to 21 years of age, and my first competition was a small regional that was to determine who would get to compete in the nationals. I won the regional, but there was only one other junior there, so I didn't think that was a big deal. At the nationals we shot seven days, and every day I'd come in second or third or fifth but never first. I was really upset because all my life I had wanted to be a winner. The last day I told my father, "I just got to win today." But I came in second again. I was really frustrated. But when they added the scores together, I had more points than anyone else. So the second match I ever shot in my life I was a national champion.

The next year I started shooting small-bore on our high school ROTC team, and the following year I became the first high school student to win the national ROTC championship, which also included college students; in fact, most of the shooters were West Pointers.

My dad then retired from the military, moved back to Texas, and decided to become a barber. He told me, "Look, I can barber anywhere, so I want you to tell me where the best college shooting team in Texas is, and that's where we're going." So I ended up at the University of Texas, Arlington.

After graduating from college in 1969, I went into the army as a second lieutenant and was sent to Fort Benning, where I had to shoot myself onto the team. From the end of 1970 until I retired in 1980, the U.S. dominated international rifle shooting, so again I was fortunate to shoot with the very best. I figured, if I were going to beat these great shooters, the only way I could do it was to learn everything they did but learn it better.

I worked very hard, and I learned everything that could possibly give me an advantage, from stock design and gunsmithing to wind reading. My wife supported me in all this. She quit college early to earn money so that I could go to rifle matches. She sewed all her own clothes so we would have money to buy bullets. She learned to make beans cheap so we could buy more bullets. We spent all of our vacations at rifle matches, where she would sit in the hotel with the kids while I was out shooting. But she never complained.

I was 25 years old when I made our 1972 Olympic team. At the trials we had five world champions competing for the two rifle spots, and I managed to finish second to John Writer, who at that time was the best in the world. He had been world champion in 1970 after winning the silver medal in 1968, and he was the favorite at Munich. But I was beating him in practice. I had it all figured out. I was going to win either the gold or the silver, and I really thought I was going to win the gold. Up to that point, I had really never experienced any kind of pressure that hurt me. I had gotten used to winning, I liked performing well, and I had never had the shakes that other people talked about.

Then something happened. On the bus on the way to the Olympic shooting range the guy sitting behind me said, "Do you realize there are 220 million Americans depending on us?" Then someone else added, "Yeah, and they're going to televise all the events." Well, I had never been on television, and I had never thought about anybody depending on me. Up to that point everything was just between Jack Writer and me. But I started to think about all this, and when I got to the range, there behind my point was a television camera: ABC Sports. It looked like a cannon.

We shoot three positions—prone, standing, and kneeling—with 40 shots in each position from 50 meters at a target with a 10 ring that is three-quarters the size of a dime. And you better hit that 38, 39, 40 times out of 40 shots in the prone to have a decent chance at the gold medal. I was a good prone shooter, and normally I shot a 390 to 400. Well, the officials said to commence firing, the camera turned on, and I started to shake. That had never happened to me before, and I couldn't understand it. I said to myself, Aww, this is silly; you can get through this. I did all kinds of things to try to settle down, but every time I put a bullet in the chamber I'd start shaking again.

It finally got to the point where I had to shoot, and I did, but I was terrible. I couldn't stop shaking, and I didn't understand what was going on. On my first 10 shots I never got a 10. So I ended up with a 90. I got out of position, went back, and sat down. I looked over at Jack, and he had 100 for his score. Now, you don't give a guy like Writer a 10-point lead, because you'll never catch him. So I knew at that point that I had lost my chance for a gold medal, and it was because of mental failure, not because of technique. At that moment I made up my mind that I was going to learn how to manage the mind under pressure and come back in four years and win the gold medal. I then relaxed and shot my normal good scores and ended up with the silver to Jack's gold.

I came home with my silver medal, and I can remember very clearly people asking, "Oh, were you in the Olympics?"

I'd say, "Yeah."

They'd say, "Did you win anything?"

"Yeah, I won a silver medal."

They'd look at me and say, "Oh, who won the gold? Tell me, is the gold bigger than the silver? Is the gold medal really gold?" For four years I had to apologize for being number two in the world. But it was very motivating. I knew that learning to manage the mind was the secret, so I wanted to take a course that would help me shoot the scores in matches that I did in practice.

You can get a PhD in physical education at any major university, but you've got to knock yourself out to find one course on how to manage the mind, and that's 90 percent of everything we do. In 1972 sports psychology was really in its infancy, and I couldn't find such a course. So I went to the only source I knew, the Olympic champions themselves. I asked them, "Hey, 95 percent of all medals in international competition are won by 5 percent of the athletes. What makes you different? Is it your blood, your background, something someone said to you? Do you have a good shrink? What's the deal? I want to know." I found out it wasn't any of those things. The difference was just in how they mentally prepared themselves.

I got little pieces of information from various athletes, and the puzzle started fitting together. What I discovered were these principles of mental management. There are laws that govern the mind just as there are laws for gravity and motion, and if you know and use them you can greatly improve your performance.

By the time of the 1976 Olympics, I was a far different person than in 1972. I won all the pre-Olympic competitions, and I had everybody in the world convinced I was going to win the gold medal—everybody except Margaret Murdock, who had beaten Jack Writer for the second spot on our team.

Margaret was a phenomenon in her own right. She was a 33-year-old nurse from Topeka. She was also the only woman of her time to shoot on par with the men. From late 1970 to 1980 I was never beaten by anyone but another American, either Lones Wigger, who was an Olympic champion in 1964 and 1972, or Jack Writer, who had won in 1972, or Margaret Murdock, who won a world championship in 1960 and should have won another in 1970.

Margaret was not as good a shooter in the kneeling position as I was, but no one was superior to her prone and standing. And sure enough, in the competition she was ahead of me going into the kneeling, but it didn't bother me too much because I thought I could catch her. Well, she shot great kneeling. I beat her, but all I did was make up the difference between her lead and where I was. When the preliminary scores were posted, Margaret had 1,162 and I had 1,161, but they had misgraded one of my kneeling targets. I had 100 on my third 10-shot string kneeling, and they had given me 99. I knew it was a mistake and that after the judges regraded the targets we would be tied. The tie-breaking procedure back then was to use the last 10 shots kneeling to decide the entire match, and I had outscored her on these.

But after those unofficial preliminary scores went up, I can remember Margaret's sister crying out, "Oh, Margaret, you're the Olympic champion." That was all UPI, AP, and ABC Sports needed. They just swarmed over her. She tried to tell them that they had to wait, but they wanted to do their interviews right then. So she sat there and answered their questions. For about three hours no one came over to me with a microphone, and I was just sitting there, thinking, This isn't the way I pictured it. You see, I knew I had won, but nobody else did.

About three hours later they changed the scores, and I was officially declared the winner. Well, Margaret aged about 10 years during that moment. She had really allowed herself to believe that she had won.

By this time everyone was gone except her sister, my wife and father, and a few others. We sat there and said, "This is really the pits. We both shot the same score." I suggested that we ask the officials either to give duplicate medals or to let us have a shoot-off. But that was against the rules. Then I thought that Margaret should refuse to take the silver medal, but she couldn't do that. We thought and thought about what we could do without bringing disgrace on the United States. For whatever good reasons, black fists in the air and that kind of thing didn't fit in with the patriotic, service-oriented, NRA member that I was. So, instead, when they put the medals around our necks, I pulled Margaret up on the winner's platform, and we stood there together while the national anthem played. That was our statement explaining how we felt, and that picture of us has become quite famous.

When I got home I guess I answered about 10,000 pieces of mail from people who wrote that they had seen it. That kind of made up for not getting all of those neat interviews and having a big crowd at my moment of ultimate victory in sports.

There is no physical advantage in being a man or a woman in shooting, but in 1984 we separated the women's shooting events for the first time. It's kind of sad. I was champion of the whole world, men and women. Now you can be only the men's or the women's champion. There was also a conscious effort made to change distances and number of shots fired so that you can no longer compare the performance of a woman with that of a man, and that was no accident.

Most of our top shooters certainly would not be bothered by shooting against women, but there are countries in the world where it is an embarrassment to have women shooting in what is often seen as a masculine sport. I now train the national champion of India. She is also the only Indian shooter who has ever won a medal in international competition. She is 19 years old, and I'm sure that there are a lot of people who would prefer that their champion be a man.

Shooting is not a man's sport, and it does not have anything to do with the military. I can remember so well when I came back from the Games, people would ask, "Well, you were in the military. Were you a sniper in Vietnam?" I was a Medical Service Corps officer, but people just assumed that the army must have used my skills for some kind of combat assignment. Or people would say, "Hey, I bet you hunt a lot. Do you go on safaris and all that good stuff?" One day I just answered, "Let me ask you something. Did you ask the javelin thrower how many animals he killed with his spear?"

Our sport is really about learning how to control the body and the mind. The rifle is a micrometer to see how well you are able to stand still when you pull the trigger and how well you plot the wind, because the wind moves the bullets. And there's another important point that often gets overlooked. I've been involved with shooting for almost 30 years, and in that whole time I've never even seen a Band-Aid necessary because somebody got hurt. We have the safest sport, bar none. My own kids are involved with two sports: shooting and soccer. One got his nose broken in soccer, but he never got it broken in shooting. When your kids go to the rifle range in some NRA or junior Olympic program, they will come home all in one piece. It's a sport that tries to help children control themselves. I tell parents all the time that we've got a sport that helps kids be still. We teach them control under pressure and how to focus their concentration. That's one of the reasons these kids are all good students in school.

After I won the Olympics in 1976 my next biggest goal was to be free of other people telling me all the time, "Captain Bassham, this is what you have to wear. Here's where you have to live and what you have to do, and here's what you are worth." Now, there's tremendous security in all this, and the army treated me well all nine years that I was in. I'm proud to have served in the nation's armed forces and would again in a minute. I hope that my children do. But I really missed the freedom of doing what I want to do. I also wanted a nice home with a horse ranch because I've always loved horses, as do my father and wife. I also liked to be around quality. I've always wanted to drive a Mercedes Benz, but in the military I could afford only Volkswagens. And I always wanted my own shooting range. I worked hard from 1978 to 1980, and I acquired all these things, half from Amway and half from my work in mental management.

Actually, I left the army in 1978 because at that time winning the world championship meant more to me than a career in the military. I needed more time to practice than the army was willing to give me. One problem was that I had to find something else to make a living. I didn't know how to do anything else but shoot.

Photo courtesy of the National Rifle Association

Lanny Bassham on the victory stand with Margaret Murdock.

In the army I had become an expert in advising the corps commander what to do with his nuclear dead, but no one on the outside was going to hire me for that kind of work. I did have a degree in computers, but it was obsolete because I had not worked with them for 10 years. I could put holes in a paper from 50 meters better than anybody else in the world, but there was no professional shooting, and I never got a Wheaties contract. So I really didn't know what I was going to do.

One day a friend of mine told me about Amway. I told him that I didn't want to become an Amway distributor. He said, "Yeah, but understand something. They make real good money in a short amount of time. They'll teach you what to do, and you don't have to invest any money." I got to thinking, Well, that's the best offer I've had so far.

I've now been doing this for about eight years. It pulls in about 60 percent of our annual income and all of our retirement income. We have a very nice network of about 10,000 distributors worldwide, and I draw a very small residual on all of their sales. We're marketing things that people want to have anyway at a price they're willing to pay, and it's enough so we can make some money and yet provide them with a good value. That's just the American way.

Amway also provided the financial nest egg that allowed me to test this mental management thing. My goal was to shoot through the 1980 Games and to get some students who wanted to learn mental management. I had put all my principles down, and now I wanted to start applying them. I began with shotgun shooters because I didn't know anything about shotguns technically, so if everything worked it was because of mental management skills rather than technique.

Everything was going just great. I had what I always wanted. In the morning I could shoot, in the afternoon I had my mental management students, and at night I did my Amway work. Everything was perfect until about the middle of February of 1980 when President Carter, in his infinite wisdom, decided that the only way he could hurt the Russians over Afghanistan was to keep me from going to Moscow.

President Carter may be 10 times smarter than I am, but that decision didn't make any sense to me as an Olympian. I was really hurt and upset. If you only knew how many times I dreamed of going to Russia and cleaning their clocks on their home range. If you want to hurt the Russians, what better way than to go over there and just wipe them out? We did that in 1972. They invited us over, and Jack Writer and I just thoroughly whipped them. They didn't get over that for three or four years.

The minute Carter announced that his decision was final, I took my rifle, cleaned it, stuck it in the closet, and booked business for all my previously planned training days. I did go to the trials, but I didn't train for them, and I didn't do well. I finished third or fourth, and you had to finish first or second to make the team. Of course, there wasn't any Olympic team to make.

Right after 1980 I developed a disease in my eyes. I couldn't focus properly. My left eye finally stabilized, but not my right. I pulled off our national team in 1981 because of this problem, and I've been kind of medically retired ever since. I'm not too old, but my eyes are not good enough for me to continue.

I now run an international shooting school, and I teach my mental management courses. I've got a top-selling video on mental management and one on Olympic rifle shooting. I've also taught the Olympic teams of the United States, Taiwan, Canada, Japan, Australia, and Korea.

You see, the principles of mental management have nothing to do with individual cultures. For example, I'll give you a principle. The more you think, talk, and write about something happening, the more you improve the probability of its actually happening. So be careful what you think about. You're going to get it. And if you talk to me about something you're doing wrong, you're improving the probability that you are going to do the same thing wrong again. The subconscious mind moves you to do whatever the conscious mind is picturing. The subconscious has all your power, so it's going to move you toward what you're picturing. You heard about this guy in Oklahoma who went into the post office and did everyone in. The psychologists will tell you that mass killers like that are constant complainers. They start talking about how the world is against them and how they're so depressed and down. They talk about how persecuted they are. Finally, one day they get back. That is the opposite of what I'm trying to do. I'm trying to get people to ask themselves what they are doing right instead of what they are doing wrong.

Another principle is, if you want to get what you want, help somebody else get what they want. This isn't new. I didn't invent any of this stuff. I've got my handle—the way I package and present it—and that's what people are paying for. I'm an interpreter. Here it is. Come get what you want.

I work hard at what I do. I treat my students and my Amway partners the same way I treated myself when I was driving for the Olympic gold medal—and I'm a formidable partner to have.

I feel very blessed, and I thank the good Lord for allowing me to have this kind of life. I don't know why things have happened to me exactly the way they have, but I appreciate the parents I've had, the people I've known, and being an American. In any other country I wouldn't have had the opportunity to have trained with the best. I'm even happy with my failure in 1972. I think if I had won then there's no way I would be as well off as I am today. I wouldn't have searched things out. If I had won, I also might have stayed in the army, and today I might be a young lieutenant colonel making a tenth of what I now do and living a tenth as well. Not that there's anything wrong with being a lieutenant colonel, but I now have a richer life because I failed in 1972. So I have a message: don't give up when you run into a wall. There's a way around it. And maybe there's a reason why you have to find your way around, through, or over that wall.

MAC WILKINS

Gold Medal, Discus, 1976
Silver Medal, Discus, 1984

Mac Wilkins began his track and field career at the University of Oregon as a javelin thrower who threw 257 feet as a freshman. An elbow injury in his second season led him to concentrate on throwing the discus and putting the shot, and in his senior year he won the national NCAA and AAU championships in the discus.

In 1976 Wilkins not only won the Olympic gold medal in the discus but also set four world records, the best of which was a throw of 232 feet, 6 inches.

At Montreal Wilkins gained the reputation of a rebel for his independence and outspokenness. A maverick in his training and lifestyle, and intimidating in appearance, Wilkins was frequently at odds with team officials.

In 1984 at the Los Angeles Games, Wilkins fouled on two throws, either of which would have won the gold medal, and as a result he had to settle for a silver with a throw of 217 feet, 6 inches, 1 foot short of the winning throw.

At present Mac Wilkins is involved in establishing an Olympic development program in San Jose for young athletes. He has produced two instructional videotapes on discus throwing and shot putting and conducts clinics and fulfills speaking engagements throughout the U.S.

There are always people in sport, like Olympic administrators, who think they know what is best for athletes. Their actions indicate, however, little awareness or concern for athletes' needs, in spite of the fact that they are charged with serving the athletes and that the games are for the athletes. Look what happened to Al Feuerbach and me when we were training for the Montreal Games. We had been at the Olympic track team training camp at Plattsburgh, New York, for about a week. The time came when the

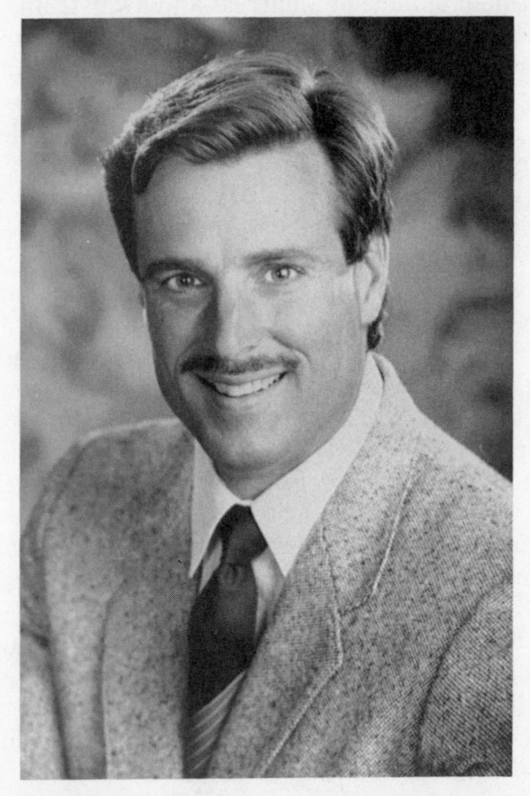

Mac Wilkins in 1985. Photo courtesy of Mac Wilkins

officials decided that the team had to leave for the Olympic Village in Montreal. Now, that was 4 or 5 days before the opening ceremonies and 10 or 11 days before our event was on the schedule. Al and I decided we didn't want to check into the Village that far ahead of our event. I knew what it would be like; it would be mass chaos and constant stimulation, and when you get too much of that your mind goes blank, and you don't know what you're doing, so you can't concentrate.

We knew that the East Germans and the Russians and even some western European teams had training camps outside of Montreal where their athletes could stay in order to avoid the kind of atmosphere that existed in the Olympic Village. These countries would send their athletes into the Village a day or so before the competition. Al and I often trained together, and we knew how to train and eat in a way that was best for us, so we had decided to get an apartment outside of Montreal and away from the Olympic Village. As self-coached world record holders in our events, we were solely responsible for our training and performances. To give up this control to some stuffed shirt who wasn't an athlete and didn't know anything about training was unthinkable, especially 10 days before we competed.

We had tried to arrange this in advance, beginning the previous fall, but of course that didn't work. Al and I asked the officials at the national championships in 1975 for permission to get a place of our own away from the Village so that we could train the way we knew we had to to be in peak condition. We asked again in the spring of 1976 and then later that summer. But nobody did a damn thing about it. They just listened and said, yeah, they'd look into it, but they didn't. Then, when the time came to go to Montreal, these coaches and Olympic officials told us that they couldn't do anything. They had a whole caravan of Chevy trucks and cars there at Plattsburgh to take the team to Montreal, and they told us we all had to go as a team. To hell with that. Al and I told them we weren't going, and we didn't; we stayed in Plattsburgh that first night.

The next night about 11:00 P.M. they called us up and said that I'd been selected for doping control and that I had to get up to the Olympic Village to take the tests. That was baloney! I knew from my German contacts that, first of all, I didn't have to check into the Village until maybe two days before my competition, and second, if I didn't check into the Village, I didn't have to take the doping test until I did check in. Now they could have kicked me off the team if they wanted to, but I was willing to take my chances with that if push came to shove. Traditional American Olympic officials are very conservative, and in this case either they were ignorant or they were lying, and there's no excuse for either.

I told the person who called, "OK, you can send a car for us and take us to Montreal, but we're not staying in the Olympic Village." He said that would be all right; they'd put us up in a hotel and try and get this thing squared away. By that time I was beginning to feel like some kind of criminal. I half expected the FBI to nab me and take me by force to the Olympic Village. The car came, and we went up to Montreal and met with the officials and explained our position. They gave us a pretty good runaround that day, but a couple of days later their lawyers decided that, yes, I didn't have to check into the Village until two days before my event, and that, no, I didn't have to worry about some yo-yo at doping control saying that I had to go through dope testing just because the whole U.S. team checked into the Olympic Village. Al and I already had an invitation to stay with the West Germans at Trois-Rivières, about two hours from Montreal. At the end of that first-day meeting with the officials they told us it was OK for us to go up to Trois-Rivières, but we had to leave our address and tell them when we would be back to check into the Village.

Dope testing is supposed to be done on members of the Olympic team selected at random. However, the list of people selected for testing in Montreal was made up of those whom the doping control officials suspected of taking drugs, and my name was on the list. Why? Because I had broken the world record four times, and that made me a suspect. The most successful athletes are always the ones accused of taking drugs or taking the most drugs.

Al and I had rented an apartment in Trois-Rivières, and we had great training sessions and workouts while we were there. We got back to the Village on the following Wednesday and checked in. It was perfect timing for me because once you check in you get a real adrenaline rush, and you can hold that for only so long. If you get it too soon, you're going to be flat for your competition. But it came at just the right time for me. I did a little workout on Thursday, and I had a great workout on Friday. I hit 230 feet with a left-hand wind, which was a handicap. It was one of those times when, after the workout, you sit down to write in your diary, and you realize what you've done and what you're capable of doing. It's kind of overwhelming, and it brings tears to your eyes. This happens rarely, and I think it does because at those moments you are facing the fear of success, and you're accepting it and realizing that you can overcome it and reach your potential, which is usually beyond what you ever imagined. My competitions were scheduled for Saturday and Sunday, and after that workout on Friday I realized that I would probably win if I did well, and basically that's the way I've always felt: if I did well, I'd win.

I had just one goal at the Montreal Games—to throw the discus as far as I could—and I knew what I had to do to accomplish that. I had to prepare psychologically as well as physically, and I had to keep my attention focused on that goal. Meantime I'm getting all this hassle from the officials. I wasn't at Montreal to march in parades or to trade pins; I was there for one reason, to throw the discus.

The qualifying round was on Saturday at 9:00 A.M. Everything is new, and you get all keyed up because finally this is your chance to go. Afterward there's a natural letdown, and then you have to come back on the second day, and that's when what you do really counts. I took two throws just to warm up, and for me that's a short warm-up. On my first warm-up throw I hit 230 feet, and the second, someone said, was 236 feet.

After we entered the stadium we had to sit in a little room for about 20 minutes while someone checked our equipment to make sure we didn't have too much gear, or Adidas name tags showing, or our numbers on upside down, things like that. I went out onto the field and watched John Powell and Jay Silvester throw. They were very tense and dumped their throws, hitting 150 to 160 feet. You've got to throw 200 feet or so to qualify automatically. As I watched them, it was very clear to me what I had to do to win, and I remember thinking, What is this with these guys? Get them out of there; I can show you how to do it. Let me in there. I was just bursting with eagerness, but I knew I had to be very conservative and restrain myself.

When my turn came, I threw 224 feet, 5 inches, which wasn't the best I could have done that day, but if you throw over 200 feet, the qualifying distance, that's the only throw you get because either it's over the line or it's not. That 224-foot-5-inch throw is still an Olympic record, but I was a little disappointed because I knew I could have done better.

The next day I wasn't as sharp; I didn't feel the same kind of energy I did on Saturday, but I was still at such a high level that it didn't matter that much. On my first throw I was trying to get cute, and I did something different with my technique, and that throw went about 201 feet. That made me a little nervous. We had about 25 minutes between throws, and that gave me some time to think about what was going on. I thought, Come on, don't blow it. You've got this thing right here in your pocket. Twenty-five minutes is a long time to think. Well, I went easy on my second shot, and I had that effortless feeling at the finish of the throw, which means that everything was fine, perfect, and the discus went out 221 feet, something. Again it wasn't as far as I was capable of throwing, and I wasn't pleased with my performance because of that. It gave me a comfortable margin of victory, but it just wasn't a particularly satisfying throw. Of course I was happy and satisfied to have won; I enjoyed that tremendously.

John Powell was second, and Wolfgang Schmidt of East Germany, who was a good friend of mine and a real tough competitor, was in third place. Then on his last throw Schmidt moved ahead of Powell. I went over and picked Schmidt up and gave him a big hug, and guess what? Everybody around there thought I had insulted Powell, my fellow countryman. John Powell was not my friend, but Wolfgang was. I wasn't looking at what country Schmidt was from; I was just looking at the terrific performance he had made, coming through on his last throw like that to take a silver medal. He was great, but a lot of stuffed shirts were upset with me then, and even more so a bit later.

On the victory stand I was laughing and chuckling to myself and thinking, So this is what it's all about. This is what you see on TV, and it comes down to this. This is easy and no big deal. Of course, the performance itself was relatively easy. The hard part was preparing physically and mentally to get to the level needed to make that performance. A day or so later I was hanging over a balcony at the dorms when Bruce Jenner walked by. He lived a few blocks from me the previous year, in San Jose, and my roommate was his training partner. They'd get together every morning and go out for a run. So Bruce and I were friends. We looked at each other, and a kind of knowing smile came over our faces, and Jenner said, "Well, what did you expect?'

I said, "Yeah, I know." It turned out exactly the way I thought it would, and that was because I had a clear picture of my performance in my mind, and I knew precisely what I had to do to throw far. It seemed so easy: all I had to do was follow the plan I laid out for myself. The bad thing was that a lot of officials seemed to be trying to prevent me from following my plan, as if they knew better than I how to throw the discus.

In many ways I was the bad guy, the black sheep of the '76 Olympic Games. First, I was big and strong and had long hair and a beard, and that probably intimidated some people. Then, when they found out I wasn't going to check into the Olympic Village with the rest of the team, they created a big to-do about it. And of course the Olympic officials didn't like it when I told them I hoped the East Germans would win all the medals except in the discus because the U.S. didn't deserve to win. What we were doing was a travesty. East Germany and many other countries, including some in the West, support their athletes. Our athletes weren't getting any support at all from the Olympic people. They were just wasting the potential of these athletes. All I got from the Olympic officials was an airline ticket and a uniform. They didn't support me; they didn't help me. I got to the Olympics on my own. When I was asked whether I won the gold medal for myself or for my country, I had to say that, basically, I won it for myself. I was the one who did the work to earn it, and, if other people are going to be inspired by what I did, then that's fine; I'm glad to have them share in it. I'm proud to be from this country, and I'm proud to represent it at the Olympics, but the Olympic officials are not the country, and they don't represent the country; they represent themselves.

After the Olympics I got a lot of hate mail. Many people wrote letters telling me what a jerk I was and asking why I don't go to Russia. Milt Richmond wrote all kinds of nasty things about me and said that I was a spoiled brat. And then at a press conference shortly after the Games, I said that I was embarrassed to be associated with people who are as incompetent as are the people who organized my part in this Olympics, and I mentioned some of the bullshit I had to go through and the lying and the deception. One reporter asked me why I was laughing on the victory stand. If I had been thinking, I'd have said, "Well, do you think I should have cried because I was sad? No! I laughed because I was happy. Wouldn't you be happy if you had just won an Olympic gold medal?" But I didn't say that. What I did say was "I think John Powell farted." Of course it came out in the papers that when asked why I was laughing I "replied with a crude remark." It was pretty interesting.

Mac Wilkins in 1976. Photo courtesy of Mac Wilkins

A little later I read in a magazine that I was spoiled and selfish and that I drove around San Jose in my Porsche. Yeah. I was driving a 1966 Volkswagen Bug. John Powell and Bruce Jenner had Porsches, but I had an old Volkswagen that cost $600. After that magazine article appeared I got more hate mail for driving a Porsche. That was pretty interesting, too.

It was ironic. I always tried to do things properly, with integrity and honesty. In this case, however, by doing so I was the bad guy. I had put myself into that role. How? It was easy. I didn't have to manufacture anything. By speaking the truth about U.S. Olympic sports, I was attacking an American myth. The public, the USOC, and the media don't like their myths destroyed. However, later in the fall of that year, 1976, the President of the U.S. Olympic team issued a statement in which he said that we had to do more to help the athletes. Basically he said the same things I had said earlier, even though back in July he had said that I was a grandstander and that saying the things I did was like expressing hatred for your parents. But that's part of the problem I was complaining about. The Olympic officials always took a paternalistic, condescending attitude toward the athletes. They treated us as if we were 14-year-olds who had no experiences in life and no knowledge about what was going on. Sure, some of the swimmers and gymnasts were young and may have led sheltered lives, but I was 25 years old and had been taking care of myself for a long time, and that was true of many others. I had gotten to the Olympics not because of the Olympic people but in spite of them.

I have to say that in the years since the '76 Games there has been a dramatic change in the position of many coaches and Olympic officials. They have learned that U.S. athletes can't compete successfully in international competitions like the Olympics unless they get some support, and I don't mean only financial support. They need the lastest information about nutrition and about preventing and treating injuries, and they need facilities where they can practice and develop their potential. Some of this is beginning to happen. There are still some old fogies around, but there have been some positive changes, particularly since track and field got out from under the control of the AAU and now has its own federation, The Athletic Congress—TAC. Athletes have a major influence on the direction of TAC.

The '76 Games were the highlight of my athletic career, but that whole year was great. I continued to have terrific performances. One of the honors of 1976 that I'll always cherish was not being nominated for the Sullivan Award. I consider that a real honor because it was undoubtedly the result of the political statements I made and the reaction of the people in charge of selecting Sullivan Award nominees. Now, if I had come out of the Olympics waving the flag and sounding all gushy, I probably would have been nominated. I attribute my non-nomination to my integrity. But I'm also proud of another distinction: I've never been invited to train at the Olympic facilities at Colorado Springs. Now, that's not so much because of politics as it is because of a lack of any facilities that would benefit a discus thrower. The field there is Astroturf. If you want to throw the discus, you have to go three miles down the road to a high school field. Also, you have to work out in the off-season, which is in the winter, and the weather in Colorado Springs is not always pleasant at that time of year.

I had a good year in 1976. I wanted to keep going up and up, but you really can't do that. On a daily basis you have ups and downs, hard days and easy days, and the same thing applies to weeks and months and even years. But I didn't know that at the time, or maybe I preferred to ignore it. Anyway, at the end of 1976 I started throwing the shot, too, and in 1977 I did a lot of indoor shot-putting. I even won the national indoor championships with a throw of 69 feet, 1½ inches. That was a very long season for me, from December 1976 when I began to throw the shot to my last discus competition in September 1977. I was in 60 or 70 competitions that season, and they were all over the world, including some in Europe and in New Zealand. The promoters would invite me and pay all the expenses and give me something for appearing. But I was getting emotionally run down throwing the discus. I had a couple of long throws but couldn't maintain that good feeling that tells me when I'm doing everything right. Also, in 1977 I went to a lot of parties and generally goofed off.

In 1978 I got things back together. I worked hard, and I was emotionally rested. I had better performances in '78 than I did in '76 because the quality was more consistent. I lost only one competition all year, and I was quite satisfied with my performances.

Toward the end of 1979 I began my serious training for the 1980 Olympics; then, in February, President Carter announced the boycott of the Moscow Games. That was a real pain in the rear, but it didn't surprise me. It was just the continuation of the kinds of policies whereby the people who have no power, in this case the athletes, get the shaft. Since we athletes had no power, it was easy to sacrifice us so that the politicians and the businesspeople could go on and make whatever point they were trying to make by calling a boycott. If they had bothered to take a poll of the athletes who were going to be affected by the boycott, they would have found they had almost no support.

At the Moscow Games the officials blatantly cheated in favor of the Soviet athletes. It was incredible that that could have happened, but it did, and the worst of it occurred in the track and field events. After three or four days of this there were enough protests that international judges were put on the field with the Soviet judges. That kind of thing wouldn't happen here because U.S. judges bend over backward to be fair to everybody, even if that means that sometimes they are harder on American athletes.

But even without the Olympics, 1980 was a good year for me. I threw a life record in the discus of 232 feet, 10 inches in Helsinki, and that was with a strong wind coming from the left side. With a good wind it might have gone 240 feet. I had decided that, since I couldn't go to the Olympics, I'd retire at the end of that season, and I wanted it to be my best year ever. That was my goal, and I met it. I had set my lifetime record, and I had several throws in practice that went 237 feet. But after I decided to retire, I had a bittersweet feeling. My performances were good, but I wasn't getting much satisfaction from them, probably because I wasn't sure what I would do when I retired. I even took a career-planning course, but nothing much came of that.

After the season I really didn't do much of anything, except get on everybody's nerves. I just couldn't seem to find anything I really wanted to do, and I was unhappy. So in 1981 I started throwing again. After the '78 season I wanted to change my technique because I thought some things I was doing were not correct. So in 1981, '82, and '83, my technique was somewhat better, but it wasn't as effective as it had been. I was improving physically, but I wasn't as consistent, confident, and uninhibited as I had been, and you need those qualities to perform well. Those years weren't very satisfying, even though I was still among the top two or three discus throwers in the world.

In 1984 I felt things coming together for me, as they had in '76, though not quite as clearly. In the '84 Olympic Games my bad throws were much better than my bad throws in '76, and my good throws were also better. I had a foul at 220 feet, which would have won, and I had another when I just barely touched the top of the rim of the circle on a throw of 225 feet, which would have been an Olympic record. Those throws didn't count, and I ended up with a silver medal. I went into that Olympics knowing that it would be my last one, and I wanted to get as much out of it as possible. I tried to be more aware of the things going on around me, and I was. I wasn't as cold as I was in '76 and not as single-mindedly focused on my goal as I had been. In some ways my performance in '84 was better than it was in 1976, despite the fact that I didn't win. My throws were better, and I got tremendous satisfaction from that. Also, my parents and many of my friends were watching, and sharing the experience with them was deeply emotional and very gratifying. I felt satisfied in throwing very close to my best. The color of the medal was not as important as that satisfaction. Even today, I think of that satisfaction and not of losing the gold.

At Los Angeles I was completely ignored by the media because at the same time that the discus event was taking place Mary

Decker fell down in her race, and that was a media event. I've never really appreciated what ABC does to sport, particularly the Olympic Games and track and field. They've commercialized the Games by showing mostly those events that sell the most advertising time. That has helped some sports such as women's gymnastics, but they haven't done anything to increase the awareness and appreciation of many other sports such as archery or equestrian events. They've also created a star system, which means that just a few athletes determine whether a sport lives or dies on TV. Two or three star athletes can command more money than the rest of the athletes combined. And finally, the throwing events get little media attention anyway, unless, of course, there's a big, hairy, bearded guy saying unpleasant things to people and throwing world records at the same time.

FRED NEWHOUSE

Gold Medal, 4x400-Meter Relay, 1976
Silver Medal, 400-Meter Dash, 1976

Fred Newhouse exemplifies the individual who is able to combine world-class athletic ability with an equally enthusiastic commitment to off-track excellence.

After failing to make the 1968 and 1972 teams, and after completing an undergraduate degree in engineering and a master's in business, Newhouse made a comeback in 1976 in Montreal, where he narrowly lost to Alberto Juantorena in the 400-meter finals before running a leg on the winning 4x400-meter relay team.

For the past 15 years, Newhouse has worked as an engineer and manager for the EXXON Corporation in Baton Rouge and Houston, where he now specializes in employee relations. He is also a member of the executive boards of The Athletic Congress and the U.S. Olympic Committee.

My parents died when I was seven years old, and I grew up with my grandparents in Hallsville, Texas, about 50 miles from the Louisiana border. Their names were David and Bennie Newhouse, and not even my real parents could have loved my brother, Lucious, and me more than they did.

We lived eight miles outside of town on a farm where we had one basic rule: if you were not participating in a school activity, you came home and worked. Now anyone with any brains would rather participate in choir, band, athletics, or whatever than come home and plow mules, pick cotton, and things like that. So we had a good incentive to do well in school, and no excuse was good enough for either my brother or me to make only a B grade. My grandparents were great motivators, even though they never scolded or threatened us. My grandmother had a way of talking to you after you had done something wrong such that you'd much

Fred Newhouse in 1986. Photo by Fogarty and Carlson

rather she just spanked you.

I really started running while chasing after my brother. We used to get up every morning and milk the cows by hand. In the winter we took them to a pasture that was about two miles from our house. On the way home my brother would give me about a 100-yard head start, and we'd race back home to catch the school bus at quarter to seven. I'd do anything to keep him from catching me, but since he was four years older than I, he would always catch me about 25 or 30 yards from the house. But one day he didn't catch me—so he stopped giving me a lead.

I didn't formally compete in track and field until my junior year of high school. Baseball was the major spring sport, and the coach, W. B. Edwards, would pick the fastest guys off the baseball team to run track on the weekend. I ran the 100 and the 220, long-jumped, and high-jumped, but I never made a state championship. You had to win a first in the district meet to qualify for state, and I never did. My best time was probably a 10.2 or 10.3 in the 100 and about 22.2 in the 220.

During my second semester at Prairie View A & M, when I felt I could handle engineering school, I went out for the baseball team. That was in the spring of 1967. I was a walk-on and I guess the third-string right fielder. One day the coach decided that the reason we were losing was because we were not in good condition. So he took us over to the track and told us he was going to run us into shape, but that whoever won the quarter-mile would not have to run anymore that day. He also asked Hoover Wright, the track coach, to time us. Wearing a baseball suit, tennis shoes, and on a cinder track, I ran my quarter in 52 seconds. Wright said, "Hey, I got guys out here on scholarship who can't do that." Strangely enough, I had only run one quarter in high school, and that was about a 56.3. But I had grown about an inch and a half my freshman year in college, and mentally I was much more mature.

That ended my baseball career, especially after Coach Wright promised me a track scholarship if I could get a point in the conference meet against the likes of Texas Southern, Southern University, Grambling, and Jackson State and their big-name stars such as Winston Short, Jack Phillips, Grundy Harris, Clyde Duncan, and Jimmy Hines. All I had to do was get a sixth place in the 100 for my point, so I felt, Hey, sixth place, anybody can do that. Well, I came in last in the first heat, even though I ran a personal best of 9.6. Hines ran 9.2, and there were six other people between us. That experience left me feeling that it was all over for track and me.

But later that year, we sent a relay team to the NAIA championship, and Coach Wright looked at me again and said, "OK, Little Pony, you've got the same chance once more." We ended up getting a third or fourth place—and six points—which meant that I got a point and a half and my scholarship.

That was a great relief because I was going to school on a work-study program in which I worked during the summer to pay my fall tuition; then in the spring semester they gave me a loan. My grandparents couldn't afford to pay my way through school, so I was happy to remove any burden from them. My first priority was to get that engineering degree in four years, and the scholarship allowed me to do that.

I was the 16th and final 400-meter runner to qualify for the 1968 Olympic trials in Los Angeles. I had to compete against such guys as Larry James, Lee Evans, and Vince Matthews, but at the time I had never heard of any of them. I read technical journals, not sport magazines. But on the way to LA, I picked up this old *Sports Illustrated* that featured an article about Larry James, and I'll never forget it. The writer called him the "Mighty Burner." He had run 47.2 indoors to set the world's record. I thought, Jesus Christ, nobody will ever beat that time. The guy is untouchable. And there I was on the same track with him.

Well, in the prelims I led him to the tape. Twenty yards from the finish I was leading the race. He was right behind me. After the race he came up to me and said, "You've got some talent. You ought to work at it a little bit. I was really impressed with the way you took the race out."

This was Larry James—the guy I had just read about in the magazine, the Mighty Burner. I didn't make the team, but I started thinking that I had been selling myself short. Back at school I started taking myself a bit too seriously. My name was in the school paper, and the girls were starting to give me more attention. I began thinking of myself as a big man on campus, and I really got the big head. Partly because of this, I didn't apply myself that next year. Then my wife-to-be, Rhonda Marshall, joined me at school. She cut out some of my courting activities. I also began to grow a little and started to dedicate myself to track and field and to my studies.

In January of my senior year I set a world record in the 400 meters of 45.6. I kept thinking to myself, The Mighty Burner ran only 47.2. That was 1970, and I also made my first international team that year. Two years later I was one of the favorites to make our Olympic team.

Unfortunately, at the trials I allowed my ego to overrule my better judgment. In the semifinals I ran a really easy 44.1, hand-timed, so I felt like I was already on the team. I started talking to the press, or they started talking to me, asking if I was going to break the world record. I also started reading the papers. I had never read the sports page in my life, but I saw where Coach Jim Bush of UCLA told some reporter that his guys would still win. I took that personally and got angry. I was determined that I was going to break the world record even though I was probably already running above my head. I had broken a bone in my left foot in May and still wasn't in top condition.

I took the finals out entirely too fast. There were several people who later said they timed me anywhere from 20.5 to 20.8 for the first 200. Someone said I could have won the open 200 with my split. My coach timed me at 29.8 for 300 meters. But the last 20 meters turned out to be the longest 20 meters of my life. It was like a never-ending nightmare. I was leading by 7 or 8 meters, but in those last 20 meters everybody but one guy passed me, and I ended up seventh.

At that point I wanted to give up track and field. I really was ready to quit. If it were not for my wife, I don't think I ever would have made an Olympic team. For several weeks after that I couldn't sleep, and when I did I would have horrible nightmares. I was really hurting, and all I wanted to do was cry. It had all been right there. I had run fast enough in the semifinals to be solidly on that team. But I had ruined everything when I ran out of control.

My wife kept telling me, "Don't quit. You owe it to yourself to keep on going. Let's do it together." She was right there with me.

I was in the U.S. Army at the time. I got out the following September and enrolled in the MBA program at the University of Washington. I also resumed my training and worked as a graduate assistant in track. After I received my master's I went to work for EXXON in Baton Rouge, Louisiana, where Willie Davenport, Rod Milburn, and I started the Baton Rouge Track Club.

Baton Rouge was good to me. It was a family town. You could be anywhere in town in 20 minutes, so I could work out at either LSU or Southern University and get back and forth to home and work without much trouble. Neither school would give me locker facilities, but I would change clothes in my car after work and then train on my own.

But that became a problem. I didn't have anybody to train with. Willie and Rod were hurdlers and didn't have to do the distance work. I was also having trouble finding races. The universities wouldn't let me run in their collegiate meets because they claimed I messed up their scoring system and hurt their guys' egos. One night I was sitting home, and on the television there was a documentary about the Ethiopian marathoner, Abebe Bikila, entitled "You Must Run This Race Alone." I adopted that as my theme. That very next day I wrote on my blackboard at work, "You Must Run This Race Alone." And every time I would start feeling sorry for myself, I'd look up at that blackboard and think, Nobody's going to have any sympathy for you, and nobody's going to help you. You must run this race alone.

I didn't have a coach or anybody, but there was a gentleman there at work who loved track. His son-in-law had run on the LSU team, and he had been a judge and timer at some of the LSU meets. I told him that I was having trouble with my training, and he told me he would come over and time me. His name was W. R. Lewis, and he gave me everything I needed. I knew what to do, but he'd always tell me I could do more. I'd finish a run and be standing there, bent over, with hands on my knees, and he'd say, "Come on, you can do it. One more. Come on, you can do it." He gave me that little extra push when I was ready to say, "I've had enough for today," even though I hadn't finished my schedule. He had nothing to gain from all this. He was just a good man who was willing to come out because I asked him to—and he did make a difference.

All I needed was a little encouragement. I knew that I had everything it took to be on the team. By that time I had the mental maturity, and I had experimented over the past four years with running my race using various strategies and styles. I'd go out and purposely run a slow race in the beginning just to see if I could finish in the money. The next race I'd reverse that strategy. Regardless of the conditions, the weather, or what lane I was in, I could finish in the money. So it took me four years after 1972 to develop this confidence, this mental tenacity, so that I knew that nowhere in the world on a given day were there three quarter-milers who were better than I; in fact, I had come to believe that no one was as good.

When I got to the Olympic trials in 1976, I established the pace in every race. In the finals I drew lane eight, which is usually undesirable, but I said to myself, Hey, that's good. Anywhere out front, because Fred Newhouse has a reputation of going out fast, and everybody is going to let him take it out and sit on his heels and then try to blow him away in the stretch. So in the first 100 meters I really took it out just like they wanted me to. Then on the backstretch I slowed it down to a snail's pace. Coming off the turn I was still in first place, and I knew I was on the Olympic team. It was my race, my strategy. There was never any doubt. The rest of the guys followed me right to my spot on the team. It was a slow race. I ran 45.6 and finished second, but I didn't care. I had accomplished my goal, and I was on the team.

That was one of the happiest days of my life. Making the team was better than winning the medal when you're in a country like this one, where there are so many great athletes running the 400 meters.

I have to say that I ran extremely well at Montreal even though I did not win the 400 meters. It was my lifetime best race. I ran the race exactly as my coach, Dr. Leroy Walker, and I had laid it out. We had planned our splits by 100-meter segments, and I was within three-tenths of a second on each of the four. It was just that Cuba's Alberto Juantorena was ahead of me at the end of the final segment.

I knew he was a fantastic runner even before the race, and although I had never run against him, there was never any doubt in my mind that I could beat him. That doubt just didn't exist. So I was extremely surprised to see him there on my shoulder when I was 50 meters from the tape. Dr. Walker and I had thought that 44.6 would win the race. I ran 44.4, but Juantorena ran 44.26. Obviously we had underestimated his talent. He had already run the 800, and we felt he would be drained.

Juantorena was not a seasoned 400-meter runner, and he did not know pace. He just ran to win, and he was a phenomenal athlete. Ronnie Ray had beaten him at the Pan-Am Games the year before because Ronnie got lane eight and Juantorena was in lane two, way back, and he couldn't feel where Ronnie was. In the finals, I got lane six, Herman Frazier was in lane five, and Juantorena was in three, where he could see every move we were making. And with his power and his ability to maintain contact he just overpowered us at the tape. In the last 100 meters of the 400, it is not who accelerates, but who slows down the least, and he had that ability to maintain his peak speed much longer than anybody else I've ever seen.

I got to know him pretty well. He's a super guy. The American women went wild for him, and he went wild for a few American women as well. I can remember on the track he would ask me, "Who is that? Where's her boyfriend?" I could never dislike the guy. I was never one to take my races or competitors personally and let that damage relationships off the track. On the track it was every man for himself, but off the track we could talk and be friends, and Juantorena and I were, and still are, friends.

He was here at my home in Houston in December of 1985. As a Vice President of The Athletics Congress, I had initiated contact with him about a goodwill trip to the United States. Castro gave his OK, and I extended an invitation through the State Department that he come as a guest to our national convention. Juantorena, Herman Frazier, and I—the three medalists—appeared on the podium together. We took him out to dinner one night at a very, very nice place. We talked a lot about the politics of sport, but I don't think he liked that much. The next day I brought him to my home, where we had hot dogs and potato chips and talked about old times. He enjoyed that a lot more. He's a normal, regular guy who prefers to keep sports separate from politics.

I did not support the 1980 Olympic boycott for similar reasons. It did not change anything, and it was not fair to the athletes who trained all those many years. There are a lot of bitter athletes running around in this country because they didn't get their chance in 1980. It was a matter of pure politics. In hindsight a lot of people believe we did not make the right decision. My attitude toward a problem has always been: let me be on the inside trying to solve it rather than on the outside complaining about it.

We made the decision not to go at the April 1980 meeting of the Executive Committee of the USOC. Before he knew the outcome of the vote, filmmaker Bud Greenspan made a speech about what a great thing it was in this country to have so many people volunteering their time for an ideal, to promote goodwill among people and to further excellence among athletes. His speech was so touching that people were literally crying in the audience because their consciences were bothering them. These were all good patriotic Americans. I mean, these were people who believe in apple pie and who, if Reagan asked them to don their armor and go fight, most of them would. So when Carter said, "Hey, guys, you're hurting our nation. Don't do that. It's not good for the country," they had a

Fred Newhouse in 1976. Photo courtesy of Fred Newhouse

hard time saying no to him. They thought he was in a better position to make a decision on this matter than they were, so as good, obedient Americans they voted to go along with the boycott.

There was tremendous pressure put on the committee, pressure you wouldn't believe. I just never thought my government would stoop to such tactics. We had direct accounts from corporations that had been told not to follow through with their pledges to the USOC. That in itself was intimidating. Our people saw the entire Olympic program going down the drain. We were told by Mr. Carter that he would put $30 million into our future Olympic programs, and I think he would have done so, but he didn't win the election. It was hardball he was playing, real hardball.

Personally, I felt that as an American I had the right to express my difference of opinion. Just because he was the president of the United States made him no more an American than I am. He's got one vote; so do I. His might be bigger than mine, but I still had the right to say whatever I believed in a peaceful, tactful manner, and I had a right to vote on that issue as I saw fit. In hindsight I think most of those voting for the boycott wish they had the opportunity to remake that decision, and that includes Mr. Carter.

At the time, I had people at work who entirely forgot that I had won an Olympic gold medal. They just saw me as being anti-American. I mean, people in my community wouldn't talk to me. For them it was black or white—either you're American or you're not. So they thought I was just another of those selfish athletes who could only think of himself.

There was, of course, some selfishness there. People were thinking of themselves, not because they were so self-centered, but because they and their families had put in such long hours of suffering. Lots of people were involved and affected. It was not like going to just another track meet. Those on the outside could not begin to understand what it means to compete in the Olympics. It's not even winning the gold medal. It's just being able to compete and be one of the best and knowing what it took to get there—that you were able to make it.

The entire matter of so-called amateur sports and money is another difficult question because of the traditional values we equate with the word *amateur*. The values of the Avery Brundage era came right out of the movie *Chariots of Fire*. Olympic sports were something that rich gentlemen did. Because of this kind of tradition, we have a tough time accepting the way we handle track and field and some of the other sports today. But it's time for that to change because there is no reason why an athlete who represents America, and who has worked diligently for long hours, over long periods of time, should not get rewarded for it in a country that has always rewarded people for being successful. This is a capitalist nation. Supply and demand determine who gets paid and who doesn't. The best guy at the top of the heap can demand more money. This has been true everywhere you can think of—except in amateur athletics.

Many of the educational institutions make money from sports, and sometimes they plow it back into other sports. That's the good thing about the NCAA. But what of the athletes themselves? Athletes sign a pact with a college that states in return for four years of competition they get an education. Now for football that may be great because after college I can play pro if I'm good enough. But for track and field I can give you four years, and at the end of that time, if I don't get my degree, somebody didn't live up to their end of the bargain because at that moment I don't have a skill that I can sell. So I go out and keep running track, and maybe if I'm lucky I can skim a dime under the table from a meet promoter. If I'm an average athlete, in a good year I might make $3,000 or $4,000 dollars. If I'm a Carl Lewis type of superstar, that's a far different story. But most amateur athletes today still don't make enough money to survive. They retire from competition, and if they didn't get their college degree, a large number of them will have to go back to the streets with no salable skills.

Another change that we're going to see is the increased use of drugs in amateur sports. Now, don't get me wrong. I've fought against drugs for years, but it's sort of like what the guy told me when I said I wasn't going to let my daughters wear makeup. He said, "You can resist that now, but understand, you're fighting a losing battle. You're just going to lose that one."

We're going to lose the war on drugs in amateur sports. We can fight it, but we're going to lose. It's simply a choice that athletes are going to have to make. You don't have to take drugs to be successful. There are thousands of examples that demonstrate this. But there are other people who feel that drugs enhance their performance, and maybe they do. But so does hard work, longevity in training, and determination. If you are willing to pay the price, you'll get there.

Some Americans think that drugs explain the great athletic success of the Eastern Europeans, but I believe that's due to more than just the use of drugs. They have well-coordinated, totally integrated programs. This is especially true of the East Germans. When you look at their programs, you know that drugs cannot do all this. They start very early with the athlete, and they teach good, solid techniques. We need to do more of the same thing in this country.

As I now look back on my Olympic experience I know that my

gold medal is not as important as the silver because the silver came in an individual event. The relay was a team effort. It was an exciting race. We had a fantastic team. Our strategy was simple—get out so far ahead that not even Alberto Juantorena could catch us, and it turned out just that way. Herman Frazier, Benny Brown, and I gave Maxie Parks at least a 30-meter lead. He could have run backward to the tape.

It was kind of a pacifier for not having won my individual gold. I got the silver medal for running my lifetime best race. So I can't really complain about anything except that I didn't win. Even today when I look back on that race I can think of things I could have done differently that might have changed the outcome. But it doesn't bother me because I know I executed the strategy we had planned. A slightly different strategy might have changed the outcome. I could have run the first 200 meters in 21.3 instead of 21.4. We're talking about tenths of seconds here, but they might have made the difference.

15 LOS ANGELES, 1984

The 1984 Los Angeles Olympics marked the third successive Games in which sizable numbers of countries refused to participate for political reasons. This time it was the Soviet Union and most of its Eastern Bloc allies who decided to boycott: the Soviets insisted that they feared for the safety of their athletes, but their action was obviously intended as a retaliation for the American boycott of 1980. Once again, it was the victimized athletes who suffered the most, but a record 140 countries did send 7,800 competitors.

Peter Ueberroth, the President of the Los Angeles Olympic Organizing Committee, was determined to put the Games—called the "No-Frills Olympics"—on a solid financial footing. Many existing facilities were used, including the Coliseum that was originally constructed for the 1932 Games. Ueberroth did such a masterful job of raising money from corporate sources that the Games turned a handsome profit of several million dollars. Some critics, fearing what they perceived to be excessive commercialism, maintained that Ueberroth's actions were tantamount to selling the Games to the highest bidder.

Without competition from the Soviet Union and its allies, the

U.S. proved overwhelmingly dominant in such traditionally strong areas as track and field, boxing, basketball, freestyle wrestling, diving, and swimming. But the boycott also resulted in an unusually strong showing in gymnastics, cycling, volleyball, and Greco-Roman wrestling, events in which Americans had seldom enjoyed any kind of success.

Among the great individual accomplishments were Edwin Moses's 90th straight 400-meter hurdle victory and Carl Lewis's four gold medals, matching Jesse Owens's feat in Berlin in 1936. In winning the 100- and 200-meter dashes and the long jump and anchoring the world-record-setting 4x100-meter relay, Lewis's victories were arguably even more impressive than Owens's, not only because the competition was tougher but because the media expected it. Lewis's counterpart among the women was Valerie Briscoe-Hooks, who set American and Olympic records in the 200 and 400 meters as well as in the 4x400-meter relay. Tiffany Cohen, Mary T. Meagher, and Tracy Caulkins each won two individual golds in swimming, and Meagher and Caulkins picked up a third in the 4x100-meter medley relay. But it was gymnast Mary Lou Retton who emerged as the darling of the media, winning a gold in the all-around, plus two silvers and two bronzes. No American woman had previously won an individual medal in gymnastics. In Los Angeles the U.S. women won seven medals plus the team silver. The male gymnasts did even better. They dethroned the reigning world champions from the People's Republic of China in the team event and went on to win seven individual medals.

Perhaps the most dramatic moment of the Games occurred when Jeff Blatnick mounted the victory stand and broke into tears. Two years earlier he had been victimized by a form of cancer called Hodgkin's disease, but he battled back to become only the second American ever to win a gold medal in Greco-Roman wrestling.

Defeat also brought its dramatic moments. Millions of stunned viewers watched Mary Decker's dreams of victory end in disaster when she fell after tripping over Zola Budd in the 3,000-meter race. Decker had missed the '76 Games because of injuries, and the boycott had ruined her chances in 1980. It was equally devastating to Budd, who so admired Decker that she had her picture on her bedroom wall back home in South Africa.

All kinds of adjectives, many of them contradictory, could be used to describe the closing ceremonies at Los Angeles. They were bombastic, chauvinistic, colossal, glittering, and, to some, tasteless. Originally, the Games were to have closed with a parade of America's former gold medalists. The oldest winners would have marched first into the stadium followed by the champions from more recent times. But someone had a better idea and substituted an exhibition of breakdancing. The results were unrestrained and spectacular, but many observers thought the parade of the champions would have made a more fitting tribute to the dignity and historical continuity of the Olympic Games.

CARL LEWIS

Gold Medal, 100-Meter Dash, 1984
Gold Medal, 200-Meter Dash, 1984
Gold Medal, Long Jump, 1984
Gold Medal, 4x100-Meter Relay, 1984

At the 1984 Games in Los Angeles, Carl Lewis became only the third track and field athlete to win four gold medals in the same Olympics. The University of Pennsylvania's Al Kraenzlein did it in 1900; the immortal Jesse Owens, in 1936. Owens won the 100- and 200-meter dashes, the long jump, and the 4x100-meter relay, the same events in which Lewis achieved his victories.

Carl Lewis, who won the Sullivan Award in 1981 as the year's best amateur athlete and the Associated Press's "best male athlete of the year" in both 1983 and 1984, is arguably the best track athlete in the world, but he is far from the best liked. He has been accused of being arrogant, self-centered, and aloof. Tom Callahan, writing in Time *magazine on February 18, 1985, quotes Lewis's answer to his critics: "Looking back, I think the trouble was just the fact that I had been number one in my events for three years, and there was nothing new to say about me. When you can't find something new, it's time to find something wrong."*

Some of the criticism stems from Lewis's strong sense

of independence. Carl Lewis does things his way, not the traditional or expected way. He was frequently at odds with his coaches, first at Kennedy High School in Willingboro, New Jersey, where he hurdled, long-jumped, ran the sprints, and played junior-varsity soccer, and later at Willingboro High, where he specialized in the long jump and sprints. His refusal to bow to authority was not only condoned by his parents but actively encouraged by them. He and brothers, Machie and Cleve, and his sister, Carol, were raised to act and think for themselves.

Early, aggressive efforts to promote and market Lewis and his own lavish lifestyle—expensive home, furnishings, car, and clothes—have also contributed to the media's image of a self-indulgent and spoiled athlete. In reality, Lewis is a complicated, intelligent, multitalented man who easily accepts the wealth that his athletic abilities and their commercialization provide. But this seems to bother many reporters and fans who can accept the high-salaried professional football, basketball, and baseball players, but who still view track and field athletes as somehow "purer"—meaning virtually unpaid—and if they are not, they are expected to have the grace to pretend that they are and to act accordingly. But that's not Lewis's style; he's comfortable with himself, and he is not one to adjust to the expectations of others.

At the 1968 Olympic Games in Mexico City, with an altitude of over 7,000 feet, Bob Beamon set an Olympic and world record of 29 feet, 2½ inches in the long jump. Competing under perfect jumping conditions, he became the first person to break the 28- and 29-foot marks. Beamon never broke 28 feet again. There was considerable expectation among the spectators and the press at Los Angeles that Lewis, whose personal best was 28 feet, 10¼ inches, would make a serious effort to break Beamon's record. Earlier in the Games he had won the 100-meter dash, and earlier on the day of the long jump, he had run and won two preliminary heats in the 200

Carl Lewis in 1985. Photo courtesy of Joe Douglas, Athletes International

meters. His first jump was 28 feet, ¼ inch. He fouled on his second and passed on his next four jumps. This caused a spectator reaction that Lewis had never before experienced.

Yes, some people in the stands booed me during the long jump competition. I think the main problem was that the stadium was full of people who did not know much about track and field. I would say at least 60 percent really didn't know much at all and probably 20 to 30 percent had never seen a track meet before. My mother was sitting in the stands, and when the athletes were taking their sweat clothes off, many of the people around her said, "Oh, my God! Why are they getting undressed?" Also, when it was announced that the first run of the 3,000 meters was canceled, one lady said, "I hope that Mary Decker will be given the gold medal anyway." It's unbelievable that people could say such things, but they did. Those who booed probably felt that they had paid to see a full six jumps. I think many of them didn't understand that it only took one jump to win.

But another problem was the press. The press jumped on the booing thing and the fact that I didn't take the last jumps and made a big issue of it. They didn't try to educate the crowd. They didn't explain that I had two more events to compete in and that I might have been pacing myself so I'd be in good shape to run the next two heats in the 200 and then run the relay. They alluded to that fact, but they really didn't explain the situation.

By the end of the 200, even though many of the people didn't really understand track and field, they saw me winning and they began to comprehend why I didn't compete more. When I stepped onto the track for the semifinals, the crowd was kind of silent. There were no boos when I won that; and when I won the gold medal, they roared and cheered and celebrated. You could hear people saying, "Okay, I see what's going on here. The long jump was like the second period of a basketball game. This was the third period, and he still has the fourth period to go." The people began to understand what was happening. The press continually went on about the long jump. I didn't enter the long jump event in LA to beat Beamon's record. I entered it to compete and to win, which I did.

Every time the media suggested that I should be going after Beamon's record, I said that the Los Angeles Coliseum was not conducive for records. The Coliseum winds swirl in such a way that you can run down the runway and have a tail wind for the first five strides, have a dead wind for ten yards, and then during the last five strides have a head wind. That's just how the winds were swirling, and that made it very difficult to get your steps right. So I was pleased to get off the first jump. I was really excited. I thought to myself, "Great! I have one." As it turned out, everyone jumped below par throughout the competition.

I was born in Birmingham, Alabama, but we moved to Willingboro, New Jersey, a suburb of Philadelphia, when I was just two. My parents were both high school teachers and were both fine athletes. My father had run track and played football at Tuskegee Institute, and my mother, who also graduated from Tuskegee, had been a nationally ranked hurdler. When she could not get a girls' track team started at the school where she was teaching, she and my dad started their own track club. That was 1969, but my sister Carol and I didn't start our serious training at the club until a couple of years later, when I was ten and she was only eight. I began competing in certain meets, and I did just about everything. I jumped, sprinted, and ran the mile. I won medals throwing the discus and putting the shot. I even pole-vaulted in one meet. When I would finish one event, I just would run over and enter the next.

In high school I concentrated on the sprints and the long jump. I set a national high school record in the long jump of 25 feet, 9 inches. In 1979 I went to the University of Houston on a track scholarship. I liked it a great deal at first. The atmosphere was good, people were happy, I enjoyed school, and I met some very nice professors. Coach Tom Tellez and his staff were great. I enjoyed it all very much in the beginning. I did well in school and in track, and I enjoyed the city. You can't beat that.

But later it got to the point where it became difficult for both the university and for me. Certain members of the athletic department felt they had to control my scheduling and the things I was doing, in part because I was able to earn money running outside of the university. But Coach Tellez and I had a wonderful understanding in that respect. We never had a problem. If he asked me to go to a meet, that he needed me, I was there. And if I went to him and said, "Look, I'd like to go to this meet," he'd say, "Okay, we only have a dual meet. Go on and go. No problem." We had a great understanding. I never missed a major meet, and I set conference records for points scored. So I was really into the team. But when the athletic directors started telling me that I couldn't go here and I couldn't go there and that I had to do what they told me, I said, "Enough." Coach Tellez and I had a long talk, and we agreed that it was best if I didn't continue on the team.

Coach Tellez told me to keep my life going and that I was more than just a university athlete—I was a person. So I kept going, and even now I still learn more things about him and he learns more things about me, and we are still maturing as though nothing ever really happened. Actually, his role became even bigger after I left the team. Because I didn't have the university restrictions, I needed more advice, encouragement, and guidance than when I ran for the varsity, and he gave all of this to me. Joe Douglas, the president of the Santa Monica Track Club, was also very supportive, and I did my competing for the Santa Monica A.C. Joe is also my manager.

My first Olympics were the 1984 Games. I had qualified for the 1980 Games in Moscow, but the U.S. boycotted those Games. I thought at the time that the boycott was a campaign move on the part of President Carter. I tried to look at that decision from both sides, and still I felt it was strictly a political move by Mr. Carter. He had been accused of backing down on several issues and of not being a strong president. I think he used the Soviet invasion of Afghanistan as an excuse to boycott the Games. That way he could show that he could stand strong and get the country behind him and win his election in the fall. So the United States backed out of the Olympics, and the athletes suffered the consequences.

The problem I see is that the government, whether through Carter or Reagan or whoever, doesn't pay attention to sports unless they can be used for some political purpose; then the government pays a lot of attention. If the government wants to use athletes for political purposes, it should support and promote them right along, like the Soviet Union does. It just doesn't make sense for the government to use sports for political ends but not to support the overall concept of sports. I think President Carter's decision to boycott the 1980 Games was a mistake, but when the athletes complained, they were made to appear as unpatriotic, bickering, young brats.

One of the consequences of that decision was that the Soviets and most of their allies boycotted our Games in '84. They were getting even for our boycott; that was their main reason for not coming. But there was also another reason. I don't think they were really ready for the '84 Games. Many of their athletic programs were in a period of transition. They were conducting a lot of new experiments, and I just don't think they were ready. At the 1983 track and field world championship they didn't do well at all. So they had two reasons for not coming, but the main reason was that they were reacting to our boycott of their Games.

Of course, I continued to compete after the '84 Games. In 1985 I pulled a hamstring early in the year, and that interfered with my performance the rest of the season. I still came back and ended up number one in the world in my events; so it was a successful year, but it just wasn't my type of year because of the injury.

In the first half of the '86 season, I competed in a few meets, but my left knee bothered me, and in the second half I was nothing. I competed but I wasn't anywhere near healthy. I ended up having arthroscopic surgery in September, and I took three months off after that. So far in 1987 I've done very well in all my events.

I am involved in other things besides athletics. I've been interested in the entertainment industry for some time. I began taking acting lessons a few years ago, and I'm continuing with that. I was in a movie called *Dirty Laundry*, which was released in the California area in the spring of '87, and I'm playing a dance instructor in a Warner Brothers film that starts production in September of '87. It's a much bigger role than I had in *Dirty Laundry*.

I made a recording before the '84 Games called *Going for the Gold*. It was released in Europe but not here. Believe it or not, I don't even have a copy. The producer in California, Narada Michael Walden, probably has some. It's funny; I wish we had done the record this year because he's one of the hottest composer/producers out there right now. He produced *Freeway of Love* for Aretha Franklin and Whitney Houston's new album. *Going for the Gold* might have been a huge hit if it were produced now.

I've continued recording. We're just finishing an album for the European market. We have two songs left that we're going to do in July, so the album should be released at the end ofAugsut 1987. There are nine songs, two of which a California producer, David Jones, and I are producing with my band, The New Generation. I'm working with producers in Europe on the other songs, some of which may be released in this country. But the album is being produced primarily for European markets because it was a European producer who contacted us. He had heard *Going for the Gold*, which did pretty well in Europe. Last fall we did a single with him, "Break It Up," which ended up going gold in three markets there and making money in all the markets where it was released.

Winning those medals in the Olympics has given me an opportunity to experience many things. Companies have contacted me about sponsoring their products. I just finished working with Nike, and I'm talking to other companies now. People often walk up to me and say how much I inspired them, and that's a good feeling. It was just something I wanted to achieve—my ultimate goal. It's like someone who starts working for a company and says,

"One day I'll be president." When they achieve that goal, they sit back and enjoy the feeling of accomplishment that comes with that, but then they say, "Okay, now that I'm president, I've got to make something happen as president." That is where I am now. I achieved something in '84, but now I've got to do something, make something happen, make that achievement mean something. One thing I'd like to do is repeat that achievement at Seoul in 1988. That's what keeps me inspired to compete.

PETER VIDMAR

Gold Medal, Gymnastics, Team All-Around, 1984
Gold Medal, Pommel Horse, 1984
Silver Medal, Gymnastics, Men's All-Around, 1984

Between 1932 and 1984 the best finish by an American gymnast was Peter Kormann's bronze in the floor exercises in 1976. All that changed in Los Angeles when the American men, led by Peter Vidmar, won the team gold and then added seven medals in individual events. The boycott of most of the Eastern Bloc countries unquestionably played a role, but the People's Republic of China was there, and they had won the world championship the previous year.

Vidmar currently serves on the Board of Directors of the U.S. Gymnastics Federation. He also does motivational speaking, gives exhibitions, and does some television commentary for ESPN and NBC.

All of us were disappointed when we first heard that most of the communist nations were going to boycott the 1984 Games in Los Angeles. You want everybody to be there because that's what the Games are all about. But we felt great about our team victory because we defeated the People's Republic of China, and they had beaten the Soviets for the world championship the year before. At the same time, we realized that some of the medals we won would have gone to Soviet athletes because they are great gymnasts. But that doesn't detract from our performances. You compete against those who show up. You make no allowances for those who cannot compete because of injury, missing a time slot, disqualification, or

Peter Vidmar in 1984. Photo © Dave Black

retirement. No one puts asterisks beside the names of those who competed, and nothing on the gold medal states who was there and who wasn't.

The seven nations who weren't there were the real losers in 1984, just as we were losers for not going in 1980. Boycotts do absolutely nothing but hurt athletes. The 1976 boycott against

South Africa did not end apartheid; it just prevented some great African athletes from going to the Games. The killing is still going on in Afghanistan despite our boycott. The Soviet boycott failed miserably. The Los Angeles Games were a tremendous success in fueling American patriotism, in large part because our athletes won 82 gold medals.

Our American gymnastics team placed fourth in the 1983 world championships, and we were determined to win a medal in the 1984 Games, no matter what color it might be. I trained for those Games almost exclusively with Tim Daggett. He's my best friend, and my son is named after him. Together we carefully planned a routine that we hoped would prepare us for the Games.

When we walked into the gym at the beginning of the day, we would really be fired up, but by the end of a six- or seven-hour workout, our enthusiasm had understandably diminished. You normally practice your events in the order they appear in competition, and the last event is usually the horizontal bar. To keep up our motivation, we would try to put imaginary pressure on ourselves. We'd turn the radio off, and everything would get real quiet. Then one of us would say, "It's the final event of the men's team finals, and the USA is tied with the People's Republic of China. The last two gymnasts for the U.S. team in the horizontal bar are Tim Daggett and Peter Vidmar."

Actually, we had not yet even made the team. But we would go through this routine at the end of our daily workout. I would just close my eyes and imagine I was in Pauley Pavilion in front of 10,000 people, with millions more watching on television, and I had one final chance to make my team win or lose. My heart would began to pound, and I'd really get nervous. Tim would be the announcer, and he'd say, "Next up from the USA is Peter Vidmar."

I'd raise my hand and signal my coach as if he were the head judge. Then I would begin my routine on the horizontal bar. If I fell off, I felt like I had lost the Olympics, and it ruined my day. It didn't matter how good the workout had been up to that point; it was now ruined. And if I did that final routine successfully, I really felt great because I imagined that I had just won the Games for my team and my country.

Of course, it was just practice, and we never really thought we would have to confront such a situation in the Olympics. But that is precisely what happened. Going into the final event, the scoring between China and us was very close, and Tim Daggett and Peter Vidmar were the final two on the horizontal bar. Normally there would have been less pressure because only five out of the six scores count, with the lowest one being dropped. But Scott Johnson, who led off and who had enjoyed a fine overall competition, made a mistake, so we knew that most likely the scores of the next five of us would have to count. We rallied ourselves. Jim Hartung went up and scored a 9.8; Bart Conner improved that to a 9.9; Mitch Gaylord did that crazy Gaylord flip of his and scored a 9.95; Tim then did his routine with a double layout with a full twist dismount. He landed perfectly and earned a 10. Then it was my turn.

I can remember pacing back and forth, waiting for Tim's score to flash. All kinds of things were racing through my mind, things like your prayers being much more sincere when you are in a difficult situation: "Heavenly Father, if I can make this routine, I'll be so much better for the rest of my life, and I really mean it this time." Then I remembered, Hey, the competition doesn't depend just on me. The Chinese also have to do well. Maybe they're having problems on their last event, and I can relax. I glanced over my shoulder and saw Li Ning in the floor exercises do a perfect double-twisting, double back flip and land flawlessly, so I figured that hope was gone.

Just before the green light went on for my turn I looked at my coach, Makoto Sakamoto, the man with whom I had been working for 12 long years. I gave him a smile, and he smiled back and said, "OK, let's go. Just like in the gym. You've done this a thousand times." That's when it hit me. "Of course I'm prepared. I've done this every day at the end of my workouts."

In practice I had always tried to imagine myself in competition, and now it was the other way around. I was mentally trying to take myself out of Pauley Pavilion and its 10,000 noisy fans and back into the UCLA gym with 2 or 3 people watching.

It worked. When I grabbed the bar, I really felt like I was home. I did my routine and scored a 9.95. Now there was no doubt. We had won the team gold.

The team victory is always the most coveted by gymnasts, and the U.S. had never previously won, so it is pretty easy to understand why we were so elated with our performance in Los Angeles.

Of course, the women got much more media attention than we did. Women's gymnastics has become an American glamor sport, and, at times, we men jokingly resent all the coverage that's given them. Every year I was on the USA team we always placed higher in international competition than did the women, but they always got the attention. And in Los Angeles we finished first in the team competition to their second, but they got most of the television and press coverage.

It's a funny thing. Most Americans think Mary Lou Retton won every event in 1984. They think she really cleaned up. Actually, she won only the all-around, and she won it by five-hundredths of a point. That was her only individual gold. Romania's Ecaterina Szabo won four golds to Mary Lou's one, but America scarcely noticed.

In the 1968 and 1972 Games the media also fell in love with Cathy Rigby, although she never won a single medal. Make no mistake about it, both Mary Lou and Cathy were tremendous athletes who did great things for the sport of gymnastics. And it's largely because of athletes like them that in this country we now have 10 times as many women competing in gymnastics as men.

Male gymnasts tend to reach their peak after they have physically matured. Women reach theirs before. Once they mature, women tend to gain more weight in their hips and busts. That changes their center of gravity and makes it more difficult to do certain routines. Men need strength, power, and explosiveness; women require more flexibility.

A great coach and very supportive parents made my gymnastics career possible. My father had done some gymnastics in high school, and his taking me to a gymnastics exhibition when I was about nine really got me interested in the sport. A couple of years later I heard about tryouts for the Culver City Gymnastics Club. I went and was one of five boys picked.

When I was 16 I qualified for the U.S. championships, and I placed 13th. That was a big breakthrough because the top 14 made the 1978 national team. But Coach Sakamoto had me decline, because when you prepare for a competition you have to slow down your acquisition of skills, and he wanted me to become better prepared for international competition. I think I was the only person in history to turn down an invitation to be on our national team.

The following year I again placed 13th and that was a real blow. Young guys are supposed to improve. I think I had fooled myself into believing that I was really working hard enough, but I wasn't.

I knew I could work harder. That was the summer of 1979, and the final trials for the world championship were going to be in the fall. Coach Sakamoto now told me he wanted me to be on the team. I thought he was out of his mind because they take only six and I had placed 13th. So I had just four months to move up seven places. That summer was a real test for me, and I trained like a maniac.

That kind of training meant both quantity and quality. I would do my routines over and over again, as many as 30 repeats. Then, at the end of this four- or five-hour workout at the UCLA gym, I would go back to my club gym and do weight training. I really pushed myself to the breaking point, but it did bring its rewards.

At the fall trials I placed sixth and made the team. So I knew that I had a chance to be one of the big boys. The following year I was a freshman at UCLA, and Sakamoto was now also there as the assistant gymnastics coach. I won the USA all-around and I made our 1980 Olympic team. Of course, that was the team that didn't go.

The boycott was a disappointment, but it wasn't the blow to me that it was to other athletes, because I was so young. Some of the others had decided to hang around for four more years and had really made tremendous sacrifices and then didn't get to compete. There were others who were in their prime and would probably have won medals. At the time, I was in neither category.

I do know that the boycott really hurt our sport, because in every Olympiad little kids sit in front of their TV sets, watch the gymnastics competition, and then run out and join gymnastics clubs. That didn't happen in 1980, and some clubs even had to close down because they depend on that big boost in enrollment they get every four years.

At Los Angeles, I did win an individual gold in the pommel horse, and I came within twenty-five thousandths of a point of winning the men's all-around, which is the most coveted individual crown. I was leading after the first day, but Japan's Koji Gushiken had a great final round and nosed me out for the gold. Going into my final event on the parallel bars, I needed a 9.95 to win, and I scored a 9.9. I did a very good routine, and if I had stuck my dismount I probably would have scored a 10 and won, but on landing I took a little hop, and there went the gold.

I can go back and think of all the little things I could have done better, a little knee bend here or a small hop there, but at the same time you can look at all the other gymnasts and say the same thing. Koji Gushiken could have done better as well. Li Ning was the favorite, but he took the bronze because he made mistakes. So you cannot go back and say, "What if, what if?" I try not to do that. If I permitted myself to think of that twenty-five thousandths of a point, it would bother me the rest of my life.

Two nights later I did win the pommel horse. Starting into my final routine, I knew I had to score a 10 to defeat Li Ning and Tim Daggett, who was our national pommel horse champion. Because I knew I had to achieve perfection, I expended too much effort in the first half of my routine, and I started to tire as I broke into my scissors sequence. I thought, Oh, no, I can't fall apart now. I can't make any mistakes. Then, as I picked up to do my circles to finish my routine, I started to rationalize and say, Maybe I should do a simpler dismount and not go for the tougher one I planned because I can't afford any mistakes.

So many things race through your mind when you're competing. You plunge deeply into your emotional psyche, and your entire gymnastics life flashes before your eyes. You even look at your coach, and for a brief moment you think, For 12 years of my life I spent every day with this man. And you look at your parents or you hear your father's voice in the stands. You think of all the sacrifices they've made for you, and you become concerned about their welfare because you don't want to disappoint them. You even think, Come on, Dad. Don't be nervous.

I had to do the more difficult dismount because I knew that the judges would notice if I did something easier, and I wouldn't get my 10. I went for it, and I hit it. That was so satisfying because I especially wanted to win a gold medal for my coach. We had gone through so much together. The best present I could have given him was that all-around title, but I knew that this would also mean a great deal to him. He grew up and trained at a time when American gymnastics wasn't all that good. We were maybe 10th-best in the world. He was a fine gymnast, but it is impossible for anyone to win individual gold medals if his team is mediocre. If the other scores on your team are very low, the judges won't jump yours to the level they might deserve. That's just the way judging is. They won't jump from an 8.8 to a 9.9 for members of the same team. Makoto Sakamoto was deserving, but he never had the same chance for a medal that I did, so in a way I won that medal for both of us.

DARRELL PACE

Gold Medal, Archery, 1976 and 1984

At the age of 15, Darrell Pace just missed making the 1972 U.S. Olympic Archery Team, but he has made every Olympic team since.

Pace took up archery in 1970, and less than two years later he was the United States champion. In 1975 and again in 1979, he won the world title, the first person in the "modern" era of archery to win that title twice.

The U.S. boycott of the 1980 Games in Moscow thwarted Pace's hope to win three consecutive Olympic gold medals, but he plans to compete in the '88 Games in Seoul, Korea, and may yet win that third medal. Pace and Edwin Moses are the only Americans who won gold medals in both '76 and '84.

I started archery in a pretty unusual way. I was in a lot of other sports as a youngster, like baseball and bowling. But I found out that, because I was so small and skinny, like the little kid who always got sand kicked in his face, I could perform better when I did something as an individual. If I did poorly, it was my fault; if I did well, it was my own doing. Whenever I played team sports, I had trouble distinguishing how I did because it was dependent on whether the team won or lost.

We had this coupon book in the house, one of those "buy one, get one free" things. We would try something different in it every week. There was one in it for archery, so I told my father that this week I was going to try archery, and I asked if he would take me to this archery range where you get to shoot for a second hour free if you pay for the first hour. That was in Cincinnati at Pierson Archery Lanes, which was run by Mildred and Charlie Pierson. The first time I shot an arrow was on May 2, 1970, at 9:30 in the morning, and I was 13 years old. Afterward the Piersons asked me to come in and shoot in a junior development program they had for children up to 18 years.

I started in their program every Saturday morning, and I progressed very rapidly. They were rather surprised. Within about six months I had achieved all the ranks there were: normally it

Darrell Pace in 1984. Photo by Ron Stevens

takes years to get to the top rank. I started shooting in tournaments and kept working my way up. Starting from scratch, within two years I was the national champion. The score I got in winning my first national championship stood for close to eight years. I was 15 at the time. I shot in the intermediate class in that nationals, and I also outshot the men's score. *Sports Illustrated* picked that up in their "Faces in the Crowd" section. I turned to the men's division after that. The following year, when I was 16, I set a new national record. When I was 17, I set another national record and a world record. When I was 18, I broke the world record again.

I made my first world team when I was 16 years old in 1973, and I've made every international team since then. That means every world championship team and every Olympic team since 1973. That's still a long-standing record.

I ate, slept, and drank archery in those years. I probably lost a lot of the years of my youth because in archery you are usually around adults. Archery has always been thought of as an older person's sport because it is something you can do all your life. There are excellent shooters in their 40s and 50s.

The funds for world-class archers are almost nonexistent. That's why we're living in this trailer. Some of the trips to meets are weekenders, and you can pretty much handle those on your own. But the longer ones, and especially to the world meets, are very expensive. I just recently got a job with the Ohio Department of Natural Resources as a radio technician. Before that my wife pretty much supported me, and when I was younger my parents did. I've always had a hard time keeping a job because a lot of times I have to tell them that I'll be gone three or four months out of the year, and I need to train three or four hours a day when I'm getting ready for major meets.

We shoot indoors in the winter. There's a pretty good winter season, and it's a good time to rest and experiment. I drop down about eight pounds in bow weight in the winter and let the muscles have some relief, then build back up sometime in May.

When I first started shooting, there were weekends when I would shoot 12 or 14 hours a day—from sunup to sundown. It's hard to find a good, safe place to shoot 100 yards, or 90 meters. You need safe surroundings. About the only safe place you can find is a football field, but then there are always people running around the track. The last few years I've been going out to my in-laws' 130-acre farm, which is real nice because I can go up there and get some private practice. You need to be alone for serious practice, yet the longer I've been shooting, the less I actually train. But I do a lot of mental training; I psych up for the tournaments.

When the Olympic trials came around in 1972, I was only 15 and had been shooting less than three years. At the trials I was the youngest, skinniest, smallest athlete on the field. I was 5 feet, 10 inches tall and weighed 115 pounds. I missed making the team by 10 points. I'll never forget that. My first two arrows missed the target completely. See, I don't remember my good shots, just the poor ones. You really learn from the things you do wrong. I promised myself then that I would never get nervous on the first shot again—and I haven't.

I made my first world championship team in 1973, but because it was my first world-class competition I didn't do very well; I placed something like 23rd. World championships are something else. It's a shocking experience, but once I had that international exposure, I was different. I won that championship for the first time in 1975 by something like 90 points, a pretty good margin at that level of competition. I won again in '79, was second in '81, and tied for first in '83.

I made the Olympic team in 1976 and went to Montreal. Archery is always among the last events in the Olympics, and we had to wait almost a month before we got to shoot. It seems like an eternity, and then when the time comes you shoot for six or seven hours a day for four days. Then it's over, but once I get going I don't want to stop.

At Montreal the teams from the various countries stayed pretty much to themselves. They seemed afraid to mingle because of the fear of terrorism. Remember, these were the first Games after the terrorists attacked the Israeli team in Munich. There were military guards everywhere. When we rode our bus to the shooting area, there would be guards in the front and rear of the bus. You had this feeling that you were being protected, but that also made you worry that someone really might try to attack. Our shooting field was out near a woods, and there were guards in the trees and in the fields around the whole area. I was assigned both a military and a civilian guard, who were with me at all times. It created a feeling of security and insecurity at the same time.

There's no other feeling like winning the Olympic Games. You stand on the podium and know that you are the best in the world, but you also know that you may never be there again.

The hardest thing after you've won an Olympic medal is to regroup and start over again. Four years is a long time to wait for another chance. For four years I worked hard; I made the team in 1980, and I was ready. But there were no Games for us. That meant I would have to wait another four years, for the 1984 Games, to get a second chance.

I really have strong feelings about our country's boycott of the 1980 Games. I was in the Air Force in 1980, and I was trained to obey my superior officers and to do whatever my commander-in-chief asked me to do for the good of my country. I still believe that way. There's no one more patriotic than I am, but, speaking as an athlete and competitor, the boycott was a mistake. The Olympic

Games exist for one purpose, and that is to find out who is the best in the world in his or her sport, period. Politics should never enter the Games. All that the athletes want to do is to compete—to find out who is the best in the world. You really can never know who is the best unless they are all there. I'll fight for my country, and I'll pull the trigger against any enemy my government so declares, but let's not use the Olympics for political war games. That's not what the Olympics are all about.

I won the Olympic trials again in 1984. The atmosphere at Los Angeles was unique. It had been eight years since we had competed in the Olympics, and the mood was entirely different than it was in Montreal. The Russians were wrong when they said that the security would be insufficient at LA. The security was fabulous, and, unlike Montreal, you never really saw the security people, but they were all over the place. To show how good and unobtrusive security was at Los Angeles, I'll tell you what happened to me. I'm an amateur ham radio operator, and I took some of my equipment with me to the Games. I was talking to someone about 90 miles away one evening, and I went out on the balcony to get a little better reception. Within three minutes three SWAT team members came up to me. One came up the steps, one came down the steps, and one came through the door where I was—all three at the same time. I had to convince them that I was legitimate. They were very professional about it, but they wanted to know why I was standing out on the balcony with a radio in my hand. Once they knew, they were very nice.

All of the athletes at Los Angeles mingled with each other and celebrated. It was wonderful! It didn't matter where you were from; everyone got along well with each other. It was as if brothers and sisters had met again after a four- or eight-year separation. And the people in Los Angeles were just marvelous. They couldn't do enough for you. If they saw you walking down the street carrying a credential tag, they would give you a ride or help in any way they could.

I may decide to retire after the '88 Games. I can't afford to live the rest of my life in poverty. I'll work 8 hours a day or 50 hours a week in electronics or something. I want a house, and I want to live a more or less normal life.

JEFFREY BLATNICK

Gold Medal, Greco-Roman Wrestling, 1984

One of the most dramatic moments in the 1984 Los Angeles Games occurred when a 26-year-old Greco-Roman wrestler mounted the victory stand and began to cry. These were not simply tears of joy. Two years earlier Jeff Blatnick had contracted a form of cancer known as Hodgkin's disease, and now he had come back—all the way back to become an Olympic champion.

Friends and family certainly supported him in his struggle, but it was the lessons learned in wrestling itself that made his comeback possible.

I learned to win by learning to lose—that means not being afraid of losing. That probably helped me more than any other single thing. When people found out that I had lost matches before the Olympic Games, they just couldn't understand how I could become an Olympic champion. I happen to base everything on performance. You want to win, but if you perform well there isn't much more you can do. When Larry Bird scores 50 points but the Celtics lose, are you going to tell him that he's had a poor performance? The statistic of winning or losing seems to be so much more important to fans than what they actually see. But that was how I always came back from a loss. Big deal. I lost this one match, but that doesn't mean I won't get another chance to try again.

I got into wrestling in the 10th grade because of a series of bomb scares. When we evacuated the building, the wrestling coach, Joseph Bena, convinced my brother Dave and me to quit basketball and to substitute mat burns for bench splinters. I started out losing 9 of 16 starts as a sophomore, including getting pinned my first two tries, which cost the team the matches. But Coach Bena stuck with me. I was 33 and 0 my senior year, but I was certainly no natural.

Bena was a real motivator. He managed to get all of us to think for ourselves and to understand why we were doing the things we were doing. We used to practice in the cafeteria because we had no space in the gym. We moved all the tables aside, swabbed the floor, and moved the mats out. There was only room for about half the guys actually to scrimmage, so the other half would run through the hallways of the school. I also started working out on my own because I realized that's the only way I was going to improve.

There were no college wrestling coaches beating on my door with scholarship offers, and I had no opportunity to go to a Division I school. I wound up going to Springfield College on a football scholarship, despite my high school counselor telling me that I probably wouldn't make it.

At Springfield I enjoyed wrestling much more than football. I even used to wear my wrestling shoes to football practice; in fact,

Jeff Blatnick in 1984. Photo courtesy of Jeff Blatnick

by my senior year I was wrestling between double sessions of football simply because, after you get back from a national summer camp headed by Dan Gable, going to a football practice was not what you would call hard work.

Gable is an intense individual. I always admired him. I'm a firm believer that a lot of times it isn't so much what they are doing to your body as it is what they are doing to your mind. Gable has this ability to push you beyond what you think you can do. When you think you can't do anything more, you look at him, and there he is doing everything he's telling you to do. He would do all this conditioning and then get on the mat and wrestle with us. He used to beat me up when we first started. Things have changed a little, but he could certainly do a number on me when I first went to his camps in the late 1970s.

Unfortunately, in this country we have three styles of wrestling: we have the two international styles of Greco-Roman and freestyle, and then we have our own folklore or high school and collegiate style, which no one else in the world practices. Most of our collegiate wrestlers go right into freestyle in international competition because the techniques of grabbing and securing legs are very similar to those they already know. The major difference is that our folklore style is based on control. Roll-throughs across the back and quick movements are not necessarily rewarded. To gain points you have to put the guy on his back within a 45-degree angle of the mat and hold him there, demonstrating control. In freestyle, if you get him anywhere near his back, you score points because it's a 90-degree angle you have to break, and you don't have to show control.

Our American style invites more stalling and blocking, and you're allowed to back out of bounds. In international competition, if a move starts in bounds and travels out of bounds, it is scored, and there is no such thing as an escape. Once you are on the bottom your sole purpose is not to be turned—period! For 15 seconds the guy on top will do anything he can to turn you, and you have to do anything you can not to be turned. If you stop a couple of attacks and show that you defense well, you're brought to your feet, and you start again.

Greco-Roman never really got a fair shake because most of our wrestlers were freestylers, and those who didn't make the team would then try to make it in Greco. It wasn't until the early 1970s that people really started to train specifically for Greco. They were known as the Minnesota Group or the Minnesota Wrestling Club, and I eventually trained with them.

I was doing my student teaching in 1979 in Boston, and I used to go down to the Boston Union to train with Jim Peckham, who was the athletic director at Emerson College and who had been the Greco coach of our '76 Olympic team. I competed in the nationals and took second to Brad Rheingans, who had finished fourth in the '76 Games and was an excellent wrestler. Because of that match, Brad asked me to try out the next summer for our Greco-Roman world championship team. In the tryouts I wound up finishing second to Bob Walker, who beat me two out of three. He pinned me twice in 30 seconds, but I beat him in the middle match, 8–7. This showed that I could win the matches that went the distance but that I had to avoid getting caught in an early move. In Greco, if both of your shoulder blades are down, you're pinned. There's no count. Naturally, this success was very encouraging to me, so I made the permanent switch from freestyle to Greco.

It was a good move because I had great hand speed and great endurance. I also had wide hips for a better base and an extremely flexible back. And I had long arms, which meant I could tie up in a body lock at a greater distance. In freestyling you have to protect your legs and be able to execute good leg shots, and I lacked this. I was the kind of guy who was always nitpicking around the outside, and, if I got you down, I could turn you on the mat. I was a good mat wrestler, and that was the one thing I loved about folklore wrestling. In Greco you don't have to defend your legs, and you don't have to attack legs; then, too, you have a lot more initial success simply because not that many people in this country train Greco.

In 1979, Brad brought me to North Dakota State at Fargo, where I got a graduate assistantship and coached, and we continued to train together. Once the wrestling season ended in February, we moved to Minneapolis to join the rest of the club. We had a tremendous group of individuals. I think there were seven Olympians training in Greco-Roman and nothing else. These guys passed their knowledge on to me, and I still had the best workout partner in the country, so naturally my wrestling improved. As it turned out, both Brad and I made the 1980 Olympic team. Brad would have been this country's first medalist if he had been given a chance to compete. He had just taken a bronze medal in the 1979 world championships, but after the boycott he decided to retire.

So I was doing quite well until 1982, when I came down with Hodgkin's disease. I was 24 years old. I was in North Dakota when I noticed bumps on my neck, and I knew that something was wrong. The doctor who performed the biopsy didn't know quite how to tell me. I'll always remember. He and his nurse stood on the other side of the desk. They probably anticipated some show of emotion and were not sure what I would do. Of course, it's a shock when you first hear it simply because you don't understand how you could have contracted it. It's a strange disease. No one really has any answers. There is increasingly better understanding and treatment, but I don't think we've reached the point we want to—which is to eradicate it. That's going to take time.

At that point, my biggest concern was how to tell my parents. My brother Dave had been killed in an automobile accident in 1977, just before the junior world tryouts. Immediately after the funeral, my parents told me to go ahead and try out. That's what Dave would have wanted. In fact, he had written me a letter saying that he was going to come to Las Vegas and watch me. So they had lost their first-born son, and now number two was on the line. And besides that, my dad had had a rocky childhood in which he had lost his brother Russell. All the suffering they would have to go through really bothered me. And you can't help feeling guilty for having to put them through all this, even though you certainly did nothing to bring it on.

The doctors told me that treatment was possible, and I felt that, given this opportunity, plus the fact that I really do enjoy life—and living—and because I am not afraid of losing, I could beat this thing. It isn't something you sit down and plot. It's just an attitude that is bred within. It's an instinct of faith. Fear is something within the head. After wrestling 400-pounders and doing things people didn't think I was capable of, I had gained a positive attitude and a certain confidence.

As I already mentioned, when I first started wrestling I didn't have much success. I'm not gifted with a very powerful body in terms of either looks or actual muscle, but wrestling was an activity I became able to do with a great deal of success. I surprised people. All my life I always heard comments like, "You got to be kidding; that's him?" People were just not very impressed with me and my body, and it gave me such a rush to be able to go in there and tie people up in knots who looked physically superior.

So I attacked Hodgkin's disease just like I would any challenge.

I said, Hey, this is what I have to go through. If I can make it through this, I am supposedly in the clear. You have to visualize yourself getting through the treatment, getting to where you want to be, and then getting your life back on track. This is what I had to do. I tried to attack everything with a lot of optimism.

I continued to wrestle only in a token sense. I had had my spleen removed, and the radiation treatments really knocked me down physically. You really don't know what that's going to do to you until you actually experience it. You have to start all over again with your wrestling and have the patience to understand that the opponents you once took for granted you can no longer defeat. But once again, because I was not afraid of losing, I was able to go out and measure myself not in terms of winning or losing but in how well I had performed.

I would assess where I had breakdowns and where I had positives. I worked this into my training schedule and eventually was able to come back. The first major tournament I won after my bout with Hodgkin's disease was the Olympic trials. And the first international meet I won after my illness was the Olympics. I don't know if I could do it again. That's a big if. I would like to think that if I decided to try again I would do things the same way and hopefully with the same results.

I've watched the videotape of myself during that moment on the victory stand, and it's tough. A lot of people have asked me, "How can you be embarrassed?" I'm not ashamed of it, but how many times do you see a tape of yourself crying? I had a lot to be thankful for. That moment was shared not only by me but by a lot of my friends and family. Without them and their help it would have been a difficult road back.

Oh, sure, millions of people shared that moment. Hey, this guy did something you're not supposed to do—he beat cancer. But the people who really understand what that moment was all about were those who started out seeing me high, then go low, and then get back on top again. Those are the people who don't think I'm some kind of human phenomenon—because I'm not. There are three million other people who have beaten cancer. So what happens is I became not a famous wrestler but a famous cancer patient.

Many people think I was the first American to win a gold medal in Greco-Roman wrestling. Well, that's not true. Steve Fraser won our first gold medal in Greco the night before I did. Steve Fraser had a 5 and 0 record in the Olympics, but Steve Fraser didn't receive a bit of publicity. Steve Fraser didn't have cancer. On that I rest my case.

It is very evident that cancer told the story, and this is only because of the fear we attach to that word. I now go around educating people. I tell them, "Hey, the fear's in your head, not in that word." Treatments have gotten better. And if you really believe you want to continue to live, you'll do what you have to do—and not be afraid. You'll believe that there is life not only after cancer but during. You're not written off and thrown into a leper colony or something. People can do whatever they want to do as long as they put their minds to it. And that doesn't just go on the athletic field. I think I was better prepared, having come from athletics and having been put in adverse situations that required a lot of internal motivation, but I don't claim to be an inspiration. People who had Hodgkin's disease 15 years ago come up and talk to me. Now, who's inspiring whom? I see my future in front of me. And I would not have that future if it were not for those people already having done the same thing that I'm doing now.

In 1984, I was named Man of the Year in amateur wrestling, and I was stripped of my amateur status because I competed in the Superstars competition. At the time, I wasn't sure whether or not I was going to retire, and I saw this as an opportunity to compete against some very well-known athletes. I wanted it known that wrestlers are athletes, that we don't grunt and groan for our daily bread, and that we're not just something you lock up in a cage at night.

I took 7th out of 20 and made $5,000. Phil Mayre, Greg Foster, and others made a lot more money, but they're still competing as amateurs. When you look at this, you say, Hey, wait a minute. There's got to be something fairer than this.

I came out of the Olympics and received some fame. I felt that I could make this work for everybody. I could work for the American Cancer and Leukemia Societies, I could work a little for myself, and I could help put wrestling on the map. I thought I might even find a sponsor for amateur wrestling, but then wrestling turns around and sanctions me. They called me a "non-amateur," which is a worse insult than being called a professional. It was the so-called "contamination theory." Because I had competed against professionals, I was somehow "contaminated."

It aggravated me, and I had to sit back and take a look at the situation. I said to myself, Well, right now I'm not ready to compete, and I don't know when I will be ready. I'll just let it rest. It's not going to do the sport any good for me to throw a lawsuit at the U.S. Amateur Wrestling Association just because somebody on their law committee decided that what I was doing was not in their best interest.

Some changes have occurred in the administration of amateur wrestling. I think the executive committee realized that, if we were going to compete with other sports for national interest and sponsors, we had to work together. We need to train together with permanent coaches and facilities, and we must do this on a full-time basis. I see what other sports can do just because they label something an exhibition. If we're going to promote wrestling, inevitably we're going to have to promote wrestlers. Just because you didn't make a buck when you were wrestling doesn't mean you should hold that against those who are now competing. Times have changed.

I haven't made a killing as a wrestler. I've made more money making public appearances as a former cancer patient. I earned more money in the last year than I had in the previous eight, but I lived on $5,000 or less for each of those eight years, so making $40,000 in one year is like hitting a gold mine. It's a tremendous amount of money, and I do feel a little guilty, knowing that people die from cancer and knowing people who have beaten it who don't get any recognition. I've met too many people with stories tougher than mine. There's that guilt, so I feel a lot better when I've done a good day's work and really helped someone.

I continue to be a volunteer for the American Cancer and Leukemia societies, and I continue to promote amateur wrestling. I give speeches to corporations and to community and civic groups. I do some broadcast work. Whoever wants me to speak to them about whatever, I can do it. For some reason I came out of the Olympics with the gift of gab. I was never a public speaker, and now all of a sudden I can talk to the public and do it very well. This is all new to me, but it's an exciting thing. I'm talking to people whom others wait years to see. I can just walk in, and these people want to hear what I have to say. It's great, but it makes me sit back and think, Just what is going on with these people with their millions of dollars wanting me to talk to them? Really, what it comes down to is the fact that I have something that money can't buy. I have an Olympic gold medal and the story behind it as well.

Professional wrestling is a whole different matter. It is entertainment, and as long as it doesn't steal the wrestling name, I don't object. In fact, I thought before the Games that if I couldn't find a $20,000 coaching job after the Olympics, I would go into pro wrestling. If amateur wrestling had just one-fiftieth of their pie, we could run all our programs. And it should work that way. The wrestling that people see on television gives them a false impression of what real wrestling is. When they see that the amateurs don't punch each other around and don't do comedy, they just don't understand. The public needs to be educated, because the professionals are stealing our name. Unfortunately, they direct their promotions to kids, thereby distorting their impression of wrestling for life. So we do have an identity problem.

If it came down to a real match, and I got on the mat against Hulk Hogan—or, better yet, let Bruce Baumgartner, the 1984 super-heavyweight freestyle gold medalist and the 1985 world champion, go to the mat with him—you could tell the Hulk, "Hey, you can do whatever you want. You want to hit him with a chair, fine, try to hit him with a chair, but when this is over, you're going to be on your back, and you won't be let up until you publicly admit that you can't move." Most professional wrestlers would never get off their backs. We could put them in more pain than they could ever take, but that's not our intention. We just want them to recognize the legitimacy and financial needs of our sport.

There are a few of the pros who really did know how to wrestle at one time. Mike Rotunda was a Syracuse wrestler. Brad, of course, now wrestles as the Olympic Boy. Steve Williams, Dr. Death, used to wrestle for Oklahoma. But most of the pros were never even amateur wrestlers. They were football players or just somebody with a body and a mouth to go along with it.

I don't consider myself the greatest wrestler the country has ever produced. I do consider myself among the best, but definitely not *the* best. No way in the world. We're family, and that's the one thing that's held wrestling together all these years—the closeness of the sport. You're literally sweating on somebody else. You can't get any more literal than that. The closeness, the intimacy, the pushing yourself to the point where you're so angry you want to take a shot at the other guy, but you don't—this is something you find only in wrestling. You talk about competition in other sports; hey, when you're touching your opponent, when his energy can be felt right at your fingertips, that's something else; it's a one-on-one sport within a circle, and you can't get away from your opponent. That asks a lot of you, and wrestlers understand that. We don't preach that we're the toughest. We just work together. . . .